Lisa

To help when planning your next trip to Aus.

love
Nickie
2024

ULTIMATE Coastal Road Trips

AUSTRALIA

LEE ATKINSON

Hardie Grant

EXPLORE

Introduction	iv
Acknowledgement of Country	v
Helpful information	vi
Driving tips	viii
Family road trip survival guide	x
Map of Australia	xii

NEW SOUTH WALES	**1**
The Lakes Way	3
Central Coast to Nelson Bay	9
Laurieton to South West Rocks	17
Coffs Coast to Yamba	23
Byron and beyond	31
Grand Pacific Drive	39
Jervis Bay and the Eurobodalla	45
The Sapphire Coast	51
VICTORIA	**59**
Great Ocean Road	61
Beyond the Great Ocean Road	69
Phillip Island	77
Mornington Peninsula	83
Bass Coast	91
East Gippsland	99
SOUTH AUSTRALIA	**107**
Fleurieu Peninsula	109
Kangaroo Island	117
Limestone Coast	123
Yorke Peninsula	131
Eyre Peninsula	139
The Great Australian Bight	145

Opposite Driving along Great Ocean Drive near Esperance, WA
Left The Great Ocean Road, Victoria

WESTERN AUSTRALIA — 153
- Indian Ocean Drive — 155
- Coral Coast — 163
- Pilbara Coast — 171
- Kimberley Coast — 179
- Cape to Cape — 187
- The South West Edge — 195

NORTHERN TERRITORY — 205
- Gove Peninsula — 207

QUEENSLAND — 215
- Gold and Sunshine coasts — 217
- Great Beach Drive — 225
- Capricorn Coast — 233
- Whitsunday Coast — 241
- Great Green Way — 249
- Great Barrier Reef Drive — 255
- Norfolk Island, South Pacific — 263

TASMANIA — 271
- The deep south — 273
- Turrakana/Tasman Peninsula — 279
- East Coast — 285
- The north-west — 293
- Flinders Island — 299
- King Island — 305

Index — 312
Photo credits — 328
About the author — 329

INTRODUCTION

This book is dedicated to my father, Dave, who died in December 2020. Road trips with you were always an adventure, Dad.

Our family holidays were always the same when I was growing up. A summer road trip to a friend's holiday house by the sea. In order to beat the holiday crush my parents would arrange with Santa to come to our house before Christmas. Sometimes Santa came so early we'd still be at school and we'd get an extra few days off. We'd load up the car and head off, full of excitement, my sister and I crammed in the back seat with my baby brother and as many of our pre-Christmas presents as we could squeeze in. A road trip with Dad was all about getting there as quickly as possible – up before dawn to beat the traffic and heat so the big grey Valiant's radiator wouldn't boil on the way there. The only time we'd stop was when my little brother was – both inevitably and frequently – car sick, or to cool the engine if it started to steam, but those coastal road trips are still the ones I remember most fondly.

Everybody has a story to tell about their first road trip without their parents and it's always a tale about the exhilarating and intoxicating taste of freedom of having your own wheels. And just like a lot of people, one of my first road trips with friends was north out of Sydney/Warrang up the coast to Byron Bay.

More like my dad than I ever intended to be, the first few hours passed by in a blur of singing along to loud pop music and a no-stopping-under-any-circumstances determination to get as far from Sydney as soon as we could. We made it to Coffs Harbour before I insisted that everyone get out of the car for a chocolate-coated frozen banana on a stick at the Big Banana (proving, no doubt, that I wasn't nearly as grown up or sophisticated as I thought I was). But then we chilled, and the surfers of the group made us stop at almost every beach, it seemed, along the way and it took us a couple of extra days to get where we were going – but we couldn't have cared less. We were on our own and we could do whatever we liked, whenever we liked, and camp wherever we wanted to.

It's still the best way to approach a drive up the NSW north coast, taking your time to get off the highway to explore the laid-back beachside towns that all end in head: Crescent Head, Hat Head, Nambucca Heads, Brooms Head, Brunswick Heads. Nothing much has changed in these places – the beach and surf is still the main attraction, the local pub's still the only entertainment option and the caravan parks still have the best views in town. The cafes serve better coffee these days though.

Sun, sand and sea; a road trip up, down, or along the Australian coast is not just a rite of passage, but the great Australian holiday dream. With more than 50,000km of coastline and close to 11,500 beaches, Australia's magnificent shoreline has some of the most scenic coastal driving routes in the world.

A beach holiday can also be so much more than just a pretty place for a dip and a sunbake and a game of beach cricket; a coastal road trip can offer some once-in-a-lifetime wildlife encounters, off-beat adventures and genuine back-to-nature experiences. One of the things that makes a coastal road trip in Australia so unique is that you don't have to spend a fortune to wake up to a great view. There are plenty of beachside caravan and camping spots around the country where you can get a million-dollar beachfront view and still get change from a $50 note.

This book is a comprehensive guide to Australia's best coastal road trips, offering up a deep dive into some of our most spectacular stretches of coastline with 40 seaside road trips around the country.

The road trips featured are a mix of long-time favourites like Victoria's Great Ocean Road and the Grand Pacific Drive south of Sydney, lesser-known routes like WA's Pilbara Coast and bucket-list destinations such as the Kimberley in WA and Arnhem Land in the NT. You'll also find driving routes across most of the country's iconic islands, including K'gari (Fraser) and North Stradbroke/Minjerribah in Queensland, King, Flinders and Bruny islands in Tassie, and even a road trip around Norfolk Island, as well as a few sand-under-your-wheels adventures to challenge your beach-driving skills. Covering all corners of the continent, these great ocean roads all have one thing in common – plenty of great ocean views.

In this guide you'll find everything you need to know to help you plan the perfect coastal road trip. Each chapter includes information on things to see and do, route maps and a handy list of distances to help you plan your trip, as well as lots of useful advice on the best time to go, activities like walks and cultural tours, family-friendly attractions, where to eat and a selection of some of the best hotels, guesthouses, caravan parks and camping spots. And because even in the most beautiful places you can still end up with lousy weather, I've included rainy day options and hinterland excursions.

The pandemic has changed the way Australians travel – while international borders were closed we rediscovered the joy of road tripping and the delights of exploring our own backyard but with so many people doing the same, planning – and booking – ahead has become essential.

Keep this book in the car for when you're out on the road or curl up with it at home and dream about your next coastal road trip holiday. You don't have to get wet to enjoy a day beside the sea.

Lee Atkinson

ACKNOWLEDGEMENT OF COUNTRY

I'd like to acknowledge the Traditional Owners of the many different beaches and coastal hinterlands that I visited while researching this book, and their continuing connection to the land, waters and culture. I'd also like to acknowledge the Traditional Owners of the Country on which this book was written, the Dja Dja Wurrung People, and pay respect to Elders past and present.

Taking advantage of the surf at Bells Beach, Victoria

HELPFUL INFORMATION

BUSY TIMES AND SCHOOL HOLIDAYS

Summertime is holiday time in Australia. Peak season in most coastal areas is the month from Christmas to Australia Day – 25 Dec to 26 Jan, which roughly coincides with summer school holidays too. Easter is also peak holiday time and it's also when ocean temperatures, in the southern states at least, are at their warmest, unless the four-day holiday falls in late Apr, when you really need a wetsuit to enjoy being wet. During these holiday times it can be hard to secure accommodation or a campsite, and prices are generally higher too.

SWIMMING AND BEACH SAFETY

Most popular surf beaches near coastal holiday towns are patrolled by lifeguards and surf lifesavers during peak holiday times and summer weekends, so swim in the patrolled area between the red and yellow flags and if you get into trouble, raise your arm. If you see a red flag, the beach is closed because conditions are too dangerous for swimming. A red and white flag means you should evacuate the water immediately. A black and white flag means the area is off limits to surfers.

But outside of those busy times many beaches, including most beaches in national parks year-round, won't have lifeguards on duty. Tragically, in the year before this book was written, 399 people lost their lives by drowning. More than one-third of them died at least 50km from home, most likely on holiday. No matter how experienced you are as a swimmer, never swim alone and never at an unpatrolled beach.

Try to identify any potential undercurrents, sandbars or rips before you enter the water – a rip is a narrow current of water that can sweep you swiftly out to sea. The water in a rip is often calmer than the surrounding water, so avoid any sections that have no breaking waves, and can sometimes look darker in colour. If you do get caught in a rip, stay calm and swim across the current, rather than trying to swim against it back to shore.

Always check the depth of water before diving in, wear a lifejacket when boating, and be aware of waves when rock fishing – it's always good to check conditions with local fishers first.

For beach safety advice, and to find the nearest patrolled beaches to you while travelling, go to Beachsafe (beachsafe.org.au).

As tragic as the drowning statistics are, though, the main killer on Australian beaches is the sun. Australia has some of the highest UV levels in the world, and the highest rate of skin cancer in the world, too. The UV radiation in Australia is strong enough to cause sunburn in just 10 minutes. Always wear sunscreen and cover up with a hat, even on cloudy days.

That said, there are some marine nasties out there to be careful of too. Despite all the publicity, shark attacks are quite rare. Many beaches in larger towns and cities have shark nets to deter sharks, and in some coastal areas 'shark spotter' helicopters patrol in summer holidays too, but it's still wise to avoid swimming or surfing at dusk and near river mouths. In the tropical waters of northern Australia, marine jellyfish are common in the ocean between Oct and May. The sting from a box jellyfish or the Irukandji jellyfish are extremely painful and can be fatal. Swim only in netted areas or wear a stinger suit, usually available at local shops or on tours. If you are stung, treat affected areas immediately with vinegar (most beaches have bottles at beach entry points) and do not rub the area. And of course, avoid going anywhere near the water – creeks, rivers, estuaries or beaches anywhere in the top half of the country – if there are crocodile warnings. Always follow local signage and, if in doubt, ask for local advice.

EMERGENCY CONTACTS

The emergency number to call in Australia is 000 (triple zero) – for ambulance, police or fire.

If you are a member of an auto club the number for roadside assistance is 13 11 11.

Summertime is not just a busy time on Australian beaches, it's also bushfire season. If you're road tripping in summer be aware of the Fire Danger Rating each day and download the appropriate fire emergency app – there's a different one for each state – for safety alerts. In recent years, flooding has inundated many Australian towns and devastated communities. It's always good to check ahead with local authorities before travelling to impacted areas to ensure that roads are open and towns and attractions are operational – and ready to welcome travellers back.

The local ABC radio is your best place to keep up to date with emergency weather and bushfire announcements or go online (abc.net.au/emergency).

NATIONAL PARKS

Many of the beaches in this book are in national parks. While some national parks are free to visit, many have entry fees and camping fees. Pre-booking a campsite – either by phone or online – is mandatory in all national parks in Queensland, NSW, NT and SA, and in selected parks in other states. Be aware that there may not be mobile phone coverage in most national parks, so you'll need to book before you arrive. Some coastal parks in Victoria have a ballot system for securing a campsite during peak holiday times.

If you are planning on spending more than a few days or nights in national parks, buying a park pass will save you money.

For more information and updates on park closures, beach driving permits, and to buy park passes or book a campsite, visit the relevant state or territory website below.

- NSW   nationalparks.nsw.gov.au; 1300 072 757
- Vic   parks.vic.gov.au; 13 19 63
- SA   parks.sa.gov.au; (08) 8207 7700 (business hours only)
- WA   exploreparks.dbca.wa.gov.au; (08) 9219 9000
- NT   nt.gov.au/parks; 1300 281 121
- Qld   parks.des.qld.gov.au; 13 74 68
- Tas   parks.tas.gov.au; 1300 827 727

ROAD TRIPPING WITH PETS

Our pets are part of our family and nobody likes to leave family members behind. In recent years more holiday houses, caravan parks and even some hotels have begun to welcome pets, but it's not universal so you'll need to seek them out when planning your road trip. Websites such as holidayingwithdogs.com.au and holidaypaws.com.au can be useful.

Many caravan parks will accept well-behaved pets on a leash, but always check before you book rather than on arrival. Pets are not allowed in national parks, even for day visits or picnics.

Opposite Tranquil beach on the NSW Lakes Way *Left* SA's Great Australian Bight

Helpful information

DRIVING TIPS

DRIVING ON UNSEALED ROADS

Many of the roads in coastal national parks and country areas are unsealed: they can be bumpy and dusty but unless otherwise signposted are generally fine for conventional two-wheel-drive (2WD) vehicles when conditions have been dry. After heavy rains they may take a few days to dry out, and getting stuck or bogged is never much fun. Travelling on roads that have a 'closed road' sign, even if you are in a four-wheel-drive (4WD) vehicle, not only damages the road for future users, but you'll also incur a substantial fine.

DRIVING ON THE BEACH

Driving along an empty stretch of beach is one of life's great pleasures, but in most cases you'll need to get a permit from the relevant authority first, usually the local council or from national parks. The trickiest thing about driving on beaches is planning around the tides, as quite often your beach highway can completely disappear when the tide comes in. You'll need a 4WD and drop your tyre pressures to 20psi or so to avoid getting bogged, so carry an accurate pressure gauge and a quality air compressor to reinflate your tyres when you leave the beach. Generally, you don't need to brake on sand – sudden braking can bury the nose of the vehicle, particularly when driving in dunes. Be aware that some driving beaches are also swimming and fishing beaches, so watch for people sitting or walking on the beach too. If you do get into trouble in sand a pair of recovery ramps, which you put under the wheels when you're bogged in sand, give the tyres something to grip and, as a rule, will launch you out of trouble. Carry a long-handled shovel for digging and a snatch strap for those moments when all else fails – all you need then is somebody else to come along to pull you out. In remote areas it pays to travel with friends or family so there's two vehicles for this reason!

TOWING A CARAVAN

Unless otherwise noted, most of the roads covered in this guide are suitable for caravans, but road conditions can and do change, so always check local conditions before setting out, particularly if it has been raining recently.

Be aware of your van's height and weight – you'll often come across low-level bridges in country areas. Before you leave home measure the height of your van or motorhome, including any rooftop air conditioners and so on, and put it on a sticker on your windscreen to remind you. Do the same with your total laden weight, as some bridges have a 3-tonne limit, as do some country roads after rain.

ROAD CLOSURES

Some roads in national parks and outback areas can close due to seasonal weather conditions or for maintenance. National park authority websites will show park alerts for when roads – or walking tracks – are closed, and state and territory authorities will have information about other road closures.

MAPS, APPS AND PLBS

Taking the right maps or a good sat nav is key to a successful and happy road trip – as fighting over which is the right way to go is a major cause of holiday (and marital) breakdown. There is a range of free apps, like Google Maps, available to help you navigate coastal roads, but don't rely on them if you are heading away from towns, into remote areas or national parks, because phone coverage can be non-existent outside of urban areas and larger towns. Invest in a good sat nav that doesn't rely on a phone signal – we use Hema Navigator – but it pays to also carry paper maps in your car because sometimes you need to see the bigger picture, rather than just the next couple of turns.

Opposite WA's South West Edge *Above* Point Moore Lighthouse, Geraldton, WA

If you're a member, maps produced by your state automobile association (NRMA, RACV, RAC, etc) are always accurate, as are Hema maps.

If you're camping, Wikicamps is a handy app when looking for somewhere to pitch for a night. Hipcamp – like Airbnb for campers – is a network of campsites on private property. It's particularly useful if you don't fancy caravan parks, roadside rest stops or national parks, which are off limits if you're travelling with pets. And just as I'd never leave home without Google Maps or a sat nav, I can't even imagine setting up camp without checking out a weather app first – life's too short to camp in the rain.

Personal Locator Beacons (PLBs) or a satellite phone are recommended in remote areas, especially when hiking.

BEING ROAD READY

Before you leave home, give your car the ten-step once over.

1. Service please – get your vehicle serviced by a licensed mechanic before you leave home.

2. The good oil – engines like fresh oil, so treat your engine to a lube. And check it regularly while on your road trip to make sure it doesn't get low.

3. Keep your cool – check your radiator coolant level and top it up if necessary. If you're heading a long way from help (away from towns), carry some spare hoses and a bottle of coolant with you.

4. Power rangers – you'd be amazed how many people get stranded with a flat battery, especially if they are running portable fridges, chargers or night lights. Carry a spare and turn off appliances overnight.

5. Keep the pressure on – most of us forget to check tyre pressure. Carry, and use, a tyre gauge. Before you leave, check the tread and make sure you have a spare in good condition.

6. The right tools – a basic tool kit should include a jack, jacking plate and wheel-replacement tools, spare tyre, fire extinguisher, emergency fuel supplies if heading off the beaten track, engine oil, coolant, jumper leads and spare radiator hoses and fan belts and the tools you'll need to replace them.

7. Pack the essentials – never travel without a first-aid kit, always carry extra drinking water and plenty of sunscreen of course.

8. Pack it in – don't overload your car or carry unrestrained items in the back seat – even a flying book can cause serious injury in a crash. If it won't fit in the boot, don't take it. If you're travelling in a wagon or 4WD, install a cargo barrier.

9. Play it safe – make sure your vehicle (car and caravan) and home insurance is up to date. Cancel any home deliveries, get the neighbours to collect your mail, organise who will look after your pets (if you have them), and install a timer switch on a light or two (or get a reliable friend or relative to house sit).

10. Be prepared – join your state auto club before you leave home, such as the RAA or NRMA, to help you out in the event of a vehicle breakdown.

FAMILY ROAD TRIP SURVIVAL GUIDE

Road tripping with kids can be great fun. Here's some tips to make sure everyone enjoys the drive.

PLAN AHEAD

The secret to successful road tripping with kids is not to be too ambitious in terms of how far you think you can get in one drive. Allow twice as long for the journey as you normally would – especially if your kids are pre-school age – allocating plenty of time for rest breaks and planning them in advance. Take the time to get off the highway and research ahead to stop at a park or swimming pool, rather than a roadhouse. It goes without saying that wherever you choose to stop should have toilets, but try and choose places with playgrounds or at least an expanse of grass where the kids can run around and burn off some energy. Bring games for park stops (inflatable balls are a good space saver) to play with.

MAP IT OUT

Get the kids involved in planning your trip – maybe they could make a map of your trip before you leave home (older kids might like to map the route using Google Maps) and let them pick out a couple of things they'd like to see and do along the way. Decorating a map with drawings or stickers of what they see, or encouraging them to keep a journal/scrapbook of places you go to (they can glue in postcards and ticket stubs, etc), can be a good way to keep them occupied. Collect postcards at each town you drive through – buy a book of stamps before you leave home and the kids can post them off on the spot. Another option is to create a treasure list of things to find at each stop. If the kids are old enough, let them navigate and then they can answer your 'are we there yets'.

STAY HEALTHY

Make sure you have medication if your kids get car sick – dose them up before you hit the road, not once they feel unwell. Carry a plastic bucket (with a lid) and plenty of wet wipes just in case. Roadhouse food is often atrocious, unhealthy and expensive. Pack a bag of healthy snacks, sandwiches and drinks – but go easy on the sugar and anything that can spill or stain. Make sure your kids have water bottles in the car too.

KEEP KIDS AMUSED

Pack some toys and games but don't even think about asking them to share – give each child their own bag of things to pull out as they want; older kids might like to pack their own bag of activities. Books are great for long car trips as they can keep kids occupied but avoid them if your kids are prone to motion sickness; and also avoid anything hard, sharp or tricky to clean if spilt (or doodled) on upholstery. With kids of any age, you can have a storytelling competition or make it a team effort, where each person adds a line. Read younger kids a book (if you're the passenger!), listen to an audiobook or listen to a podcast with children's stories or one of the many great themed family-friendly podcasts on topics such as science, art or music. Don't underestimate the power of old-fashioned games like I-spy, spelling bees, word games, 'who am I?' and so on – the internet is full of quirky suggestions, just Google 'road trip games'.

Older kids might like to download their own music before a road trip and even if they don't have phones you can buy relatively inexpensive MP3 players (yes, they still exist!) that store a limited amount of music. Another idea is to get kids to create a playlist on your phone on a music streaming service – giving them input helps to make them feel that they have

Opposite Rex Lookout on the Great Barrier Reef Drive, Queensland
Above The Gove Peninsula, NT

helped plan the road trip. If all else fails, put movies on to an iPad. Portable DVD players are also a lot cheaper than they used to be and most run via the 12-volt outlet in the car – don't forget headphones.

PACK A SURVIVAL BAG

Put everything you might need, like a change of clothes, towel, swimmers, jumpers, torches, even pyjamas, in a bag to carry in the car to save repacking the boot every time you need something.

AVOID DRIVING AT NIGHT

In theory, the idea that driving through the night will mean the kids sleep while you motor in peace is a tempting proposition, but in reality you'll just end up dog tired the next day while they are full of beans. Driving in the dark on country roads also means that the chance of colliding with wildlife is high.

CHOOSE FAMILY-FRIENDLY ACTIVITIES

There are endless activities and attractions in Australia that are kid-friendly, and they need not be expensive. Theme parks exist, sure, and are great fun, but there are wildlife encounters to be had, great bushwalks for families, zoos, museums and galleries that often have activities for kids, tours to learn about First Nations' culture, beachcombing, lighthouse climbs (Maritime Safety says children must be over age five), swimming with marine life, stargazing activities, whale watching boat tours, fishing, surfing lessons, boat cruises to islands, dinosaur digs, pony rides, gardens and parks to roam in, and towns to explore. Just to name a few things that you can plan to do with your kids! Many caravan parks are now pitching themselves as family friendly too, with playgrounds, jumping pillows and activities like go-karts and games rooms.

Happy road tripping!

NEW SOUTH WALES

1. The Lakes Way...3
2. Central Coast to Nelson Bay...9
3. Laurieton to South West Rocks...17
4. Coffs Coast to Yamba...23
5. Byron and beyond...31
6. Grand Pacific Drive...39
7. Jervis Bay and the Eurobodalla...45
8. The Sapphire Coast...51

VICTORIA

9. Great Ocean Road...61
10. Beyond the Great Ocean Road...69
11. Phillip Island...77
12. Mornington Peninsula...83
13. The Bass Coast...91
14. East Gippsland...99

SOUTH AUSTRALIA

15. Fleurieu Peninsula...109
16. Kangaroo Island...117
17. Limestone Coast...123
18. Yorke Peninsula...131
19. Eyre Peninsula...139
20. The Great Australia Bight...145

WESTERN AUSTRALIA

21. Indian Ocean Drive...155
22. Coral Coast...163
23. Pilbara Coast...171
24. Kimberley Coast...179
25. Cape to Cape...187
26. The South West Edge...195

NORTHERN TERRITORY

27. Gove Peninsula...207

QUEENSLAND

28. Gold and Sunshine coasts...217
29. Great Beach Drive...225
30. Capricorn Coast...233
31. Whitsunday Coast...241
32. Great Green Way...249
33. Great Barrier Reef Drive...255
34. Norfolk Island, South Pacific...263

TASMANIA

35. The deep south...273
36. Turrakana/Tasman Peninsula...279
37. East Coast...285
38. The north-west...293
39. Flinders Island...299
40. King Island...305

MAP LEGEND

PERTH/BOORLOO ○ State capital city
BUNDABERG ○ Major city/town
Lorne ○ Town
McLaren Vale ○ Other population centres

— Road trip
— Sidetrack route

- Caravan stay
- Camping area
- Information
- Roadhouse (RH)
- Airport
- Attraction
- Ferry
- Lighthouse
- Mountain, hill
- Cave
- Gorge, Pass

xii

Map of Australia   xiii

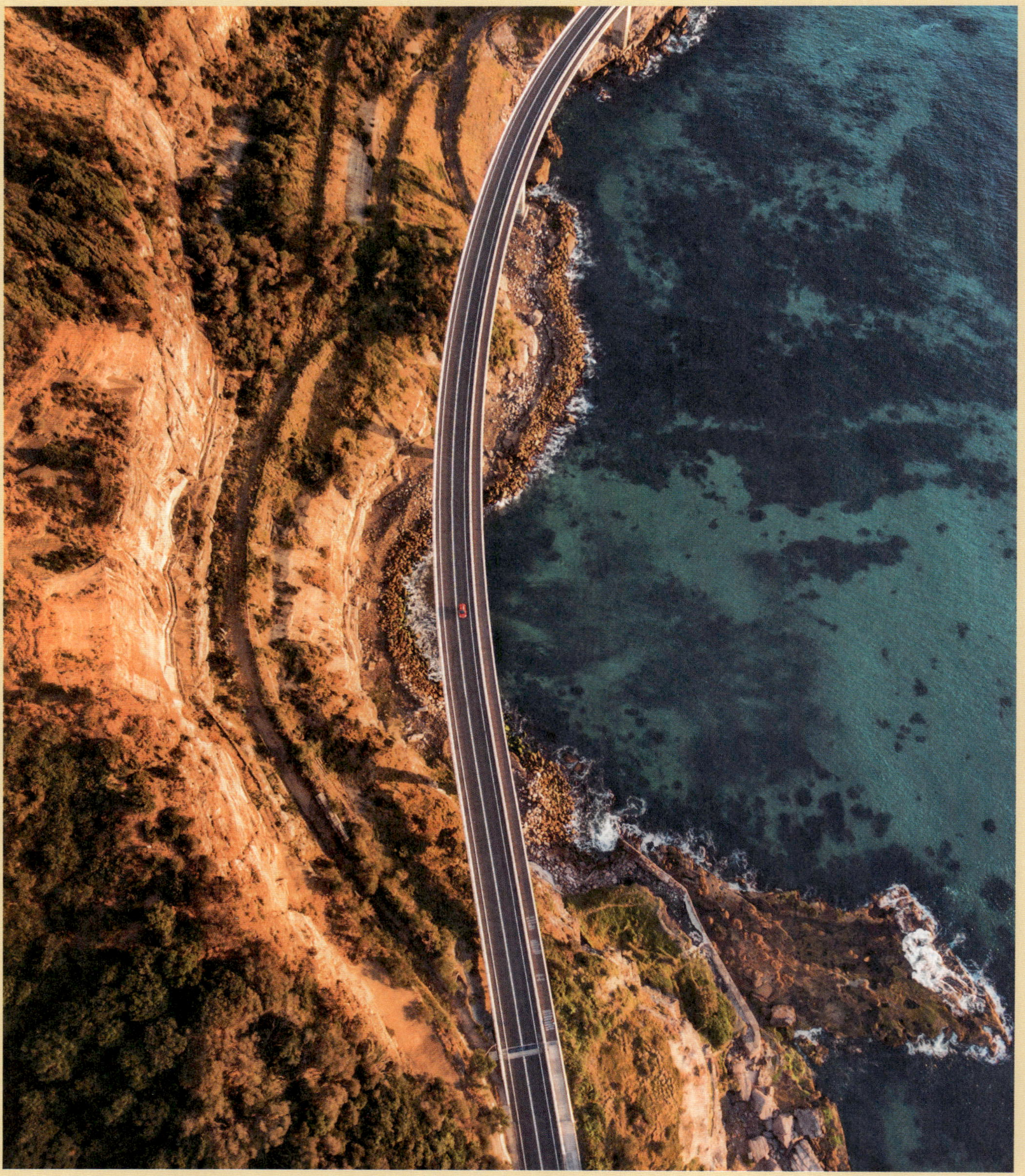

New South Wales

World-class surf and coastal wilderness.

A15
Lake Glenbawn
Mount Woolooma
Mount Barrington
Rawdon Vale
Barrington
Burrell Creek
TAREE
Harrington
Dangarfield
Aberdeen
Davis Creek
BARRINGTON TOPS NATIONAL PARK
Mount McKenzie
Gloucester
Purfleet
KIWARRAK SF
A1
Old Bar
Wallabi Point
GONDWANA RAINFORESTS OF AUSTRALIA WHA
AVON RIVER SF
Rainbow Flat
Krambach
Big Buzz Fun Park
Diamond Beach
Hallidays Point
Mount Royal
Stratford
Blue Top Mountain
Nabiac
MUSWELLBROOK
Salisbury
Prickly Peak
Craven
DARAWANK NR
National Motorcycle Museum of Australia
Wards River
Bunyah
FORSTER–TUNCURRY
Ravensworth
Dawsons Hill
Eccleston
Williams
Karuah
GHIN-DOO-EE NATIONAL PARK
Myall
Lake Liddell
Lake St Clair
Bandon Grove
Coolongolook
Wallis Lake
Cape Hawke
Halton
Lostock
Upper Myall
Coomba
Stroud Road
Wootton
Whoota Whoota Lookout
St Clair
Green Point
Hunter
Ravensworth
Winns Mountain
Wallingat River picnic area
Tiona
Dungog
Jerrys Plains
Camberwell
Gresford
East Gresford
Stroud
Grandis
Elizabeth Beach
Pacific Palms
B84
A15
Bulahdelah
Blueys Beach
Trevallyn
MYALL
Bungwahl
Smiths Lake
Warkworth
Brookfield
Booral
LAKES
Myall Lake
Smiths Lake
SINGLETON
Vacy
NP
Seal Rocks
Mount Thorley
Clarence Town
Submarine Beach
Sugarloaf Point Lighthouse
Bombah Point
WOLLEMI NP
Belford
Paterson
Limeburners Creek
Black Knob
Branxton
Glen Oak
A1
Tamboy
Mungo Rainforest Walk
North Rothbury
Mungo Beach
Lochinvar
Myall
Broke
Seaham
Mungo Brush
M15
A43
Dark Point
Broughton Is
YENGO NATIONAL PARK
Karuah
Tea Gardens
Rothbury
MAITLAND
Morpeth
Hawks Nest
POKOLBIN STATE FOREST
Port Stephens
HUNTER
Abermain
RAYMOND TERRACE
Lemon Tree Passage
Nelson Bay
CESSNOCK
Beresfield
Shoal Bay
Paynes Crossing
Bellbird
Kurri Kurri
A1
Anna Bay
Weston
NEWCASTLE AIRPORT
Anna Bay
Hexham
Millfield
PORT STEPHENS–GREAT LAKES MARINE PARK
Wollombi
Stockton Bight
Ellalong
B82
A15
THE GREATER BLUE MTNS AREA WHA
Nobbys Head
M1
WATAGANS NATIONAL PARK
NEWCASTLE
AWABAKAL NR
Murrays Run
Toronto
Rathmines
RANGE
Bucketty
Cooranbong
Lake
YENGO NP
OLNEY SF
Morisset
Macquarie
Swansea
JILLIBY SCA
Mannering Park
Kulnura
Catherine Hill Bay
St Albans
Wyee
Lake Munmorah
Central Mangrove
TASMAN
Wyong
Toukley
Tuggerah
Norah Head
Peats Ridge
Tuggerah
Wisemans Ferry
Lake
The Entrance
SEA
Ourimbah
Long Jetty
Hawkesbury
Mount White
Gosford
Brisbane Water
Terrigal
Woy Woy
Kincumber
MARRAMARRA NP
M1
Umina
Bombi Point
Cowan
Barrenjoey Head
Galston
KU-RING-GAI CHASE NP
Palm Beach
Bangalley Head
Hornsby
N
Newport
Mona Vale
Frenchs Forest
A1
M2
Long Reef Point
Dee Why Head
0
10
20 km
A3
Manly
North Head
South Head
SYDNEY/WARRANG
SYDNEY AIRPORT
Randwick
M5
Botany

An easy trip from Sydney/Warrang or Newcastle, follow the shoreline of the NSW Great Lakes and you'll discover an untouched paradise of waterways, beaches and rainforest.

The Lakes Way

HOW LONG?
The Great Lakes region is really best explored in two sections over two days – unless of course you give into temptation (and I recommend you do) and decide to stay longer.

WHEN TO GO
Unless you like crowds, try and avoid the peak summer holiday season. Summer temperatures peak at around 27°C, winter temperatures range from 8 to 18°C.

Sugarloaf Point Lighthouse is a great spot for whale watching between May and Aug.

LOCAL SECRET
While it may lack designer bling, it more than compensates with a killer view – the **Pacific Palms Recreation Club** (aka the Recky) is right on the edge of Wallis Lake at Elizabeth Beach and is the best spot for sunset drinks. The food is cheap and cheerful and attracts good live music most weekends, and there's a courtesy bus if you don't want to drive.

👁 SNAPSHOT
Just an hour's drive north of Newcastle, or a 3hr drive north of Sydney/Warrang, the region known as the Great Lakes is one of NSW's unsung treasures. Here, a narrow strip of palm- and fern-covered land separates a dazzling undeveloped stretch of coastline from shimmering, shallow inland waterways that connect the three large lakes: the magnificent Wallis, Smiths and Myall lakes.

Drive rating
Easy. Mostly sealed roads with some gravel sections.

Acknowledgement of Country
This is the Traditional Land of the Awabakal and Worimi Peoples and extends further north into Biripi Country.

Distance planner
Sydney to Forster: around 324km
- Sydney to Hexham: 166km
- Hexham to Mungo Brush: 90km
- Mungo Brush to Forster via Seal Rocks: 68km

More information
There are visitor information centres in Forster (12 Little St) and Bulahdelah (Crawford St); 1800 802 692; barringtoncoast.com.au

Previous Sea Cliff Bridge near Clifton

SYDNEY/WARRANG TO MUNGO BRUSH (AND BOMBAH POINT)

With much of the coastline protected by three national parks, this paradisaical chain of beaches that stretch north of Newcastle to Forster has managed to escape the ravages of high-rise waterfront development that blights much of East Coast Australia. That's not to say it's an unknown slice of paradise: this beautiful region with its long expanse of pristine surf beaches, spectacular headlands and tree-fringed lakes draws thousands of people during the height of the summer holiday season.

During these times, almost every available corner becomes someone's idea of holiday heaven – whether it be floating in a forgotten cove in a luxury houseboat, camping on a shady lakeside beach, waterskiing, bushwalking, four-wheel driving on the beach, fishing, sailing, canoeing, swimming, surfing or picnicking.

But visit the area on a summer weekday, or an autumn or spring weekend out of school holidays, and you'll be sharing this piece of water wonderland with only a handful of others; in fact, you'll be lucky to see them at all.

From Sydney, head north on the Pacific Motorway and Pacific Hwy. After three hours of cut-and-thrust traffic, you'll be ready for a break, so take the turn-off to Tea Gardens and Hawks Nest, 50km north of the Hexham Bridge, on the outskirts of Newcastle.

Wedged between the ocean and where the Myall River spills into the sea on the northern entrance of Port Stephens, the twin towns of **Tea Gardens** and **Hawks Nest** are classic summer beach holiday territory – just ask former Prime Minister John Howard, he holidayed here every summer for more than 20 years. As I'm sure he'd agree, it's the place to go to kick back and relax, eat fish and chips at the water's edge, and generally do not very much at all.

Beyond the beautiful beaches, lakes and waterways, the area is home to a large colony of koalas and you can often see them ambling around backyards and wandering along the top of fences. The **Jean Shaw Koala Reserve** is on the corner of Ibis and Kingfisher avenues in Hawks Nest, just after you cross the bridge.

The bridge over the Myall River does more than just connect the two towns of Hawks Nest and Tea Gardens. When the wind blows the right way (from the south-west), the railings vibrate like a wind harp producing musical sounds, earning it the nickname of the **Singing Bridge**. You can often see dolphins in the water below the bridge, which is also a favourite fishing spot with locals.

Drive north from Hawks Nest on Mungo Brush Rd and it will lead you deep inside **Myall Lakes National Park**, home to the largest coastal lake system in NSW as well as extensive sand dunes and stretches of rainforest. The wetlands here are internationally recognised by Ramsar and are culturally significant to the Worimi People. There are middens throughout the national park that demonstrate a connection to this Country for millennia, with **Dark Point Aboriginal Place** a significant headland that has seen cultural gatherings for at least 4000 years. In spring the heathlands are ablaze with scented wildflowers, banksias, flannel flowers, lilies and flowering gums. There is an abundance of wildlife as well – kangaroos, wallabies, possums, bandicoots, gliders, echidnas, goannas and a wide variety of birdlife, and there's a good chance you'll see plenty of these during this section of the drive.

The road winds its way between the lakes and the beach, under a canopy of feathery casuarinas, peeling paperbarks and nutty banksias towards Mungo Brush. Along the way, countless walking and 4WD-only tracks spear off over the sand dunes towards the beach – you will need to get a permit from the National Parks and Wildlife Service to drive on the beach – or delve into the rainforest to meander around the lake foreshores.

Mungo Brush is one of the most popular spots in the park. It's a shady lakeside camping and picnic spot with electric barbecues and picnic tables, where pelicans lazily fish in the shallows as black swans gracefully glide by and opportunistic goannas prowl the grassy clearing once the visitors have packed up for the day. This is the place to launch yourself into the water. Children can splash about in the clear shallows and it's a great place to jump in a canoe for a leisurely paddle around the edge of the lake. **Mungo Rainforest Walk** is an easy 1.5km-long loop but it can be as long or short as you like as the paths branch off to other paths.

Opposite Bennetts Head Lookout, Forster *Right* White sand beach near Mungo Brush, Myall Lakes National Park

SIDETRACK

From Mungo Brush, the road continues on just a few kilometres to **Bombah Point**, where you can catch the vehicle ferry (leaves every half hour 8am to 6pm) to rejoin the highway and then and follow the dirt road signposted north of Bulahdelah through the forest to the **'Grandis'**, an 84m-high flooded gum thought to be the tallest tree in NSW. You'll find it around 100m east of Stoney Creek Rd and there is a viewing platform at the base of the tree.

The Lakes Way 5

Opposite left The Green Cathedral *Opposite right* Paddling on Wallis Lake *Left* Sugarloaf Point Lighthouse at Seal Rocks

BOMBAH POINT TO FORSTER–TUNCURRY

The highlight of the northern section of Myall Lakes National Park is Seal Rocks and Sugarloaf Point Lighthouse. To get here, either head back to the Pacific Hwy from Bombah Point to Bulahdelah and then turn onto the Lakes Way (the back road to Forster) just a few kilometres north of the town and wind your way along the northern shore of Myall Lake, or take the road through the national park from Mungo Brush.

Seal Rocks is a tiny fishing village perched on a headland, surrounded by the national park. Chat to the local fishers tending their lines knee-deep in the surf or take a 10min walk up to **Sugarloaf Point Lighthouse**, built in 1875, for sweeping views of the coastline.

Although you can't get inside the lighthouse, you can walk around the buildings and climb the unusual stairway on the outside of the tower. There is also a path here that leads to a lookout over Seal Rocks, a collection of rocky islets which are home to the northernmost colony of Australian fur seals – bring your binoculars for a better look.

Back on the Lakes Way the road skirts around the edge of a second lake, **Smiths Lake**, and then spears through dense pockets of coastal banksias and tall stands of cabbage tree palms to emerge on the shores of lake number three, aka **Wallis Lake**, a broad stretch of shallow crystal-clear water, no more than a few inches deep for the most part, that spreads all the way north to Forster.

At **Tiona**, just north of Pacific Palms, you can hire a surf ski and paddle the shoreline or sit by the grassy edge with a coffee at a lakeside cafe and watch the kids splash about. At **Booti Booti National Park**, take a walk through the rainforest to the **Green Cathedral** – an al fresco church where timber pews look out over the lake under a rainforest canopy – or head to one of a number of pristine surf beaches.

Continue north along the very slender strip of sandy heath, the tranquil lakes on your left, the crashing surf just out of sight, but not out of earshot, on the other side of the dunes until you get to the twin towns of **Forster-Tuncurry**. This is the hub of the Great Lakes area and there's all the usual seaside diversions, including dolphin watching cruises, oyster farms, cafes and restaurants. The Pacific Hwy's just down the road, and Sydney's an easy 3hr drive away, but hey, take an extra day and go back the long way.

SIDETRACK

Take a detour along Sugar Creek Rd (sometimes called Wallingat Forest Dr) just north of Bungwahl, spearing off into the rainforest to wind your way up to **Whoota Whoota Lookout** for breathtaking views over the three lakes and coastal beaches. Wallingat River picnic area is a nice spot for a swim. It's a 25km loop on narrow unsealed roads, but fine for 2WDs.

Kids' spot

If you ever holidayed in this part of the world when you were young, chances are you'll remember the **Big Buzz Fun Park** north of Forster, which has been going since 1984. It's still delighting kids of all ages with its waterslides, toboggan run, go-karts, laser tag and putt putt golf, as well as a barbecue and picnic area.

Good for a rainy day

You don't have to be a bikie to get a kick out of The **National Motorcycle Museum of Australia** at Nabiac. The ultimate bike shed, this vast, purpose-built complex houses more than 700 motorcycles, some dating back to the early 1900s, and boasts an enormous array of motorcycle memorabilia, toys and a library of motorcycle books and magazines.

BEST BEDS

- In Tea Gardens, the **Boathouse Resort** overlooks the river and has a range of one, two and three-bedroom apartments. Facilities include undercover parking, a heated swimming pool and bike hire. boathouseresortteagardens.com.au
- **Mobys Beachside Resort** began as a traditional caravan park on the edge of Boomerang Beach in the 1960s and is now a beach-house resort. Accommodation is in one-, two- or three-bedroom townhouses. Facilities include a licensed bar and restaurant, tennis courts and heated swimming pool. The beach is just 50m from the resort. mobys.com.au
- **NRMA Myall Shores Holiday Park** is a lakeside park with plenty of accommodation options, including camping and caravan sites, villas and glamping. Facilities include jetty access, a cafe, pool and playground. nrmaparksandresorts.com.au
- Soak up the ocean views from your balcony in the modern **Dorsal Boutique Hotel** opposite Forster Main Beach. dorsalhotel.com.au

VANLIFE

Mungo Brush in Myall Lakes National Park is very popular with campers and caravanners, so you'll need to book ahead: call 1300 072 757 or see NSW National Parks and Wildlife Service (nationalparks.nsw.gov.au).

The Lakes Way

New South Wales

Deserted beaches and prolific wildlife just a short drive north from Sydney/Warrang and Newcastle.

Central Coast to Nelson Bay

HOW LONG?
So close to two major cities, this stretch of the coast is the perfect destination for a long weekend or short break; two or three days is ideal.

WHEN TO GO
Average summer temperatures are around 25°C, winter temperatures range from 9 to 17°C. In winter and spring (late May through to Nov), Port Stephens is an excellent place to see whales during the annual migration when more than 11,000 humpback whales swim by close to shore.

LOCAL SECRET
The half-hour ferry ride from Ettalong Beach to Palm Beach is one of the country's prettiest boat rides, and makes for an enjoyable car-free day out. Check timetables and tours online (fantasea.com.au/palm-beach-ferries).

SNAPSHOT
With a natural harbour two and a half times as large as Sydney's, Port Stephens is an aquatic playground, less than a 3hr drive north of Sydney. Take the coastal route rather than the motorway to get there and you'll discover a string of beautiful beaches – many flanked by national parks – along the way.

Drive rating
Easy. Sealed roads.

Acknowledgement of Country
This is the Traditional Land of the Kuringgai, Awabakal and Worimi Peoples.

Distance planner
Gosford is 80km north of Sydney. The southern side of Port Stephens (Nelson Bay and Shoal Bay) is approximately 200km north of Sydney, via the M1 Pacific Motorway, around a 2.5hr drive, depending on traffic.
- Gosford to The Entrance, via Patonga: 80km
- The Entrance to Newcastle: 64km
- Newcastle to Nelson Bay via Stockton: 60km

More information
- The Entrance Visitor Information Centre, Memorial Park, The Entrance; 1800 035 377; lovecentralcoast.com
- Newcastle Visitor Information Centre, 430 Hunter St (former Civic Railway Station); (02) 4974 2109; visitnewcastle.com.au
- Port Stephens Visitor Information Centre, 60 Victoria Pde, Nelson Bay; 1800 808 900; portstephens.org.au

Opposite 4WD fishing on Stockton Beach

GOSFORD TO NEWCASTLE

Most people begin their Central Coast trip at Gosford, just off the M1 motorway. From here you can head south past Woy Woy to the waterside hamlets of Patonga and Pearl Beach, before looping back towards Ettalong Beach. Often overlooked in favour of the busier, ritzier Terrigal to the north, **Ettalong Beach** is a more budget-friendly place to stay; it's less frenetic and is a good family-friendly option, especially if you're looking for somewhere to stay for a while.

If you have come to the Central Coast for the beaches you won't be disappointed. Follow the rather aptly named Scenic Rd north from Killcare through **Bouddi National Park**, a beautiful pocket of bushland surrounded by urban development, 20km south-east of Gosford. Highlights include deserted beaches flanked by rainforest and eucalypt forests, steep hills and sandstone cliffs. More than 100 First Peoples cultural sites have been identified in the park, including rock engravings of fish and whales, some up to 20m long, as well as axe grinding grooves and middens. There are also a number of walking tracks that lead down to the sea, although what goes down must also come up, and many of the tracks can be quite steep in places. The most popular is the **Maitland Bay Track**, a half-hour (each way) walk from Maitland Bay Information Centre that winds down to Maitland Bay, a lovely crescent-shaped beach named after the paddle steamer *Maitland*, which was wrecked on the rocks in 1898 with the loss of 26 lives. The rusting remains are still visible at low tide. Maitland Bay is a good swimming spot, as is Putty Beach. Be careful if you decide to swim at Tallow Beach, as it often has strong rips and currents. None of the beaches are patrolled.

There's a string of laid-back seaside suburbs north of the national park. Stop at **Captain Cook Lookout** on the headland between Avoca Beach and Copacabana: on a good day you can see south down the coast to Sydney and north to Terrigal. During whale season (June/July and Oct/Nov) it's a good place to see humpback and southern right whales on their annual migration to and from Antarctica.

Avoca Beach fronts a 2km-long golden stretch of sand bookended by rocky headlands and bordered by a grassy foreshore and Bulbararing Lagoon and Avoca Lake. No family holiday here is considered complete without a couple of hours spent exploring the lake on an aquabike or pedalboat. The waters off Avoca Beach are home to one of the only military dive sites in NSW, the sunken naval warship **HMAS Adelaide**. The 138m-long naval frigate, which served from 1980 until Jan 2008 in the Gulf War and East Timor, was scuttled in Apr 2011 and now rests on the seabed in around 32m of water 1.8km off Avoca Beach. Unlike most wrecks, which can be difficult to access, diver holes were strategically placed

Maitland Bay

Central Coast to Nelson Bay 11

throughout the vessel before it was sunk to allow for greater exploration, and it's open to advanced divers. Highlights include the captain's chair, helicopter hangars, bunkrooms and the operations room with weapon shells. There are a few companies that offer dive tours here.

The fashionable village of **Terrigal** with its boutiques, restaurants and cafes is the next beach to the north, followed by **Wamberal**, **Forresters** and **Shelly Beach** – three good spots for those keen to surf. **The Entrance** is a family holiday favourite, with lots of great swimming options, including **Vera's Water Garden**, a free splash pool with lots of colourful sculptures to climb on. Kids also love the pelican feeding at The Entrance, when scores of squawking pelicans swarm the shores of Memorial Park.

From The Entrance, continue north along the narrow strip of land that separates Tuggerah Lake from the sea, through Wyrrabalong National Park and take the turn-off to **Norah Head Lighthouse**. Built in 1903, it is open for tours if you book ahead (norahheadlighthouse.com.au), and the view both north and south is beautiful. A walking track skirts around the side of the lighthouse and leads to stairs which climb down to the rock platform below and to **Lighthouse Beach**, a popular fishing spot.

It's around a 50min drive north to Newcastle from here, and half of that is along a narrow strip of land between Lake Macquarie and the sea, so there's plenty of places to pull over and admire the view, or go for a paddle, along the way.

Opposite The view from Tomaree Head *Above* Australian Reptile Park, near Gosford

Kids' spot

If you've got kids on board your first stop should be the **Australian Reptile Park** at Somersby, just off the Gosford exit from the M1. More than just a zoo, it is the sole Australian provider of venom for snakes and funnel-web spider anti-venoms. It's one of the only places in the country you can watch snakes being milked of their deadly poison. Children love meeting platypus, kangaroos and wombats here, and having their photograph taken with a huge python or one of the koalas.

Head into the hills

Driving Central Mangrove to Wisemans Ferry is less than 65km, but you'll feel like you're travelling back to a time 200 years ago when all the buildings were built by convicts and the only way across a river was by punt. The road winds through orchards and farms and then descends in a series of twists and turns to Mangrove Creek. From here on in you follow the water to **Spencer**, where you meet up with the Hawkesbury River, which you trace to **Wisemans Ferry**. To reach the village of Wisemans Ferry you must catch the ferry - it's free and it runs all day. From Wisemans Ferry it is only 20km or so to the village of **St Albans**, where almost all the buildings in town are convict built and classified by the National Trust. Half the drive is on gravel, but it is in good condition and the drive through the Macdonald River Valley is worth it.

NEWCASTLE TO NELSON BAY

Great coffee, good restaurants and an exploding creative arts scene, combined with plenty of beaches within walking distance of the city centre, make Newcastle a fantastic place for a coastal city break.

You're never very far from a beach in Newcastle. Follow the waterfront promenade and walk along the convict-built breakwall up to the lighthouse on **Nobbys Head** at the harbour entrance for some great views. Nobbys is linked to the string of beaches to the south by the **Bathers Way**, a 5km-long coastal walk. Stop for a swim at the Art Deco **Newcastle Ocean Baths** or head to the **Bogey Hole** at the southern end of Newcastle Beach. It was carved out of the cliff-face by convicts in 1819. There's another ocean pool at **Merewether**, the largest in the Southern Hemisphere, and most of the beachfront parks along the way have barbecue and picnic facilities.

Continue north on the B63 towards Nelson Bay via Williamtown, where you can get in touch with your inner

'Top Gun' at **Fighter World**, an aviation museum located next to the entrance of the Royal Australian Air Force Base, the home of Australia's Strike/Fighter Force. There's a huge collection of real fighter jets here, including a Meteor, Vampire, Sabre, Mirage, Macchi, Winjeel, Bloodhound and Mig to name but a few, as well as interesting replicas of a Spitfire Messerschmitt and Fokker. You can actually climb into the cockpit of some and there is a vast array of related exhibits.

Port Stephens claims it is the 'Dolphin Capital of Australia' and the bay is home to a resident pod of around 150 bottlenose dolphins. There are several operators offering dolphin cruises, but if you want to get really close join a dolphin swim tour with **Imagine Cruises** (imaginecruises.com.au) and ride the bow wave with the dolphins while tethered to the moving catamaran. Whale and dolphin watching cruises depart from Nelson Bay Marina.

If you'd rather keep your adventures on land, **Tomaree Head** is part of an extinct volcano which guards the southern entrance to Port Stephens. The half-hour walk from the beach at Shoal Bay to the summit is steep but not as hard as it looks and the views from the top over the bay, beaches and offshore islands make the climb worthwhile. Keep your eyes on the trees, as you may be lucky enough to spot a wild koala or two. For guaranteed koala sightings, drop into the **Port Stephens Koala Sanctuary** and climb the elevated viewing platform and visit the Koala Hospital; you can also glamp here (*see* p.15).

You may be just a few hours from Sydney, but this coastal road trip is proof that you don't need to go far to really get away.

Good for a rainy day

Newcastle is one of the biggest coal exporting ports in the world, and the city has always been well known for its hot and heavy industry, including steelmaking. Grab a stool at one of the riverside bars or cafes in Honeysuckle and watch the massive freighters being guided in and out of the harbour by tugboats. **Newcastle Museum** has a good display on the industrial heritage of the city including a (very noisy) sound and light show that features molten steel being poured from a furnace.

New South Wales

SIDETRACK

The **Stockton cycleway** starts at the Stockton Bridge and follows the harbour around to Stockton Breakwall. It's nice and flat, so ideal for families, and if you want to shorten the ride you can catch the ferry across the river to Stockton and bikes travel free. Head out along the breakwater and you'll see the rusted remains of a number of ships that came to grief here, including the *Adolphe*, wrecked in 1904.

The **Stockton Dunes**, which stretch almost all the way north from Newcastle to Nelson Bay is the largest mobile sand system in the Southern Hemisphere and the biggest sand dunes in Australia, with some more than 40m high. Part of the **Worimi Conservation Lands** the area is home to a huge number of Worimi cultural sites. You can explore the dunes on a range of both cultural and adventure tours, from quad bikes and 4WDs to sand boarding adventures: **Sand Dune Adventures** is owned and operated by the Worimi Local Aboriginal Land Council. Book ahead (sandduneadventures.com.au or worimiconservationlands.com).

You can also visit **Tin City**, a small cluster of rusty tin shacks half buried by the constantly shifting sands at the northern end of the Stockton Bight. It was established as a squatter's village during the Depression in the 1930s.

BEST BEDS

- Built in a giant terraced horseshoe shape that cradles a seriously large pool, most of the 236 rooms at **Mantra Ettalong Beach** enjoy picture-perfect views of Brisbane Water and Broken Bay, across towards Lion Island and Palm Beach beyond. mantraettalongbeach.com.au
- **Crown Plaza Terrigal Pacific** is right at the centre of the action in Terrigal and all rooms face the ocean. terrigalpacific.crowneplaza.com
- Most rooms at the **Novotel Newcastle Beach** have balconies with great views overlooking either Newcastle Beach or Nobbys Headland and the harbour entrance, and it's an easy walk into the centre of town. accorhotels.com.au/hotel/novotel-newcastle-beach
- A great family option, **NRMA Stockton Beach Holiday Park** is a 5min ferry ride from Newcastle's CBD. Two- and three-bedroom cabins feature a full kitchen, living room, laundry facilities and decks. Park facilities include outdoor electric barbeques and playgrounds. nrmaparksandresorts.com.au/stockton-beach
- Wake up with the koalas when you stay in one of the luxe glamping tents at **Port Stephens Koala Sanctuary**. portstephenskoalasanctuary.com.au

VANLIFE

The Central Coast has always been popular with campers and you'll find good commercial caravan parks in almost every coastal town, with a good cluster of parks in and around **The Entrance** where you can choose to set up lakeside, or closer to the beach. If you don't mind a short walk from the car to your tent, **Putty Beach** campground in Bouddi National Park is a nice place to go wild. Bookings are essential for all campgrounds in NSW national parks. See NSW National Parks and Wildlife Service (nationalparks.nsw.gov.au).

Opposite top left Strolling along Stockton Beach *Opposite top right* Wreck of the *Adolphe* at Stockton *Opposite bottom left* Scenic coastline of Bouddi National Park *Opposite bottom right* Quadbiking on Stockton Dunes

New South Wales

16

Small-town charm and beautiful uncrowded beaches with legendary surf and great camping.

Laurieton to South West Rocks

HOW LONG?
Laurieton is roughly a 4hr drive north of Sydney/Warrang. From there it's just a little more than a 1hr drive from Laurieton to South West Rocks if you stay on the Pacific Hwy, but that's not the point. With beaches this good you can stretch it out over a long weekend, or even make it a two-week holiday trip.

WHEN TO GO
Summer temperatures hover around 27°C, winter temperatures range from 8 to 18°C. Generally, the water in the ocean is warm enough for swimming between Sept and Apr. If you want to see whales, go in winter/spring between June and Nov.

NEED TO KNOW
The track through Limeburners Creek National Park between Port Macquarie and Crescent Head can be impassable after rain.

Aside from the beaches in the coastal towns, many of the beaches on this route are unpatrolled.

LOCAL SECRET
Trial Bay Kiosk in Arakoon National Park near South West Rocks is one of the coast's best-kept secrets and a favourite eating place for locals. If you haven't had the chance to try much of the local seafood, the platter for two here, best eaten on the deck while sipping a local white wine and staring out across the bay, usually showcases the best of whatever's fresh. As a bonus, it's one of the few spots on Australia's east coast where you can watch the sunset over the sea. Book ahead at trialbaykiosk.com.au

SNAPSHOT
Get off the highway and chill out on this family-friendly, back-to-nature coastal road trip through national parks and beguilingly low-key towns and villages on the NSW mid-north coast. Forget glitzy high-rise hotels – the camping grounds and caravan parks here have the best views, and fine dining is fresh fish and chips eaten with salty fingers while overlooking the sea.

Drive rating
Easy. Sealed roads with optional 4WD section.

Acknowledgement of Country
This is the Traditional Land of the Birpai, Dunghutti and Ngaku Peoples.

Distance planner
Laurieton to South West Rocks via Crescent Head: around 148km
- Laurieton to Port Macquarie, via the coast: 30km
- Port Macquarie to Crescent Head via Point Plomer (4WD): 46km (65km via the highway)
- Crescent Head to South West Rocks: 73km

More information
- Port Macquarie Visitor Information Centre, cnr Clarence and Hay sts; 1300 303 155; portmacquarieinfo.com.au
- Macleay Valley Coast Visitor Information Centre, 490 Macleay Valley Way, South Kempsey; (02) 6566 6692; macleayvalleycoast.com.au

LAURIETON TO PORT MACQUARIE

The fun begins on this little coastal roadie when you turn off the Pacific Hwy at the Big Axe in Kew (361km north of Sydney/Warrang, around a 4hr drive or a half-hour drive south of Port Macquarie airport) and head east along Ocean Dr to **Laurieton**, one of three villages at the mouth of the Camden Haven River – the other two are **Dunbogan** on the south side of the inlet and **North Haven** on the north – collectively known as the Camden Haven.

The lookout at **North Brother Mountain** in **Dooragan National Park** on the road into Laurieton has good views over Camden Haven and its expanse of waterways and beaches and is worth the short detour. There's a lovely little rainforest walk at the summit, as well as picnic tables, and it's a great spot to watch the fearless hang gliders take off.

Back at sea level, follow the walking path along the Camden Haven River in either direction to Dunbogan or North Haven and watch the pelicans swoop down to steal scraps from the fisher folk cleaning their catches – on any given day you'll usually find dozens of locals casting their lines along the breakwall, off the beaches and from tinnies, hoping to reel in a monster-sized bream, blackfish, snapper or crab, or probing the sandbars during low tide for bait. You can hire fishing gear, boats and kayaks at the **Dunbogan Boatshed**. More often than not you'll see a dolphin or two here as well.

Apart from during peak holiday time, the beaches in and around Laurieton are almost always deserted: for surf head to **North Haven**; for sheltered swimming, rockpools and shade **Pilot Beach** on the Dunbogan side is the spot. The local fish co-op down on the river, **Laurieton Seafoods** invariably has a line of hungry locals out the front, and **Armstrong Oysters** sells fat, creamy oysters from its riverside shed. The Art Deco **Plaza Theatre** shows good art house movies – Baz Luhrmann's father was a projectionist here and this is where Baz was first smitten by the motion picture industry.

From Laurieton, the coast road north to Port Macquarie cuts through heath-covered sand dunes, over headlands with views along endless stretches of beach, and skirts the shores of **Lake Cathie** (pronounced '*cat-eye*'). In spring, the bushland beside the road is carpeted with Christmas bells and flannel flowers.

In Port Macquarie, stretch your legs along the boardwalk at **Sea Acres Rainforest Centre**, the second largest coastal rainforest reserve in NSW, or on the 3hr coastal walk, where five beaches are linked by wooden walkways over rocky headlands. The pathway starts at Lighthouse Beach and finishes at Town Beach, where you can walk along the breakwall to the grassy park at the mouth of the Hastings River known as the Town Green. Do it in the afternoon so you can time your arrival at the **Beach House Hotel** to enjoy a cold beer or cocktail at an outdoor table on the edge of the green as you watch the sun sink into the river while surveying the passing parade of people and pelicans.

The **Town Green** is Port's heart and soul. It's where everyone takes their takeaway fish and chips, kids ride scooters and tricycles and chase seagulls, families dangle fishing lines from the wharf and it's practically mandatory to lick an ice-cream while reading the graffiti along the breakwall.

☺ Kids' spot

Two attractions at Wauchope will appeal especially to children. **Timbertown** is a re-creation of a 19th-century timber-getting village, complete with steam train rides, horse and carriage rides, and whip and timber-cutting displays.

Bago Maze and Winery has the largest hedge maze in NSW, and kids love discovering the giant musical chimes, recycled bells (made from gas cylinders) and marimba (a cross between a piano and a xylophone) along the way.

Billabong Zoo Koala and Wildlife Park between Port Macquarie and Wauchope is a popular family attraction, but ask a local and they'll point you to the **Koala Hospital** in the grounds of Roto House in Lord St in Port. It's the only one of its kind in the country that is open to the public every day and its cheerful band of volunteers care for up 250 sick and injured koalas each year. There's a free tour daily at 3pm.

Opposite Camden Haven, from North Brother Mountain *Top* Bago Maze, Wauchope *Bottom* Port Macquarie breakwall

◯ Head into the hills

The other 'back way' to Port (locals always drop the 'Macquarie') is via **Tourist Drive 8** (which has some unsealed sections), from Taree via Wingham and Wauchope. Take a walk through **Wingham Brush** with its resident flying foxes and visit **Ellenborough Falls**, one of the largest single-drop waterfalls in the Southern Hemisphere. The village of **Comboyne** is perched high on an open plateau and from there the road winds its way back down the mountain rainforest towards **Wauchope**.

PORT MACQUARIE TO CRESCENT HEAD

If you have a 4WD you can take the Settlement Point ferry from Port Macquarie to North Shore to rock and roll your way across the sand ridges and through the banksia forests and heathlands of **Limeburners Creek National Park** and on to Crescent Head on the sandy Plomer Rd (expect some very big, rather deep puddles after rain). If you don't have a 4WD, take the same ferry and follow the Maria River Rd. It's unsealed, but as long as there hasn't been too much bad weather lately it's usually okay. If in doubt, stick to the Pacific Hwy and take the turn-off to Crescent Head just south of Kempsey.

Keen surfers will probably already know that **Crescent Head** is home to one of the best right-hand surf breaks in the country (**Killick Beach** is a National Surfing Reserve) and a favourite with longboard riders around the world. But it's not just about the surf. Here, life is just like it used to be before fishing villages became seaside resorts: just one long beach and a casual, laid-back attitude where shoes are definitely optional and everyone has salt-stiffened hair.

Good for a rainy day

Ricardoes farm, just a 10min drive from Port, is home to the best tasting tomatoes you'll ever eat. Grab a bagful at the farm, or buy a batch ready-made into soup, sauce or relish in the shed-like Cafe Red, which also has a good range of strawberry treats; you can also pick strawberries here.

If you're a country music fan, you'll enjoy the **Slim Dusty Centre and Museum** in South Kempsey (the singer grew up in Kempsey).

CRESCENT HEAD TO SOUTH WEST ROCKS

From Crescent Head drive north along the banks of the Belmore River through lush dairy country studded with black and white cows. You'll reach the tiny hamlet of **Gladstone**, where the Belmore River converges with the broad Macleay River and you'll find several very good riverside cafes, galleries and boutiques. Follow the twists and turns of the Macleay River towards South West Rocks – if you're self-catering pick up some fresh fruit and vegies at the many **farm gate stalls** that line the riverside along the way.

Strung out along the shores of Horseshoe Bay at the mouth of the Macleay River, **South West Rocks** is another idyllic place, where the waterfront caravan park has the best view in town, the **Seabreeze Beach Hotel** not only lives up to its name but does a great lunch, and if you time your stay to avoid the holidays and summer weekends the town can be blissfully crowd-free.

Drive up to **Smoky Cape Lighthouse**, built in 1891 (it's good odds you'll see whales between May and Nov) and **Arakoon National Park** to wander around the very photogenic sandstone ruins of historic **Trial Bay Gaol**. Built in 1877, closed in 1903, and reopened in 1915 to hold internees from Germany during World War I – who were allowed out onto the beaches during the day but locked up at night – this is a gaol with a view. It's now a museum and you can walk through the old cells.

The surrounding beachside picnic and camping area is a popular spot during summer holidays and the **Trial Bay Kiosk** is a top spot for feasting with a view (*see* p.17) and just like the rest of this road trip, is proof that you don't need to be glamorous to be good, because sometimes the simple things really are the best.

SIDETRACK

Of all the half-forgotten out-of-the-way villages studded along this section of the mid-north coast, **Hat Head** is one of my favourites. It's just a clutch of holiday houses and a store where you can stock up on essentials like bait, burgers or beer, but it's surrounded by national park and offers a range of camping options that are guaranteed to remind you that all you really need to be happy is some sun, sand, surf, grilled sausages and maybe some fish and chips. It's also at the beginning of one of the best cliff-top walks in the region, the 3km **Korogoro Walking Track** that loops around the hat-shaped (if you squint) headland.

BEST BEDS

- From the outside the **El Paso Motor Inn** in the centre of Port Macquarie is your quintessential mid-20th century motel, although a recent refurb has given the interiors a fresh start. elmotorinn.com.au
- **Heritage Guest House** Located in the heart of South West Rocks, this guesthouse has nine large ensuite rooms. See if you can nab rooms 5 or 6 as they open out onto the sun-soaked balcony. heritageguesthouse.com.au

VANLIFE

There's no shortage of great places to park a van or pitch a tent on this part of the coast. The **NRMA Port Macquarie Breakwall Holiday Park** between Town Beach and the river has one of the best views in town. The **Crescent Head Holiday Park** overlooks the beach, and the camping spots at nearby **Point Plomer** in Limeburners Creek National Park are popular with surfers. **Horseshoe Bay Holiday Park** in South West Rocks offers waterfront spots opposite the pub. **Hat Head Holiday Park** is delightfully old school, but it does have powered sites and hot showers, and is just a hop, skip and jump from the beach. For wow factor though, it's hard to go past **Trial Bay Campground** in Arakoon National Park, where you can set up camp overlooking the water in the shadow of the sandstone ruins of historic gaol. Bookings are essential for all campgrounds in NSW national parks, whatever the time of year. See NSW National Parks and Wildlife Service (nationalparks.nsw.gov.au).

Opposite Trial Bay Gaol *Left* Horseshoe Bay, South West Rocks

New South Wales

Discover some overlooked and underrated seaside gems on this slow but scenic meander along the NSW mid-north coast. There are family-friendly holiday towns, magnificent coastal national parks and fabulous seafood; what more could you want?

Coffs Coast to Yamba

HOW LONG?
It's only a few hours' drive between Macksville and Yamba but there's lots to explore on this part of the coast, and towns like Nambucca Heads, Coffs Harbour and Yamba are each worth spending a few days in. Allow at least a week for this road trip.

WHEN TO GO
Like much of the NSW north coast, the ocean water is generally warm enough for swimming between Sept and Apr, but summer holidays can be very busy. If you want to see whales, go between June and Nov.

LOCAL SECRET
The best place to buy prawns in Yamba (along with a wide range of fresh and filleted fish, ocean bugs and cooked fish and chips) is from the **Clarence River Fishermen's Co-op** at the Yamba Marina on Yamba Rd. The seafood comes straight from the fishing trawlers, and you can't get much fresher than that.

SNAPSHOT
Highlights along this stretch of coast include World Heritage–listed rainforests, world-class surfing, sensational seafood, and wonderfully wild and deserted beaches in coastal national parks.

Drive rating
Moderate. Mostly sealed roads, apart from those in Yuraygir National Park, which can be a little sandy and get boggy after rain.

Acknowledgement of Country
This is the Traditional Land of the Dunghutti, Gumbaynggirr and Yaygirr Peoples.

Distance planner
Macksville to Yamba: around 300km, including coastal detours in Yuraygir National Park. Coffs Harbour is 530km north of Sydney, around a 6-7hr drive.
- Macksville to Coffs Harbour: 61km
- Coffs Harbour to Wooli: 106km
- Wooli to Yamba via Sandon and Brooms Head: 140km

More information
- Nambucca Valley Visitor Information Centre, cnr Giinagay Way and Riverside Dr, Nambucca Heads; nambuccavalley.com.au
- Coffs Coast Visitor Information Outlet, Coffs Central Shopping Centre, 35-61 Harbour Dr, Coffs Harbour; (02) 6648 4990; coffscoast.com.au
- myclarencevalley.com

Opposite Marcel Island, Nambucca Heads

MACKSVILLE TO COFFS HARBOUR

Macksville, on the Nambucca River, is around a 5hr drive north of Sydney/Warrang via the M1 and Pacific Hwy. If you're coming from interstate you can fly into Coffs Harbour and pick up a hire car there – you'll be backtracking for the first 56km, but it's worth it because Macksville is home to one of my favourite road-side eating stops, the **Macksville Star**. You can't miss it, it's the big white two-storey pub beside the river near the bridge, adorned with lots of beautiful iron lace. They do the best hamburgers on the coast. Beyond the rivers and the beaches, there's some interesting antique shops in town, and the **Mary Boulton Pioneer Cottage and Museum** is worth a look if it's open when you're there (usually Wed and Sat afternoons, but not always).

Often overlooked by travellers heading north to Coffs Harbour and beyond, **Nambucca Heads** is just a few minutes' drive off the highway. Nambucca is a local Aboriginal word that translates to either 'entrance to waters' or 'crooked river'. Nambucca is one of the mid-north coast's hidden gems, although guesthouses here have been welcoming tourists since the 1930s, and the north coast's first private caravan park opened here in 1953. Even so, Nambucca feels like a real town rather than a tourist town, and is one of the prettiest spots on the coast.

Nambucca Heads is a place with two hearts, there's the town centre high on the hill, and the caravan park, pub and a couple of holiday units down on the waterfront where the Nambucca River seeps into the sea. In between is a dense pocket of rainforest called Gordon Park, once laced with walking tracks, now home to a large colony of flying foxes. If you're a keen fisher, it's one of the best flathead holes on the coast. Otherwise, activities are all about swimming, surfing, long walks on empty beaches, admiring the public 'art' left by generations of holidaymakers on the v-wall, and strolling along the foreshore boardwalk. There's more than 80km of linked kayaking trails and the remarkably clear river is renowned for its sea life, including turtles and tropical fish. There's a golf course on its own island, dolphins are routinely spotted in the river and five headland lookouts – all great winter whale watching spots.

Way Way Creek Road drive, near Macksville

Head into the hills

The late great Slim Dusty famously crooned about the pub with no beer in 1958, giving birth to one of Australia's top 50 biggest selling singles and an Australian icon. According to the legend, the pub with no beer in the song of the same name is the **Cosmopolitan Hotel** at **Taylors Arm** – a beautiful half-hour drive through a bucolic valley west of Macksville – and it ran out of beer once when cut off by floods. Of course, like all good legends the actual facts are a bit hazy, such as when this catastrophic event occurred, but local country and western music star, Gordon Parsons, aka the Yodelling Bushman, penned a ditty and his mate Slim Dusty, a Kempsey boy, recorded it in 1958, and the rest, as they say, is history … if not myth. But the mythical pub does exist – it's now called the Pub Without Beer – and it has plenty of beer, as well as good lunches and there's often live music on the verandah.

Coffs Coast to Yamba   25

SIDETRACK

If you're coming from the south – either Sydney or South West Rocks (see p.17) – or don't mind backtracking a little, there's a fabulous little scenic loop that winds through the rainforest of Yarriabini National Park out to the coastal hamlets of **Stuarts Point**, **Grassy Head** and **Scotts Head**. The beaches are long and deserted, but the real drawcard is the lush tall rainforest, especially along **Way Way Creek Road drive** and **The Pines picnic area**, and the views from **Yarriabini lookout**. It starts at Albert Dr in the south and reconnects with the Pacific Hwy 5km south of Macksville at Scotts Head Rd. You'll find a good map at NSW National Parks and Wildlife Service (nationalparks.nsw.gov.au, search for Way Way Creek Road drive).

Head into the hills

Spend a day browsing the museums and art galleries at **Bowraville**, a 20min drive west of Nambucca Heads. Known as the 'verandah post town', the main street is lined with historic shopfronts. The **Bowraville Folk Museum** has just about everything on display, from old wedding dresses to tractors. **Phoenix Gallery and Cafe** is a community-owned social enterprise that shows off the work of people with an intellectual disability and the **Frank Partridge VC Military Museum** is a hit with war buffs.

Urunga, a 15min drive north of Nambucca, is another place on the Pacific Hwy that many road trippers drive on through, although invest the two or three minutes it takes to turn off the highway and you'll find a charming village with one of the best over-water boardwalks in the state. The **Urunga Honey Place** – a giant beehive-shaped roadside attraction where you can buy honey and watch bees at work – is worth a stop if you like honey. The Kalang and Bellinger rivers converge at Urunga, spilling out into the sea a kilometre from the village, and you can follow the boardwalk along the river and over the dunes to the beach. A second boardwalk leads off into the mangroves of the Urunga Lagoon.

If you're hungry, or in need of a coffee, make a beeline for **Sawtell**. I'm not sure the locals would entirely appreciate the comparison, but sitting at a table on the footpath sipping coffee and eating cake, watching the passing parade of holidaymakers browse the boutiques on either side of the cafe, you can't help but think that Sawtell is the NSW mid-north coast version of Noosa. Just a 15min drive south of Coffs Harbour and only 5km off the Pacific Hwy, the fig-lined main street of this pretty little seaside town is packed with restaurants, cafes, fashion boutiques, quirky homewares stores and day spas. Unlike Noosa, though, there's no traffic jams and prices are affordable.

Coffs Harbour has been a popular beach holiday spot for decades, and it's easy to see why. Beyond lazing around on the beaches, there's plenty of things to do in and around

Coffs, including white water rafting on the nearby Nymboida River, sea kayaking tours and learn-to-surf schools. You can also go snorkelling and diving in **Solitary Islands Marine Park**, where you can see hard corals and grey nurse sharks. If you're there between May and Nov, there are some good whale watching vantage points around the beaches and on the headlands like Muttonbird Island, near the marina.

Up on the mountain-top behind the city centre **Sealy Lookout** in Bruxner Park is cantilevered more than 20m out over the edge of the Great Dividing Range with views of Coffs Harbour and the coast. There's a network of good short rainforest walks here as well.

One thing you shouldn't miss in Coffs is the **National Cartoon Gallery** (nationalcartoongallery.com.au). Housed in an old World War II bunker, it's home to a staggering collection of 16,000 cartoons and caricatures – mainly political and satirical – and exhibitions change monthly.

Good for a rainy day

The Pet Porpoise Pool - now called the **Dolphin Marine Conservation Park** (dolphinmarineconservation.com.au) - has been a Coffs Harbour institution since 1970. These days the focus is on rescue and rehabilitation, but there are still daily presentations where you'll learn all about dolphins and sea lions, penguins and turtles. There are also premium experiences such as the Ultimate Dolphin Swim, where you can swim with the marine mammals.

Head into the hills

From the sea to the rainforest, or Coffs Harbour inland to Dorrigo, it's around a 1hr drive along the **Waterfall Way**. Stop in Bellingen, a dreamy Byron-must-have-been-like-this-once town tucked into indecently green hills 35km south-west of Coffs. Those same emerald hills are home to an eclectic mix of artists and alternative lifestylers, tree changers and dairy farmers. The historic main street, all verandahs and iron lace, is lined with galleries and boutiques, and there's no shortage of places to get a good meal.

Dorrigo National Park is one of the most accessible national parks in the state, and is ideal for either a quick 1hr visit or you can spend all day here on one of the longer 5hr walks. The first place to go is the **Rainforest Centre**, which has a good interpretive display on the history of the area and the types of plants and wildlife you're likely to see while you're here. You can also learn more about the Gumbaynggirr People's culture and millennia-old connection to Country by joining a guided tour led by a local First Nations park ranger. Straight out the back of the Rainforest Centre is the **Skywalk**, a dramatic boardwalk above the rainforest canopy that leads way out over the edge of the escarpment. The views of the Gondwana Rainforests World Heritage area and across to the coast are spectacular. If you only have an hour or so to spare, make sure you do the **Walk with the Birds** boardwalk. The track to the **Glade Picnic Area** is suitable for strollers and accessible for wheelchairs, and takes around 20min. There are tables, toilets and barbecue facilities here, but be warned, the scrub turkeys are not shy and can smell a picnic a mile away. On the outskirts of Dorrigo is **Dangar Falls**, which is also another nice picnic spot (not to be confused with the similarly named Dangars Falls nearer to Armidale).

Kids' spot

You can't drive through Coffs without a visit to the **Big Banana**, the 'Big Thing' that's credited with starting the craze in building super-sized roadside attractions across the country, back in 1964. If you haven't been here for a while you'll find there's a lot more to the 'biggest banana in the world' than a place to have your photo taken. There's ice-skating, toboggan rides, mini golf, laser tag, a fun park and a water park with four thrill rides and slides. Mind you, the frozen chocolate-coated bananas on a stick have always been worth stopping for if you ask me. You'll find it on the Pacific Hwy, just north of town. Admission is free, although rides are extra.

Opposite Boardwalk at Urunga *Above* The orginal 'Big Thing'

COFFS HARBOUR TO YAMBA

There's a procession of seaside towns and villages as you follow the highway north, including Woolgoolga, famous for its annual **Curryfest** (Sept) and the twice-monthly **Bollywood Beach market**, thanks to the large Sikh and Punjabi community that settled here in the mid-20th century.

The stretch of rocky headlands, cliff-top lookouts and beaches flanked by wetlands and forests between Corindi Beach and Yamba – roughly 70km as the crow flies – is almost entirely protected by **Yuraygir National Park** and free of any kind of development at all, aside from a couple of tiny beach villages surrounded by the national park. In the south you'll find **Wooli** (home to the annual Australian National Goanna Pulling Championships, held on the Oct long weekend – and don't worry, no reptiles are involved), and **Minnie Water**. To get there you'll need to turn-off the Pacific Hwy (it's signposted), and then retrace your way back to the highway to continue north as there is no road that traverses the park from south to north. The upside, though, is that these little coastal hamlets seldom get crowded and have some fabulous beachside caravan and camping spots.

To explore the northern section of the park, turn off the highway at Maclean, following the signs to **Brooms Head**, a delightfully laid-back coastal village with a couple of basic shops and a seaside caravan park. Continue south, and you'll reach the mouth of the **Sandon River**, which claims to be the cleanest river in NSW. With a network of good walking trails, kayaking spots and great fishing, it's a popular camping spot, especially in summer, and where it seems almost everyone has a boat and a couple of rods. These isolated beaches are some of the few places in the country where you'll see emus on the beach.

Take a short detour off the road that leads back out of the park to check out the astonishing views from the lookouts at **Red Cliff** on the headlands south of Lake Arragan and spend some time on the pebbly beach beneath the (you guessed it) red cliffs at low tide, exploring countless rockpools. This is another place with fantastic seaside camping.

Back on the highway, stop at riverside **Maclean** – the self-styled Scottish capital of Australia, you can't miss the tartan-painted power poles. It's also the best place on the coast to stock up with haggis (probably the only place) should you be craving some. Then, head east to Yamba.

Situated at the mouth of the Clarence River, 63km north-east of Grafton, **Yamba** has always been top of the hit list for surfers and beach-goers. **Angourie Point** is celebrated for its much-revered right-hand break and the point became the first dedicated National Surfing Reserve in NSW in January 2007. With six beaches all within walking distance of the town centre, plus the plunge-worthy **Blue Pool** – a huge rock quarry which filled with fresh water when an underground spring was disturbed sometime last century – and an enticing saltwater rockpool on Main Beach, there's no shortage of places to get wet, and to surf. Yamba has become a popular alternative to Byron, with its surf culture, great cafes and a weekly Wednesday farmers' market. Yamba is also home to the country's most delicious king prawns, although the folks from Mooloolaba on Queensland's Sunshine Coast (*see* p.217) will probably argue the point.

SIDETRACK

Ditch the car for a day and jump aboard the little wooden ferry from Yamba for a 30min trip across the Clarence River to the village of **Iluka**. Departing from the jetty at the river end of River St in Yamba, it's one of the best-value cruises around, and from there you can stroll into World Heritage-listed rainforest at **Iluka Nature Reserve**. Part of the Gondwana Rainforests of Australia, it's the largest remaining littoral rainforest in the state. The 1hr walking trail through the centre of the narrow rainforest strip winds past massive buttressed strangler figs and lilly pillies covered in vines, emerging at the beach near Iluka Bluff - the lookout is a good whale watching spot in winter - a stone's throw from the **Sedgers Reef Hotel**, a great spot for fish and chips. See clarenceriverferries.com.au for timetables and cruise information.

BEST BEDS

- **The White Albatross** holiday park - one of five scattered around Nambucca - has the best location in town, sprawling over the knob of land between the river mouth and the ocean beach, and almost every cabin and caravan parking spot has a knockout view. Even better, the V-Wall Tavern - named after the v-shaped breakwall it overlooks - does fabulous steaks, super-sized schnittys, fish and local oysters and is right at the park's front gate. ingeniaholidays.com.au
- In Coffs Harbour there's a string of beachside resorts just north of town; pick of the bunch is the **Pacific Bay Resort** with beach access, three pools, tennis courts, day spa, restaurant, nine-hole golf course and aquarium. pacificbayresort.com.au
- A great family option in Yamba, the pet-friendly **Blue Dolphin Holiday Resort** features a range of villas, many with river views, as well as caravan and campsites. It's in a great location a short walk to the centre of town, and kid-friendly facilities include go-karts, a climbing wall, pump track, jumping cushion, games room, water slides and a water park. For adults, there's a snooker room and a pool bar. bluedolphin.com.au

VANLIFE

There's no shortage of great places to park a van or pitch a tent on this part of the coast, with every town along the way featuring at least one caravan park, often more, and usually with fabulous waterfront views. Top spots in Yuraygir National Park include **Illaroo** in the south and **Sandon River**, **Lake Arragan** and **Red Cliffs** in the north, where the headland campsites offer gorgeous ocean views, although the more sheltered lakeside spots are a better choice if there's a wind blowing. **Pebbly Beach** (in the south of the park) is a great spot for fishing, swimming and whale watching from nearby headlands but you'll need a 4WD - to get there you'll need to drive along the beach and cross a saltwater creek and it's only possible at low tide. Bookings are essential for all campgrounds in NSW national parks. See NSW National Parks and Wildlife Service (nationalparks.nsw.gov.au).

Overhead view of Yamba Main Beach

Coffs Coast to Yamba

New South Wales

Byron Bay is one of the country's most famous beach holiday hot spots, but this coastal road trip makes getting there just as good as being there.

Byron and beyond

HOW LONG?
Resist the temptation to get to Byron Bay as quick as you can. Kick back and go with the flow and allow at least a couple of days to really explore this stretch of coast, longer if you want to stay in one of the other beachside holiday towns for a while.

WHEN TO GO
Generally, the water in the ocean is warm enough for swimming between Sept and Apr, but summer holidays can be very busy. Winter is pleasantly crowd free and temperatures only occasionally sink into single figures. If you want to see whales, go between June and Nov.

NEED TO KNOW
The Northern Rivers region experienced major flooding in 2022. Some inland towns like Lismore will likely take several years to rebuild, although most coastal communities are largely unaffected and welcoming visitors. Be aware that some minor roads, particularly in national parks, were damaged and some may still be closed due to landslides or damaged bridges.

LOCAL SECRET
The riverside beer garden at **Hotel Brunswick** in Brunswick Heads gets my vote as one of the best in the state. Is there any greater way to spend a summer Sunday afternoon – or any summer afternoon for that matter – than sitting under the shade of a flowering poinciana tree and tucking into a plate of super fresh fish while a guitarist belts out tunes from the makeshift stage in the corner? I think not.

SNAPSHOT
From Hollywood celebrities to hippy-trippy free spirits and tree-changers, almost everyone who spends time on the beaches and in the rainforest-clad hills of the hinterland in and around Byron Bay falls in love with the place. Find out why on this coastal road trip that will take you off the beaten track and show where the locals hang out.

Drive rating
Easy. Mostly sealed roads.

Acknowledgement of Country
This is Traditional Land of the Yaygirr People, Arakwal People, Minjungbal People and Widjabul People of the Bundjalung Nation.

Distance planner
Maclean to Tweed Heads: around 190km, plus detours. Byron Bay is 760km north of Sydney, around an 8hr drive via the Pacific Hwy.
- Maclean to Ballina: 94km
- Ballina to Byron Bay via Lennox Head: 31km
- Byron Bay to Tweed Heads: 66km

More information
- Ballina Visitor Information Centre, cnr River St and Las Balsas Plaza, Ballina; 1800 777 666; discoverballina.com.au
- Byron Visitor Centre, 80 Jonson St, Byron Bay; (02) 6680 8558; visitbyronbay.com

MACLEAN TO BALLINA

Travelling up the NSW north coast it feels like you cross an imaginary line when you drive across the Harwood Bridge over the Clarence River, a few kilometres north of Maclean, into a world of sugar cane, rainforest and tropical trees, where all the towns have a flower-child counter-culture vibe. Maclean is 641km north of Sydney/Warrang, but you could also fly into Grafton, which is just a 40min drive to the west of Maclean along the Grafton River, and hire a car there, or fly into Ballina and do the trip in reverse.

Bundjalung National Park, on the northern side of the Clarence, is a beautiful expanse of undeveloped coastline that runs north almost all the way to Evans Head near Ballina to Iluka, just across the wide mouth of the Clarence from Yamba. The Bandjalang People's (of the broader Bundjalung Nation) Native Title rights have been recognised in the national park and you can visit Gummigurrah, a winter camping ground of the Bundjalung. The Esk River, the largest untouched coastal river system on the north coast, runs through the southern half of the park, which also contains the World Heritage-listed **Iluka Nature Reserve**, the largest remaining beachside rainforest in NSW. Take a stroll along the walking track that spears through the centre of the narrow rainforest strip, past massive buttressed strangler figs and lilly pillies covered in vines – you'll probably hear the calls of whipbirds ringing through the dense forest – to emerge into the sunshine on the beach near Iluka Bluff, where the lookout is a great spot to watch whales in the winter months. There's a popular picnic and grassy camping area here at Woody Head, just a few kilometres to the north of the bluff, with beaches and rockpools at your doorstep.

Unless you have your own kayak or canoe and are happy to paddle the Esk River you'll need to backtrack out to the Pacific Hwy and take the Gap Rd (turn off just past Woodburn, around 31km north of where the Iluka Rd joins the highway) to get to the northern section of the park.

It's worth the effort, because this section of the park is quite spectacular. **Black Rocks Campground** is hidden in a banksia forest behind the dunes of Ten Mile Beach. It gets its name from the Coffee Rock formations on the beach – sinuous, rather surreally shaped cliffs made from a crumbly coffee-coloured soft rock formed from ancient river sediments. Nearby **Jerusalem Creek** is a terrific paddling spot and you can launch your kayak or canoe from the pontoon. It's a lovely waterway, lined with flowering banksias and tea trees. Landlubbers can follow the 8km-return walking track along its banks. You can also walk along the beach for hours, and more than likely you'll have it entirely to yourself, although don't be surprised if you get buzzed by a fighter jet or two, as they often practise their manoeuvres in the airspace above the beach.

SIDETRACK

If you haven't been to **Yamba** before, follow the Yamba Rd along the southern side of the Clarence River out to the coast to one of the best little seaside towns in the state, especially if you like surfing, beachcombing, rainforest walks and the world's best prawns. See Coffs Coast to Yamba road trip on p.23.

SIDETRACK

For some lovely picnic sites head to **Evans Head**, a sleepy little village at the mouth of the Evans River. Picnickers can choose from many shaded sites along the river bank, the lookout, or nearby at **Dirawong Reserve**, a place of cultural significance for the people of the Bundjalung Nation - the dirawong is a powerful goanna spirit, protector and creator that resides in the headland here, and there are many sacred and ceremonial sites in the reserve. There are several good walking tracks here, and the country puts on a show in spring when the headland is carpeted in wildflowers.

The reserve is also the site of a horrific massacre of First Nations People in the 1840s and you can find out more about it - other local First Nations sites at the **Evans Head Living Museum**.

Also in Evans Head is the **Heritage Aviation Museum**, where you can climb into the cockpit of an F111 to learn more about those jets that buzzed you on the beach near Jerusalem Creek (see p.32).

Opposite Woody Head, Bundjalung National Park *Top* Cape Byron, the most easterly point on mainland Australia

Head into the hills

A cute town full of historic buildings halfway between Ballina and Lismore, **Alstonville** offers the best of both the coast and the hinterland. It's less than 20km from the beach, only half an hour from Byron Bay, and makes a great base for exploring the charming villages and scenic drives of the Northern Rivers region. Among garden lovers it's famous for its annual autumn purple haze when the tibouchina trees that line the town's streets burst into bloom with big purple and mauve flowers. The world's first commercial orchard of macadamia trees was planted near Alstonville in the early 1880s and it's now one of the region's largest industries. Take a drive round the area and you'll pass by dozens of farm gate stalls that sell buckets of nuts for just a few dollars. BYO nutcrackers. Around 150 years ago, before the cedar cutters arrived, most of the area around Alstonville was covered in rainforest. Known as 'The Big Scrub', it was one of the largest areas of subtropical rainforest in eastern Australia although, sadly, most of it had been cleared by the turn of the 20th century, beyond a few patches here and there. One of those remnants is now part of **Victoria Park Nature Reserve**, an 8ha area of rainforest that contains a staggering 152 different species of trees. It's just 8km from town (via Wardell Rd) and features a wheelchair and stroller-friendly boardwalk that winds through the rainforest.

Byron and beyond

New South Wales

This part of the north coast is known as the Northern Rivers region, and just about every town is beside one, including **Ballina**, on the mouth of the Richmond River. You can explore the town's wonderful beaches on the walking and cycle track which hugs the coastline and along the river wall. The best time is early morning, so you can stop halfway at one of the cafes on the beach for breakfast while you watch dolphins surf the waves only metres from your table. Don't leave town without snapping a selfie in front of the Big Prawn, one of Australia's many Big Things – this one is 9m high and weighing in at a whopping 35 tonnes. Rather weirdly, you'll find it outside of Bunnings on River St (it predates the hardware store by a couple of decades), and freshly pink from a much-needed makeover.

BALLINA TO BYRON

From Ballina take the coastal road north to Byron Bay, through the beachside communities of Lennox Head and Suffolk Park, past secluded and isolated beaches accessible only by hiking tracks. This might be one of the most popular and well-known beach holiday destinations in the country, but it's surprising how undeveloped the coastline actually is – long may it stay that way.

Byron Bay is the most easterly point of mainland Australia. Claim bragging rights about being the first in the country to see the sun rise and head to **Cape Byron Lighthouse** before dawn – you can take the walking track (sometimes steep) from Main Beach, via Wategos Beach, or drive up to the lighthouse carpark. The lighthouse headland is also a great place to watch whales between June and Oct. Byron, as it's fondly known, might be famous for its alternative therapies and wellness retreats, but there's also plenty of good retail therapy opportunities, with a range of boutiques and homewares stores, more cafes, restaurants and bars than you can count, a famed farmers' market, and several swimming and surfing beaches within easy walking distance of the town centre.

The Farm at Byron is in Ewingsdale, just north of Byron, and offers coffee, the Bread Social artisan bakery, a flower shop, Three Blue Ducks restaurant, farm animals, kids activities and farm workshops for adults (book ahead at thefarm.com.au). Most of all it's a chance to slow down and walk around a working farm.

Opposite top left Cape Byron Lighthouse *Opposite top right* Tweed Regional Gallery, Murwillumbah *Opposite bottom left* Tropical colour in Brunswick Heads *Opposite bottom right* Counter culture in Nimbin

Kids' spot

Summerland Farm is a working avocado and macadamia farm on the outskirts of Alstonville. It's run by the House With No Steps, which supports people with disabilities throughout NSW, and its 7000 trees produce close to 100 tonnes of macadamias each year, and about the same volume again of avocados. Meet the farm animals and take a tractor tour through the farm's orchards. Kids will love the adventure playground and water park. There's also a cafe and licensed restaurant, surrounded by gardens.

Head into the hills

The former dairy-farming village of **Nimbin** in the hills behind Byron Bay became the heart of the hippy movement when it hosted the Aquarius Festival in 1973. Don't be shocked if you are politely offered cannabis whilst wandering down the main street. Despite this, it's still worth a visit; the shopfronts in the main street are decorated with colourful, psychedelic murals and there is a range of shops selling New Age goods and some good cafes selling organic and vegetarian food. Take a scenic drive through the maze of local roads that wind through the valleys around here, in and out of pockets of rainforest, along ridge tops and through sleepy villages.

While you're there, drive out to the site of one of the first successful environmental protests in Australia. Back in the 1970s a group of conservationists fought to save the rainforest and the pretty **Protesters Falls** on Terania Creek in what is now **Nightcap National Park** (and part of the Gondwana Rainforests World Heritage area) from logging. It's a lovely drive, via the villages of Dunoon and The Channon that tunnels through the rainforest, past massive tree ferns and tall trees festooned with staghorns and birdsnest ferns. Once at the falls it's a 30min walk to the cascades. It was closed due to flood damage at the time of going to print, but will hopefully reopen in mid to late 2023.

Whatever you do, don't miss the weekly **The Channon Craft Market** (second Sun of each month), when locals and visitors flock to the open field to set up and browse the 250-plus stalls offering everything from home-grown organic food to handmade clothes, woodwork, art, candles and just about anything else you can imagine. Despite being one of the region's most popular events, it hasn't lost its bohemian vibe, although parking can be difficult to find unless you get there early. If you miss the markets most stall holders move with the markets between Byron Bay, Nimbin, Bangalow and The Channon on alternate weekends.

BYRON TO THE BORDER

Byron Bay may get all the celebrities and Instagram glory, but for my money **Brunswick Heads**, 18km north, is a more pleasant place. You won't find traffic jams in Brunswick Heads, nor will you find high street chain stores, parking meters or anyone begging for your spare change – you'll need to go to Byron Bay for that. Although just like in Byron Bay, you will find some great surfing beaches at Brunswick Heads, as well as gorgeous coastal scenery, some fantastic restaurants and cafes and even a couple of places where you can get your tea leaves read or your fortune told. What's more, Brunswick Heads has plenty that Byron doesn't – like a broad river running through the heart of town that's perfect for fishing and kayaking and splashing about. And plenty of things that Byron Bay used to have in abundance, but has since lost – like a genuine laid-back come-as-you-are, we're-all-equal-in-our-Speedos kind of holiday vibe, where the local pub is still the town's meeting place, the caravan parks have the best views, and the local bike hire people really don't mind if you bring their bike back late as long as you let them know.

Take your time as you make your way north towards Tweed Heads on the border of NSW and Queensland and explore some of the roads that spear off the highway out to quiet coastal towns and long, deserted beaches at places like **Pottsville**, **Cabarita** and **Kingscliff**. The bright lights and glittering high-rise towers of the Gold Coast might be shimmering on the horizon but, so far, the NSW side of things is still delightfully low key.

Head into the hills

The area known as the Tweed Valley is actually the crater of a massive volcano - a caldera - more than a kilometre deep and 40km wide, and long-since extinct. You can explore it by car on the **Tweed Range Scenic Drive**, a mostly unsealed 64km loop from Kyogle that follows the edge of the caldera most of the way. A highlight is the 20min Pinnacle Walk in **Border Ranges National Park**, which leads to a lookout platform perched at the edge of the escarpment. From here you have spectacular views of Wollumbin (Mount Warning) and the Tweed Valley 1000m below. Other good walks in the park include the 3hr Brindle Creek walking track and the shorter Rosewood and Red Cedar loops, which all wind through beautiful World Heritage-listed rainforest - the latter leads to a giant red cedar tree thought to be around 1000 years old.

SIDETRACK

Simply called Mullum by the locals, the hinterland town of **Mullumbimby** in the shadow of Mount Chincogan is more authentically alternative than Byron, but not quite as free-range as Nimbin. Hard hit by the 2022 floods, the charming town is working hard to rebuild, and is keen to welcome visitors who come here to admire the historic buildings and browse the many art galleries, and New Age shops. The Friday morning farmers' market is the place to pick up some genuine home-grown organic fare, and the people watching is always entertaining.

Good for a rainy day

If you're an art lover don't miss the **Tweed Regional Gallery and Margaret Olley Art Centre** near Murwillumbah. Olley's famously cluttered Paddington art studio has been re-created here - including original architectural features like doors and windows relocated from her Sydney home and more than 20,000 items the late artist had collected over the years. Also worth a look is the new **M Arts Precinct** (m-arts.com.au) in Murwillumbah, where you'll find a collection of local artists - printmakers, sculptors, painters, photographers, weavers and leathermakers - hard at work in studios made from repurposed shipping containers. Many offer half-day workshops, too.

BEST BEDS

- Live it up in one of the luxury villas at **Elements of Byron** beachfront resort. Featuring a beguiling mix of rainforest and bush-flanked beach, facilities include a Miami-glam adults-only lagoon-style infinity pool - heated for year-round pool parties - sybaritic day spa and fine-dining restaurant. elementsofbyron.com.au
- Chill out riverside in great-value self-contained, air-conditioned cabins at **Massey Green Holiday Park** in Brunswick Heads. reflectionsholidayparks.com.au/park/massy-greene
- Stay at Insta-cool **The Sails Motel & Pool Club** in Brunswick Heads. The rejuvenated roadside motel has coastal chic rooms, a small pool and bar and brilliant burgers out front at Old Maids Burger Store, or stroll a few steps from your room to get a pizza at Saint Maries Pizza Restaurant. It's a great budget-friendly but comfortable place for couples or families. thesailsmotel.com.au
- **Peppers Salt Resort & Spa** A massive beach lagoon pool, complete with sand, lifeguard and deck chairs is just one of the attractions at this Kingscliff resort. Rooms are huge, with one-, two- and three-bedroom options, and some even have their own private plunge pools. pepperssalt.com.au

VANLIFE

This stretch of coast is beach holiday heartland and there's usually a caravan park near the water in even the smallest town, but the region does book out well ahead during summer and school holidays. In **Bundjalung National Park**, the campground at **Woody Head** has hot showers, flushing toilets and level sites. Further north, a less crowded option is **Black Rocks**, roughly midway between Iluka and Evans Head, with 49 sites behind the dunes of Ten Mile Beach. **Evans Head Holiday Park** faces both the mouth of the Evans River and the main beach in Evans Head, and is dog friendly. Byron has a choice of caravan parks but the closest national park camping to the town is the rainforest at **Rummery Park** in Whian Whian State Conservation Area adjacent to Nightcap National Park. Bookings are essential for all campgrounds in NSW national parks. See NSW National Parks and Wildlife Service (nationalparks.nsw.gov.au).

Opposite top Main Beach, Byron Bay *Opposite bottom* Brunswick River *Left* Wollumbin and the Tweed Valley, Murwillumbah

Byron and beyond

New South Wales

Short but sweet, it's simply one of the best coastal drives in NSW.

Grand Pacific Drive

HOW LONG?
An easy day drive or a great weekend away from Sydney/Warrang.

WHEN TO GO
Any time of the year is a good time to do this drive.

LOCAL SECRET
The Famous **Berry Donut Van** at Berry Service Station (73 Queens St, Berry) has been frying up cinnamon-dusted circles of sweetness for more than 60 years, but don't make the mistake of thinking you'll grab some to take home because I guarantee you'll have eaten the lot before you get to the edge of town.

SNAPSHOT
A cliff-hugging, breathtakingly scenic route that meanders along the coastline just south of Sydney. A highlight is the cantilevered Sea Cliff Bridge that curves around the cliffs.

Drive rating
Easy. Sealed roads with some winding sections.

Acknowledgement of Country
This is the Traditional Land of the Dharawal People.

Distance planner
Sydney to Berry: 155km if you follow the coast.
- Sydney to Wollongong: 100km
- Wollongong to Berry: 55km

More information
- Southern Gateway Centre, Princes Hwy, Bulli Tops; (02) 4267 5910; visitwollongong.com.au
- Kiama Information Centre, Blowhole Point Rd; 1300 654 262; kiama.com.au
- grandpacificdrive.com.au

Opposite Garie Beach, Royal National Park

SYDNEY/WARRANG TO WOLLONGONG

This fabulous little road trip begins on the southern edge of Sydney's suburban sprawl in Australia's oldest national park and the world's second oldest national park, **Royal National Park**, founded in 1879 (Yellowstone in the United States is seven years older). Deep inside the park, Lady Wakehurst Dr winds through eucalypt forests, over windswept heathlands and across low-level river weirs. Sidetracks spear off to beaches and lookouts and there are dozens of great picnic and swimming spots along the way. Being so close to Sydney, the park is a popular place on sunny weekends, when traffic snarls can be frustrating, but if you can time your drive for a weekday, you'll pretty much have it to yourself. You can also do a tour with an Aboriginal Discovery ranger to learn about the area's cultural sites, including middens and engravings.

Leaving the 'nasho', as it's known to locals, the road, now called Lawrence Hargrave Dr, bursts outs of the bush at the cliff-top vantage point of Stanwell Tops, high on the edge of the **Illawarra Escarpment**. Paragliders and hang gliders soar on the thermals rising from the ocean below, emulating aeronautical pioneer, Lawrence Hargrave, who made aviation history here by rising 5m above the ground strapped to a huge box kite in 1894. On a clear day, you can see as far south as Wollongong and enjoy a great view of the route, over the Sea Cliff Bridge and the beaches beyond.

The coastal road (Lawrence Hargrave Dr) was originally built in the 1860s to service the coalmines that had already hollowed out the inside of the Illawarra Escarpment. Carved into the cliffs 40m above the surf, the road, although breathtakingly scenic, was at times breathtakingly dangerous. The cliffs, especially along the section between Coalcliff and Clifton, had a terrifying tendency to slide into the sea, sometimes taking sections of the road with them. Boulders would plummet downhill, narrowly missing school buses and family cars on their way to the local shops. After dozens of such incidents, the road was finally closed in 2003 while a solution was formulated: the Sea Cliff Bridge, a 665m-long multi-span cantilever bridge that curves around the cliffs 50m out to sea – out of the way of any errant rockfalls.

Kids' spot

Symbio Wildlife Park in Helensburgh is a down-to-earth zoo where you can unpack a picnic or fire up a barbecue, check out the crocodiles, koalas, meerkats or any of the other 1000 animals in the park and cool off in the swimming pool.

The scenic Sea Cliff Bridge

Grand Pacific Drive

Continue south along the coast, past crumbling, down-at-heel pubs atop headlands with million-dollar views, and seaside cafes doing a roaring trade in coffee and gelato overlooking the golden sands. **Thirroul** is about as resort-like as you'll get on this section of the coast – there are a couple of boutiques and cafes here – and then the road hits a succession of increasingly suburban towns – all with great beaches and ocean swimming pools – until it delivers you into the heart of Wollongong.

The third largest city in NSW and a major coal, iron and steel producer, the 'Gong is, despite all that heavy industry, a very attractive place to spend a night. Explore the horseshoe-shaped cove of **Wollongong Harbour**, with its lighthouse, fishing fleet, fish markets and wonderful city beaches. Linger over coffee in one of the many cafes along the foreshore or stockpile some inner harmony at the eight-storey **Nan Tien Buddhist Temple** – the largest Buddhist temple in the Southern Hemisphere. Or, if that sounds a little too serene for you, join a fascinating guided tour of the massive steelworks and working port at **Port Kembla**. Bookings are essential online (insideindustry.org.au/tours).

Good for a rainy day

Not just for rev heads and car enthusiasts, you'll find a massive collection of much adored cars, motorcycles and all manner of jaunty jalopies on show at the **Australian Motorlife Museum** in Kembla Grange, as well as lots of other 'automobilia' - signs, accessories, promotional items, tools, badges and petrol pumps, caravans and books.

Kids' spot

Jamberoo Action Park is the largest water-based theme park in NSW. Teenagers love the Funnel Web, a monster-sized, cone-shaped ride and the Perfect Storm, a thrilling vortex water ride. Banjo's Billabong has waterslides, cannons, sprays and buckets. Other attractions include a wave pool and a 'rapid river' ride, as well as bobsleds, racing cars and a chairlift. It's open mid Sept to the end of Apr.

Head into the hills

The wheelchair-accessible boardwalk in Minnamurra Rainforest leads from the Rainforest Centre in Budderoo National Park through subtropical and temperate rainforest to **Minnamurra Falls** and is great for little legs and strollers. The much steeper walk to the falls can be hard going, but the stunning view of Minnamurra Falls and the canyon at the end is worth it. There's a cafe on site, as well as good picnic facilities, and you're almost guaranteed to see lyrebirds and wallabies. .

If you've a head for heights, head up to the top of **Illawarra Fly**, a 500m-long, 25m-high elevated tree-top walk a short but twisty drive away along Jamberoo Mountain Rd. Climb the 45m-high lookout (if you dare), get bouncy on the edge of the springboard cantilevers or fly through the canopy on the zipline tour. On a clear day you can see all the way to the coast, 35km away. It's in Knights Hill, a 10min drive from Robertson. At the time of going to press the Jamberoo Mountain Rd between the falls and the fly was closed due to flood damage, so check local information before you travel.

WOLLONGONG TO BERRY

Follow the coast south, skirting the shoreline of Lake Illawarra to **Shellharbour**. Surfers should make a beeline to the beach called **The Farm** at Killalea Regional Park which, along with neighbouring **Mystics Beach**, was declared a National Surfing Reserve in 2009. If you haven't surfed before, it's a good place to learn as the waves break further out so you get more time to try and stand up. **Pines Surfing Academy** (pinessurfingacademy.com.au) runs lessons at The Farm, book ahead.

According to locals, **Kiama** is a Dharawal, Wadi Wadi word meaning 'place where the sea makes a noise', and when you're standing beside the **Kiama Blowhole** – the largest blowhole in the world – getting soaked by the 30m-high jet of spray, you'll understand why. It's at its most impressive when there's a south-easterly wind blowing.

Kiama is a coastal town known for its picturesque beaches, village of shops and cafes and holiday vibe – make a beeline to the **Historic Terrace Houses** on Collins St for some electric retail therapy.

A quieter version of Kiama, the small hilltop town of **Gerringong** overlooking the golden arc of Werri Beach – a favourite with long boarders – is just a short drive south, but you can also walk – the **Kiama Coast Walk** is a spectacularly scenic 20km coastal walk that links the two towns. It's broken up into three sections so you don't have to do the whole thing; otherwise, leave your car at one end and either catch a taxi or a train back to it at the end of the walk.

There's no prize for guessing how **Seven Mile Beach National Park**, just south of Gerringong, got its name, but a beach this long is never going to feel crowded. Swim at the patrolled section, surf, have a picnic or barbecue, watch the birds – and whales in winter – and hit the bushwalking trails.

The end point on this road trip, the historic village of **Berry** is just a short drive inland. You could spend hours browsing the boutiques and antiques stores here, but the real reason to go is for the food and nearby wineries. There are half a dozen scattered around the district, but favourites include **Crooked River** with its fabulous restaurant and **Coolangatta Estate** with its beautifully restored convict-built village.

From Berry it's a 2hr drive back to Sydney via the M1, but the views on the Sea Cliff Bridge are even better going north, so if you have the time, take the long way home.

BEST BEDS

- **Novotel Wollongong Northbeach** The great rooms here have balconies overlooking the beach. novotelnorthbeach.com.au
- **Pilgrim Lodge** Nan Tien Buddhist Temple offers peaceful accommodation in this motel-style retreat. nantien.org.au
- **Tumbling Waters Retreat** Perched on the edge of the escarpment, the retreat offers superb ocean views. tumblingwatersretreat.com

VANLIFE

Killalea Regional Park near Shellharbour has some nice camping spots around a 10min walk from the beach; facilities include hot showers (killalea.com.au). You'll also find several good beachfront caravan parks in Kiama and Gerringong.

Opposite Thirroul Beach *Top* Nan Tien Temple, near Wollongong *Bottom* Shopping in Kiama

Grand Pacific Drive

New South Wales

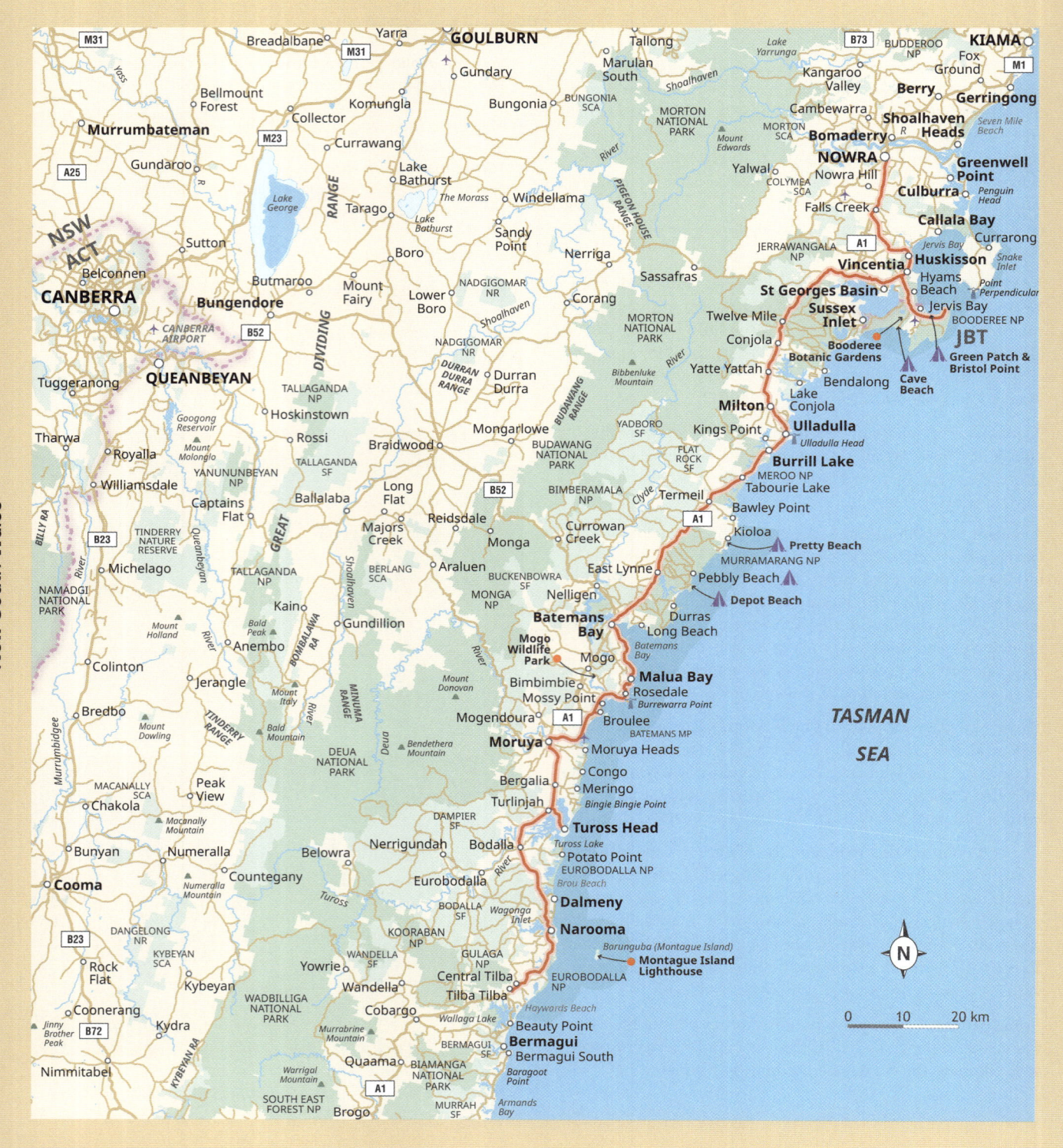

This stretch of coastline between Batemans Bay and Narooma has more beaches, rivers and ocean waterways than you can count.

Jervis Bay and the Eurobodalla

HOW LONG?
This is prime beach holiday territory, so don't rush it. Take at least a couple of days and go exploring, a week or two if your idea of a good time is chilling out in a beautiful place doing not much at all.

WHEN TO GO
This drive is great year-round, although summer is the best time if you plan to swim. If you want to see whales, travel between June and Nov.

Most of the coastal towns along this route are busy during school holidays, so book accommodation or campsites ahead for these times, especially in summer.

LOCAL SECRET
Narooma is home to one of the most scenic public golf courses in the country, where even non-golfers will enjoy the 'sea-forever' views on the cliff-edge top six. Watch out for the terrifying third, aka Hogan's Hole (actor Paul Hogan once filmed a cigarette ad here), where you have to hit your ball over a cliff to a distant green.

SNAPSHOT
Surrounded by national parks, a maze of beautiful waterways and a string of fabulous beaches, a road trip up or down the south coast of NSW is all about getting back to nature. And with a range of great value family-friendly accommodation on offer in the many waterfront holiday parks in the area, it doesn't have to break the bank either. If the lure of the world's whitest sand in Jervis Bay doesn't seduce you the beaches of the Eurobodalla – the 'land of many waters' – will.

Drive rating
Easy. Mostly sealed roads.

Acknowledgement of Country
This is the Traditional Land of the Yuin People.

Distance planner
Around 200km, not including detours. Nowra is 163km south of Sydney, via the M1 and Princes Hwy, around a 2.5hr drive, depending on traffic.
- Nowra to Huskisson (Jervis Bay): 23km
- Huskisson to Batemans Bay: 108km
- Batemans Bay to Narooma and Tilba Tilba: 85km

More information
- jervisbaytourism.com.au
- eurobodalla.com.au

NOWRA TO BATEMANS BAY VIA JERVIS BAY

Don't be surprised if it seems like every car on the road on your way to Jervis Bay, around a 30min drive south of Nowra, is from Canberra/Ngambri/Ngunnawal, because Jervis Bay is actually a separate Commonwealth territory, administered by the ACT. If you're a local, your car will have ACT plates; if you get in trouble, it will be the Australian Federal Police, not the NSW officers, that will sort you out. It stems back to 1915, when the country's capital city decided it needed a port. You can tell who comes from where by the accent: NSW folk say *jar-vis*, locals say *jer-vis*, the Navy that runs the place – most people who live here work in Defence – side with the Sydney-siders. Even more confusingly, the holiday town isn't called Jervis Bay, so follow the signs to Huskisson or Vincentia.

Whatever you do, make sure you take the turn-off to **Hyams Beach** on the way. It's reputed to have the whitest sand in the world – although Whitehaven in the Whitsundays (*see* p.244) and Lucky Bay in WA (*see* p.203) make the same claim. The devil may be in the detail – or the scientific composition of the silica – but one thing's certain, you'll need a pair of sunglasses because it is definitely dazzling. The beach is unpatrolled, but because it faces east and is protected by Point Perpendicular it rarely receives any swell which makes it a great spot for a swim – though there are some steep drop-offs into deep water (check beachsafe.org.au).

Activities here are all either on, beside or in the water. Jervis Bay offers beaches, rocky platforms and reefs, extensive seagrass beds, estuaries and deep-water cliffs, so naturally scuba diving, swimming, surfing, boating and fishing are all popular pastimes. The bay also has a resident pod of dolphins and is an excellent place to go on a whale-watching cruise during the winter months.

Nearby **Booderee National Park** is worth exploring. Highlights include coastal walks with fantastic views, a ruined lighthouse and **Booderee Botanic Gardens**, the only Aboriginal-owned botanic gardens in Australia. Booderee in the Dhurga language means 'bay of plenty', and was chosen by the Wreck Bay Aboriginal Community for the former Jervis Bay National Park and Jervis Bay Botanic Gardens following the handback of the area to its Traditional Owners. Here you'll find a number of self-guided trails lined with interpretative boards that explain how the Traditional Owners used the plants for food and medicine. There's a lovely rainforest boardwalk and you'll almost always see kangaroos grazing on the grassy picnic areas. Cultural tours are available during the school holidays.

One of the most popular spots for a picnic (and camping) is **Green Patch**. It's another good spot for swimming: there's a floating safety net to keep out any unwelcome marine predators. Kids love meeting the wildlife here – especially the birds and kangaroos in the early morning and late afternoon. During school holidays the park rangers have a range of special kids' activities.

Back on the highway you'll find detours out to charmingly sleepy lakeside hamlets and coastal villages all the way south to Ulladulla and beyond to Batemans Bay, and there are plenty of ways to enjoy the beaches, lakes and lagoons with boat ramps, wharves and jetties in almost every coastal community, as well as good snorkelling, swimming and surfing and a range of bushwalks. Much of this often rugged coastal strip, flanked by spotted gum forests and rainforest gullies, is part of **Murramarang National Park**, well-known for its water-loving kangaroos – you'll often find them paddling at the water's edge in the early morning and late afternoon, particularly at **Pebbly Beach**.

At the mouth of the Clyde River, **Batemans Bay** is the largest town on the Eurobodalla Coast. It's a great place to throw in a fishing line – or head out to sea on a fishing charter – go kayaking, stand-up paddle-boarding, sailing or just laze around on a beach.

BATEMANS BAY TO TILBA VIA NAROOMA

In 1851 gold was discovered just south of Batemans Bay, near the present-day village of Mogo, and by the 1860s more than 30,000 diggers were working the goldfields. Today **Mogo** is a popular pit-stop, with an eclectic range of shops selling everything from New Age crystals and handmade jewellery to antiques.

Kids' spot

Don't leave Mogo without visiting **Mogo Wildlife Park**, where the animals include Nepalese red pandas, white lions, snow leopards, bears and tigers. There's also a range of animal encounters, with meerkats, snakes and lemurs, and you can hand feed the big cats and go behind the scenes to become a keeper for a day.

Head into the hills

Canberra might feel like it's a long way from the sea, but it's actually only a 2hr drive from Batemans Bay, along the Kings Hwy. It's a pretty drive down the Great Dividing Range. Highlights include shopping for art and crafts in **Bungendore**; don't miss **Bungendore Wood Works Gallery**. Housed in a beautiful purpose-built gallery it specialises in Australian-made wood craft, with everything from fine furniture to rustic bush craft and beautiful sculptures. The town of **Braidwood** is also worth stopping at for a wander around. Classified by the National Trust, most buildings date to the 19th century - from grand public buildings and hotels to workmen's cottages - and many now house art galleries and cafes. Most of the buildings on the main street have been restored and are painted in heritage colours. The small museum, which began life as a hotel in 1845 and was bought by the Oddfellows in 1882, is also an information centre, and make sure you visit the kitchen exhibit out the back.

Opposite Hyams Beach *Above* Central Tilba

There are more wildlife encounters waiting for you at Narooma but take your time and follow the coast road and explore **Broulee**, **Moruya** and **Tuross Head** on the way. If you're a keen paddler you'll enjoy kayaking the waterways around here: the waters teem with fish and birdlife is prolific. A favourite is **Tuross Lake**, where an intricate system of channels, backwaters and eddies has been formed by the Tuross River as it carves its way east to spill into the sea at Tuross Head, and there are countless good launching spots all along this section of the coast. If you don't have your own kayak or canoe you can hire one at Mossy Point – or join a guided tour with **Region X** (regionx.com.au).

From Narooma, head south to the twin villages of **Central Tilba** and **Tilba Tilba**, around 20km south. If you're a garden lover, you'll enjoy the **Foxglove Gardens** at Tilba Tilba. These extensive private gardens are open to the public Thurs through to Mon and feature several shady arbours, ponds, a 'ruined church' folly, rose gardens and a multitude of showy flower beds. For more about these villages, *see* p.49.

From here, if you want to go back to Sydney via the highway it is around a 5hr drive. Or continue south to the border on the Sapphire Coast road trip (*see* p.51) – for even more sea, sand and surf.

SIDETRACK

In Narooma you can take a tour out to **Barunguba (Montague Island)** 9km offshore and the second largest island of NSW's islands. Its granite lighthouse, built in 1881, with a visible horizon of 36km, stands sentinel above the island, appearing to guard not only the treacherous passage between the island and the coast, but also the wealth of wildlife found on the island which includes around 8000 pairs of little penguins as well as colonies of Australian and New Zealand fur seals. You'll also find crested terns, silver gulls and three different species of shearwaters here during the nesting season and it is a great spot to watch whales between Sept and Nov. In summer you can snorkel with seals and most tours include access to the lighthouse. Contact **Narooma Charters** (naroomacharters.com.au) or call 0407 909 111 to book tours.

Good for a rainy day

Central Tilba and **Tilba Tilba** are both heritage-listed villages, and the vibrantly painted weatherboard houses and shopfronts look much the same as they would have at the turn of last century. The main street of Central Tilba now houses a range of galleries, gift shops, leather and woodwork showrooms, but the vanilla slice from the **Tilba Bakery** is the drawcard for many visitors (and locals). The village is also home to the **Tilba Real Dairy**, in the historic ABC Cheese Factory. Get there on a Mon or Wed before noon and you can watch the cheesemakers at work. It's a great spot to stock up on picnic supplies - and ice-cream.

BEST BEDS

- Go wild in comfort at **Paperbark Camp**, one of Australia's first eco-friendly luxury camps. Each of the 12 'tents' have open-air private ensuites - enjoy some birdwatching while you wash - wraparound decks, insect screens and solar-powered lighting and are stylishly furnished with locally handcrafted furniture. Dining is in the Gunyah, a chic space built high off the ground in the treetops. The beautiful beaches of Jervis Bay are only 4km away and there are complimentary bicycles and canoes. paperbarkcamp.com.au
- **NRMA Murramarang Beachfront Holiday Resort** The one- and two-bedroom villas sit right on the edge of the sand, and there are also powered caravan sites, a licensed restaurant, a playground and a swimming pool. An added attraction is the resident mob of kangaroos, and the sheltered beach is ideal for kids. nrmaparksandresorts.com.au/murramarang
- **Lakesea Holiday Park** Wedged on to a triangle of land between Durras Lake and the Tasman Sea, this holiday park is just a few kilometres north of Batemans Bay. There's powered caravan and camping sites and a range of cabins from simple to seriously luxe. lakesea.com.au
- **The Whale Inn** at Narooma has great value large rooms with water views and a pool. merivale.com/stay/the-whale-inn-narooma

VANLIFE

You'll find good caravan parks at most towns and there are lots of camping options in the national parks, but you'll need to book well ahead during summer, when all these places are very popular. In **Booderee National Park** near Jervis Bay, top camping spots include **Green Patch**, **Bristol Point** and **Cave Beach**. In **Murramarang National Park**, the largest campground, **Pretty Beach**, has 70 sites (including powered caravan sites) and facilities include hot showers. **Pebbly Beach** is the best place to go to see kangaroos on the beach and has 20 sites, cold showers and gas barbecues, but is not suitable for caravans. **Depot Beach** is another good spot and also has powered caravan sites and hot showers. Bookings are essential for all campgrounds in NSW national parks, whatever the time of year. See NSW National Parks and Wildlife Service (nationalparks.nsw.gov.au).

Opposite Admiring the rock formations near Wasps Head, Murramarang National Park *Left* Tuross Head

Jervis Bay and the Eurobodalla

New South Wales

50

Named for the brilliant blue of the sea and sky, this stretch of the NSW South Coast between Batemans Bay and the border really is a natural paradise.

The Sapphire Coast

HOW LONG?
You could drive this stretch of coastline, from Bermagui to Green Cape, easily in a couple of hours or so but stretch it out over a couple of days – or longer if you have the time – because there's some really lovely national parks to explore.

WHEN TO GO
Summer and autumn are the best times if you plan to swim – locals say the water is actually warmest in autumn. If you want to see whales, travel between June and Nov. Most of the coastal towns along this route are busy during school holidays, so book accommodation or campsites ahead for these times, especially in summer. The cooler months are perfect if you don't fancy battling crowds and are happy to rug up.

LOCAL SECRET
No matter where you are on the South Coast the locals will tell you that their oysters are simply the best on the coast ... probably the best in the country, even the best in the world. Pop into one of the 'shellar doors' between Tathra and Wonboyn Lake to see if they are telling the truth, join an oyster tour or try some oyster shell gin.

SNAPSHOT
The sparkling beaches and annual whale migration are two of the Sapphire Coast's biggest drawcards. Every town and village seems to have its own fishermen's co-op selling fresh catches of the day, the dairy farms in the lush hills produce some fantastic cheeses and the fertile fields yield an amazing array of fresh fruit and vegetables. So grab yourself a blanket, an empty picnic basket, and head here. Oh, and did we mention the oysters? They're pretty good too.

Drive rating
Easy. Mostly sealed roads with some gravel sections in national parks.

Acknowledgement of Country
This is the Traditional Land of the Yuin, Dhurga, Thaua and Bidawal Peoples.

Distance planner
Around 140km, if you take the coast road, plus a few extra for detours and sidetracks. If you follow the highway from Bermagui to Green Cape it's 156km. Bermagui is 380km south of Sydney, via the M1/A1 and Princes Hwy.
- Bermagui to Merimbula (via Tathra): 68km
- Bermagui to Merimbula (via Bega): 92km
- Merimbula to Green Cape: 69km

More information
- Eden Visitor Information Centre, Weecoon St, Snug Cove, Eden; (02) 6496 1953; visiteden.com.au
- sapphirecoast.com.au

Opposite Tathra Wharf

BERMAGUI TO MERIMBULA

The starting point for this coastal road trip is the small seaside town of Bermagui, around a 15min drive south-east of heritage town of Tilba Tilba on the Princes Hwy – the end point of the Eurobodalla drive (see p.45). Of course, that's 15min only if you don't get distracted snapping a pic at popular photo spot **Horse Head Rock** – a huge horse-shaped rock accessed by an elevated walking track between Camel Rock and Muranna Point at beautiful **Wallaga Lake** – or the beaches at **Horseshoe Bay** along the way.

Bermagui is famous for its fishing – between the beach, harbour, estuary, nearby rivers and lakes there are plenty of places to throw in a line, and plenty of fishing charters available too if you like the idea of big game deep-sea fishing. It's also famous for its bottom-of-the-cliff swimming pool, known as the **Blue Pool** – a very photogenic natural rockpool that is also a popular snorkelling spot with lots of anemones, sea stars, nudibranchs and other colourful marine creatures.

Continue south, hugging the coast on the road to Tathra, past undeveloped beaches and secluded bays. Stop at **Michael Lerner Lookout** for great views, before winding through the forests of **Mimosa Rocks National Park**. Keep your windows open and you'll be serenaded by bellbirds almost the entire way. Named for a paddle steamer that was wrecked on rocks in 1863, the Mimosa Rocks walking track in the northern section of the national park is an easy 2km-return walk that leads to a lookout where you may, if the tide is right, see the shipwreck on the rocks below. The national park is on Yuin Country, and on the Mimosa Rocks walk you'll learn about the Yuin Dreaming stories that tell of its creation. Guided bush-tucker tours led by an Aboriginal Discovery ranger are available during school holidays, as well as traditional weaving workshops. Book at nationalparks.nsw.gov.au.

Tathra is another normally quiet (except during summer and Easter school holidays) seaside village where most of the action seems to be on the historic wharf – the only deep-sea timber wharf remaining on Australia's East Coast – where dozens of hopeful anglers line the edge of the high platform, usually hauling in impressively sized catches. It's a good spot to watch whales during spring, and you'll sometimes see penguins and seals in the water below. There is a cafe here that also hires fishing rods and sells bait and a small museum upstairs. If you're feeling really energetic, you can tackle the 27km **Wharf to Wharf** walk from Merimbula Wharf to Tathra Wharf, or hit the **Bundadung Trails** for mountain biking – there are more than 55km of MTB trails winding through the bush near town.

Horse Head Rock, Wallaga Lake

The Sapphire Coast   53

South of Tathra, **Bournda National Park** features not just saltwater and freshwater lakes, but also a lagoon, a creek and plenty of beaches. The clear tea-tree-stained waters of **Wallagoot Lake** are great for swimming, there are two lovely lakeside beaches and small kids love splashing in the shallows. The Traditional Country of the Dhurga and Yuin Peoples, guided cultural tours and workshops are available during school holidays: book at nationalparks.nsw.gov.au. The park is also popular with anglers (as is Bournda Beach) and kayakers, and there are some good walks, ranging from an easy 1km stroll from Bournda Lagoon to North Tura Beach via Bournda Headland to the 5hr **Kangarutha Track**, along an often rugged coastline with hidden beaches and spectacular cliffs. Eastern grey kangaroos are common in the park (they can be annoying in the campground as they will try and steal your food as soon as your back is turned – we had to shoo one out of our campervan), and birdlife is prolific, particularly waterbirds and sea eagles.

From Bournda it's a 15min drive south to **Merimbula**, a popular holiday spot at the entrance to Merimbula Lake. Stretch your legs on the lakeshore boardwalk that winds through mangroves and past oyster farms. It starts near the Merimbula Bridge and is around 3.5km return and will take around 90 leisurely minutes. It's stroller (and wheelchair) friendly and dogs are fine too, as long they are on a leash. The wharf is another popluar spot, especially in the hour or so before sunset, for fishing. There is whale watching here between Sept and late Nov.

Head into the hills

The coast is flanked by lush dairy farming country, and at Bega on the Princes Hwy, 18km inland from Tathra, you'll find the **Bega Cheese Factory**, which opened in 1899 and became one of Australia's biggest cheese producers. The heritage centre - a faithful reproduction of the original co-op creamery - has an informative museum. The cafe has a shady verandah overlooking the Bega River - great for a ploughman's lunch of Bega cheese and pickles or a cheese toastie.

A further 20km inland, at the northern end of the Bega Valley, surrounded by Wadbilliga National Park, **Brogo Dam** is a lovely spot for a picnic, a spot of fishing - the dam is stocked with trout and bass - or a paddle, and you can hire a canoe from **Brogo Wilderness Canoes**. If you're here in Sept, keep an eye out for flowering rock orchids in the cliffs.

Kids' spot

Most kids love splashing in the shallows of the lakes and beaches in and around Merimbula, but if they are craving a bit more excitement, **Merimbula's Magic Mountain** could be the answer. A waterslide, jumping castle, mini golf, rollercoaster, fun rides, dinosaurs and high ropes adventure course are just some of the attractions, as well as good picnic and barbecue facilities and a toddler pool and playground.

Opposite Blue Pool, Bermagui *Above* Bar Beach, Merimbula

SIDETRACK

Gabo Island is just on the Victorian side of the border, and managed by Parks Victoria, but unless you have your own boat the easiest way to access to this small island is on a scenic tour with **Merimbula Air Service**, based at Merimbula Airport. The half-day tours include a scenic flight over beautiful Twofold Bay before circling Gabo Island and its tall, pink granite lighthouse and landing on the small grassy airstrip in the middle of the island. At 49m high, Gabo is the second tallest lighthouse in Australia (the tallest is only one metre higher on King Island). Hewn from the surrounding granite rocks it took four years to build, and finally began operating in 1862. Fur seals sun themselves on the rocks below and huge waves pound the shoreline. A gourmet picnic lunch under the wing of the aircraft is included in the tour. Other attractions you'll see on Gabo include a shipwreck and historic cemetery. Book flights ahead of time at mairserv.com.au/gabo-island.

Good for a rainy day

The **Eden Killer Whale Museum** on Imlay St details the history of Eden and the role whales have played in the town's fortunes. One of the most interesting stories is that of Old Tom, leader of a pack of killer whales (orcas) who, in a strange example of human and animal symbiosis, would help the whalers hunt and kill the huge baleen whales in the harbour by rounding them up and directing them towards the whalers waiting with harpoons in exchange for unwanted whale scraps. There are also displays on shipping, fishing and associated maritime industries, as well as local history. The museum sounds a siren whenever a whale sighting is made in the bay - chances are, if you are here in spring, you'll hear it quite often. Thankfully, a lot has changed in 100 years and whale watching rather than hunting is now the attraction here.

MERIMBULA TO GREEN CAPE

Nicknamed the 'Humpback Highway' there are countless good places between Bermagui and the border where you see whales during their annual Antarctic migration, but one of the best is **Eden**, on the shores of Twofold Bay. Only 100 years ago, Eden was one of the most important whaling centres in the country.

Another legacy of the whaling era is **Davidson Whaling Station** historic site, in Beowa National Park (formerly Ben Boyd National Park), just south of town. Beowa means orca in the Thaua language and the park is rich in cultural sites, including rock shelters, middens and traditional travel routes.

The park was renamed at the request of First Nations and South Sea Islander communities in 2022. Ben Boyd, after whom the national park was formerly named, was a cruel colonist who enslaved Aboriginal, Māori and Pacific Islanders into labour.

Not far from Davidson Whaling Station, off Edrom Rd, is **Boyd's Tower**. This imposing square tower was built in 1846 and was originally intended to be a lighthouse, but the government would not give permission to use the privately owned structure as a lighthouse and instead it was used as a lookout for whales. Continue down Edrom Rd and take the turn-off to Green Cape. The road is unsealed and can be slippery after rain but is in otherwise good condition. **Green Cape Lightstation** was built in 1883. This was once one of

New South Wales

the most treacherous and dangerous sections of the coast, ruled by the strong East Australian Current. The lighthouse stands on a headland that juts out unexpectedly from the coastline, which many ships would hug in order to avoid the current. The nearby bay, aptly named Disaster Bay, is littered with wrecks – there is a good lookout on the road to the lighthouse. Just below the carpark is a cemetery with the graves of some of the 71 people who drowned when the *Ly-ee-Moon* was wrecked here in 1886, despite the lighthouse being operational at the time. Guided tours of the lighthouse are available on request; contact NSW National Parks and Wildlife Service (nationalparks.nsw.gov.au).

You can walk between Green Cape and the campground at **Bittangabee Bay** via a 7km walking trail, following the old horse-drawn track that the lightkeepers used to collect supplies that were offloaded in the bay. It's part of the longer 30km multi-day **Light to Light Walk** between Boyd's Tower and Green Cape Lightstation.

The view overlooking the cliffs from the point in front of the lighthouse is spectacular. Seals frolic in the white water of the waves below, the odd dolphin, or whales in season, swim by. Sea eagles, shearwaters, cormorants and occasionally even albatross soar above the waves.

If you're continuing south, it's a little less than an hour's drive back out to the highway and down to the Victorian border.

BEST BEDS

- **Clifftop at Tathra Beach** Revel in the retro beach house vibes at this '60s holiday house with a view; see Airbnb or Facebook.
- **Coast Resort Merimbula** Set in native gardens between Merimbula's lake and beach and opposite a good playground, it has a range of one-, two- and three-bedroom apartments, swimming pool and tennis court, as well as a Tesla EV charger. coastresort.com.au
- **Green Cape Lightstation** The historic lighthouse keepers' cottages have been restored and are available for accommodation. The three cottages - one three-bedroom and two two-bedroom - have a fully equipped kitchen. Linen is provided but bring your own food, and a book as there is no TV. Green Cape Lighthouse Rd, Beowa National Park; 1300 072 757; nationalparks.nsw.gov.au

Vanlife You'll find good caravan parks at most towns and there are lots of camping options in the national parks as well. At Mimosa Rocks National Park near Bermagui, you can park your van at **Gillards Beach**; **Aragunnu and Picnic Point campgrounds** are not suitable for caravans but camper trailers are okay. **Hobart Beach campground** in Bournda National Park, wedged between the surf beach and beautiful Wallagoot Lake is the only campground in the park, but it does have space for caravans (no power), hot showers, gas/electric barbecues, and drinking water. In Beowa National Park near Eden you can camp at **Bittangabee Bay** and **Saltwater Creek**. Both are great for swimming and snorkelling, and have gas/electric barbecues and rainwater tanks. Neither are suitable for caravans, but camper trailers and small campervans are okay. As you would expect, however, all national park campgrounds get very busy in summer and you'll need to book ahead during those times; bookings are essential for all campgrounds in NSW national parks, whatever the time of year. See NSW National Parks and Wildlife Service (nationalparks.nsw.gov.au).

Opposite top left Tathra Wharf *Opposite top right* Pambula River
Opposite bottom left Hiking to Green Cape Lighthouse, Beowa National Park, part of the Light to Light Coastal Track
Opposite bottom right Humpback whales

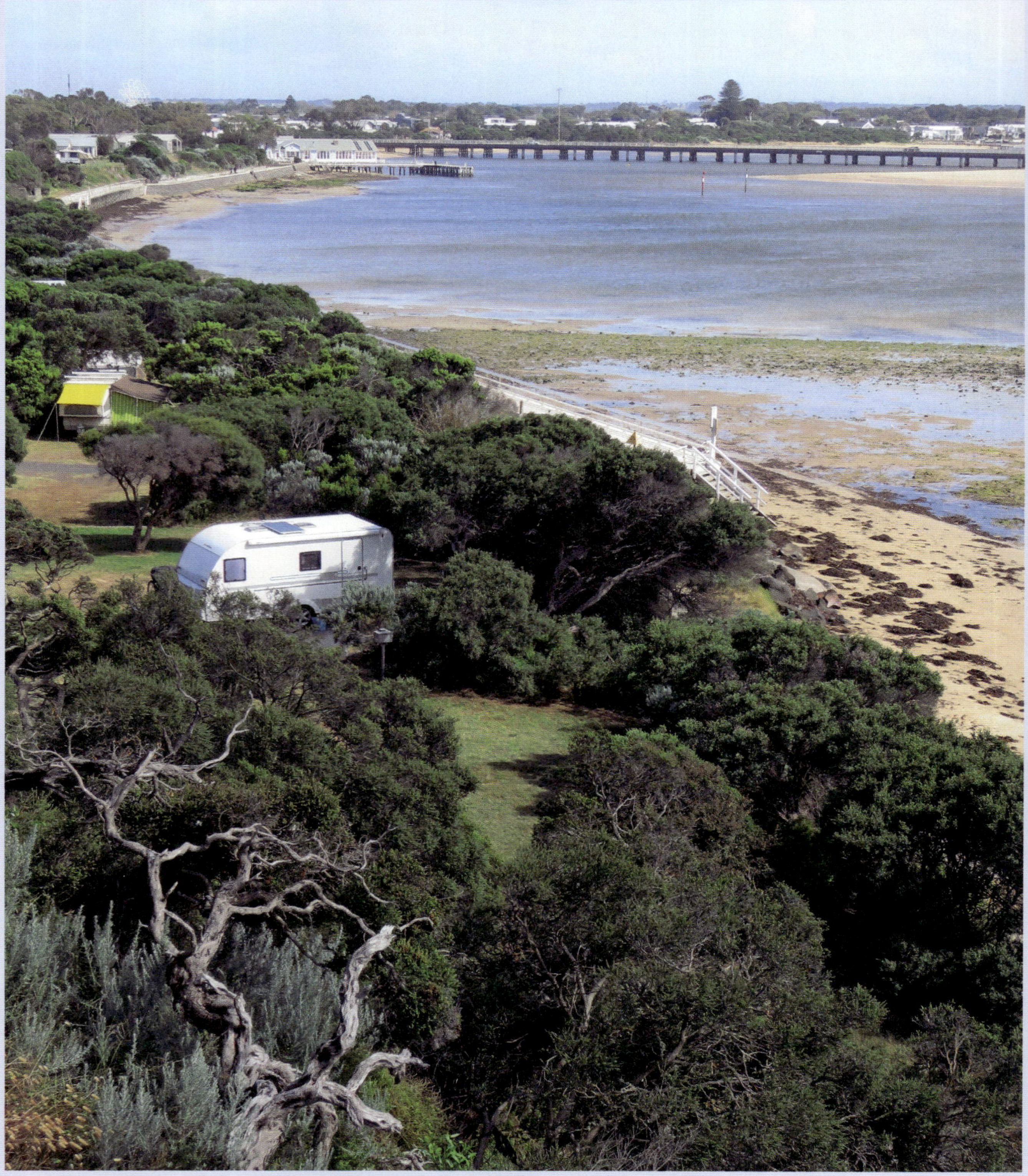

Victoria

Nature, wildlife and iconic rock formations.

Victoria

This is one of the world's greatest coastal drives, following the south-west coast of Victoria past countless beaches, along stunning stretches of cliff-top road, through beautiful rainforest and, of course, those famous rocky sea stacks known as the Twelve Apostles.

Great Ocean Road

HOW LONG?

You can easily drive the Great Ocean Road in one day – and many people even do the return trip to Melbourne/Naarm in one (very long) day – but this a drive best taken slowly, allowing time to explore the many beaches and coastal towns along the way, so make it a two- or three-day trip.

WHEN TO GO

If you can, try to avoid holidays and weekends, when the traffic along the Great Ocean Road can be frustrating. Midweek in midwinter is a glorious time to drive the route, as you'll have the road almost to yourself, and it's the best time to see whales, although it's too cold to swim. Summers are dry and warm; most rain falls during winter, when temperatures can be quite chilly, and also in spring.

NEED TO KNOW

Book ahead for accommodation and activities if you are planning on driving the Great Ocean Road during school holidays or on a weekend. Most people drive the route from east to west: go against the flow and you'll have less traffic. But note that if you drive west to east (Warrnambool to Torquay), you'll miss out on many of the roadside lookouts, as the only places to pull off are on the ocean side of the road and crossing the double lines is both foolhardy and illegal. Whichever direction you travel in, the cliff-hugging road is narrow and there are vertiginous drops to the ocean below – making for spectacular views but hairpin corners, limited places to pass other vehicles, and often slow driving. Take it easy and watch out for wildlife, cliff-stabilising works and roadworks.

◉ SNAPSHOT

Top of any list of great Australian coastal drives is the Great Ocean Road. Built between 1919 and 1932, the cliff-hugging road was hewn from the rock using picks, crowbars and shovels by 3000 returned World War I soldiers, who dedicated the 14-year project as a memorial to their mates who died in the war. There is a memorial arch at Eastern View, just past Fairhaven and Moggs Creek, if you're travelling from Torquay.

Drive rating
Easy. Sealed roads with extensive winding sections.

Acknowledgement of Country
This is the Traditional Land of the Eastern Maar, Gunditjmara, Gadubanud and Wadawurrung Peoples.

Distance planner
Torquay to Warrnambool: around 260km, without detours.
- Melbourne to Torquay: 104km
- Torquay to Apollo Bay: 94km
- Apollo Bay to Port Campbell: 97km
- Port Campbell to Warrnambool: 66km

More information
- Lorne Visitor Information Centre, 15 Mountjoy Pde, Lorne; (03) 5289 1152, also 1300 891 152; iamlorne.com.au.
- Great Ocean Road Visitor Information Centre, 100 Great Ocean Rd, Apollo Bay; 1300 689 297.
- Warrnambool Visitor Information Centre; 89 Merri St, Warrnambool; 1800 637 725.
- visitgreatoceanroad.org.au

Previous The holiday town of Barwon Heads
Opposite top left Live Wire Park near Lorne
Opposite top right Cape Otway Lighthouse
Opposite bottom left Australian National Surfing Museum, Torquay *Opposite bottom right* The beach at the bottom of Gibson Steps

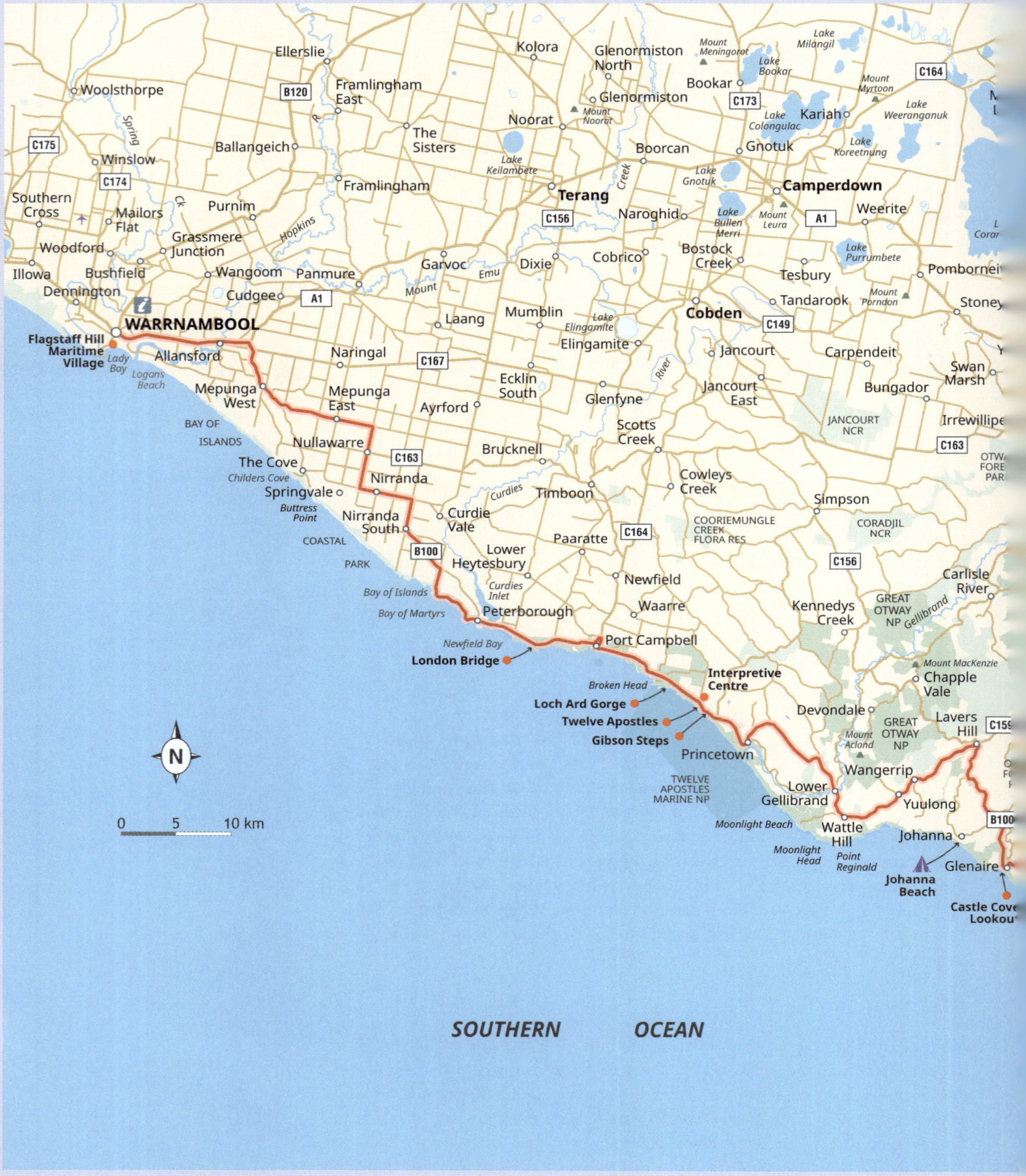
Ellerslie
Kolora
Glenormiston North
Mount Meningoort
Lake Bookar
Lake Milangil
C164
Woolsthorpe
B120
Framlingham East
Glenormiston
Bookar
Mount Noorat
C173
Mount Myrtoon
Noorat
Lake Colongulac
Kariah
Lake Weeranganuk
C175
The Sisters
Boorcan
Gnotuk
Lake Koreetnung
Winslow
Ballangeich
Lake Keilambete
Lake Gnotuk
Camperdown
C174
Framlingham
Creek
Terang
Southern Cross
Purnim
Lake Bullen Merri
Mount Leura
A1
Weerite
Mailors Flat
Hopkins
C156
Naroghid
Grassmere Junction
Bostock Creek
Woodford
Garvoc
Dixie
Cobrico
Lake Purrumbete
Illowa
Bushfield
Wangoom
Panmure
Emu
Tesbury
Pomborneit
Dennington
Cudgee
A1
Mount
Mount Porndon
Tandarook
Stoney
Laang
Mumblin
Cobden
WARRNAMBOOL
Lake Elingamite
C149
Flagstaff Hill Maritime Village
Lady Bay
Allansford
Elingamite
Carpendeit
Logans Beach
Naringal
C167
Jancourt
Swan Marsh
Ecklin South
River
Jancourt East
Mepunga West
Mepunga East
Glenfyne
Bungador
Ayrford
JANCOURT NCR
Irrewillipe
BAY OF ISLANDS
Scotts Creek
Nullawarre
Bucknell
C163
C163
The Cove
Cowleys Creek
Childers Cove
Nirranda
Timboon
Curdies
Springvale
Simpson
Buttress Point
Curdie Vale
Nirranda South
COORIEMUNGLE CREEK FLORA RES
CORADJIL NCR
COASTAL
C164
Paaratte
B100
Lower Heytesbury
C156
PARK
Newfield
Carlisle River
Bay of Islands
Curdies Inlet
Waarre
Kennedys Creek
GREAT OTWAY NP
Gellibrand
Bay of Martyrs
Peterborough
Newfield Bay
Port Campbell
London Bridge
Mount MacKenzie
Interpretive Centre
Chapple Vale
Broken Head
Loch Ard Gorge
Devondale
Twelve Apostles
GREAT OTWAY NP
Lavers Hill
Gibson Steps
Mount Acland
Princetown
Wangerrip
TWELVE APOSTLES MARINE NP
Lower Gellibrand
Yuulong
B100
Moonlight Beach
Wattle Hill
Johanna
Moonlight Head
Point Reginald
Glenaire
Johanna Beach
Castle Cove Lookout
N
0
5
10 km
SOUTHERN OCEAN

Great Ocean Road   63

TORQUAY TO APOLLO BAY

The starting point of the Great Ocean Road, **Torquay** can easily claim to be Australia's surfing capital – **Bells Beach**, one of the most famous surf beaches in the country and home of the world's longest running professional surfing event, the Rip Curl Pro, is just down the road. Two of the world's leading surfwear brands, Rip Curl and Quiksilver, were born here, and their flagship stores remain, along with a whole lot of other surfing and skateboarding brands.

From Torquay head south, along what is known as the Surf Coast, to the holiday town of Anglesea, where the road hits the coast and you first enjoy the spectacular views that make the Great Ocean Road famous.

At **Aireys Inlet**, drive up to Split Point Lighthouse for a fine coastal panorama and you can climb the lighthouse on a tour too. At Eastern View, just a few kilometres on from Aireys Inlet, is the **Great Ocean Road Memorial Arch** – a popular place to stop for a souvenir photo, but please don't try to snap a selfie in the middle of the road (you'll be amazed how many do!).

The stylish resort town of **Lorne** is not far away; it's great for a stroll, a spot of boutique shopping and coffee or lunch at one of the many restaurants that line the main street. Pop into the **Great Ocean Road Heritage Centre** inside the Lorne Visitor Centre to see The Great Ocean Road Story, a fascinating exhibition that tells the story of how the famous road was built.

Good for a rainy day

Torquay's **Australian National Surfing Museum** claims to be the largest surfing museum in the world. It encompasses interactive exhibits, memorabilia, a Surfing Hall of Fame and lots of surf art and kitsch. Don't miss the Waves and Wheels exhibition about surfers and their cars, and the road trips they took, the Great Ocean Road being up there with the biggest and best of course.

SIDETRACK

The **Surf Coast Walk** follows the trail blazed by the surfing pioneers. Stretching from Torquay all the way to Aireys Inlet, the entire walk is 44km but there are 12 trailheads along the way so you don't need to do it all. Wherever you pick it up you'll find gorgeous clifftop views, as well as tracks and staircases that lead to hidden beaches that only the locals know about, such as the one that winds down the sandstone cliffs to the surf beach of Jan Juc just on the edge of Torquay.

Opposite Hopetoun Falls *Below* Loch Ard Gorge

Wedged between the coast and the Otway forests, Lorne is also a good base for short excursions into the hinterland. **Erskine Falls** is just a few minutes' drive from the village centre and there are well-made walking tracks though the rainforest past the falls, huge tree ferns and towering trees. Stop on the way at **Live Wire Park** (you can book ahead at livewirepark.com.au) for some high-flying thrills that range from elevated boardwalks through the canopy and high-rope adventure courses to extreme zip-lining fun on the Shockwave Zip Coaster that winds at speed through the treetops. There's a range of experiences, suitable for all ages, even youngsters. If you'd rather remain on land, there's sweeping views to enjoy at **Teddy's Lookout** in Lorne, and another nice easy walk at **Sheoak Falls**, between Lorne and Cumberland River.

The town of Apollo Bay is around an hour's drive from Lorne, and the road hugs the coast the whole way. En route, drive through the pretty hamlet of Wye River and stop for a great coffee or meal at the **Wye General**. Look for koalas at **Kennett River** and pull over at **Cape Patton Lookout** for a fantastic coastline view and yet another great photograph.

Apollo Bay curves around the beach and is, like Lorne, full of shops, cafes and restaurants. It is also home to a lively fishing industry and you can watch the fleet unloading its catch at the wharf, or buy some of the local speciality, crayfish (lobster), at the fisherman's co-op down at the harbour, to eat beside the beach. Keep an eye out for the resident seals that are often snoozing in the sun at the end of the wharf.

Head into the hills

The coastal route might get all the glory, but this little daytrip through the rainforest is an absolute corker of a drive, and one that gets overlooked by all the tourists on the bus trips. Take the C159 from Lavers Hill on the Great Ocean Road and wind your way north-east through the forests to the hamlet of Beech Forest and then the C119 north to the township of Forrest. It's less than 60km and sealed all the way but will take you twice as long as you expect because it's very narrow - take it slow and be prepared to move over if you meet an oncoming vehicle - very twisty and incredibly scenic. Reasons to go beyond immersing yourself in the lush rainforest are the spectacular **Hopetoun Falls** - there's a platform that looks out over the 30m-high falls, and a good walking track that leads to a fern-fringed pool at their base. The stunning **Redwood Forest** beside the Aire River is a forest of massive Californian Redwoods that was planted in 1936 but has never been logged, and some of the trees are now more than 60m tall - it's one of the most photogenic spots in the Otways. The former logging town of Forrest has a network of forest and waterfall walking trails, as well as **Forrest Brewing Company** for dining and drinks, and **Forrest General Store** cafe and local information. Nearby **Lake Elizabeth** is a great spot to walk and try to see a platypus, although your best chance is at dusk or early in the morning. Forrest is also one of the state's best mountain-biking destinations - bike hire is available from **Forrest MTB Hire** (forrestbikehire.com.au).

Kids' spot

A fun family attraction on this stretch is the **Otway Fly** (otwayfly.com.au), a 1hr rainforest walk that includes an elevated boardwalk through the rainforest canopy, 25m above the ground. If you have a head for heights, climb the 47m-high lookout tower for stunning views. Thrill-seekers can join a 2.5hr zip-line tour that flies through the treetops. It's well signposted, 12km from Lavers Hill.

Foodie trail

It takes roughly 45min to drive the C151/152, a lovely winding road that twists through the rainforest hinterland behind Lorne to Birregurra, a tiny little town that punches well above its weight when it comes to eating out. Most famous of them all is **Brae** (braerestaurant.com), Victoria's best regional restaurant and also world-renowned. It's a set menu of 14 or 15 small courses that changes daily according to what chef Dan Hunter has harvested from the organic garden adjacent to the farmhouse dining room, and takes around three to four hours to eat. For drivers the non-alcoholic drinks that match each course are arguably more exciting than the wine, and there are six suites onsite if you want to stay overnight. It's a bucket-list experience worth every cent but you'll need to book several weeks in advance.

APOLLO BAY TO PORT CAMPBELL

At Apollo Bay the road leaves the coast and cuts through lush green farmland and the dense rainforest of **Great Otway National Park**, before emerging on the western side of Cape Otway headland at **Port Campbell National Park**.

Maits Rest Rainforest Trail is a 30min boardwalk stroll through beautiful rainforest, where giant myrtle beeches tower above a delicate understorey of tree ferns, lichens and mosses. It's just off the Great Ocean Road around 16km from Apollo Bay.

Take the turn-off to the tip of Cape Otway, around 12km from the Great Ocean Road. The site houses one of the best-preserved groups of historic lighthouse buildings in Australia, built in 1848. **Cape Otway Lighthouse** is open daily for self-guided tours, or you can join one of the history talks that depart regularly throughout the day (usually when there are enough people) and include climbing the spiral staircase to the top of the light tower. There are also lighthouse keeper's cottages if you want to stay onsite and a cafe with a view of the lighthouse. Keep a lookout on the drive in, as you will often see koalas asleep in the trees beside the road.

West of Lavers Hill the road cuts across a heath-covered plateau to **Princetown**, where the coastal plain borders sheer cliffs, sometimes just metres from the edge of the road. Take the time to check out the view from **Castle Cove Lookout** and the often-overlooked wave-wracked expanse of **Johanna Beach**, before heading to the star attraction of this trip, the **Twelve Apostles**. Originally called the Sow and Piglets, there are actually only eight remaining, as a few have tumbled into the sea in recent years. Carved out of the adjacent cliffs by wind and wave erosion, the cliffs rise to nearly 70m in some places and the highest Apostle is around 50m from base to tip. There's a short wheelchair-accessible walk from the carpark to a lookout. If you'd like to get a closer view (without the crowds that you'll often find jostling for space and taking selfies at the viewing platform), backtrack to **Gibson Steps** (they're signposted on the Great Ocean Road a kilometre east of the main lookout). These steps are carved into the side of 70m-high cliffs and lead down onto the beach and to the foot of two giant rock stacks, nicknamed Gog and Magog, and it's a completely different view of the Great Ocean Road's most famous sight.

Alternatively, splurge out on a short **helicopter flight**, available near the Interpretive Centre at the Twelve Apostles (12apostleshelicopters.com.au).

Most of the buses and daytrippers don't go beyond the Twelve Apostles, but the grand views continue as you head to **Loch Ard Gorge**, site of a tragic shipwreck in 1878 that left just two survivors out of 54 passengers and crew, and then on to **London Bridge**, which dramatically lost one of its arches in 1990, stranding two startled sightseers on the newly formed tower, and the **Bay of Islands Coastal Park**. All of these major natural attractions are well signposted and offer good lookout points and short but very scenic walks.

PORT CAMPBELL TO WARRNAMBOOL

After Peterborough the road leaves the coast once more to meander through beautiful pastoral lands and rich dairy country before hitting the coast again at the regional city of Warrnambool.

If you are driving the Great Ocean Road between June and Sept, head for **Logans Beach** at Warrnambool, where you might be lucky enough to see one of the many female southern right whales that come here each year to give birth – this is one of the best shore-based places to see these whales and their calves in winter. The whales stay in the bay for around two or three months, so frequent visitors to the whale-watching platform in the dunes can watch the calves grow, which are around 5–6m long when they are born – by the time they head back to the Southern Ocean they are almost double that size. Though the whales come close to shore, you'll get a much better look if you have binoculars.

There is a lot more to do in Warrnambool and the city's attractions and activities are included in the Beyond the Great Ocean Road (see p.69) itinerary. From Warrnambool it is 260km back to Melbourne via the M1, around a 3.5hr trip, depending on traffic. Or go a little further on another road trip: Beyond the Great Ocean Road starts where this one stops.

✕ Foodie trail

If you're a food lover – or just enjoy strawberries and ice-cream, whiskey, cheese, beer or chocolate (and who doesn't enjoy one or all of those!) take the road to **Timboon**. It's home to cheesemakers, an ice-creamery, distillery, and a number of artisan producers and growers, many who have been farming here for generations. If you're wanting to discover more foodie stops in the Otway Ranges, follow the **Otway Harvest Trail** (otwayharvesttrail.org.au).

☺ Kids' spot

Warrnambool's **Flagstaff Hill Maritime Village** is an open-air museum created around the original lighthouses and fortifications that gave rise to the town of Warrnambool in 1859. The Great Circle Gallery tells the story of the more than 180 shipwrecks along this section of coast. The star exhibit is the Loch Ard Peacock, a Minton porcelain peacock – one of only nine in the world – that was destined for the Melbourne International Exhibition in 1880 and miraculously washed up unscathed when the *Loch Ard* came to grief near Port Campbell in 1878. The nightly sound-and-laser show, Tales of the Shipwreck Coast, brings the story of the shipwreck to life.

BEST BEDS

- **Anglesea Riverside Motel** Fabulously retro and channelling the mid-20th century motel vintage vibe, this waterfront drive-in gem is in the middle of Anglesea. Laze about on sun lounges beside the outdoor pool, stroll across the road to the river, or round the corner to the beach. angleseariversidemotel.com.au
- The kookaburras provide the wake-up calls at **Lorne Bush House**. Built into the side of a hill, these glamping retreats have a big double bed complete with ensuite and kitchenette, but you'll probably spend most of your stay sitting out on the deck, admiring the view and counting the 'roos. lornebushcottages.com.au
- **Chris's Beacon Point Villas** Perched in high bushland above the Great Ocean Road, near Apollo Bay, the villas and studios offer spectacular views of the ocean and Otway Ranges, with an onsite restaurant. chriss.com.au
- **Deep Blue Hotel and Hot Springs** You don't have to be a guest to enjoy a therapeutic soak in one of the geothermal mineral pools at this Warrnambool hotel, but it's nice not to have to stumble too far back to your room. thedeepblue.com.au

VANLIFE

There are caravan parks at Torquay, Anglesea, Aireys Inlet, Lorne and Warrnambool, but two of the best spots are **Cumberland River Holiday Park**, 7km west of Lorne, where you'll find a lovely grassy camping area set beside the river (unpowered sites only), and beachfront **Kennett River Family Caravan Park** between Lorne and Apollo Bay, where powered sites are available. You can also bush camp at **Johanna Beach** and **Lake Elizabeth** near Forrest, perfect if you plan to do a little platypus watching early in the morning or late in the afternoon. Book both through Parks Victoria (parks.vic.gov.au).

The famous coastline and rock formations along the Great Ocean Road

Victoria

The Great Ocean Road might get all the Insta fame and glory, but the coastal scenery gets even better (and less crowded) the further west you go. This trip takes you from lovely coastal hamlets to a unique cultural World Heritage Site, with stories of shipwrecks along the way.

Beyond the Great Ocean Road

HOW LONG?

At less than 200km this is not a long trip, and you can easily drive it in a couple of hours. It makes a great one- or two-day extension to a Great Ocean Road trip (*see* p.61), or a scenic byway between Melbourne/Naarm and Adelaide/Tarndanya.

WHEN TO GO

Summers are dry and warm; most rain falls during winter, when temperatures can be quite chilly, but that's also the best time to see whales and their calves at Logans Beach near Warrnambool. The Port Fairy Folk Festival is in Mar and the Koroit Irish Festival is in Apr.

LOCAL SECRET

For lunch with an unbeatable view, drive straight to the **Bridgewater Bay Cafe** in Cape Bridgewater (you can't miss it, it's pretty much the only thing there, apart from a clutch of holiday houses). Order a glass of wine and some fresh fish and chips, grab a table at the edge of the sand, and watch the whales go by (hopefully). No shoes required.

SNAPSHOT

The highest sea cliffs in Victoria, the state's oldest town, lots of whales, shipwrecked treasure and the country's newest World Heritage Site are just some of the reasons why it's worth going a little further on your drive down the Great Ocean Road. Throw in the chance to drive around the inside of an active volcano, and it's a great ocean road trip to remember.

Drive rating
Easy. Sealed roads.

Acknowledgement of Country
This is the Traditional Land of the Gunditjmara People.

Distance planner
Warrnambool to Nelson: 189km
- Warrnambool to Portland: 102km
- Portland to Cape Bridgewater: 22km
- Cape Bridgewater to Nelson: 54km

More information
- Warrnambool Visitor Information Centre; 89 Merri St, Warrnambool; 1800 637 725.
- The Port Fairy and Region Visitor Information Centre; Railway Place, Bank St, Port Fairy; (03) 5568 2682.
- Portland Visitor Information Centre; Lee Breakwater Rd, Portland; 1800 035 567.
- visitgreatoceanroad.org.au

Opposite Discovery Bay Coastal Park

WARRNAMBOOL TO PORTLAND

Starting at the end of Victoria's famous Great Ocean Road (*see* p.61), this coastal road trip goes where many travellers don't. As the most well-known 'must see' spot on the iconic coastal drive, many Great Ocean Road trippers turn around at the Twelve Apostles and head back to Melbourne, not realising that some of the south coast's most underrated bits are lurking further west, in Warrnambool, Port Fairy and beyond.

In **Warrnambool, Flagstaff Hill Maritime Village** – an outdoor museum built around the 1858 heritage-listed lighthouse and home to Victoria's largest shipwreck collection, including the *Loch Ard* treasures (*see* p.67 for more detail) – is the regional city's most popular attraction but it's not the only one.

The **Foreshore Promenade Walk** is a 7.5km sealed coastal trail suitable for walkers, cyclists, prams, wheelchairs and rollerbladers, that includes the historic breakwall – built in 1890 it was one of the most important maritime engineering projects in Victoria in the late 19th century – parklands and surf beaches. The star attraction is **Logans Beach**, where, between June and Sept, you might be lucky enough to see one of the many female southern right whales that come here each year to give birth. **Middle Island**, just a few hundred metres from Warrnambool foreshore, is home to a colony of little penguins, uniquely guarded by Maremma sheepdogs: you can meet the four-legged change to sentries on a guided tour during summer.

If you have always dreamt of finding a secret hoard of loot there's buried treasure hidden in the sand dunes west of Warrnambool, or so the legend goes. In the 1830s some shipwrecked sealers found a decaying wreck in the Armstrong Bay area, and a story grew that it was the remains of a 16th-century Spanish or Portuguese galleon full of treasure. Sometime in the 1880s the wreck seems to have disappeared, possibly covered by shifting sands, and ever since the story of the so-called Mahogany Ship has become more mysterious with each retelling. If you fancy a bit of treasure hunting, follow the **Mahogany Ship Walking Track**, which traces the coast between Warrnambool and Port Fairy and passes sites where the mythical ship may rest. The trail is 22km long and is mostly on the beach, but if you want to concentrate your search efforts head to the area east of Gormans Rd and west of Levys Point near Dennington – at least that's what the treasure hunters on the online forums suggest!

Port Fairy Lighthouse

Beyond the Great Ocean Road   71

The historic seaside village of **Port Fairy** is an easy 30min drive from Warrnambool, and it too has a strong link to Ireland, despite being originally settled by a Scottish whaler in the 1820s. It was the Irish who flocked here during the potato famine of the 1840s that built the town's many magnificent buildings, most of which still remain today. Back then, the surrounding land was owned by one man, Sydney solicitor James Atkinson, who converted the sealing and whaling community into a modern port by draining the swamps around the town, subdividing and selling or leasing the land and building the harbour on the Moyne River. Named Belfast after Atkinson's Irish home, the fledgling fishing village at the mouth of the Moyne River became one of the colony's largest and busiest ports, supplying Melbourne with boatloads of fresh fish and produce from the surrounding farmlands. It also became Australia's largest privately-owned town.

Today it's a very pretty place with many historic buildings housing restaurants, boutiques and art galleries – more than 50 of the buildings are classified by the National Trust. Take an early morning walk along the historic wharf and watch fishermen unload their catch of crayfish and abalone among the bobbing cruising boats and racing yachts, and chat to some of the anglers that line the riverside boardwalk, all hoping to catch their own breakfast fresh from the sea. Continue on past the wharf towards the harbour, following the track to **Griffiths Island**, where you can walk along a short causeway to the historic **Griffiths Island Lighthouse**, built in 1859, or wander along the dune paths.

One of the best places in Australia to witness one of nature's great migrations, 40,000 short-tailed shearwaters (mutton birds) fill the sky above Griffith Island in the mouth of the Moyne River each summer. So punctual you can almost set your watch by them, they arrive, en masse, from Alaska on or around 22 Sept, a remarkable bit of timing given they've flown more than 16,000km. They return, with the same partner, to the same nest they had on the island the year before, and stay until Apr, when they go back to Alaska, leaving the chicks behind. Stroll out to the island via the causeway around sunset, when they return to their nests, for a truly spectacular show.

Settled in 1834, **Portland** is Victoria's oldest European town. Many of the grand historic buildings in town – mostly built with distinctive bluestone – date back to then. It was – and still is – the only deep-water seaport between Melbourne and Adelaide, and you can watch the big ships loading and unloading in the harbour from **Whalers Bluff Lighthouse**.

It's also a good spot to watch whales, with southern right whales visiting the coast – sometimes even seen in the harbour – during the winter months, and Earth's largest mammal, the blue whale, in summer. If you see a yellow flag flying outside the visitor centre it means that whales have been spotted in local waters.

Good for a rainy day

You can enjoy a session at the **Deep Blue Hot Springs Sanctuary** in sunny weather, but soaking in a hot pool while it rains is a delightful way to while away an inclement day. Surrounded by gardens, there are 15 open-air geothermally heated mineral pools, many fed by waterfalls or featuring a swim through caves. Relax with a therapeutic soak and float in the warm pools or take a deep dive into the various wellness therapies, including aromatherapy pools, colour therapy, infrared sauna and a purpose-built salt room.

Opposite Thunder Point Walk, Warrnambool *Above* Exploring Princess Margaret Rose Cave

SIDETRACK

If you're not keen on the idea of walking all the way to Port Fairy, the **Warrnambool to Port Fairy Rail Trail** is a 37km cycle way that follows the route of a disused railway line. The best thing about rail trails is that they are traffic free, and because those old trains couldn't haul uphill very well you don't have to either – this rail trail is gentle and suitable for all levels of fitness and riding abilities, which makes for a great family day out.

Head into the hills

There aren't that many places in Australia where you can drive into the crater of a dormant, rather than extinct, volcano. Roughly halfway between Warrnambool and Port Fairy, **Tower Hill Wildlife Reserve** is actually inside the volcano, last thought to have erupted around 32,000 years ago. The crater – a giant nested maar – is more than 3km wide, and has since filled with water, from which rise volcanic cone-shaped hills. Called Koroitj by the Gunditjmara People, who would have witnessed the last eruptions and who still tell stories about the events, the area is rich in archaeological artefacts that date back to the time of the eruption, including ancient middens that contain the bones of Tasmanian devils, as well as axes and other tools found buried under volcanic ash. Worn Gundidj at Tower Hill run 2hr culture and nature tours which focus on the Gunditjmara history and culture of the area, as well as Traditional lifestyles. It became a national park in 1892, making it the oldest in Victoria, and is a popular spot for wildlife viewing, including koalas, possums, kangaroos and wallabies. Worn Gundidj also run nocturnal wildlife walks in the evening. There's also a range of good short walks, including the lava tongue track to the most recent flow of lava. The Tower Hill Circuit Drive takes you around the rim, following for the most part Lake View Rd, before winding down deep inside the crater to the wildlife reserve and visitor centre in the middle of the crater.

On the northern edge of Tower Hill, the sleepy town of **Koroit** appears snapped frozen in time. If you're a fan of mid-century vintage, you'll love Koroit – it's all shabbily authentic. Settled by Irish immigrants in the 1840s, Koroit still beats to an Irish drum – called a bodhran in this neck of the woods. Potatoes are big business around here, and if you pass a farm gate stall selling bags of spuds grab some to take home. Pop into **Mickey Bourke's Koroit Pub** for some Aussie craic, and if you're in town in Apr when the town celebrates all things Irish, including the Australian Danny Boy Championship, get ready for plenty of singing and dancing and lots of spud picking and peeling fun.

Beyond the Great Ocean Road

☺ Kids' spot

The giant 33m slide in the sand dunes at **Yambuk** (a 10min drive west of Port Fairy) is great fun for kids of all ages. There are also amazing views out to Deen Maar (Lady Julia Percy Island), Australia's oldest offshore volcano, which is home to around 27,000 fur seals, the largest breeding colony in the country.

Aside from the lovely sheltered beach and expansive grassy foreshore, family-friendly attractions in **Portland** include the hop-on-hop-off **Cable Tram**, a lovingly restored old Melbourne tram that trundles around a 7.4km route along the foreshore, stopping at the town's most popular museums, model train centre, lookout and the botanic gardens. If you only get off at one stop, make it the **Maritime Discovery Centre**. Full of local history, a highlight is sitting inside the belly of a sperm whale.

SIDETRACK

Inscribed on the UNESCO World Heritage List in July 2019, **Budj Bim Cultural Landscape** near Heywood is, at the time of writing this guide, the only World Heritage Site in Australia listed purely for its Aboriginal cultural values. At around 30,000 years old, Budj Bim's lava fields at its base allowed the Gunditjmara People to trap, store and harvest kooyang (freshwater eels) long before the pyramids of Egypt were even contemplated. The Budj Bim landscape provided an economic and social base for Gunditjmara People for more than six millennia, making it one of the world's oldest and most extensive freshwater aquaculture systems and human settlement sites. You need a guide to see it though; aside from a couple of story boards at the beginning of the walking trail, there's little interpretative information. This is a place that needs a local - someone who grew up with the stories of how the rocky landscape was formed by volcanic eruptions as recently as 8000 years ago and how the people lived and farmed here - to bring it to life. Book ahead online for a tour (budjbim.com.au). You can also visit the newly opened **Tae Rak Aquaculture Centre** that houses a tour desk, cafe and souvenir shop.

Top Cape Bridgewater *Bottom* Cruising the Glenelg River Gorge

PORTLAND TO NELSON

For more great ocean views – and possibly a whale sighting or two – take a 15min drive out to **Cape Nelson Lighthouse**, (guided tours available). You can also stay in the lighthouse keeper's cottages (*see* Best beds section).

From Cape Nelson, head west towards **Cape Bridgewater**. Victoria's south-west coast is blessed with some pretty impressive cliffs – if you've driven the Great Ocean Road you'll have already seen some spectacular crags, bluffs and precipices – but those at Cape Bridgewater take the crown. At more than 130m high, these are the tallest sea cliffs in Victoria and, like much of the surrounding landscape, this was once a volcano – the western edge of a volcanic island that over millennia has become joined to the mainland by calcified sand dunes. It's a bit of an uphill slog to get there – about a 2hr walk – but from the top you can peer down to a large colony of fur seals, so don't forget your binoculars.

Nearby, at the end of Blowholes Rd, are (you guessed it!), the **Bridgewater blowholes**. They can be a bit underwhelming on a calm day, but during high seas the spouts can be quite spectacular. If you see any similar 11m-high spouts at sea level, it will be from a blue whale.

One of the coast's weirder natural phenomena are just a 5min walk away. Despite their misleading name, the solidified columns and tubes of the **Petrified Forest** are not fossilised tree trunks but the dissolved rocks that have formed a forest of hollow tubes, some more than 20m high.

Nelson is the last town (or at least the most westerly) in Victoria. In fact, it is so close that you can walk to South Australia and back in one afternoon on a pretty wildflower-lined cliff-top walk above the Glenelg River Gorge in **Lower Glenelg National Park**, which is not far from the edge of town. You can also cruise through the gorge, which has cliffs as high as 50m in some parts, with **Nelson River Cruises** (glenelgrivercruises.com.au) – half-day trips can include a tour of **Princess Margaret Rose Cave**, one of the most richly decorated limestone cave systems in Australia , but check ahead as at the time of research the cave was closed due to repair works.

If you really want to experience a great ocean road trip without crowds, this is the drive for you, but don't leave it too long, because it won't stay this underrated for long.

SIDETRACK

If you've got a 4WD, spend some time exploring **Discovery Bay Coastal Park**, a 50km-long sweep of ocean beach backed by huge dunes and coastal lakes that stretches between Cape Bridgewater and Nelson. Highlights include lakeside camping, deserted beaches, rockpools and sandy 4WD tracks.

BEST BEDS

- The bedrooms in the attic at the **Merrijig Inn** in Port Fairy might be small, but what they lack in space they make up for in charm. Built in 1845 opposite the town's original jetty, it's the oldest inn in Victoria and the place to go for early evening cocktails in the fruit and flower-filled garden, and seriously fine food in the historic dining room or cosy front bar. merrijiginn.com
- There are five two-bedroom cottages for overnight stays at **Cape Nelson Lighthouse**, near Portland. All include a fully equipped kitchen, TV, open fireplace and wraparound views. capenelsonlighthouse.com.au

VANLIFE

There are several commercial caravan parks in Warrnambool, Port Fairy and Portland. **Killarney Beach Caravan Park** is an old-style, pet-friendly camping reserve beside a sports oval with powered sites and hot showers. It's in a handy location between Warrnambool and Port Fairy. You can bush camp at **Lake Mombeong** in Discovery Bay, and there are paddle-in camping sites spread out along the river, as well as caravan sites at **Princess Margaret Rose Cave** and **Pritchards**, in **Lower Glenelg National Park**. Book through Parks Victoria for all of them (parks.vic.gov.au). **Kywong Caravan Park** in Nelson has a large bush camping area as well as powered caravan sites.

Beyond the Great Ocean Road

Victoria

A tiny island packed with wildlife, wild views and family-friendly fun, less than a 90min drive from Melbourne/Naarm.

Phillip Island

HOW LONG?
Visiting Phillip Island is a popular daytrip from Melbourne/Naarm, but there's so much more to see here than just the Penguin Parade. Two or three days here would be ideal.

WHEN TO GO
Summers tend to be short on Phillip Island, and winters can be wet, cold and windy, which means Dec to Mar is the most popular time to visit. Go in winter though, and you'll have the place almost to yourself – just be sure to have warm woollies for cold nights and for penguin-watching. The Australian Motorcycle Grand Prix is in mid Oct, the Superbike World Championship is in mid Nov.

NEED TO KNOW
A Four Parks Pass gains you entry to the Penguin Parade and Antarctic Journey attraction at the Nobbies Centre, Koala Conservation Centre and Churchill Island. Aside from the timed entry to the parade, it's valid for six months and is a 20 per cent discount on the standard ticket prices. Book online (penguins.org.au).

SNAPSHOT
The little penguins might steal the limelight – or moonlight in this case – but there's much more to Phillip Island than just the famous penguin parade. Take a drive around the island and you'll discover wild coastlines with spectacular cliff-top walking trails, a wealth of wildlife beyond the waddling penguins, great food and wine, and some fantastic family-friendly attractions.

Drive rating
Easy. Mostly sealed roads.

Acknowledgement of Country
This is the Traditional Land of the Boon Wurrung People.

Distance planner
Melbourne to the Penguin Parade on the south-west tip of the island is around 150km. From San Remo, the journey to Summerlands and back to Cape Woolamai is around 53km.
- San Remo to Cowes: 17km
- Cowes to Summerlands (Penguin Parade): 12km
- Summerlands to Cape Woolamai: 24km

More information
- Phillip Island Information Centre, 895 Phillip Island Rd, Newhaven (1km over the bridge onto Phillip Island); 1300 366 422; visitphillipisland.com.au

Opposite Fishing expedition at Cape Woolamai, Phillip Island

SAN REMO TO SUMMERLANDS

Connected to the mainland by bridge at San Remo, Phillip Island – known as Millowl by the Boon Wurrung People – is 122km south-east of Melbourne via the Monash Fwy (M1) and the South Gippsland and Bass highways, around a 90min drive, depending on traffic.

Call into **Artfusion Gallery** on the way, a sculpture and glass studio and art gallery where you can watch artists at work and buy their wares at half the price that you'd find them for in Melbourne galleries. You'll find it at the roundabout at Anderson, just before you get to San Remo.

San Remo might not be very far – as the pelican flies – from the bright lights of Melbourne, but it has a genuine fishing village vibe. **San Remo Fisherman's Co-op** at the jetty beside the bridge is the spot to go for fresh fish and chips – or rock lobster – straight off the fishing boat. Time your visit for noon and you can watch the daily free pelican feeding show on the beach next door, where about 30 hungry birds jostle for a fishy feed. There's also a free **Fishing Heritage Museum** where you can learn about the history of the local fishing fleet.

From San Remo it's around a 20min drive to **Cowes**, the main town on the island and where you'll find most of the island's shops, cafes and restaurants. It's a further 15min or so to get to the Penguin Parade at the western tip of the island – but take your time, as there's plenty to see and do along the way.

Rhyll Inlet is a haven for birdlife, with thousands of pelicans, black swans, gulls and migratory waders. The walking track and boardwalk – which is also suitable for bicycles – provide a great way to explore the inlet and mangroves without getting your feet wet. You can follow the track and boardwalk all the way from Conservation Hill to the seaside village of Rhyll (allow 90min return) or just do the half-hour mangrove boardwalk.

Good for a rainy day

If you have a sweet tooth, call into **Phillip Island Chocolate Factory** - it's on the main road, not long after you've crossed the San Remo bridge. Watch chocolate being made, see the world's largest chocolate waterfall, chocolate displays, including a model train set and miniature village all made of chocolate, and a life-size chocolate version of Michelangelo's *David*, as well as a hard-to-resist chocolate cafe and shop.

Kids' spot

Kids will love **Churchill Island Heritage Farm**, where they can watch cows being milked, sheep being shorn, take a wagon ride and watch a blacksmith at work. The historic houses, which date from the 1850s, are fully furnished and open for self-guided tours. During school holidays there are a range of special activities, including old-fashioned games, ranger walks and activity tables.

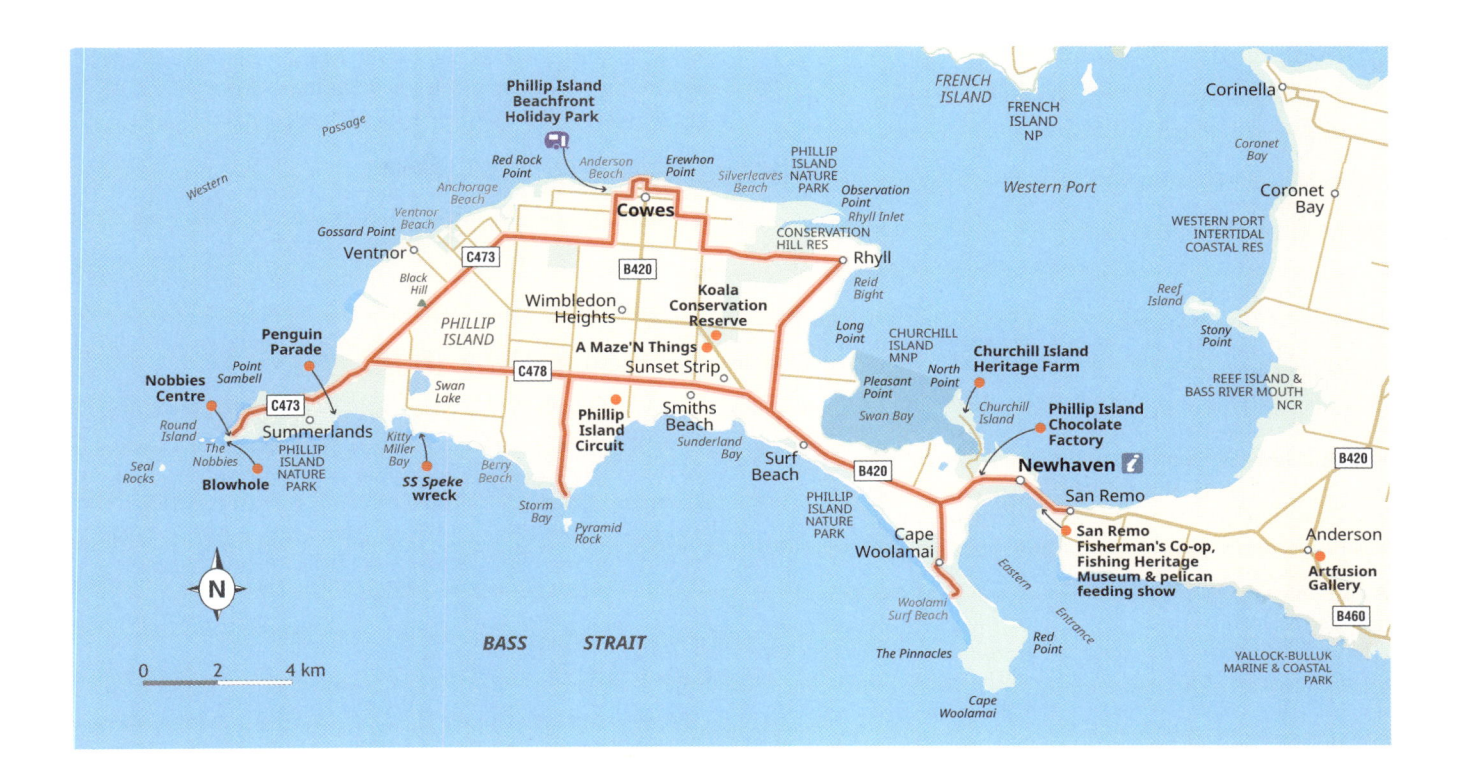

About halfway between Rhyll and Cowes you can see koalas in the wild at the **Koala Conservation Reserve**, where two elevated boardwalks let you get close to the koalas perched in the treetops. The centre also has a breeding program and if you're lucky you may catch a glimpse of a joey emerging from its mother's pouch as it learns to climb the towering eucalypts to forage for food. Both walks are wheelchair accessible – and good for those pushing prams as well as those on little legs – and both take around 20min. There are also wallabies, echidnas and lots of colourful native birds in the reserve.

As an added bonus to its holiday town vibe, Cowes has a lovely north-facing beach – a rarity in Victoria. Flanked by a shady expanse of grass, the beach is a sheltered swimming spot, and there's a fishing jetty nearby.

No first-time visit to Phillip Island is complete without a ringside seat at the nightly **Penguin Parade** (penguins.org.au), when hundreds of little penguins (that's their official name, although they used to be called fairy penguins in less politically correct times) come out of the sea at Summerlands Beach at dusk and waddle up the hill to their burrows. It attracts thousands of visitors each night and is one of Victoria's most popular attractions. Keep an eye on the time because the road to the Penguin Parade and the nearby Nobbies Centre closes one hour before sunset in order to protect the wildlife. Make sure you book your tickets online ahead of time and arrive at least an hour before sunset, or you may find yourself without a seat. That said, some positions on the boardwalk leading down to the viewing platforms can give you a better view of the penguins as they head up the hill to their burrows.

There are two viewing platforms and a number of tours, but the best is the **Penguin Plus** – it ensures a prime viewing position and you'll only have to share the experience with 150 others, rather than the bigger crowds at the main platform. The penguins start arriving at sunset, which in summer is around 9pm, and the lights are turned out 50min after the first penguin arrives, so it can be a late night for little kids. It also gets cold, even in summer, so bring warm clothes, and a cushion or blanket to sit on – those bench seats get hard after an hour or so! When you leave, don't forget to check under your car for stray penguins and keep an eye out for wildlife on the drive home.

Opposite Walking trail at Pyramid Rock

Phillip Island 79

😊 Kids' spot

Just across the road from the Koala Conservation Reserve, the **A Maze'N Things** theme park is always a hit with kids. There's a maze, of course, as well as mini golf and the Magic Manor, which has magic rabbits, a time machine and a flying chandelier and nothing is quite as it seems. You have to see it to believe it!

The **Nobbies Centre** is a 5min drive beyond the turn-off to the Penguin Parade. It can be tempting to dismiss the Nobbies Centre as just a ticket outlet, tourist information centre and souvenir shop, but the displays inside on the local marine life, including penguins and seals, are really informative. Inside, you'll find the **Antarctic Journey** attraction where you can get a taste for what life is like in the frozen south – kids love the 'chill zone'.

Australia's largest fur seal colony lives at **Seal Rocks**, just beyond the headland. Head out to the boardwalk outside: it's a fantastic cliff-top walk along the headland and if you've got binoculars you'll have a good view of the seals. During big southern swells the blowhole at the end of the walk puts on an impressive display.

SUMMERLANDS TO CAPE WOOLAMAI

The island's south coast is wilder and emptier than the north. The beaches along the stretch are great for beachcombing, and at low tide you can see the rusting remains of the *SS Speke*, wrecked on the rock shelf on the east side of Kitty Miller Bay in 1906, enroute to Sydney from Peru. Don't miss **Pyramid Rock**, around halfway along the southern coast, off Back Beach Rd. It's an easy 10min walk – much of it along wooden boardwalks – to the lookout platform, which provides great views not only over the triangular pile of rocks that gives this scenic point its name, but also north and south along the coast. The rocks are the remnant of a lava flow that once formed a land bridge to the point. You can also follow a cliff-top trail to **Berry Beach**; go early in the morning and you're almost guaranteed to see wallabies on the track.

Home to the Australian Motorcycle Grand Prix each Oct, as well as the Superbike World Championship and the V8 Supercar Series, the **Phillip Island Circuit** (around halfway between the Penguin Parade and San Remo) is one of the most scenic racetracks in the world, although it's unlikely that the racers have much time to admire the panoramic ocean views; it's also one of the fastest tracks in the world. There's a display on the history of motor sport at the track, racing simulators, and you can also take a guided circuit tour, ride a go-kart or buckle up for a few hot laps with a racing driver.

Penguins aren't the only birds to call Phillip Island home. Each year 23 million short-tailed shearwaters (muttonbirds) migrate to southern Australia from the Bering Sea near Alaska, an epic 15,000km journey. Around a million of them arrive on Phillip Island in late Sept to mate, then stay until Apr raising their chicks. Watching them arrive en masse at sunset is quite a spectacle. The best place to see them is **Cape Woolamai** just south of San Remo.

Cape Woolamai is also a good spot to see humpback whales on their annual migration between May and October, and for stargazing – if you're lucky you may even be treated to a showing of the Southern Aurora and Aurora Australis (aka the southern lights). Philip Island may not be very far from the metropolis of Melbourne, but its landscapes and wildlife make it seem a lot wilder.

BEST BEDS

- **Silverwater Resort** Although the resort isn't technically on Phillip Island - San Remo is on the mainland side of the bridge but your view is all Phillip Island - it's still a great option for families, offering a mix of one-, two- and three-bedroom apartments. Facilities include two swimming pools, tennis, basketball and volleyball courts, and a playground with jumping pillows. silverwaterresort.com.au
- The **North Pier Hotel** is opposite the beach in Cowes and has a range of rooms from budget to ocean view rooms with a balcony overlooking the sea. northpierhotel.com.au
- Hide away from the world in one of the three luxe cabins at **Five Acres** on the island's west coast. Stargaze while soaking in the outdoor bath on the deck or cosy up beside the log fire and enjoy the sweeping views. fiveacres.com.au

VANLIFE

Nowhere is very far from anywhere on Phillip Island, but Cowes - the biggest town on the island - is right in the middle of things and the **Phillip Island Beachfront Holiday Park** is beside the beach, in the middle of Cowes.

Opposite top left Swamp wallaby *Opposite top right* Fur seals at Seal Rocks *Opposite bottom left* Sleepy resident at the Koala Conservation Reserve *Opposite bottom right* Little penguins on parade

Phillip Island

MELBOURNE/ NAARM
Richmond
Box Hill
Croydon
Ringwood
Camberwell
Burwood
St Kilda
Caulfield
Elsternwick
Oakleigh
Glen Waverley
Brighton
Brighton Beach bathing boxes
Moorabbin
Clayton
Hampton
Sandringham
Highett
Cheltenham
Springvale
Beaumaris
Mordialloc
Noble Park
Dandenong
Aspendale
Edithvale
Chelsea
Bonbeach
Carrum
Seaford
Frankston
Carrum Downs
CRANBOURNE
Royal Botanic Gardens Cranbourne
Cranbourne South
Clyde
Langwarrin
Mount Eliza
Mornington Peninsula Regional Gallery
MORNINGTON
Baxter
Pearcedale
Somerville
Mooroduc
Tyabb
Mount Martha bathing boxes
Mount Martha
Hastings
Bittern
Safety Beach
Dromana
Rosebud
Rye
Alba Thermal Springs & Spa
Red Hill
Merricks North
Merricks General Wine Store
Balnarring
Crib Point
Stony Point
Red Hill South
Sunny Ridge Strawberry Farm
Montalto Vineyard & Olive Grove
Merricks
Pt Leo Estate
Somers
Point Leo
Ashcombe Maze & Lavender Gardens
Shoreham
Flinders
Cape Schanck
Cape Schanck Lighthouse Reserve
Boneo
Fingal
Peninsula Hot Springs
Blairgowrie
Sorrento
Portsea
Point Nepean
Fort Nepean
Point Lonsdale Lighthouse & pier
Point Lonsdale
Queenscliff
Queenscliff Low Light
Queenscliffe Maritime Museum
Queenscliff High Light
Fort Queenscliff
Marcus Hill
Mannerim
Drysdale
Clifton Springs
Bellarine
Portarlington
Indented Head
St Leonards
Port Phillip
BASS STRAIT
Western Port
Cowes
Ventnor
Rhyll
PHILLIP ISLAND
FRENCH ISLAND
Fairhaven
Tankerton
Werribee
Werribee South
Point Cook
Altona
Williamstown
Newport
Spotswood
Laverton
Hoppers Crossing
Tarneit
Truganina
Dandenong
Hallam
Hampton Park
Lyndhurst
Narre Warren
Berwick
Beaconsfield
Warneet
Tooradin
0 5 10 km

The Mornington Peninsula is one long beach – a 100km boot-shaped peninsula jutting into the ocean on the eastern edge of Port Phillip. If the beaches aren't enough to tempt you, the array of fine wine and food certainly will.

Mornington Peninsula

HOW LONG?
You can do this drive in one day from Melbourne/Naarm, or stretch it out over two for a gourmet weekend escape. (If you want to take a ferry trip to the Bellarine Peninsula too, allow an extra day or more, *see* p.86.) For a shortcut from Melbourne to Rosebud and the southern peninsula, take the M11 Mornington Peninsula Fwy (via the M3 Eastlink).

WHEN TO GO
Summer is mild for a quintessential beach holiday; winter is more likely to be wet but offers cosy accommodation and wineries and restaurants without the crowds. Summer school holidays and long weekends can be hectic, so book in advance and be prepared for some traffic.

LOCAL SECRET
Don't be deceived by the name or the rustic exterior at **Merricks General Wine Store** (mgwinestore.com.au) – this place does seriously good food, and also has a cellar door. It's popular with both locals and visitors, so make a reservation.

SNAPSHOT
The Mornington Peninsula is around an hour's drive south of Melbourne. Colonies of seals and bottlenose dolphins frolic in the bay and the beaches are flanked by lines of brightly-coloured wooden 'bathing boxes'. In the hinterland, vineyards produce some of Victoria's best cool-climate wines and fertile farmlands yield rich crops of olives, apples and strawberries. Add to this villages full of cafes and boutique stores, a range of accommodation – from seaside campgrounds to luxe hotels – and you have yourself an all-rounder weekend or holiday destination.

Drive rating
Easy. Sealed roads.

Acknowledgement of Country
The Mornington Peninsula is the Traditional Land of the Boon Wurrung People. The Bellarine Peninsula across the bay is the Traditional Land of the Wadawurrung People.

Distance planner
Return to Melbourne: around 250km
- Melbourne to Portsea, via Bayside: 101km
- Portsea to Cape Schanck: 29km
- Cape Schanck to Hastings: 42km
- Hastings to Melbourne: 77km

More information
- Mornington Peninsula Visitor Information Centre, 359B Point Nepean Rd, Dromana; 1800 804 009; visitmorningtonpeninsula.org

MELBOURNE/NAARM TO PORTSEA

The quickest way to get to the Mornington Peninsula is via the M11 Mornington Peninsula Fwy from Melbourne (via the M3 Eastlink). If you live in Melbourne, that's probably what you'll do, as you'll already be familiar with the bayside suburbs of St Kilda, Brighton, Chelsea and beyond to Frankston. But if you're from somewhere else, follow the coastal road around the curve of Port Phillip – it'll be slower, but much more interesting than the freeway. Places worth finding a parking spot for a better look include **Brighton Beach** with its iconic colourful Victorian-era wooden bathing boxes – dating back to the 1860s they were built to protect the modesty of the swimmers who would change into their swimwear inside them – and the 17km of foreshore and coastal walking trails between Brighton and Beaumaris, and rockpooling or snorkelling at **Ricketts Point Marine Sanctuary**.

SIDETRACK

If you're a garden lover, or just a lover of Australian native plants, you'll love the **Royal Botanic Gardens Cranbourne**. Plan to spend at least a couple of hours here on the 10km of pathways and cycle tracks that wind around the beautifully landscaped gardens and feature more than 100,000 plants from almost 2000 varieties, with heathlands, arid zones, wetlands, perched swamps and woodlands. It's all native, and the Australia Garden with its Red Sand centrepiece is spectacular. There's a cafe if you get hungry, free barbecues, picnic spaces and a kid's playground.

The best way to explore the peninsula is to drive along the western shore to Portsea at the toe of the boot, stopping on the way to explore beachside towns like **Mornington**, **Mount Martha**, **Dromana**, **Rosebud**, **Rye** and **Sorrento**, which have attracted holidaymakers from Melbourne for decades. On a sunny summer day, crowds head for the sun, sand and sea, often finishing off the afternoon in one of the beachside pubs or restaurants. Snap a photo or two of the colourful bathing boxes on the beach at **Mount Martha**, a small village with plenty of cafes and shopping opportunities, or browse the upmarket boutiques, gift stores and private art galleries in **Sorrento**.

The Mornington Peninsula is a popular destination for dolphin-watching and there are around 150 bottlenose dolphins living in the bay. **Polperro Dolphin Swims** (polperro.com.au) runs summertime trips from Sorrento to swim with dolphins and Australian fur seals. Swimmers float in the water behind the boat, holding onto a rope while dolphins and seals approach; they are usually very friendly, inquisitive and playful, and will often come very close to the swimmers.

Alternatively, drop a fishing line from any number of the small-town jetties and simply sit back and watch the pelicans drift by.

Portsea is the closest town to the tip of the peninsula's boot, and you can drive out to the end along Defence Rd to **Point Nepean**, now a national park. Port Phillip was once the most heavily fortified port in the Southern Hemisphere and **Fort Nepean** has been a defence post and military fort since the days of the gold rush. It's now open for tours which include the forts, barracks, gun emplacements, old tunnels and the 19th-century Quarantine Station. The **Fort Nepean Walk** is an easy 75min one-way walk to the tip of the peninsula, and passes Cheviot Beach, where Prime Minister Harold Holt disappeared in 1967.

Good for a rainy day

Visit **Mornington Peninsula Regional Gallery** in Mornington. Renowned for its specialist collection of contemporary Australian artworks on paper, the permanent collection includes big names like Preston, Boyd, Drysdale and Blackman and has a focus on how the landscape and cultural heritage of the peninsula influenced artists such as Fred Williams, Albert Tucker and Brett Whiteley. There is also a changing program of exhibitions by Australia's leading artists.

Opposite Sorrento Back Beach *Top* Port Phillip dolphins
Bottom Waratah at the Royal Botanic Gardens Cranbourne

SIDETRACK

Situated at the entrance to Port Philip on the Bellarine Peninsula, and only a 40min vehicle ferry ride (searoad.com.au) from Sorrento, **Queenscliff** started as a fishing village then became a fashionable holiday destination for Melbourne's elite in the late 19th century. Today it still attracts holidaymakers to its beaches, galleries, boutiques and grand Victorian-era hotels. Take a walk down the historic pier that was built between 1884 and 1889, and is one of the last in Victoria to still have a Lifeboat Shed. History lovers will also enjoy a tour of **Fort Queenscliff**, a 19th-century walled artillery fort and military museum, and the **Queenscliffe Maritime Museum** down near the harbour which has a display on many of the ships that came to grief negotiating the notorious 'rip' at the entrance to Port Phillip. Check out the **Queenscliff High Light**, a dark lighthouse (there's a white one too, called the Queenscliff Low Light); it's one of only three black lighthouses in the world. If you don't want to take your car on the ferry from Sorrento, most of Queenscliff's attractions are within easy walking distance of the ferry terminal. If you do take your car across, a circuit of the Bellarine Peninsula makes for a great daytrip. Highlights include the lighthouse and pier at **Point Lonsdale**, hiking around **Barwon Heads Bluff**, feasting on fresh mussels in **Portarlington** and the coastal drive around **Half Moon Bay** from Indented Head (just east of Portarlington) to St Leonards, as well as many wineries.

ⓧ Foodie trail

If you're a chocolate lover you won't be able to resist a stop at **Mornington Peninsula Chocolaterie and Ice Creamery in Flinders**. Almost too beautiful to eat, these hand-made chocolates have won a swag of awards and gold medals. Hosted tasting sessions, and chocolate making workshops - including some just for kids aged 6-12 - are held throughout the day.

PORTSEA TO HASTINGS

Mornington Peninsula National Park, with its windswept dunes and steep cliffs, stretches along the Bass Strait foreshore (the foot of the 'boot') from Portsea, past a string of beaches and lookouts to the basalt cliffs of Cape Schanck. It's home to grey kangaroos, southern brown bandicoots, echidnas, reptiles, bats, and many forest and ocean birds. Explore it on one of the many ocean beach walks.

Around halfway to Cape Schanck is one of the peninsula's most popular destinations, the **Peninsula Hot Springs**, near Fingal. There are more than 50 pools spread across the 17ha site linked by pathways that wind through the native bushland around a chain of pools that cascade down the hillside and spill from one terrace to another. The most popular of all is the hilltop pool, where bathers can gaze out across the hills of the Mornington Peninsula. The pools may be meticulously landscaped, but the springs are natural – the geothermal waters are pumped up from wells more than 600m below ground. The water at the source is a hot 54°C, but the temperature in the pools vary from 34 to 42°C. Rich in minerals, bathing enthusiasts believe that waters will remedy just about anything that ails you – and all you have to do to reap the benefits is soak in it. Other options, beyond bathing, include hot spring yoga sessions – a novel take on aqua aerobics; fire and ice workshops that involve rotating between a sauna, ice cave, -25 °C deep freeze, cold plunge pool and hot springs; as well as guided meditation; barrel bathing; cave pools; private bathing pavilions; massage showers; reflexology walks; foot baths; waterfall bathing; a Turkish Hamman; bathe-in cinema (Fri nights during summer) and a raft of spa and massage treatments. There is also accommodation at the Hot Springs (*see p.89*). The hot springs are very popular, and a less crowded option is the newer luxe **Alba Thermal Springs and Spa**, which has 30 pools and is also located at Fingal.

Drive along the southern coast of the peninsula towards the 'heel' of the boot. **Gunnamatta Beach** is popular with experienced surfers, the cliff-top lighthouse and museum at **Cape Schanck Lighthouse Reserve** are worthy of a visit and you can join a tour to climb the lighthouse, and the rock platform at **Mushroom Reef Marine Sanctuary** near Flinders Beach is a good spot to see weedy seadragons.

Sorrento

Victoria

Meander your way north through the sleepy beachside communities of Point Leo, Somers and Hastings, where koalas saunter along the tops of garden fences and the bush echoes with the call of native birds. Fine wine and fine art collide at **Pt Leo Estate**, home to an acclaimed fine-dining restaurant and a sculpture park with an outdoor gallery with changing exhibitions of more than 60 large-scale sculptures, many by some of the biggest names in the art world.

From Hastings, it's only about an hour's drive back to Melbourne via the M1, but your time on the peninsula will make you feel as if you've been a world away from the city.

Head into the hills

The peninsula is home to more than 50 cellar doors - the region is renowned for its cool-climate pinot noir, pinot gris and chardonnay - and most are clustered in the centre of the peninsula, signposted off the Mornington-Flinders Rd. A favourite is **Montalto Vineyard and Olive Grove** in Red Hill South. The restaurant here has a beautiful view across the vines, through which winds a 1km-long sculpture trail. Much of the food is grown in the kitchen garden. You can also order gourmet picnic hampers and wine to eat at one of six special private picnic locations on the property. For details of other wineries, see morningtonpeninsulawine.com.au

Opposite left Artwork at Pt Leo Estate's Sculpture Park
Opposite right Bathing boxes on the beach at Mount Martha
Top The sprawling Pt Leo Estate

Kids' spot

Let the kids loose in Australia's oldest hedge maze at **Ashcombe Maze and Lavender Gardens** at Shoreham. At more than 3m high and 2m thick, negotiating the narrow passageways is quite the adventure. There's also a circular rose maze with 1200 rose bushes and a lavender labyrinth. Getting lost has never smelt so good.

Another family fun spot is **Sunny Ridge Strawberry Farm** - kids love picking their own strawberries. Picking season is Nov to Apr, but the cafe and store is open weekends year-round, where you can treat yourself to some rich strawberry jam, thick freshly whipped cream and homemade scones with a Devonshire tea. The homemade strawberry ice-cream is a must.

SIDETRACK

Accessible by a 15min passenger ferry ride from Stoney Point (about 5km south of Hastings), **French Island** is home to a large population of koalas. Other inhabitants include a large population of long-nosed potoroos and diverse waterbirds including sea eagles and waders, which can be seen in and around the wetlands, mangroves and salt marshes. You can't take your car across, but bus tours are available and there are walks and bicycle trails (you can hire bikes at the general store) starting at Tankerton Foreshore Reserve, next to the jetty.

BEST BEDS

- Enjoy a moonlight dip and glamp it up in a luxury canvas-walled cabin with ensuite, heated floors and a private deck at the **Peninsula Hot Springs.** Glamping, dining and spa packages are available. peninsulahotsprings.com
- **Lancemore Lindenderry Red Hill** This luxe boutique hotel is a great base if your aim is to sample local food and wine. lancemore.com.au/properties/lancemore-lindenderry-red-hill
- **Peppers Moonah Links Resort** Situated at Fingal, on the tip of the peninsula, the resort has two 18-hole golf courses and was home to the 2003 and 2005 Australian Open. moonahlinks.com.au
- **RACV Cape Schanck Resort** Enjoy long walks along the dramatic southern coastline from your base at this modern hotel-style resort. Facilities include a restaurant with great views, championship golf course, day spa, indoor heated swimming pool and good facilities for kids. racv.com.au/travel-experiences/resorts/cape-schanck

VANLIFE

No camping is allowed in Mornington Peninsula National Park, although you can pitch a tent or park the van on one of the many foreshore reserves at **Dromana**, **Rosebud**, **Rye**, **Sorrento**, **Balnarring**, **Point Leo** and **Shoreham**. You can also camp at **Fairhaven** on the west coast of French Island. There are several caravan parks on the peninsula, too: see visitmorningtonpeninsula.org for details.

If you catch the ferry from Sorrento to Queenscliff, there are seaside caravan parks in the towns of Queenscliff, Point Lonsdale, Barwon Heads and St Leonards on the Bellarine Peninsula; see visitgeelongbellarine.com.au for details.

Mornington Peninsula

Victoria

One beach after another unveils before you as you wind your way along the coast, past rugged clifftop lookouts, before reaching one of the state's most popular national parks, Wilsons Promontory.

Bass Coast

HOW LONG?
A great weekender or three-day trip, unless you get seduced by the Prom and decide to stay a little longer.

WHEN TO GO
The summer months, from the Melbourne Cup weekend in early Nov through to Easter, is when most people head to the Prom, which also means that's when it's at its most crowded. Go in late spring for masses of wildflowers in bloom and milder daytime temperatures that make for more pleasant bushwalking.

NEED TO KNOW
Campsites and accommodation at Wilsons Prom are allocated on a ballot system during the peak summer holiday season (from late Dec to 26 Jan), usually held in the preceding June. For details, see Parks Victoria (parks.vic.gov.au/where-to-stay/ballots-and-peak-season-bookings).

SNAPSHOT
This coastal drive from Melbourne/Naarm east to Wilsons Promontory might not be as well known as its more famous sibling on the western side of the metropolis, the Great Ocean Road (*see* p.61), but that means it's also less trafficked, which makes it a great ocean drive indeed.

Spend a night or two at the Prom exploring the granite headlands and unspoiled beaches, rivers and walking trails and you'll see why the Prom is Victoria's most-loved national park.

Drive rating
Easy. Sealed roads.

Acknowledgement of Country
This is the Traditional Land of the Boon Wurrung People.

Distance planner
It's about 121km from Melbourne to Anderson where this road trip starts. From Anderson to Tidal River via Inverloch, Cape Paterson and Walkerville, it's 149km.
- Anderson to Inverloch via Cape Paterson: 41km
- Inverloch to Tidal River via Walkerville: 108km

More information
- Inverloch Visitor Information Centre; 16 A'Beckett St, Inverloch; 1300 762 433; visitsouthgippsland.com.au

Opposite Wilsons Promontory National Park

Cape Paterson

ANDERSON TO INVERLOCH

This coastal road trip starts where the Phillip Island one (*see* p.77) ends, at Anderson near San Remo, around a 90min drive from Melbourne via the M1 and the South Gippsland Hwy. And while there are quicker ways to get to the Prom, as it's affectionately called by most Victorians, this way will take you along some of the state's most scenic – and underrated – coastal roads.

Follow the Bass Hwy past Kilcunda Beach, stopping to admire the impressive **Kilcunda trestle railway bridge** that spans Bourne Creek. Built in 1911, the 12m-high wooden bridge was part of the Woolamai-Wonthaggi railway until 1978 but is now part of the 16km-long **Bass Coast Rail Trail** that links the two towns. If you don't have a bike, it's still worth walking across for the coastal views.

The road hits the coast again at **Cape Paterson**, and in theory it should only take around 15min to drive the 14km between Cape Paterson and Inverloch, but it will almost certainly take you much longer, simply because it's impossible not to keep pulling over to admire the views along the way. Known as the **Bunurong Coastal Drive**, it's one of the most scenic short drives in Victoria, hugging the cliff-edged coastline the whole way and there are lookouts, deserted beaches and short walking trails along the route. The road is well signposted from both Wonthaggi (it starts/ends 8km from the centre of the town) and Inverloch, and if you're looking for it on maps it will be marked as the C435.

INVERLOCH TO WILSONS PROMONTORY

Like everywhere else in this part of the world, **Inverloch** gets very busy over Christmas and Easter, but out of season it is a delightfully laid-back place. On the shores of Anderson Inlet, the shallow protected waters are ideal for swimming, boating, stand-up paddleboarding and fishing, and the **Screw Creek Nature Walk**, an easy 40min boardwalk, is a great way to explore the mangroves and salt marshes. The ocean beach is a popular place to learn to surf as well.

Bass Coast

😊 Kids' spot

Take a trip back in time on an underground mine tour of the **State Coal Mine** in Wonthaggi. Established in 1909 when a miners' strike in NSW left the Victorian railways and Melbourne short of coal, the State Coal Mine soon had 1800 men working eight-hour shifts in almost 4822km of underground tunnels, hauling more than 660,000 tonnes of coal out of the ground each year. The mine began to decline after the Great Depression, and was eventually closed in 1968, but reopened a couple of years ago for guided tours. Each tour begins with a safety briefing and the donning of the obligatory hard hat, followed by a careful walk down the steep entrance to the mine, which is more than 60m below ground. It's a fascinating look at how the miners worked, and not much has changed since the last workers downed tools. Thankfully you don't have to slug it back uphill at the end: an old coal skip has been converted into a carriage that is winched to the surface. Above ground you can visit several historic houses, including the winder house and museum, and there are barbecue facilities on site. Note: at the time of going to press the underground tours were temporarily suspended for ongoing maintenance - aboveground sites were still open: check for updates at Parks Victoria (parks.vic.gov.au).

Head into the hills

There's much more to the small town of **Meeniyan** than meets the eye. It's home to less than 500 people, but it regularly hosts some of the biggest names in Australian music - and an impressive roll call of international stars - in its tiny wooden town hall with its cabaret-style table seating that can squeeze in 260 at a pinch. What's more, the annual garlic festival (Feb) attracts more than 8000 people keen to try garlic ice-cream and garlic beer, among other pungent delights, to town, and the Australia Day Scarecrow Competition (26 Jan), when the town's streets and parks are taken over by an army of strange straw beings and animals, also draws hefty crowds. Stroll down Meeniyan's main street and you'll find several art galleries and cafes and usually a healthy population of well-dressed crow scarers thriving in the community garden, months after the competition has been done and won.

Opposite top left Kilcunda trestle railway bridge *Opposite top right* Lazy afternoon at Cape Paterson Bay Beach *Opposite bottom left* Glennie Island Group off Wilsons Prom *Opposite bottom right* Fish Creek *Left* On the road to Cape Liptrap

Bass Coast

Good for a rainy day

In the middle of some of the most beautiful and productive dairying country in Victoria, there's definitely something fishy going on in **Fish Creek**. Maybe it's the giant mullet on top of the **Promontory Gate Hotel**, looking like it has just flopped out of the sea and been slightly surprised to find itself perched on the corner of the Art Deco pub, now known as the 'Fishy Pub'. Or perhaps it's **Orange Roughy Cafe**, the brightly painted undersea murals, **Fish Tales** secondhand bookshop, or just the fish-shaped seats scattered around town. Even the local church seems in on the fun, with a giant red Christian fish symbol painted on the roof. Fish Creek is also a magnet for artists, and there are several good galleries in town, including the **Celia Rosser Gallery.** One of Australia's great botanical artists, Celia painted all 78 known species of the banksia - there's even a banskia named after her, *Banksia rosserae*; the only other woman who has a banksia named after her is Queen Victoria.

Opposite the township of Inverloch, on the other side of the inlet, is **Point Smythe**, part of **Cape Liptrap Coastal Park** which extends all the way down the coast to Walkerville, almost 50km. Cape Liptrap isn't the southernmost point on the Australian mainland, but you can see it from there – Wilsons Prom (the official southernmost point) is just across the bay. The coastline's wild and rocky and great for beachcombing and walking, but not for swimming – although there are patrolled beaches nearby on the way to Point Smythe, and some sheltered bays on Anderson Inlet opposite Inverloch.

The seaside views continue as you head to **Wilsons Promontory**, a wild and rugged knob of land hanging like a fishhook-shaped pendant off the southernmost tip of mainland Australia and encircled by sea on three sides. The Prom's coastline is outrageously scenic; a string of dazzling white-sand beaches flanked by a jumbled mess of lichen-streaked boulders that look as if they are set to tumble into the sea the moment a breeze blows in. It's part of the same granite range that forms the mountainous spine along the east coast of Tasmania, including the famous rock peaks of the Freycinet Peninsula (*see* p.285).

Tidal River is the main visitor hub of the park, where you'll find the visitor centre, general store with basic supplies and camping gear, laundry, kiosk and expansive campground with cabins and hot showers. In summer holiday periods there's even outdoor movies and shuttle buses to some of the more popular spots. Make sure you've booked ahead (*see* p.97).

Wilsons Promontory National Park is crisscrossed by a network of trails, ranging from short 300m tracks that go to beautiful beaches to long overnight hikes. Must-see spots include **Squeaky Beach**, an arc of white sand flanked by large granite boulders that is famous for its squeaky sand; picturesque **Whisky Beach**; the panoramic views from the summit of **Mount Oberon**; and the historic 1859 **Wilsons Promontory Lightstation**, which is also available for overnight stays, but the catch is the only way to get there is by foot – it's a 19km walk and you'll have to carry all your food and gear in, and all your rubbish out.

However you decide to explore the park – by boat or on foot, camping, in a cabin, or glamping it up in the luxe wilderness retreats – it's no surprise that almost every Melburnian has at least one 'night at the Prom' story to tell. It's that kind of place.

Opposite Cleft Island, aka Skull Rock, off the coast of Wilsons Prom *Left* Cape Liptrap Lighthouse

SIDETRACK

Rising from the sea in the shape of a gigantic bird's skull, **Cleft Island** - otherwise known as Skull Rock - is the perfect bad guy's lair. As you cruise past the pointed 'beak', craning your neck to look up at the monstrous hollowed eye sockets looming above, the island slowly reveals the distinguishing feature that would make any evil mastermind in search of a secret hideout go weak at the knees. The eerily shaped granite monolith is actually hollow, a massive chamber 60m above the roiling sea. Carpeted with grass, it's large enough to hide the sails of the Sydney Opera House inside, should a Bond villain decide to. With no safe place to anchor and no safe way of scaling the sheer cliffs, Skull Rock has, according to eco-tour operator Rob Pennicott, been explored by fewer people (nine) than have walked on the moon (12). Located about 5km off the coast of Wilsons Promontory it's the star attraction of **Pennicott's Wilsons Promontory Cruise** (promcruises.com.au), a 2.5hr wildlife and sightseeing cruise aboard a custom-made amphibious boat that can drive straight into the sea. Other highlights include more birds than you can count, lots of whales in season, a visit to one of the country's largest fur seal breeding colonies, and close-up views of deserted beaches that otherwise would involve long overnight hikes to see.

BEST BEDS

- **RACV Inverloch Resort** Here you'll find stylish ocean view rooms and multi-bedroom self-contained villas, plus a caravan park, all just minutes from the beach. This is a good family option and facilities include a restaurant, pool, gym, playground and school holiday activity programs. racv.com.au/travel-experiences/resorts/inverloch
- **Ross Farm** This former dairy farm at Meeniyan delivers plenty of unexpected wow factor in three re-imagined old farm buildings with bespoke furnishings and innovative design. rossfarm.com.au
- **Tidal River** Accommodation options at the main settlement in Wilsons Promontory National Park include huts that sleep between four and six, ensuite cabins sleeping up to six people, and luxury wilderness retreats, each with ensuite and private deck. parks.vic.gov.au

VANLIFE

Tidal River Campground at Wilsons Promontory National Park has 484 camping and caravan sites, including some powered caravan sites; facilities include flushing toilets, hot showers, laundry facilities, some gas barbecues, a general store and cafe. Tidal River sites operate on a ballot system during summer, so apply well in advance with Parks Vic. You can also bush camp at **Bear Gully** in Cape Liptrap Coastal Park, on the opposite side of the bay from Wilsons Prom, and you'll need to book well ahead with Parks Victoria (parks.vic.gov.au). **Inverloch Foreshore Camping Reserve** beside Anderson Inlet is right in the middle of town and there's good beachside camping at **Cape Paterson** too: bookings for both can be made at ingeniaholidays.com.au.

Bass Coast

Victoria

Watersports offer endless activities; cafes in coastal villages serve freshly caught seafood; national parks with endless stretches of undeveloped coastline are great for bushwalking; and the many islands are home to large colonies of koalas, seals and penguins.

East Gippsland

HOW LONG?

You'll want to spend time exploring the off-the-beaten-track beaches, coastal villages and national parks on this coastal road trip, so allow at least a week.

WHEN TO GO

The Gippsland area enjoys a year-round temperate climate, with mild summers and relatively warm, but often wet, winters – the locals in Mallacoota like to boast that they enjoy Victoria's warmest winter temperatures.

NEED TO KNOW

This part of Victoria, between Bairnsdale and Mallacoota, was badly hit by the Black Summer bushfires in 2019–20 – the red skies and naval evacuation of Mallacoota made international headlines – but nature's ability to heal itself, particularly here in Australia where many of the plants rely on fire to reproduce, is amazing and the forests are green again with new growth, although the impact of the blaze on the landscape can still be seen.

LOCAL SECRET

Mallacoota is renowned for its abalone and just about everyone you'll meet is or was related to an abalone diver. Most of the abalone is exported straight to Asia, but you can try some at **Lucy's noodle house** in the main street, which has a cult following with locals for her hand-made rice noodles and silky soft dumplings.

SNAPSHOT

The north-east corner of Victoria is a vast coastal wilderness, fed by Australia's largest system of inland waterways. Alpine rivers spill into the sea from the High Country to the west, feeding a series of large lakes and a very long beach, making this area a favourite holiday destination with a wealth of sailing and fishing on offer.

Drive rating
Easy. Mostly sealed roads with some unsealed sections in coastal national parks.

Acknowledgement of Country
This is the Traditional Land of the Gunaikurnai and the Bidawal Peoples.

Distance planner
Sale to Mallacoota: around 500km, without detours. Mallacoota is roughly halfway between Sydney and Melbourne (521km from Melbourne, 560km south of Sydney) via the Princes Hwy.
- Sale to Lakes Entrance, via the coast: 293km
- Lakes Entrance to Mallacoota, without detours: 202km

More information
- Lakes Entrance Visitor Information Centre, 2 Marine Pde, Lakes Entrance; (03) 5155 1966; visiteastgippsland.com.au
- Mallacoota Visitor Information Centre, cnr Allan Dr & Maurice Ave, Mallacoota; (03) 5158 0800; visitmallacoota.com.au

Opposite top left Yeerung River Estuary walk at Cape Conran *Opposite top right* Mallacoota is perfect for messing about on boats *Opposite bottom left* Pelican on Mallacoota Inlet *Opposite bottom right* Sun orchids at Cape Conran

Mount Lookout
The Sisters
Mount Reynard
Mount Dawson
Mount Kent
Crooked River
Mount Delusion
Brookville
Doctors Flat
Ensay North
The Crinoline
Mount Tamboritha
ALPINE NATIONAL PARK
The Pinnacles
Dargo
WENTWORTH STATE FOREST
Mount Baldhead
Ensay
Ensay South
Reedy Flat
Mount Wellington
Mount Thomson
Morris Peak
Stirling
YOWEN-BURRUN SF
Hells Gate
Tambo Crossing
FAINTING RANGE SF
Mount Johnston
Mount Margaret
The Sentinels
Waterford
Mount Djoandah
Tabberabbera
Mount Sugarloaf
Licola
Mount Hump
The Razorback
VALENCIA STATE FOREST
Mount Budgee Budgee
Castleburn
The Two Sisters
Mount Welcome
B500
AVON WILDERNESS PARK
Mount Blomford
Cobbannah
The Basin
Deptford
MOUNT ELIZABETH NCR
Buchan South
Bullumwaal
C601
MITCHELL RIVER NP
Mount Little Dick
Mount Angus
Mount Difficulty
Mount Ray
Mount Alfred
KENNY STATE FOREST
C486
GIPPSLAND
Mount Taylor
Clifton Creek
Wiseleigh
Bruthen
Mount Gog
Culloden
Glenaladale
Woodglen
Sarsfield
Mossiface
C620
Nowa Nowa
Lake Glenmaggie
Valencia Creek
Stockdale
Walpa
Calulu
Glenmaggie
Coongulla
Briagolong
Coongulmerang
BAIRNSDALE
Lucknow
Nicholson
Swan Reach
A1
Boisdale
Bushy Park
Krowathunkooloong Keeping Place
Mitchell River silt jetties
Lake Tyers
Kalimna West
Fernbank
Lake King
Seaton
Newry
A1
Munro
Harrow
Eagle Point
Lake Tyers
Dawson
Heyfield
Tinamba
PROVIDENCE PONDS FFR
Forge Creek
Raymond Island
Metung
Lakes Entrance
Maffra
Stratford
Perry Bridge
Bengworden
Paynesville
Off the Wharf
Sodafish
Denison
Goon Nure
Metung Hot Springs
Cowwarr
Bundalaguah
C106
Winnindoo
Airly
Meerlieu
THE LAKES NP
Toongabbie
Nambrok
Montgomery
Lake Victoria
Clydebank
Kilmany
Fulham
Cobains
Loch Sport
GIPPSLAND LAKES COASTAL PARK
La Trobe
A1
SALE
The Heart
Lake Wellington
C485
Flynn
Rosedale
Kilmany South
Seacombe
Lake Reeve
Longford
Flynns Creek
HOLEY PLAINS SP
Lake Coleman
Dutson
Willung
C485
Paradise Beach
C482
Hiamdale
Stradbroke West
Golden Beach
Gormandale
C496
Delray Beach
The Wreck Beach
Lake Reeve
STRADBROKE FFR
Flamingo Beach
Willung South
Stradbroke
Glomar Beach
Carrajung
MULLUNGDUNG SF
A440
GIPPSLAND LAKES COASTAL PARK
Carrajung South
Blackwarry
Seaspray
MULLUNGDUNG FFR
Giffard
NINETY MILE BEACH MNP
Won Wron
McGauran Beach
Darriman
Jack Smith Lake
Greenmount
Woodside
Yarram
Woodside Beach
Hunterston
Alberton
McLoughlins Beach
Tarraville
Port Albert
Manns Beach
BASS STRAIT

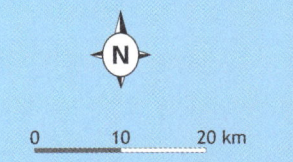

East Gippsland

SALE TO LAKES ENTRANCE

The drive along Victoria's East Gippsland coast is one of the country's great seaside road trips, but it takes a bit of effort because much of the coastline is undeveloped wilderness and there is no one coastal road that links the towns, beautiful beaches and waterways. To really see the best of this magnificent area you need to spear off the Princes Hwy, which runs inland rather than along the Gippsland coast, and often have to do a little backtracking as well. It's worth it though, because this really is a spectacular part of the country, especially if you like being on, in or near the water. The flip-side bonus is that it's really easy to escape the crowds, even in holiday season.

If you're coming from Melbourne/Naarm or even Wilsons Promontory (*see* p.91) turn off the A1 – the Princes Hwy – at Sale (around a 3hr drive from Melbourne), and point the car towards the coast.

Whoever named **Ninety Mile Beach** wasn't very good at numbers – this golden sliver of sand between the sea and the Gippsland Lakes that stretches from Port Albert north to Lakes Entrance is actually 94 miles, or 151km. It's summer holiday heartland, with lots of holiday houses and caravan parks in the villages dotted along its shore, but there are also some great camping spots just metres from the beach in **Gippsland Lakes Coastal Park**. It can be a popular spot during summer and on long weekends but go outside of peak holiday season and the beach will be practically deserted. The lower section of the park is accessible by road via the village of Seaspray, and you can drive along the narrow spit of land that separates the shallow Lake Reeve from the sea along Shoreline Dr to Paradise Beach. Beyond there, you'll need to walk or launch a boat, although there is a network of sandy 4WD tracks on the western side of the lake, many leading off Loch Sport Rd. If you have a kayak or canoe it's the perfect spot for a paddle, and it's also a top spot to try your luck catching a flathead, salmon, whiting or bream.

Circle back to the highway – or take the C106 cross country if you'd rather take the road less travelled – to the riverside town of **Bairnsdale**, the commercial hub of the region. You're on Gunaikurnai land and to find out what that means the **Krowathunkooloong Keeping Place** has guided and self-guided tours and exhibitions of traditional hunting tools and weapons, canoes and basketry, as well as contemporary Gunaikurnai art. It's part of the **Bataluk Cultural Trail** that follows the Traditional routes across East Gippsland that have been used by the Gunaikurnai People for more than 30,000 years.

The **Mitchell River silt jetties** at **Eagle Point** are the second longest silt jetties in the world (the longest are on the Mississippi in the US). Silt jetties are long, thin strips of land that have been built up over millions of years, and these on the Mitchell River are more than 8km long. You can drive out to the end and you'll get water views all the way, with the river on one side, the lake on the other. There are plenty of good fishing spots along the way too. For a good look from above, head to the lookout at Eagle Point Bluff.

Most people go to **Paynesville** to mess about on boats. The **Gippsland Lakes** are the largest inland waterway in Australia – a network of lakes and lagoons covering more than 600sqkm – and there are countless moorings and lots of islands and hidden coves to explore, as well as some great picnic spots in **Gippsland Lakes Coastal Park** and **The Lakes National Park** that are only accessible by boat. It's great for novices, so if you don't have your own boat you can hire one from **Bulls Cruisers** (bullscruisers.com.au): no license is needed and tuition is included in the fee. You can boat to pelican breeding grounds, Ninety Mile Beach and **Sperm Whale Head**, where you can go for a short walk or a swim. If you're lucky, you may even see dolphins.

It's less than a dozen kilometres across the lake to **Metung**, but by road it'll take around 40min, although the last section is very pretty as it follows the twists and turns of the Tambo River. Like Paynesville, Metung is a sleepy kind of place where entertainments include fishing from jetties and strolling the boardwalk along the edge of Bancroft Bay or a lunch with a view in places like the waterfront **Metung Hotel**. Here too you can charter a motor cruiser without a boat license or learn to sail with **Riviera Nautic**. If you like the idea of getting wet, but don't fancy a cold dip in the lake, **Metung Hot Springs** has bathing pools filled with naturally heated geothermal mineral waters.

Lakes Entrance is at the northern end of the Gippsland Lakes, and lays claim to being the seafood capital of the state. Given the size of the fishing fleet in the harbour, the number of places you can dangle a line or join a fishing charter, and the fabulous abundance of seafood restaurants and fish and chips places, it has every right to own the title. Buy fresh from the trawler at the fisherman's co-op fish shop down at the wharf (called **Off the Wharf**) or treat yourself to a meal at **Sodafish**, one of the region's best seafood restaurants. It's also easy to get to Ninety Mile Beach from here, via the footbridge across the lake, also known as Myer Street Jetty.

Good for a rainy day

Marvel at the weird, wacky and downright wonderful collection of shells and sea creatures on display at **Griffiths Sea Shell Museum and Marine Display** in Lakes Entrance. One of Australia's largest private collections, there were more than 90,000 objects at last count, so don't be too judgemental if some of the exhibits need a little bit of dusting when you visit. It's on the Esplanade and you can't miss it, there's a monster-sized octopus clinging to the roof.

Opposite West Cape, Cape Conran Coastal Park *Above* Eagle Point silt jetty

Kids' spot

Adults are just as charmed as children, but a trip out to **Raymond Island** is a terrific thing to do with kids and it doesn't cost a cent. The tiny island (it's around 6km long by 2km wide) is home to one of the largest koala colonies in Victoria and is one of the best - and easiest - places to see koalas in the wild. There's a marked koala trail you can follow. The koalas rest in the trees in people's front gardens, and you'll sometimes see them prowling along fences and ambling along footpaths. Watch where you are walking though, as it can be very easy to trip over when your eyes are focused on the treetops. The Raymond Island ferry departs every half hour from Paynesville and the crossing takes around 3min; the ferry is free for pedestrians and cyclists, and you'll see your first koalas only a block or so from the wharf, so you don't need to drive.

Head into the hills

The Gippsland region has several rail trails - cycling paths along disused railway and tram corridors - that wind their way through farmland and forests. Because they are built on old tracks there's nothing too strenuous - those old train engines weren't designed to haul heavy loads up steep hills - and are great for families as there is no road traffic to contend with. The **East Gippsland Rail Trail** is a 90km trail from Bairnsdale to Orbost, but the shorter 25km **Gippsland Lakes Discovery Trail** follows an old tramline through the Colquhoun/Boyanga Gidi State Forest, which links the East Gippsland trail to Lakes Entrance and is a good one-day option. Download a map (railtrails.org.au) or join a tour with **Snowy River Cycling** (snowyrivercycling.com.au).

East Gippsland

LAKES ENTRANCE TO MALLACOOTA

The road leaves the coast just past Lakes Entrance, but comes back to it at Marlo, where the Snowy River spills into the sea. If you can tear yourself away from the deck of the **Marlo Hotel** overlooking the river mouth (try the local pippies and mussels with lime and coconut if they are on the menu), stretch your legs on the 5km **Snowy River Estuary Walk** before driving along the coast to Cape Conran.

Cape Conran Coastal Park is just one of two wilderness parks in the area and features heathlands and bird-filled banksia woodlands, rivers and wild windswept ocean beaches. Pick a beach, any beach and you can walk for hours. Good places to start are West Cape Beach (7km later you'll end up at Point Ricardo) or East Cape where you can walk up the beach to the Yeerung River, around 90min one way. Or for something a little less strenuous, there's the **Cape Conran Nature Trail**, a pleasant 90min walk from East Cape across to West Cape along boardwalks and beaches. If you've got a 4WD, take the **East Yeerung Track** (or walk from the bridge, 4hr return) to a gorge with deep, dark rock holes. Because Cape Conran is a coastal park, rather than a national park, you can bring your dogs with you as long as they stay on a leash.

Head north to the Princes Hwy via Cabbage Tree Conran Rd, and if you're a keen fisher, take a little side trip down to Bemm River at **Sydenham Inlet** – you don't need a boat as there are several fishing platforms around town, and the main catch is bream.

Encircled by the wilderness of Croajingolong National Park, the tiny seaside village of **Mallacoota** at the mouth of the Mallacoota Inlet is just south of the NSW/Victoria border and is surrounded by water – there's more than 305km of shoreline in the two lakes that make up the waterway. It's a very popular spot with sailors, anglers eager to catch flathead (although there's plenty of bream, whiting, salmon and tailor, too), paddlers and anyone with a boat keen to explore the lakes and narrow backwaters. The area is a known habitat for koalas, and you'll also see sea eagles, azure kingfishers, white-faced blue herons and cormorants. You can hire kayaks, tinnies and stand-up paddleboards at one of the two boat sheds in town, or join a cruise aboard the *MV Loch-Ard*, a cute little ferry made of Huon pine and kauri in 1910.

Whether you're out on the water, on a beach or even on the road surrounded by bush, it's easy to see why they call this section of the state the Wilderness Coast.

SIDETRACK

Legend has it that there is $2 million of silver buried from a shipwreck in the dunes of the **Sandpatch Wilderness Area** in Croajingolong National Park, but it has never been found. The **Dunes Walk**, which starts at the Thurra River campground, is a 2hr-return walk that takes you through banksia forest to some of the tallest dunes, but take care as the dunes all look the same and it is easy to become lost and disorientated. Hikers should be well prepared and take a map, water, sun protection and good sunglasses and avoid walking in the middle of the day. The walk is one of the zones of the 100km **Wilderness Coast Walk** which stretches from Sydenham Inlet north to Wonboyn in NSW; you can find out more at Parks Victoria (parks.vic.gov.au). The lost silver is not the only local legend. The **Point Hicks Lightstation** is reputed to be haunted by Kristofferson, the ghost of a lighthouse keeper washed away while setting crayfish traps on the rocks in front of the lighthouse in 1947. His body was never found, but the sounds of his hob-nailed boots have been heard in the old pantry of his cottage and he has a penchant for shining brass doorknobs inside the lighthouse, apparently. The first part of Australia's east coast sighted by James Cook in 1770, Munda Bubul was renamed Point Hicks after his lieutenant, Zachary Hicks. Built in 1890, the 38m-high lighthouse features a cast-iron spiral staircase cantilevered from the walls (most lighthouses have stone or concrete steps built around a central column) and amazing views from the top. The lighthouse and surrounding area, including the Thurra River precinct, was impacted by both the Black Summer bushfires (see p.99) and also heavy rainfall that has caused erosion, and at the time of writing was still closed, but will hopefully reopen in 2024. Check with Parks Victoria (parks.vic.gov.au) for updates.

BEST BEDS

- **Captains Cove Resort** in Paynesville has spacious two-storey three-bedroom apartments on the canal, each with their own private jetty, a 10min walk from the town centre. captainscove.com.au
- **Waverley House Cottages** overlook pretty gardens on the edge of the forest at Lakes Entrance. Each one has a wood fire, kitchen, laundry and spa bath, and there's a pool on site. waverleyhousecottages.com.au
- **Karbeethong Lodge** Built in 1903, the lodge overlooks the serene expanse of water that surrounds Mallacoota. The 12 ensuite bedrooms all open out onto the verandah for great views. karbeethonglodge.com.au

VANLIFE

Caravanners and campers are spoilt for choice in East Gippsland. Beyond commercial caravan parks, which you'll find in most of the coastal and lakeside communities, the **Mallacoota Foreshore Holiday Park** is a favourite. There's a string of bush campgrounds along the stretch of beach between Seaspray and Golden Beach in **Gippsland Lakes Coastal Park**; around half are suitable for trailers and dogs are allowed at some, although not every campground has a toilet. There's good camping at **Corringle Slips** at the mouth of the Snowy River near Marlo, and at **Cape Conran** you can camp beside the sea at Banksia Bluff - both are dog friendly too. There are several campgrounds in **Croajingolong National Park,** including Wingan Inlet, Peachtree Creek beside Tamboon Inlet, Mueller Inlet and Shipwreck Creek near Mallacoota, although the most popular is Thurra River with sites scattered between the river and the ocean beach, although the bridge to get there was destroyed by bushfire, so check that it has been rebuilt before travelling. See Parks Victoria for further details (parks.vic.gov.au).

Hoping for a bite, Mallacoota

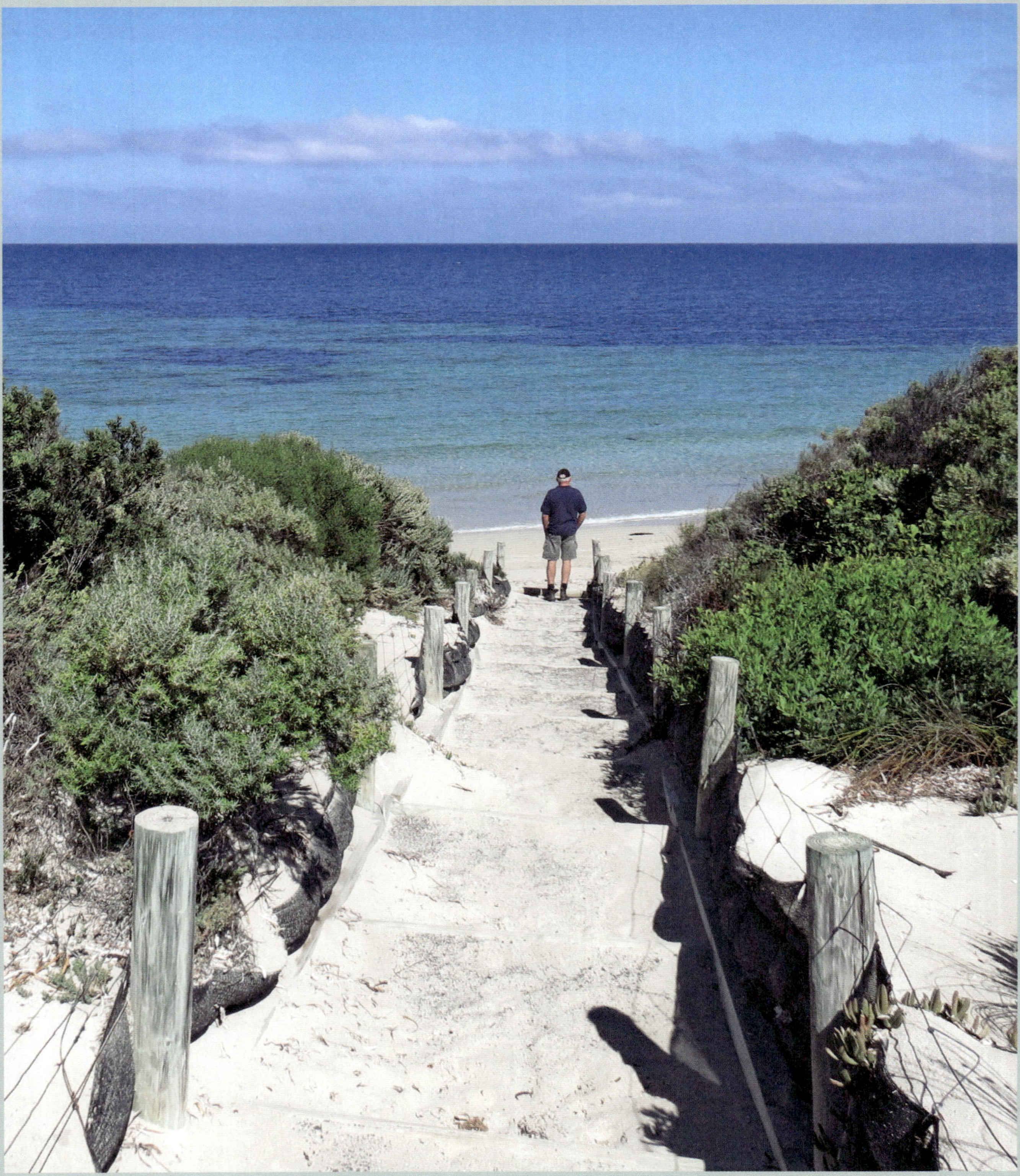

South Australia

The wild and lonely seafood coast.

ADELAIDE/TARNDANYA
Grange
Croydon
North Adelaide
Rostrevor
Lobethal
Keswick
ADELAIDE AIRPORT
Waterfall Gully
Uraidla
Woodside
Holdfast Bay
Unley Park
Summertown
Glenelg
Edwardstown
Belair
Balhannah
Oakbank
Hove
Brighton
Seacliff
Glenalta
Mount Lofty
Stirling
Bridgewater
BELAIR NP
Aldgate
Hahndorf
Blackwood
STURT GORGE RP
Mylor
Littlehampton
Happy Valley Reservoir
SCOTT CREEK CP
Mount Barker
Reynella
Lonsdale
Clarendon
Mount Bold
Echunga
Christie Downs
Morphett Vale
Wistow
Christies Beach
ONKAPARINGA RIVER NP
Mount Bold Reservoir
Port Noarlunga
Noarlunga Centre
Blewitt Springs
Kangarilla
GULF
ST VINCENT
Seaford
d'Arenberg Cube
Meadows
Macclesfield
Old Noarlunga
McLaren Vale
McLaren Flat
Mount Wilson
Ochre Point
Maslin Beach
Port Willunga
Port Willunga Beach Caves
Aldinga
Willunga
KYEEMA CP
Strathalbyn
Aldinga Beach
Ashbourne
Silver Sands
Yundi
Aldinga Bay
Mount Compass
COX SCRUB CP
BULLOCK HILL CP
Sellicks Beach
Sandergrove
Mount Compass
Nangkita
Myponga Beach
Tooperang
Finniss
Myponga
Myponga Reservoir
Mount Cone
Gilberts
Haycock Point
Carrickalinga
ENCOUNTER MARINE PARK
MYPONGA CP
Currency Creek
Normanville
Yankalilla Bay
Yankalilla
SPRING MOUNT CP
Finniss River
HMAS Hobart wreck
Hindmarsh Valley
GOOLWA AERODROME
Currency Ck
Clayton
Second Valley
Rapid Head
Rapid Bay
Middleton
Goolwa
Rapid Bay
FLEURIEU PENINSULA
Hindmarsh Island
Mount Rapid
Victor Harbor
Fishermans Bay
Port Elliot
SIR RICHARD PENINSULA
Delamere
Granite Island
Encounter Bay
Murray Mouth
Cape Jervis
Cape Jervis
Stringybark
Waitpinga
Rosetta Head (The Bluff)
Cape Jervis Lookout
Lands End
TALISKER CP
Deep Creek Waterfall
DEEP CREEK NP
NEWLAND HEAD CP
King Head
West Is
Fishery Beach
Tapanappa
Boat Harbour Beach
Tunkalilla Beach
Tunk Head
Parsons Beach
Waitpinga Beach
Newland Head
Cobbler Hill
Trig
Porpoise Head
Tapanappa Lookout
Backstairs Passage
ENCOUNTER MARINE PARK
SOUTHERN OCEAN
N
0
5
10 km
A15
B23
B34
B37
B27
B33
M1
M2
A13

Located practically on the outskirts of Adelaide/Tarndanya, the Fleurieu Peninsula is famous for its wine, scenic coastline and gourmet produce.

Fleurieu Peninsula

HOW LONG?
So close to Adelaide/Tarndanya, the Fleurieu is a popular weekend getaway spot, and you can explore most of it in two or three days.

WHEN TO GO
The Fleurieu Peninsula is relatively mild during both summer and winter. It's at its most dramatic during the winter months, when wild seas pound against towering cliffs, and during spring, when the grassy hills and coastal heathlands are blanketed with wildflowers. May through to Oct is also the best whale-watching time.

LOCAL SECRET
Originally carved out of the cliff-face by fishermen to house their boats, the **Port Willunga Beach Caves** are the perfect hidey hole for a seaside picnic when you want to stay out of the sun.

SNAPSHOT
Explore the Fleurieu Peninsula on this drive that follows the dramatic coastline, where grassy hills spill into the sea over sheer rocky cliffs. The heart of the wine-growing area is McLaren Vale, where olives and almond groves are scattered among the vineyards. Victor Harbor, on the southern side of the peninsula, is the most popular seaside resort with lots of family attractions.

Drive rating
Easy. Mostly sealed roads.

Acknowledgement of Country
This is the Traditional Land of the Ngarrindjeri, Kaurna, Ramindjeri and Peramangk Peoples.

Distance planner
It's about 40km from Adelaide to McLaren Vale. From McLaren Vale to Goolwa via Cape Jervis and Victor Harbor, it's 153km.
- McLaren Vale to Cape Jervis: 75km
- Cape Jervis to Goolwa via Victor Harbor: 78km

More information
- McLaren Vale and Fleurieu Coast Visitor Centre, 796 Main Rd, McLaren Vale, (08) 8323 9944; mclarenvaleandfleurieucoast.com.au
- Victor Harbor Visitor Information Centre, 2 Railway Tce, Victor Harbor; (08) 8551 0777; visitvictorharbor.com
- fleurieupeninsula.com.au

Previous Mozzie Flat, Yorke Peninsula

MCLAREN VALE TO CAPE JERVIS

Start your drive at **McLaren Vale**, a quick 45min drive from Adelaide/Tarndanya via the Southern Expressway and Main South Rd. McLaren Vale is one of the few wine regions in SA that is close to the sea, and the cool ocean breezes and sandy soils produce great shiraz, cabernet sauvignon and chardonnay wines. It's also one of the oldest wine-growing regions in Australia – the first vines were planted in 1841 – and many of the wineries feature beautiful stone and timber cellar-door tasting areas. You can easily spend a couple of days here tasting the wines at more than 60 cellar doors. It's a pretty area, a patchwork of vineyards dotted with historic wineries in a snug valley wedged between the tail end of the Mount Lofty ranges and the coast.

From McLaren Vale, head towards **Port Willunga** on the coast, following the tourist route signposted the **Fleurieu Way**, where you'll enjoy the first of the many expansive coastal views that are a highlight on this drive. Stretch your legs at **Maslin Beach**, SA's first official nudist beach, and take a walk along the edge of the multicoloured cliffs that flank the beach (the clothing-optional end is at the far southern tip). If you're a foodie, book a table at **Star of Greece** in Port Willunga. Don't be misled by the name – it's not a Greek restaurant, but it was named after a ship that wrecked itself on the beach below in 1888. Perched high on the cliff-top overlooking the sea, Star of Greece has multi-million-dollar views and offers beautiful seafood dishes and other locally sourced produce in the restaurant and simpler snacks at **Port Willy Kiosk**.

Continue south to Myponga and then take Reservoir Rd, drive across the dam wall and wind your way down the steep hills to **Myponga Beach**, a cluster of beach houses and shacks tucked away on a tiny beach. The views as you head down to the shore are fantastic. The seaside community of **Carrickalinga** is just down the road and you can follow a terrific coastal drive and walkway that leads from Carrickalinga to **Normanville**, yet another sleepy beachside town.

From here all the way to Cape Jervis (*see* p.112) on the tip of the peninsula the views are simply amazing, and you'll find yourself pulling over to the side of the road again and again to take photographs of the mostly treeless green hills dropping abruptly into the sea.

Good for a rainy day

For a wine tasting with a view head to the tasting rooms at the top of the **d'Arenberg Cube**, a five-storey complex that looks like a giant Rubik's Cube floating above the grapevines and is a bit like Disneyland for wine lovers. Entry includes a self-guided tour of the Alternate Realities Museum which includes a wine aroma room and a virtual fermenter as well as an art gallery and wine making displays. Wine tasting masterclasses and blending sessions are also available and there is a very good restaurant as well.

Foodie trail

It's not just the fabulous wines that make this area so popular with foodies - it's the almonds and olives planted by immigrant farmers from Greece and Italy in the late 1800s, and newer farming ventures that focus on venison, handmade cheeses, berries, beef, lamb, organic vegetables, trout and marron. All of these, plus freshly baked breads and tempting pies and pastries, homemade jams and preserves and delicious cakes, are piled high upon tables and trestles at the weekly Sat morning **Willunga farmers market**. On the second Sat of the month the stalls spill over into the **Quarry Markets** across the road, where you can browse bric-a-brac, secondhand books and handmade jewellery and clothes.

Opposite top Coriole Winery, McLaren Vale *Opposite bottom* Middleton Beach Huts

Fleurieu Peninsula 111

At **Second Valley** you can follow a short walk along the bottom of the dramatic cliffs, past the jetty, to a collection of very photogenic, very rusty boatsheds cobbled together with bits of scrap iron. This is a popular snorkelling and diving spot: the former Navy ship *HMAS Hobart* was scuttled off the coast here in Nov 2002, creating one of the best dive sites in Australia. As part of the preparation, many holes and hatches were cut into the wreck to facilitate access and navigation. Many of the ship's original fittings – including filing cabinets, sinks, toilets and tools – are still in place.

The road now curves inland but take a side trip down to **Rapid Bay** for more cliff-line views and to find the boulder that marks the spot where Colonel William Light first stepped ashore on his way to establish the colony of South Australia back in 1836. He recorded the event by carving his initials and the date into the boulder, now part of a grassy foreshore park and camping area.

There's not much to **Cape Jervis** – an angular lighthouse, the terminal for ferries to Kangaroo Island (*see* p.117) and that's about it, but the lookout over the point has great views across Backstairs Passage to Kangaroo Island and is a good whale-watching vantage point during winter.

Opposite Views from the Heysen Trail, near Victor Harbor
Below Carrickalinga Beach

SIDETRACK

On the southern tip of the peninsula, **Deep Creek National Park** is a wild and undisturbed area of natural bushland. It's a rugged place perfect for keen hikers, including some terrific coastal trails. For most people it's the beautiful coastal views that are the main attraction of this park, but **Deep Creek Waterfall**, one of the few year-round waterfalls in SA, is a gorgeous spot with a deep waterhole at the base. The walk to Deep Creek Waterfall from Tapanappa Lookout is a hard 3.5hr-return walk (6.6km) but well worth the hard slog. The 2.5hr-return hike (3.2km) to **Deep Creek Cove** also starts at Tapanappa Lookout and offers spectacular views of the south coast. If you're a photographer – or just want the perfect snap for your Instagram feed – you'll get a great shot of the coastline from Tapanappa Lookout, with views of the green hills and white-sand beaches stretching into the distance. It may not be your classic white-sand beach, but the pretty little rock-strewn beach at **Boat Harbour** is very photogenic, especially in the early morning or late afternoon when shadows on the rocks can produce great images.

CAPE JERVIS TO GOOLWA

Heading north-east, Range West Rd follows a high ridge through the rural heartland of the peninsula, snaking its way towards Victor Harbor (the reasons why it's spelt in the American way without the 'u' seem to have been lost in time) on the shores of Encounter Bay. Here, in 1802, Matthew Flinders, sailing around the continent, met the French explorer Nicholas Baudin, who was also circumnavigating it. Although England and France were at war at the time, their meeting was friendly and Flinders commemorated it with the name he gave the bay.

Before you get to Encounter Bay, turn down Waitpinga Rd and follow the signs to **Newland Head Conservation Park**. The centrepiece of the park are two long beaches, **Waitpinga** and **Parsons** – neither are great for swimming as they are not patrolled by lifesavers and both have strong rips that can sweep you out to sea, but the crashing waves are a magnet for experienced surfers, and during winter the wild, empty beaches are great for beachcombing and fishing: you can cast out from the shore and if luck is on your side you'll hook a salmon or salmon trout. You'll often see pods of dolphins playing in the waves. In July and Aug the headlands are one of the best places in the country for whale watching.

Fleurieu Peninsula

Victor Harbor is a favourite family holiday town with many attractions and activities. It offers cafes, restaurants and a range of accommodation for a beach break. You can learn some of the stories of the Ramindjeri and Ngarrindjeri Peoples at the visitor centre in the redeveloped Railway Goods Shed, which also has an informative display on whales, and about local history and the meeting of Flinders and Baudin at the **National Trust Museum** in the old Customs House near the Causeway (open Wed–Sun). You can also ride the country's only **horse-drawn tram** out to Granite Island. The tramway is on The Esplanade.

Just a few minutes' drive from Victor Harbor, the pretty holiday town of **Port Elliot** is full of historic stone buildings, a selection of cafes and accommodation and a fantastic seaside restaurant, the **Flying Fish Cafe**.

Historic **Goolwa**, the end point of our little coastal roadie around the peninsula, is at the mouth of the Murray River, and is full of beautiful sandstone buildings, many of them now art galleries and restaurants. You can continue from here by doing the Limestone Coast road trip in reverse (see p.123).

SIDETRACK

If you want to explore this coast in greater depth, there is a long-distance walking track that follows the shoreline from Cape Jervis to Goolwa, via Victor Harbor. It's part of the 1200km-long **Heysen Trail**, which continues up to Parachilna Gorge in the Flinders Ranges. Even if you are short of time or energy, you can still walk parts of the trail, at Parsons Beach or Waitpinga Beach in Newland Head Conservation Park, or at the Bluff on the outskirts of Victor Harbor. Simply wander along the cliff track for as long and far as you please.

Head into the hills

From Goolwa, head inland back towards Adelaide via the Currency Creek wine region and **Strathalbyn**. Settled by Scottish immigrants in the 1830s, it's an attractive heritage town with 30 or so historic buildings and a popular place to shop for antiques. The Soldiers' Memorial Garden is a lovely place for a stroll or picnic. The drive back to the city will take around 75min, if you don't stop to shop, or try some wines.

🙂 Kids' spot

Few kids fail to get excited at the sight of an old steam train and here you can even ride one. The historic **Cockle Train** - Australia's first railway - operates between Victor Harbor, Port Elliot and Goolwa. The train usually runs on weekends and Wed, and daily during school holidays or long weekends. Another family activity is the 30km **Encounter Bikeway**, a dedicated bike path between the Bluff and Signal Point at Goolwa Wharf. The sealed path is suitable for all riders wanting a gentle seaside cycle, and even families with little kids could ride part of the way. Between May and Oct you may even spot whales as you ride.

BEST BEDS

- **Anchorage Hotel** This atmospheric old stone pub on the seafront in Victor Harbor has a range of rooms from ensuite spa suites with balconies to budget rooms with shared bathrooms and self-contained cottages. anchoragehotel.com.au
- **Beach Huts Middleton** They're not actually on the beach, but these colourful candy-striped cabins certainly look like they should be and are all named after some of the country's most famous stretches of sand. The real beach is only a few blocks away and there's a restaurant on site. beachhuts.com.au
- **Mulberry Lodge** This luxury country retreat surrounded by lovely gardens on the edge of Willunga township is a great base for exploring the vineyards and cellar doors of McLaren Vale. mulberrylodgewillunga.com

VANLIFE

In Deep Creek National Park, **Stringybark camping area** is in a sheltered forest setting and has 16 sites, hot showers, toilets and rainwater, as well as unpowered caravan sites. If you'd like to be closer to the main walking trails, the **Trig** camping area has open grassy areas with 25 well-sheltered and shady sites suitable for caravans and camper trailers. There are 18 sites at **Tapanappa** with spectacular coastal views and 10 sites at **Cobbler Hill**, close to Blowhole Creek Beach. You can also camp at **Rapid Bay**. There are several commercial caravan parks in **Victor Harbor** and at **Port Willunga**.

Opposite Aerial view of Port Willunga *Top* Carrickalinga hills *Bottom* The historic Cockle Train

Fleurieu Peninsula 115

South Australia

116

A drive around wild and rugged Kangaroo Island is a wildlife safari.

Kangaroo Island

HOW LONG?
You can break this road trip into three separate day trips, using Kingscote as a base. But five days would be even better: at 155km long and 55km wide, Kangaroo Island is bigger than you think.

WHEN TO GO
Any time of the year is a good time to do this drive – temperatures are relatively mild during both summer and winter. At times, cool ocean breezes make windproof clothing necessary, while central areas of the island occasionally experience temperatures of 35 to 40°C in the middle of summer.

NEED TO KNOW
Ferries run by Kangaroo Island **SeaLink** (13 13 01; sealink.com.au) depart several times each day between Cape Jervis on the Fleurieu Peninsula (around a 90min drive south of Adelaide/Tarndanya, *see* p.109) and Penneshaw on the island, and the trip takes around 30 to 45min, depending on which ferry you take.

Australia's third largest island, more than half of KI, as the locals call it, was burnt in the Black Summer bushfires of 2019–20. Fast forward a few years and most of the infrastructure has been rebuilt, and the landscape is well and truly on the road to recovery, although you will still see traces of the devastation as you drive around the island.

The Kangaroo Island Pass provides entry to the island's parks as well as guided tours at most of its popular nature-based tourist attractions. It's available at the National Parks and Wildlife Service Kangaroo Island office in Kingscote and the Seal Bay Visitor Centre or online at Parks SA (parks.sa.gov.au/book-and-pay/kangaroo-island-tour-pass).

👁 SNAPSHOT
Kangaroo Island's gentle rolling hills, covered in rich pasture and dotted with grazing sheep and cattle, belie a wilder heart. Close to half of the island is either natural bushland or national park, and it is home to some of the most diverse wildlife you'll find concentrated in one area anywhere in Australia – fur seals, rare Australian sea lions, dolphins, koalas, kangaroos, platypuses, short-beaked echidnas, 254 species of birdlife and more tammar wallabies than you could ever begin to count. If you can't spot wildlife here then you simply aren't trying.

Drive rating
Moderate. Unsealed roads with loose gravel. A sudden swerve to avoid a wallaby or kangaroo (of which there are plenty, especially in the late afternoon or at dusk) can end in disaster. Avoid driving at dusk or night.

Acknowledgement of Country
Kangaroo Island is the Traditional Land of the Ramindjeri, Ngarrindjeri, Kaurna, Kartan and Barngarla Peoples.

Distance planner
Base point, Kingscote, is 186km from Adelaide/Tarndanya, including the ferry crossing. Indicative distances for key locations on the island are below. If you return to Kingscote each day, it's about 630km driving.
- Kingscote to Penneshaw: 58km
- Penneshaw to Cape Willoughby: 27km
- Kingscote to Seal Bay: 60km
- Seal Bay to Cape du Couedic: 82km
- Kingscote to Cape Borda (via Playford Hwy): 90km

More information
- Kangaroo Island Gateway Visitor Information Centre, Howard Dr, Penneshaw; 1800 811 080; tourkangarooisland.com.au

Opposite Flinders Chase National Park

KINGSCOTE TO PENNESHAW AND CAPE WILLOUGHBY

Kingscote is the biggest town on KI, with around 2500 people, so it is a good place to use as a base. It is also where flights arrive and depart for Adelaide/Tarndanya if you've decided to fly in and hire a car on the island. If you've travelled over on the ferry, you'll arrive and depart from the slightly sleepier town of Penneshaw, which is about a 45min drive from Kingscote.

Head east from Kingscote along Hog Bay Rd, through the pastoral heart of the island to Penneshaw.

Stop at **Pennington Beach**, a long expanse of white sand edged up against rugged limestone cliffs at the narrowest point on the island. From here, continue east through Penneshaw and onto the unsealed road that leads 30km out to **Cape Willoughby** on the far-eastern tip of the island.

The long sandy beach at **Antechamber Bay** in Lashmar Conservation Park is a great spot for a picnic and a walk along the beach, and if you have a kayak you can paddle up the Chapman River, which empties out into the sea here in the bay. It's also a good camping spot with two campgrounds, on opposite sides of the river.

The nearby **Cape Willoughby Lighthouse** is one of four on the island: it was also the first to be built in SA. The 27m-high tower is open for tours and from its top you can see across the rather descriptively named Backstairs Passage towards the mainland.

Both Kingscote and Penneshaw have colonies of little penguins, and the best way to see them is on the guided boardwalk tour in **Penneshaw**. Adult penguins spend most of the day feeding out at sea and return to land just after dark. You can watch as they come waddling out of the water and clamber up the rocky beach to their burrow-like nests in the sand dunes to feed their hungry chicks. The penguins are in residence at the colony all year, except for the month of Feb when they go out to sea, but sightings are not guaranteed. See **Penneshaw Penguin Centre** (penneshawpenguincentre.com) for tour times.

Opposite Remarkable Rocks *Top* Lookout in Flinders Chase National Park *Middle* Kangaroo Island grasslands *Bottom* Australian sea lion at Seal Bay

SIDETRACK

Emu Ridge Eucalyptus Distillery in Macgillivray is the only commercial eucalyptus distillery in operation in SA. The oil is reputed to be excellent for soothing arthritic aches and pains.

Good for a rainy day

Kangaroo Island may only be 20km from the Australian mainland, but that's too far for a bee to fly. As a result, the island is one of the world's oldest bee sanctuaries. Moreover, despite being just about as far away from Italy as you can get, the island is home to the only genetically pure population of Ligurian bees in the world. You can check them out in the glass hives at **Clifford's Honey Farm**, which is worth visiting just to taste its swoon-worthy honey ice-cream.

Kangaroo Island 119

Seal colony at Admirals Arch

KINGSCOTE TO CAPE DU COUEDIC

On your second day, head south to **Flinders Chase National Park** and **Cape du Couedic** along the South Coast Rd. At mis-named **Seal Bay**, 60km from Kingscote, you can join a tour and stroll along the high-water mark on the beach among dozens of huge, sleepy sea lions resting after spending three days at sea hunting for food. Seal Bay is the only place in Australia where you can get this close to sea lions; all other colonies are perched on inaccessible rocky headlands. If you don't want to join a ranger on a tour (they leave from the park's visitor centre behind the beach), there is a self-guided boardwalk, but it does not allow you to get onto the sand or as close to the sea lions.

As you drive across the island, watch for dawdling echidnas crossing in front of your car and, of course, the wallabies and kangaroos that are ubiquitous on the island. KI is also famous for its wild koalas, but they are not natives. Back in the 1920s, in a bid to stop mainland koalas becoming extinct, 18 koalas were introduced to the island. Over the next 100 years the population exploded and before the 2019–20 bushfires it was estimated that there were more than 48,000, far too many for the island to support. Today, there are around 8500 and although you've got a good chance of seeing koalas in the trees just about anywhere on the island, you're guaranteed to see them at the **Hanson Bay Wildlife Sanctuary**, but you'll need to book a tour (South Coast Rd, between Kelly Hill Caves and Flinders Chase National Park, hansonbay.com.au).

Flinders Chase National Park covers most of the far-western reaches of the island. More than 95 per cent of the park was burnt in the bushfires, although most of it has now re-opened. If you're on social media you'll probably recognise the Cape du Couedic Rd, its undulating waves are one of the most Instagrammed roads in SA. Wander among the **Remarkable Rocks**, a cluster of huge weather-sculptured granite boulders perched on a granite dome that swoops 75m down to the sea, then head south-west to **Cape du Couedic**. The rock platforms below the lighthouse are home to a colony of New Zealand fur seals; look for them wallowing in the sun or frolicking in the surf under the dramatic rock arc of **Admirals Arch**.

Like the koalas, platypuses were also introduced on to KI in the 1920s, and while they never quite thrived in the same way as the koala, the island is home to the only wild population in SA. Before the bushfires one of the best places to see them – especially at dawn and dusk – were in the waterholes near Flinders Chase Visitor Centre at Rocky River, which was sadly destroyed. At the time of writing a new centre was being designed and is expected to open in 2024 but check for updates at National Parks and Wildlife Service (parks.sa.gov.au) before you travel.

KINGSCOTE TO CAPE BORDA

The third driving route on KI is to the far north-west tip at Cape Borda. From Kingscote, head west on the Playford Hwy through Parndana, where in late winter and spring the roadside is carpeted with wildflowers; the last 38km or so of the road cuts through the wilderness of Flinders Chase National Park. The rather squat, square lighthouse at **Cape Borda** is 155m above sea level (book a self-guided tour before you go at parks.sa.gov.au). Only 4km to the east is **Scott Cove Lookout**, where you can see the spectacular cliffs of Cape Torrens and Cape Forbin.

Although there is no coastal road linking them, there are several lovely beaches on the sheltered north coast, and good side trips on the way back between Flinders Chase and Kingscote include **Western River Cove** – ideal for swimming and fishing – and **Snelling Beach** at the mouth of Middle River and Stokes Bay around 20km east of Western River Cove, where a walk through a headland of boulders brings you to a fine, white sandy beach surrounded by cliffs.

Emu Bay is another worthwhile detour – a lovely 3km-long beach with vehicle access on to the hard sand. Anglers can try their luck from the jetty or launch their boats from the ramp. Any of these spots on the north coast are a great place for a picnic lunch with a million-dollar view – and chances are you'll have it all to yourself.

😊 Kids' spot

Part of Seal Bay Conservation Park, the area known as **Little Sahara** (7km to the west of the Seal Bay turn-off on the South Coast Rd) is an area of massive razor-backed inland sand dunes. It's a tough climb up, but it only takes seconds to slide down on a well-waxed board and is fabulous fun, for adults and kids alike. Just resist the urge to squeal or you'll end up with a mouthful of sand. Sandboards and toboggans are available for hire from **KI Outdoor Action** (kioutdooraction.com.au). Note that sand boarding in SA is only permitted in certain areas where it's been determined there's minimal risk to the environment.

BEST BEDS

- **Mercure Kangaroo Island Lodge** Ideal for those on tighter budgets, this older-style motel in American River (about halfway between Kingscote and Penneshaw) offers affordable rooms with a pool and waterfront views. Kids will love watching the wallabies graze the lawn and the pelicans on the beach in front of the hotel. kilodge.com.au
- **Lighthouse keepers' cottages** Accommodation is available in the lighthouse keepers' cottages at Cape Willoughby. The cottages sleep up to nine adults in five bedrooms, and there is a minimum two-night stay. parks.sa.gov.au/parks/cape-willoughby-conservation-park
- **Southern Ocean Lodge** The original super-luxe cliff-top retreat above Hanson Bay on the south-west coast was destroyed in the bushfires, but is being rebuilt and will re-open at the end of 2023. It offers unforgettable ocean views and amazing food, and if money is no object it's absolutely worth the splurge. There's a minimum two-night stay. southernoceanlodge.com.au
- **Aurora Ozone Hotel** This hotel overlooking the beach in the centre of Kingscote has good-value motel-style rooms and apartments. ozonehotelki.com.au

VANLIFE

The following beaches have caravan sites: **Nepean Bay** (Kingscote), **Penneshaw**, **Antechamber Bay**, **Browns Beach**, **Stokes Bay**, **Emu Bay**, **Vivonne Bay** and **Western River**. At the time of writing campgrounds were still being rebuilt at **Rocky River** in Flinders Chase National Park, near the visitor centre. You can bush camp at **Snake Lagoon**, **Harveys Return** near Cape Borda Lighthouse and **West Bay** (4WD only), and at **Murrays Lagoon** or **D'Estrees Bay** in Cape Gantheaume Wilderness Area, but check for updates before you go, as some were impacted by the bushfires.

Mount Compass
Currency Creek
Finniss
Langhorne Creek
Milang
Wellington
Lake Alexandrina
Port Elliot
Goolwa
Hindmarsh Island
Raukkan
Narrung
Ashville
B1
B37
Victor Harbor
Murray Mouth
Mark Point
Lake Albert
Encounter Bay
FLEURIEU PENINSULA
YOUNGHUSBAND
The Coorong
Waltowa
Meningie
Long Point
Noonameena
COORONG NATIONAL PARK
Magrath Flat
Parnka Point
Woods Well
Jack Point
Policemans Point
Salt Creek
Long Bay
Chinaman Wells
42 Mile Crossing
PENINSULA
SOUTHERN
OCEAN
UPPER SOUTH EAST MARINE PARK
The Granites
Kingston SE
Big Lobster
Wyomi
Lacepede Bay
Cape Jaffa
B101
Kings Camp
Mount Benson
Boatswain Point
Guichen Bay
Robe
Cape Lannes
Lake Hawdon North
UPPER SOUTH EAST MP
Lake Eliza
Nora Creina
Lake St Clair
Lake George
Three Mile Bend
Pool of Siloam
Beachport
Rivoli Bay
Seaview Trail
Southend
Kotgee & Nal-a-wort
CANUNDA NP
LOWER SOUTH EAST MARINE PARK
Lake Bonney SE
Carpenter Rocks
Cooke Plains
Sherlock
Peake
Jabuk
Geranium
A8
Coomandook
Yumali
Ki Ki
CARCUMA CP
Coonalpyn
MOUNT BOOTHBY CP
Mount Boothby
The Monolith
Culburra
Tintinara
Kumorna
Coombe
MESSENT CP
Mount Penny
Two Wells
Baneallla
BUNBURY CR
GUM LAGOON CP
Mount Rough
Willalooka
Reedy Creek
Mount Scott
Avenue
Lucindale
Conmurra
Greenways
Bray Junction
Chinaman Wells
Clay Wells
Furner
Hatherleigh
Rendelsham
Mount Burr
Millicent
Glencoe West
Glencoe
Snuggery
Tantanoola
Wandilo
MOUNT GAMBIER
Blue Lake
Glenburnie
Mil Lel
Tarpeena
Nangwarry
Kalangadoo
Krongart
A66
Penola
Coonawarra
Glenroy
Wattle Range
Wrattonbully
Struan
Joanna
BIG HEATH CP
Naracoorte
Naracoorte Caves
Hynam
C240
Kybybolite
Binnum
Frances
Keppoch
Padthaway
Bangham
Western Flat
Custon
B57
Mundulla
Bordertown
Wampoony
Cannawigara
Wirrega
Brimbago
Lowan Vale
Keith
A66
NGARKAT CONSERVATION PARK
Mount Rescue
Mount Shaugh
Mount Edgerley
Parilla
Pinnaroo
B12
Lameroo
Murrayville
BIG DESERT WILDERNESS PARK
SOUTH AUSTRALIA
VICTORIA
Telopea Downs
Broughton
Yarrock
Lillimur
Kaniva
Lillimur South
LITTLE DESERT NATIONAL PARK
Neuarpurr
Morea
Booroopki
Bringalbert
Apsley
Edenhope
Langkoop
Kadnook
Chetwynd
Dergholm
Glenelg
C198
Casterton
B160
Strathdownie
River
Marp
N
0
20
40 km

Put the fun back into the Melbourne to Adelaide commute and follow the coast rather than the highway from the Victorian border to the Murray Mouth.

Limestone Coast

HOW LONG?
Allow two to three days.

WHEN TO GO
This is a good summertime trip, because the Blue Lake at Mount Gambier is at its bluest during summer, lobster season is Oct through to May and access to the more remote sections of the Coorong can be difficult in winter.

LOCAL SECRET
If you fancy a lunch of fresh lobster (or fish and chips), head to **Lacepede Seafood** in Kingston SE. Eat in the shady waterfront park opposite – although you'll have to fend off the hungry seagulls. You'll find it beside the jetty in the park on Marine Pde, it's open daily from Oct to May.

SNAPSHOT

The rugged eastern coastline of SA, known as the Limestone Coast, is a popular holiday destination with a string of pretty seaside towns renowned for their fishing and rock lobster. It's a place of mysteries and wonder, with some of Australia's youngest volcanoes, magical sinkhole gardens, fossil-filled caves, and mystifying lakes that change colour virtually overnight. It's also home to Australia's first saint and the country's most celebrated red wine. Spend your days on cliff-top walking trails, scenic seaside drives or tackling the sandy 4WD tracks through the dunes and along the beach.

Drive rating
Easy. Mostly sealed roads with an optional challenging 4WD section.

Acknowledgement of Country
This is the Traditional Land of the Bunganditj/Boandik, Bindjali and Ngarrindjeri Peoples.

Distance planner
Mount Gambier to Goolwa: around 435km
- Mount Gambier to Robe, via the coast: 128km
- Robe to Goolwa: 307km

More information
- Mount Gambier Visitor Centre, 35 Jubilee Hwy East, Mount Gambier; 1800 087 187; discovermountgambier.com.au
- Penola Coonawarra Visitor Information Centre, 27 Arthur St, Penola; (08) 8737 2855; wattlerange.sa.gov.au/tourism
- Robe Visitor Information Centre, 1 Mundy Tce, Robe; 1300 367 144; robe.com.au
- visitlimestonecoast.com.au

MOUNT GAMBIER TO ROBE

Located just west of the Victoria/SA border, **Mount Gambier** is roughly halfway between Melbourne/Naarm and Adelaide/Tarndanya. South Australia's second largest city is also home to some of Australia's youngest volcanoes and lots of crater lakes, caves and sinkholes, but is best known for its **Blue Lake**, a 75m-deep lake inside an extinct volcanic crater on the edge of town. Actually there are three lakes here, but only one changes colour each year: in winter, the lake is a steely grey, but over the course of a few days in Nov the water changes to a brilliant cyan blue and stays that way until Mar. Although there are lots of theories, no one is really quite sure why this happens. You can drive (or walk) around the rim of the volcano, and there are several lookouts that enable you to peer down into it. You can also take a glass-panelled lift down into the crater for a close-up view during a 45min **Aquifer Tour** (aquifertours.com).

Other must-see spots around town include the two sinkhole gardens. The **Cave Garden** – a State Heritage Area – is in the middle of town (Watson Dr) and has a free 15min sound-and-light show every night at around 8pm. **Umpherston Sinkhole**, around 2km from the town centre (Jubilee Hwy East), has trailing vines and verdant plants deep below ground, and is also worth a visit at night, when possums descend in large numbers to feed – BYO torch. Both gardens are open 24 hours and are free to enter.

From Mount Gambier head towards the coast via Millicent. Keep an eye out on the way for the prowling tiger on the roof of the **Tantanoola Tiger Hotel**. In the 1880s, after the discovery of a number of mauled sheep, locals became convinced that a Bengal tiger had escaped from a travelling circus. In 1895, several hundred sheep and a lot of hysteria later, a beast was shot by bushman Tom Donovan. It turned out though that it was not a tiger, but an Assyrian wolf, thought to have stowed away on a boat that was shipwrecked off the coast – and that the real culprit responsible for most of the missing sheep was a local thief called Charlie Edmondson. The wolf-tiger was stuffed and is still on display inside the hotel.

Beachport has one of the longest jetties in SA and some great fresh lobster shops. The **Bowman Scenic Drive** is a short but stunning coastal drive that sweeps around the beaches and dunes south of the town centre, taking in several lookouts along the way. It skirts the edge of the **Pool of Siloam**, a salt lake seven times saltier than the sea which is reputed to cure all matter of aches and pains. The high salt content makes the water very buoyant, and on a hot day it's a great place for a soak and a float.

Good for a rainy day

The ground beneath Mount Gambier's streets is a labyrinth of limestone caves. The most accessible is **Engelbrecht Cave**, which extends under seven city streets. Once used as a dump by one of the city's whisky distilleries, it's now open for tours.

Head into the hills

Known as Australia's answer to Bordeaux, the **Coonawarra** is celebrated for its red wines, particularly cabernet sauvignon, thanks to a legendary 12km-long, 2km-wide cigar-shaped strip of rich terra-rossa soil. According to the experts, this soil, which sits atop a white limestone base that was once the ocean floor, is one of the most productive *terroirs* outside Europe. More than 20 Coonawarra wineries have cellar-door sales and most are open seven days a week. The heart of the Coonawarra is the tiny township of **Penola**, which is full of antique stores, galleries and boutiques. **Petticoat Lane**, the oldest residential part of Penola, still has redgum kerbing and is lined with original timber-and-stone cottages. The township's most famous past resident though is undoubtedly Mary MacKillop, Australia's first saint. Together with Father Julian Tenison Woods, Mary MacKillop founded the religious order of the Sisters of St Joseph in Penola in 1866. You can learn all about Mary MacKillop's life and times and her many good works in the **Mary MacKillop Penola Centre**, which is full of historic displays as well as a shrine, an old schoolhouse and a gift shop packed full of every type of Mary MacKillop memento you can imagine.

Kids' spot

It's a bit of a detour, but if you're interested in fossils, or you've got youngsters with a fascination for dinosaurs and big critters - and what kid doesn't love learning about zygomaturus, marsupial lions and giant kangaroos? - **Naracoorte Caves**, SA's only World Heritage Site, is worth the hour or so drive from Mount Gambier. The caves have acted as pitfall traps, collecting animals unlucky enough to fall through the holes in the ground for more than 800,000 years and consequently preserving the bones of a range of prehistoric megafauna. There are 28 known caves in the park, and four are open for tours, including adventure caving and behind-the-scenes tours of working fossil digs and the fossil lab, as well as the above ground **Wonambi Fossil Centre**. Book ahead for tours (naracoortecaves.sa.gov.au).

Opposite Just one of the beaches on the Bowman Scenic Drive
Above Canunda National Park

SIDETRACK

There's no shortage of fantastic seaside walking trails on the Limestone Coast, but one not to miss is the **Seaview Trail in Canunda National Park** between Southend and Beachport. It starts near the carpark at Cape Buffon near Southend and takes around 3hr return. It's along cliff-top almost the entire way, and the name just about sums it up - it's one jaw-dropping sea view after another.

Home to around 1200 or so people, **Robe** is a holiday town with a handful of cafes, restaurants, shops and caravan parks, but in the 1850s it was SA's second busiest international port. There are more than 80 historic buildings and sites around town; you can pick up a heritage walking trail map at the visitor centre near the beach. Even if you don't walk the heritage trail, you can see the sandstone buildings for yourselves on the main street and surrounds. The **old cemetery** off O'Halloran St is fascinating with gravestones telling of the cause of death of early settlers and pastoralists, including wagon accidents and whole families who died of a mysterious illness.

Robe's popularity in the mid-19th century was partly the result of a £10 landing tax imposed on all gold seekers arriving in Victoria during the gold rush. For many, particularly the Chinese gold seekers, that was more than the cost of their voyage to Australia, so they chose to arrive in Robe instead and head overland to the Victorian diggings on foot. There's a monument to the 16,000 Chinese people who walked the 200mi (320km) to Ballarat and Bendigo near the tiny but informative **Customs House**, a little gem of a maritime museum.

SIDETRACK

A favourite with four-wheel-drivers the **Beach Run** between Beachport and Robe via Nora Creina is a challenging drive, with soft sand, sharp rocks and some wickedly steep dunes, but it is also great fun. It's less than 60km but will take you half a day. You need to check the tides carefully before you go, air down your tyres to around 15-20 psi and be prepared to get stuck at least once or twice. It's also easy to lose the track, so ask at the visitor centre in Robe or Beachport for the 4WD trip notes. Travel with another 4WD so you can help each other if you get stuck and there are also 4WD tours on offer.

Opposite top left One of the resident possums at Umpherston Sinkhole *Opposite top right* Engelbrecht Cave *Opposite bottom left* Old town hall, Mount Gambier *Opposite bottom right* Sunken garden at Umpherston Sinkhole *Below* Southend

Limestone Coast 127

ROBE TO GOOLWA

The Limestone Coast is famous for its southern rock lobster, and the **Big Lobster**, a 17m-high spiny red crustacean – one of Australia's many 'Big Things' – is just half an hour up the road at Kingston SE. Legend has it that the original lobster was only meant to be 17ft tall, but the builder misread the plans and used metres instead. There are plenty of places in town where you can buy real lobster, as well as fish and chips. The lobster season is from Oct through to May.

The next 150km or so of this road trip skirts the edge of the Coorong, a long lagoon and windswept beach known as Kurangk ('long narrow neck') by the Ngarrindjeri People. Today much of it is protected by **Coorong National Park** and the wealth of culturally significant sites – shell middens and evidence of campsites used over thousands of years – testify to the enduring connection to Country. The waterways attract an enormous variety of birds, and the area was made famous by the 1976 movie made from Colin Thiele's children's novel, *Storm Boy*, about a young boy who befriends a pelican called Mr Percival – one of the largest breeding colonies of the Australian pelican is at Jack Point. It's also a great spot for kayaking, boating and fishing, and the ***Spirit of the Coorong*** (spiritofthecoorong.com.au) has a range of full- and half-day sightseeing and adventure tours.

At Meningie the road turns inland, along the shores of **Lake Albert** and **Lake Alexandrina** – the original name of Queen Victoria before she took the throne – where the Murray River spreads out to become the largest freshwater lake in SA, wide and shallow and ringed with reeds and bursting with birdlife. From here, the Murray finally creeps towards the ocean, tracing one last great bend at Goolwa before seeping into the sea at the Murray Mouth on Hindmarsh Island. To get there you'll need to take the free car ferries across the Murray River at **Narrung** – birthplace of David Unaipon, the Ngarrindjeri man featured on the Australian $50 note, with the Raukkan church in the background – and **Wellington** and follow the road around the edge of the lake to Goolwa on the Fleurieu Peninsula.

Oozing history at almost every turn, **Goolwa** was once a thriving river port, where paddle steamers unloaded their cargo on to the country's first railway, which ferried the goods to the seaports of Port Elliot and Victor Harbor. Now known as the **SteamRanger Cockle Train** (*see* Fleurieu Peninsula road trip, p.109), it's been a popular tourist route since 1887, earning its rather quaint name from the large cockles found on the sandy surf beaches of Goolwa. Take a walk along the river's edge, past historic boatsheds and slipways, where paddle steamers once docked, or head out the boardwalk over the sand dunes for coastal views. The town is full of beautiful sandstone buildings, many of them now art galleries and restaurants.

To get to the Murray Mouth, cross the bridge to **Hindmarsh Island**, where you'll find a lookout platform and you can usually walk along the beach unless the area has been recently dredged, which occasionally happens during times of low water flows to prevent its closure. It might be Australia's mightiest river, flowing more than 2500km from the mountains to the sea, but its end point is not as dramatic as you might expect, although the beach is very nice.

From Goolwa, it's around a 75min drive north to Adelaide/Tarndanya, unless you get waylaid at one of the wineries or galleries along the way.

Opposite Seaview Trail, Canunda National Park *Above* The Big Lobster, Kingston SE

SIDETRACK

If you have a 4WD you can drive along the stunning narrow ribbon of sand called the **Younghusband Peninsula** for 150km, from the Granites near Kingston SE to the mouth of the Murray River. Separated from the mainland by a chain of saltwater lagoons, the peninsula has huge flocks of waterbirds, gorgeous beaches and tall dunes, but you need to be wary of wind and tide conditions and the route should not be attempted in winter.

BEST BEDS

- **Mount Gambier Gaol** Home to outlaws and the condemned from 1866 until 1995, the gaol has been refurbished and made into a boutique budget hotel, with the old bars and razorwire fences still in place. Rooms range from dormitories to self-contained family units, and while the guards' peep holes in the doors have been covered over for privacy and cells now include a toilet and basin, almost all the original gaolhouse fittings and fixtures are still in place. The difference of course these days is that all prison guests get a key. theoldmountgambiergaol.com.au
- **Robe House** Built in 1847, this was one of the first houses to be built in Robe, as the home of the Government Resident. There are four self-contained apartments in the historic sandstone house, each with queen-sized brass beds and ensuites - two rooms have log fires. robehouse.com.au
- **The Boathouse** Beautifully restored, this riverfront boathouse at Birks Harbour in Goolwa has its own private wharf. birksharbour.com.au

VANLIFE

Almost every seaside town has a good caravan park, often right on the waterfront. A favourite is the **Beachport Southern Ocean Tourist Park** but there are also several good ones in Robe. The lakeside campsites at Three Mile Bend in **Beachport Conservation Park** are just a few kilometres from Beachport town centre. You can camp at **Kotgee** and **Nal-a-wort** at the end of the Seaview Trail hiking path in Canunda National Park, but you can also get there by road from Southend. **Naracoorte Caves Campground** has powered caravan sites and in the Coorong there are a number of beachside campsites: **42 Mile Crossing**, **Parnka Point**, **Long Point** and **Mark Point** are suitable for caravans but do not have power.

Limestone Coast

South Australia

The perfect city escape less than a 90min drive from Adelaide/Tarndanya, this boot-shaped peninsula has more than 700km of coastline to explore, and is classic beach shack and summer holiday territory.

Yorke Peninsula

WHEN TO GO
Temperatures are moderate most of the year. Summer is usually much drier than the winter months, although winter is the best time for salmon fishing.

HOW LONG?
Go for a weekend – or stay for a week – the beauty of the Yorke Peninsula is its compact size. Three or four days would be ideal to do this coastal loop without rushing.

LOCAL SECRET
The unassuming **Minlaton Bakery** on the main street of Minlaton has an almost cult-like following among locals and wised-up travellers, who flock here for its meat pies (try the pepper steak or spinach and roasted capsicum, pumpkin and carrot mash if you're not a meat eater), lavish cupcakes and delightfully rich chocolate donuts. Open every day except Sun.

SNAPSHOT
This coastal road trip looping along both sides of the Yorke Peninsula delivers a beguiling mix of white-sand beaches – many littered with intriguing shipwrecks – coastal walking trails, lighthouses, fishing, and some sublime beachfront camping. With beaches facing north, east, west and south there's always a good one, no matter how the wind blows. Not the type of place to go if you're looking for racy nightlife or high-end shopping, the Yorke is charmingly low-key.

Drive rating
Easy. Mostly sealed roads.

Acknowledgement of Country
This is the Traditional Land of the Narungga (also known as Adjahdura) People.

Distance planner
Adelaide to Pondalowie and back: around 750km
- Adelaide to Edithburgh: 234km
- Edithburgh to Pondalowie Bay via Troubridge Point: 114km
- Pondalowie Bay to Adelaide via Wallaroo: 400km

More information
- Yorke Peninsula Visitor Information, 18 Main St, Minlaton; (08) 8853 3898; yorkepeninsula.com.au

Opposite Troubridge Point

ADELAIDE/TARNDANYA TO EDITHBURGH

From Adelaide head west on the A1 to Port Wakefield at the top of the St Vincent Gulf, then turn south to trace the Yorke Peninsula's eastern shore. Look at a map and you'll see the peninsula resembles a big boot, and this is the calf of the leg, although in reality it's a succession of small coastal towns, all the way until you get to Edithburgh at the heel, around a 3hr drive if you don't stop. But that would mean missing out on the stunning red coastal cliffs at **Ardrossan** and raking the beach for sand and blue swimmer crabs at nearby **Tiddy Widdy** beach (yes, that's a real place). All you need is a rake (pick one up at the local hardware store), boots that won't get sucked off in the sandy shallows, and a tub to put them in. Best time to do it is at low tide, from spring to autumn, but check online (pir.sa.gov.au) for size and bag limits before you go to make sure you keep it legal.

And while other towns across the country are showcasing their silo art, Tiddy Widdy has a **Stobie pole art trail**. (Stobie poles are termite-resistant concrete power poles invented by Adelaide man James Cyril Stobie, that were, until the 1990s, unique to SA – a useful fact to keep handy for trivia nights!) Wander along the waterfront and you'll find more than 26 brightly decorated poles.

Port Vincent's also worth a look. You'll often see dolphins in the water, there's good summertime swimming out to a pontoon, a jetty for fishing, and some lovely cliff-top lookouts and walking trails.

Dolphin Point, Dhilba Guuranda-Innes National Park

Yorke Peninsula

The Yorke Peninsula is an excellent place for walking. There's a network of walking trails and cycle paths on all three sides of the peninsula, known collectively as **Walk the Yorke**, that stretches for more than 500km. It's spilt up into 16 smaller sections, and you can download track notes (yorkepeninsula.com.au/walk-the-yorke), or pick up details from visitor information centres.

Dangle a fishing line from the jetty at **Edithburgh** – once one of the busiest ports in the country when windjammers and ketches loaded up with cargo bound for England jostled for space at the wharf – it's renowned as a place to catch King George whiting, squid and garfish, and the waters around the pylons are a popular diving and snorkelling spot, home to big-bellied seahorses and leafy sea dragons. And no visit to Edithburgh is complete without a dip in the town's **seawater swimming pool**. The unique **Mosaic Trail** is also here, a 2.9km coastal track from Edithburgh to Sultana Point – suitable for wheelchairs and prams – that features 94 mosaics.

EDITHBURGH TO PONDALOWIE BAY

This next section of the coast, west along the bottom of the boot, from Edithburgh at the heel to Dhilba Guuranda-Innes National Park at the toe, is one of the most scenic drives in SA. It makes for a fabulous daytrip, past the towering **Troubridge Hill Lighthouse** made from distinctive red clay bricks, gleaming salt flats, cliff-top lookouts and beautiful deserted beaches.

Don't be put off by the name **Mozzie Flat** (about halfway along this section), as it's a lovely swimming and camping spot and was actually named for the small flat-bottomed sailing ships – ketches – that once skimmed across the bay and were nicknamed 'the mosquito fleet'. Likewise, there's nothing foul at all about **Foul Bay**; it's a gorgeous 16km-long stretch of golden beach, named by explorer Matthew Flinders, who charted and named much of Australia's southern coast. Cruising past on his circumnavigation of the island continent in 1802 he forever unjustly maligned the shallow bay when, frustrated because he couldn't find a good place to anchor his ship, he declared it 'a foul bay'.

More than 40 shipwrecks lay off the coast of the Yorke Peninsula, many off the coast of **Dhilba Guuranda-Innes National Park** on its southern tip, which is co-managed with the Narungga Traditional Owners. The park's most famous wreck is *The Ethel*, which ran aground in 1904 during a storm – you can still see traces of the half-buried three-masted iron barque at **Ethel Beach** – but there are also a number of much more modern relics lying forgotten on various bays and beaches in the park. Where there are wrecks there are lighthouses – there are three in the park – and the one at **West Cape** is stunning. Built of stainless steel it gleams by day but is at its most impressive just before dusk when the setting sun paints it gold.

Shipwreck remains on Ethel Beach, Dhilba Guuranda-Innes National Park

If you only have time to do one walk in the national park, make it the 2hr-return walk to **Royston Head**. Highlights include panoramic coastal views of offshore reefs and islands and a short side trip for a swim in water so clear it's almost invisible at beautiful **Dolphin Beach**. Dhilba Guuranda-Innes National Park is also a place for birdwatching – eagle rays, white-bellied sea eagles, hooded plovers, ospreys, budgerigars, malleefowl and pelicans. Tammar wallabies thrive here due to a conservation program. Southern right whales can be spotted from May to Sept, and dolphins are frequently seen too.

Head into the hills

Not so much heading into the hills as across the flatlands, there are around 200 salt lakes in and around the township of **Yorketown**, around 15km inland from Edithburgh. Yorketown was established in the 1870s to harvest the salt – during World War I more than 57,000 tonnes of salt was harvested in just one year – but these days the lakes, which change from white and silver to pink and orange or blue and purple, depending on the time of year and salinity levels, are a magnet for photographers. Best photo stops are **Lake Fowler**, **Dhalliwanggu-Lake Sunday** and **Pink Lake**.

SIDETRACK

Explore land-based wrecks of a different kind in **Inneston**, a remarkably intact gypsum mining village that was once home to 200 people but abandoned in the 1970s. If you fancy the idea of spending the night in a ghost town, seven of the historic buildings are now self-contained accommodation (*see* p.137), but most likely the only signs of life you'll see are the resident emus prowling the deserted streets. There's a short walk that leads to Inneston Lake, a blue-green salt lake where you can see rare stromatolites.

PONDALOWIE BAY TO WALLAROO

From Dolphin Beach there are a maze of small gravel roads that will eventually lead you north or you can backtrack to Marion Bay and follow the Marion Bay Rd to hook back up with the coast at the top of the foot, near Corny Point Lighthouse. It's worth detouring along the way to explore the sand dunes and watch the surfers at **Daly Head**. Berry Bay, near Corny Point, is another very popular surfing spot.

The western coast of the peninsula – the shin – is washed by the waters of the Spencer Gulf, and all along this stretch between Point Turton and Wallaroo, you'll find charmingly peaceful coastal communities, where ramshackle beach shack chic is about as glitzy as it gets. Beaches and locales worth making a detour for include **Flaherty Beach**, a good sunset and swimming spot, and **Parsons Beach**.

Minlaton is the main service centre on the peninsula. There's a memorial in the centre of town to its most famous son, daring airman Captain Harry Butler. His original World War I Red Devil monoplane, believed to be the last genuine one left in the world, is on display at the edge of town. Minlaton also claims it is the Barley Capital of the World, so head to the **Watsacowie Brewery** to try a local brew.

Yorke Peninsula

Known as the Copper Coast, the north-west section of the peninsula was once a bustling mining district. Copper was discovered here in 1861 and at its peak **Moonta** was SA's largest town. Most of the miners were Cornish – the local Cornish pastries, which you'll find in every cafe and bakery, are legendary – and the Cornish heritage is still celebrated today with the **Kernewek Lowender** festival. Held every two years in Moonta, Kadina and Wallaroo, it's the world's biggest Cornish festival. Many of the old Cornish mine buildings, engine houses and infrastructure have been preserved at the **Moonta Mines State Heritage Area** and **Moonta Mines Museum**.

Finish off your Yorke coastal road trip with a drive along North Beach at **Wallaroo**. At low tide the sand on this 2km-long beach is firm enough to drive on, even for 2WD vehicles, although check the tides, as you don't want to get stranded. Facing west, it's a corker of a place to watch the sun go down.

☺ Kids' spot

Take the kids for a ride back in time on the **Moonta Mines Railway**. A round trip on the narrow-gauge train takes 50min and gives a good overview of many of the historic sites. It departs from Moonta Mines Museum and runs on weekends and during SA school holidays. Cool off afterwards at **Splash Town**, a free waterpark with slides, fountains and a tipping water bucket at the Moonta Bay Jetty.

☂ Good for a rainy day

Kadina's Farm Shed Museum tells the story of dryland farming and copper mining through a collection of historic displays that include an old schoolhouse from the 1950s, a Victorian house museum, a life-sized model of an underground mine, the game-changing stump jump plough and lots of engines and antique machinery, including a very impressive line-up of vintage tractors.

Opposite Stenhouse Bay Jetty in Dhilba Guuranda-Innes National Park *Top* Cape Spencer, Dhilba Guuranda-Innes National Park *Middle* Sooty oystercatcher *Bottom* World War I monoplane, Minlaton

BEST BEDS

- It's not particularly flash but the **Edithburgh Caravan Park** is in an excellent spot in the middle of town and has seaview cabins, caravan sites and a good kids' playground. The park is very close to the tidal swimming pool and opposite the fishing jetty. edithburghcaravanpark.com.au
- There is a range of self-contained heritage accommodation available in the abandoned township of Inneston in Dhilba Guuranda-Innes National Park. The **Engineers and Managers Lodges** both sleep 10 in three bedrooms, while the old **Post Office** is perfect for couples. Linen and bedding are not supplied so bring your own sheets, pillows, blankets and towels. Book through National Parks and Wildlife Service SA (parks.sa.gov.au).
- **Wallaroo Marina Apartments** are modern, spacious and all have great views over North Beach. Close to both the centre of town and the jetty, it's a handy spot if you're planning on taking the ferry across to the Eyre Peninsula. wallarooapartments.com.au

VANLIFE

The Yorke Peninsula has a refreshingly relaxed attitude towards campers, with a range of bush camping areas, often just metres from a dazzling beach that anywhere else would be prime real estate for the rich and famous or home to a luxe resort. You'll find most on the western side and southern tip of the peninsula - download a map with locations and pay for your permit online (visityorkepeninsula.com.au) or pick map up at the visitor centre in Minlaton or Kadina. A favourite spot is **Mozzie Flat**, about halfway along the Troubridge Scenic Dr, with sheltered sites tucked in the dunes behind a white-sand beach. Also good are the three free campgrounds clustered together around a 10min drive north of Balgowan on the north-west coast. **The Gap** is the biggest and most popular, but **Tiparra Rocks** has the best beachfront sites - although the trade off for uninterrupted water views is a lack of shelter and shade. You can also camp at several spots in **Dhilba Guuranda-Innes National Park**: **Stenhouse Bay** is on a headland with good views over the beach below, and close to the entrance of the park and nearby Marion Bay township, while **Pondalowie** is sheltered behind a large sand dune and only a short walk to the beach, which also has a boat ramp. Book through National Parks and Wildlife Service SA (parks.sa.gov.au). Most of the larger coastal towns and communities also have commercial caravan parks.

South Australia

Crowd-free beaches, waterfront campsites and good-value rooms with a view, plus beautiful walking trails, excellent fishing and great seafood.

Eyre Peninsula

HOW LONG?

The distances between towns are not vast, so you could easily drive the length of the peninsula in half a day but take some extra time around Port Lincoln to explore Lincoln and Coffin Bay national parks. Plan to spend at least a week if you combine this drive with the first half of the Great Australian Bight road trip (p.145) north along the western side of the peninsula, and allow at least a day each way to get to (and from) Adelaide/Tarndanya. To cut a corner, catch the car ferry from Wallaroo on the Yorke Peninsula to Lucky Bay near Cowell with Spencer Gulf Searoad ferries (spencergulfsearoad.com).

WHEN TO GO

Temperatures are moderate most of the year. Summer is usually much drier than the winter months. The ocean is too cold for swimming during winter unless you've got a thick steamer wetsuit. The best time to see giant cuttlefish, and swim with them in Whyalla is between May and Aug.

LOCAL SECRET

Port Lincoln's **Fresh Fish Place** is your one-stop shop when it comes to the best of the peninsula's local seafood. Housed at the front of a fish processing factory in the industrial part of town, the retail section specialises in locally caught fish, scallops, oysters, abalone, prawns, crab and crayfish. It also has a range of seafood that is pickled and smoked inhouse and a licensed cafe, or get some cooked fish and chips to take away. Behind-the-scenes factory tours and seafood cooking classes are also available.

SNAPSHOT

On this beautiful coastal drive along the eastern side of the Eyre Peninsula, you'll find beach after beach visited only by the occasional angler, screeching seagulls and very few of the holiday crowds you find along the rest of the Australian coast. Campsites are right on the edge of the sand and you're often the only ones there – and the seafood is amazing. The Eyre Peninsula is one of Australia's most underrated coastal destinations.

Drive rating
Easy. Mostly sealed roads, with some optional - but challenging - 4WD sections.

Acknowledgement of Country
This is the Traditional Land of the Nawu, Wirangu and Barngarla Peoples.

Distance planner
Whyalla to Port Lincoln: 268km. The starting point, Whyalla, is 76km south of Port Augusta, 320km west of Adelaide.
- Whyalla to Tumby Bay: 219km
- Tumby Bay to Port Lincoln: 49km

More information
- Whyalla Visitor Information Centre, Lincoln Hwy (at the northern entrance to Whyalla); 1800 088 589; whyalla.com/visitor-guide
- Port Lincoln Visitor Information Centre, 60 Tasman Tce; 1300 788 378; visitportlincoln.net
- eyrepeninsula.com

WHYALLA TO TUMBY BAY

If you're coming from Adelaide/Tarndanya the Eyre Peninsula officially begins at the shipping and iron ore–mining town of **Whyalla**, which in recent years has become famous as a place to witness the annual migration of giant cuttlefish, thanks to a ban on commercial fishing that has allowed the once dwindling population to recover. Now, hundreds of thousands of the chameleonic cephalopods converge at the top of the Spencer Gulf between May and Aug to breed, and it's one of the only places in the world where you can join diving and snorkelling tours to watch their elaborate underwater mating rituals, which include changing colours and shape. If you don't fancy getting wet, glass-bottom boat tours are also available. If you miss the cuttlefish, other attractions in town include tours of the steelworks and the **Maritime Museum**, which features the *HMAS Whyalla*, the first modern warship built in SA. Ask at the Whyalla Visitor Centre at the Maritime Museum for details of tours.

Cuttlefish aside, the best bits of the peninsula are to be found further south along the Lincoln Hwy, in places like **Cowell**. The pristine waters of the Eyre Peninsula produce some of the best oysters in the world, and you can buy them almost anywhere in this sleepy town – direct from the oyster farmers along Oyster Dr, from the bakery, the cafe, on the jetty or cooked and covered in sauces from one of the hotels. If oysters aren't your favourite food try the whiting, another Eyre Peninsula specialty. While in Cowell, drop by the jade showroom at the **Jade Motel**. The local nephrite jade is one of the oldest and largest deposits in the world.

SIDETRACK

Almost all of the coastal towns on the Eyre Peninsula have long wooden jetties, usually lined with hopeful anglers and danglers of hand lines. Originally built to service the grain ships back in the mid-19th century, most of the jetties are very long because many of the towns are on shallow bays. The longest of them all is at **Germein Port**, at the top of Spencer Gulf. Although on the wrong side of the gulf to be part of the Eyre Peninsula, you'll pass by on your way from Adelaide and it's the perfect place to stretch your legs. Originally built in 1881, it's a whopping 1680m long, so long that from the start you can't see the end. There's a good display of historic equipment at the entrance to the jetty, and undercover picnic tables too.

Opposite View over Sleaford Bay from Wanna Lookout, Lincoln National Park *Above* Tumby Bay

Continue south to Tumby Bay but take Beach Rd rather than the highway out of Cowell and follow the curve of Franklin Harbour, through the hamlet of **Port Gibbon**, past **The Knob** and other spectacular beaches, on to **Poverty Bay**, **Red Banks Beach**, **Arno Bay** and **Port Neill**. Most of the beaches are unpatrolled, so not recommended for swimming, but they are lovely places for long walks, and Red Banks is good for surfing if you know what you're doing. If you're keen to try your luck at catching your own seafood feast, the beaches are also all good spots to cast a line, or head to the nearest jetty. Most of the time you'll find these wooden piers lined with local fishers who'll give you the run down on what fish are biting where, and often try to give you the fish they caught as well!

The days of the Great Grain Race in the early 20th century – when windjammers jostled for space at the end of the jetties before competing to see who could get their cargo of wheat to England in the fastest time – may be long gone, but grain production is still one of the region's main industries: the peninsula yields more than 45 per cent of SA's wheat crop, and you'll often see the towering silos on the edge of town long before you get there. Like elsewhere in Australia, many now sport **marvellous murals**, including the one at Tumby Bay, painted in 2018 by Argentinian street artist Martin Ron, of two young local lads joyfully jumping off the Tumby Bay jetty on a hot day. It's just one of several eye-catching murals you'll find around town. **Tumby Bay** is a small holiday town and the main street follows the curve of the bay. The best food in town (fresh local seafood, of course) is at either of the two hotels. Alternatively, buy some wine and takeaway from one of the seafood shops in town and dine out at one of the picnic tables along the shoreline.

Good for a rainy day

Take a quick detour inland on the Bratten Way to the **Smithy Museum** in Koppio. It focuses on farming prior to the late 1940s, and the complex includes a pine-log, thatched-roof shepherd's hut, a schoolhouse, blacksmith's shop, lots of old rural machinery and tractors, and a woman pioneers' room. It's worth visiting just for the Bob Dobbins barbed wire collection.

TUMBY BAY TO PORT LINCOLN

Tumby Bay to Port Lincoln on the tip of the peninsula is an easy half-hour drive.

Just 6km before you get to Port Lincoln, drop into **Boston Bay Wines** for a wine tasting and one of the best cellar-door views in the country.

Port Lincoln is the largest town on the peninsula and has plenty of good restaurants, cafes, galleries and shops. It is home to the largest commercial fishing fleet in the Southern Hemisphere and is renowned for its tuna. The annual **Tunarama Festival** is held on the Australia Day long weekend at the end of Jan (complete with the World Championship Tuna Toss). Ask at the visitor information centre for details of fishing charters and behind-the-scenes tours of fish processing plants and aquaculture cruises.

The best part of this bit of the world is the scenery and nearby **Lincoln National Park** is a must-see. There are a number of scenic drives that are fine for 2WD, as well as a challenging 4WD-only one to the rugged southern section of the park that is largely along cliff-edges to the **Sleaford sand dunes** – an endless expanse of towering white dunes bordering beaches pounded by enormous waves. The more sheltered, northern section of the park (2WD accessible) has a string of pretty bays and calm beaches – most with camp and picnic sites. If you have a 4WD, head to **Memory Cove**, but you'll need to get a gate key from the visitor centre in Port Lincoln before you go.

Port Lincoln is at the southern tip of this triangular-shaped peninsula, but if you have the time, head north along the western coast to **Ceduna**, rather than retracing your route, along the Great Australian Bight road trip (*see* p.145). But be warned, with scenery and seafood this good, the Eyre Peninsula can be a very hard place to leave.

Good for a rainy day

Port Lincoln is the place to come face-to-face with a great white shark on a cage dive and since you're going to get wet anyway, it really doesn't matter what the weather's like. You don't have to be a certified diver to do it - but you may have to be certifiably crazy. There are several companies that offer shark-cage dive tours out of Port Lincoln, but ask whether they bait or feed the sharks when you book, as this practice has been linked with increasing shark attacks. A less scary alternative - if you can forget for a moment that these waters are home to great white sharks - is swimming with sea lions. Known as the puppy dogs of the sea, they are insatiably curious, love to play and will often mimic your actions, circling when you do and diving and surfacing with you; the same companies that run the shark dives also run half-day swim with sea lion tours.

SIDETRACK

The **Whalers Way** is a 14km cliff-edge drive through private property south of Port Lincoln and is worth the $40 it costs to get a key and camping permit from the visitor centre in Port Lincoln. It's sublimely scenic, tracing the coastline the entire way, with several good picnic spots. You can camp behind the dunes at Red Banks Beach near the end of the drive, a magical spot that never gets crowded out, with sensational views (but there are no facilities) and a ladder to climb down to the rockpools on the beach.

BEST BEDS

- **Donington Cottage** If you really want to enjoy Lincoln National Park, but camping is not your thing, you can stay at this historic cottage, which sleeps six people. You will need to bring your own linen and food, but it's worth it for the views alone. Spalding Cove, Lincoln National Park; bookings via the Port Lincoln Visitor Information Centre or kataandbelle.com.au.
- **Port Lincoln Hotel** The hotel is already in a great location, in the heart of town opposite Boston Bay, but it's worth paying extra for an ocean-view room with a balcony - otherwise all you'll enjoy is a view of the carpark. portlincolnhotel.com.au
- **Tanonga Luxury Eco Lodges** The two hilltop eco-friendly cabins in Charlton Gully, a 35min drive from Port Lincoln, have knockout views of the surrounding 200ha property. tanonga.com.au
- **Tumby Bay Hotel** This lovely old pub built in 1904 offers cheap, cheerful and comfortable accommodation and the views from the hotel verandah look clear across the bay. There are also self-contained seafront apartments. tumbybaypub.com

VANLIFE

There are caravan parks in most coastal towns, and some fabulous coastal camps near **Port Gibbon**, strung out along cliff-tops and behind the dunes alongside Beach Rd. Beachside camping is available in both **Lincoln and Coffin Bay national parks**. The most popular site in Lincoln National Park is **Memory Cove** (4WD only: book at Port Lincoln Visitor Information Centre), but other good spots include **Fishermans Point**, **Surfleet Cove**, **Taylors Landing** and **Sept Beach** (each with toilet facilities) and the beach-side bush camps at **Carcase Rock**, **MacLaren Point**, **Spalding Cove**, and **Woodcutters Beach**. The best campgrounds for caravans are at Sept Beach or Surfleet Cove, although neither has power. In Coffin Bay National Park the most popular campground is at **Yangie Bay**, a sheltered bay surrounded by dense shrub. All other campsites in the park are 4WD only and most have no facilities. Sensation Beach is lovely, but quite exposed so best in calm weather, while **Big Yangie**, **Black Springs**, **Morgans Landing** and **The Pool** near Point Sir Isaac all offer more sheltered beachside campsites.

Opposite Red Banks Beach on the Whalers Way near Port Lincoln *Top* Cuttlefish, Whyalla *Middle* Fishing fleet, Port Lincoln Marina *Bottom* Silo art by Martin Ron at Tumby Bay

South Australia

144

Experience outback Australia's vast open space and enjoy endless views from cliff-top vantage points on this epic drive around the eastern arc of the Great Australian Bight.

The Great Australian Bight

HOW LONG?
It's at least a five-day drive, one way, from the tip of the Eyre Peninsula to the western end of the Bight near the WA border, and you'll need to add on two more days to finish crossing the Nullarbor at the end (or turn around and come back).

WHEN TO GO
Summer is the best time for swimming on the Eyre Peninsula, although these waters are famous for their great white sharks; winter is relatively mild and beachside campsites are usually deserted. The best time to travel across the Nullarbor is during the winter months, when days are dry and warm, though nights can be very cold. Whale season is between June and Oct.

NEED TO KNOW
Don't drive the Nullarbor at night: wandering stock are a real hazard, as are wild camels. The longest sections without fuel are around 200km. Carry plenty of drinking water: if caravanning or camping, make sure you have enough water to last the trip as most roadhouses along the way rely on tank water and will not allow you to fill up your water tanks for free.

SNAPSHOT
Driving across the Nullarbor might not seem like an obvious choice for a coastal road trip, but while you can't see the sea from the road, it's actually quite close to the coast with lots of access to the longest unbroken line of sea cliffs in the world. Combined with the scenic cliff-top roads and tracks that wind along the western side of the Eyre Peninsula, driving the Great Australian Bight really is one of Australia's ultimate seaside drives.

Drive rating
Moderate. Sealed roads with long distances between stops, and optional 4WD sections.

Acknowledgement of Country
This is the Traditional Land of the Nawu, Barngarla, Wirangu and Mirning Peoples.

Distance planner
Port Lincoln to Eucla: around 900km
- Port Lincoln to Ceduna: 402km
- Ceduna to Eucla: 492km

More information
- Port Lincoln Visitor Information Centre, 60 Tasman Tce; 1300 788 378; portlincoln.com.au
- Ceduna Visitor Information Centre, 58 Poynton St, Ceduna; (08) 8625 3343; cedunatourism.com.au
- eyrepeninsula.com
- nullarbornet.com.au

Opposite Australia's longest straight road

South Australia

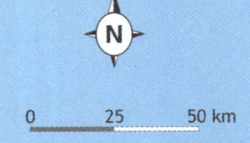

NULLARBOR PLAIN (WA / SA)

- Nullarbor Regional Reserve
- Nullarbor National Park
- Nullarbor Wilderness Protection Area
- The Catacombs
- Nullarbor Roadhouse (RH)
- Yalata self-service fuel
- Yalata (RH)
- Border Village
- Eucla
- Eucla Telegraph Station
- Bunda Cliffs
- Head of Bight
- Far West Coast Marine Park
- YALATA
- NUNDROO
- WAHGUNYAH CONSERVATION PARK
- Great Australian Bight Marine National Park
- Coora...
- Cape Adieu
- NUYTS ARCHIPELAGO MARINE PARK

Great Australian Bight

SOUTHERN OCEAN

N

0 25 50 km

146

The Great Australian Bight 147

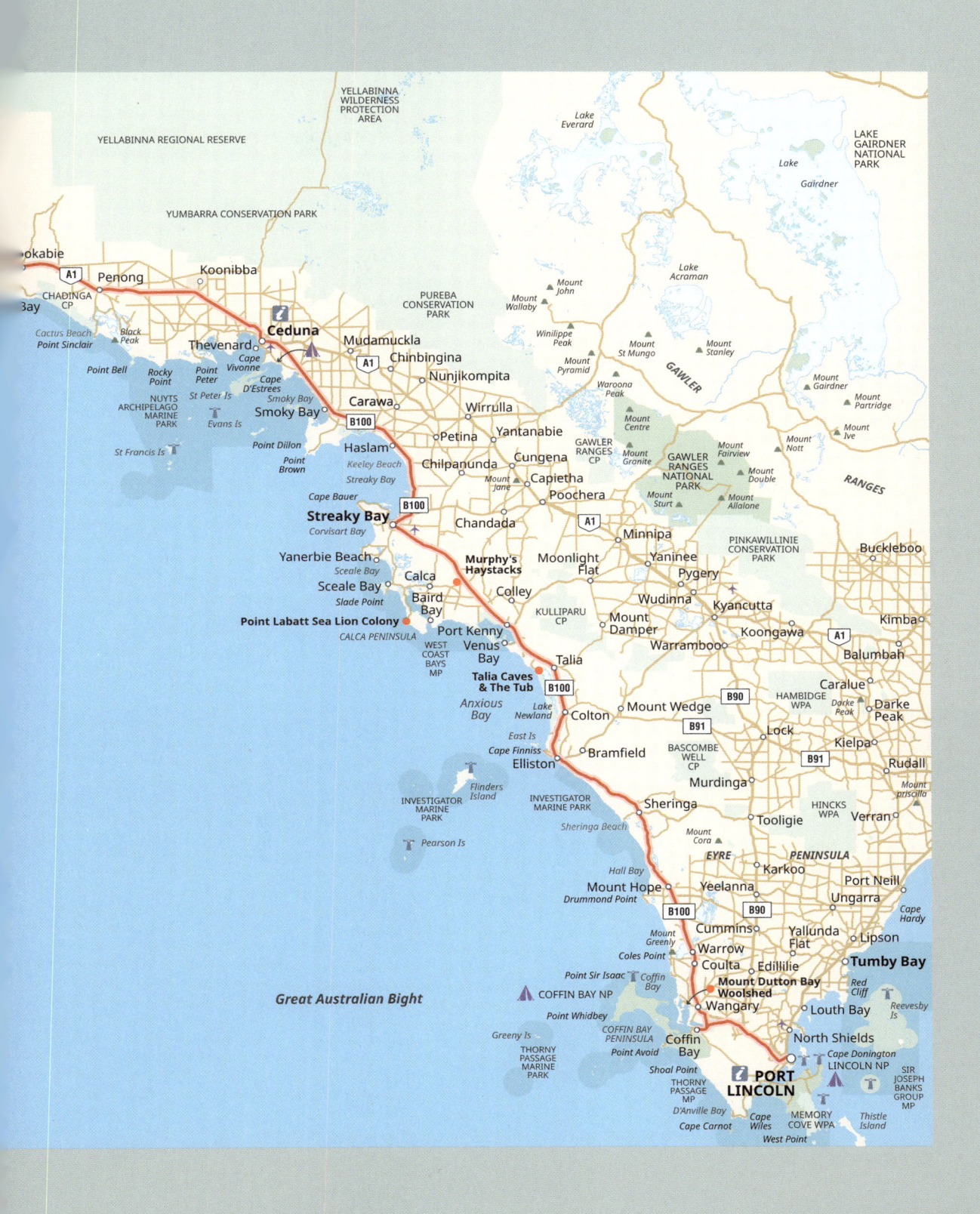

PORT LINCOLN TO CEDUNA

From Port Lincoln on the southern tip of the Eyre Peninsula, head north along the western edge of the peninsula in the direction of Streaky Bay. **Coffin Bay National Park** is about 40km from Port Lincoln and is great for 4WDs. You can drive the length of the park to Point Sir Isaac, but be warned, the sand can trap even the most experienced off-roader. Lower your tyre pressure and carry a compressor to reinflate them – you will need to do this several times during the trip. It's only 55km from the ranger station, but it will take around 3hr each way. Much of the road is actually on the beach, so check the tide chart before you set off. There are good camping spots along the way at **Black Springs** and **Point Sir Isaac** – both sites are practically on the beach and the fishing is good. If you're in a conventional car there are also plenty of great beaches and lookouts you can visit – and a campground at Yangie Bay – although you will not be able to get deep inside the park without a 4WD.

If you're an oyster lover you'll be familiar with Coffin Bay oysters, arguably some of the world's best. In the township of **Coffin Bay**, ask one of the locals for directions to where you can buy some freshly shucked oysters (lots of local oyster growers sell them from backyard sheds for just a few dollars) and find a shady spot on the **Oyster Walk** that skirts the edge of the bay for a five-star lunch. There's also a range of oyster farm tours.

Further north, **Elliston** is home to a very scenic cliff-top drive, with cliffs as sensational as those you'll see on the Nullarbor, except these ones are decorated with some quirky sculptures. A highlight of the next section is **Talia Caves**, which were hollowed out of the granite and limestone cliffs by the sea. There are steps down to a large cavern in the cliff base and a ladder to **The Tub**, a large, crater-like hole around 30m deep and 50m wide.

All along this section of the coast you'll see turn-offs to small coastal communities and deserted beaches, and if you are not in a rush (and it would be a shame to rush this trip) it's fun to explore them. One not to miss is **Venus Bay**, where the general store (there's only the one) sells quite possibly the world's best fish and chips, locally caught King George whiting, perfectly battered and super fresh. That said, the seafood – from oysters and prawns to abalone and fish – everywhere on the Eyre Peninsula is superb: don't go home without eating as much as you can. The jetty in Venus Bay is a good place to catch squid and whiting, and the **South Head walking trail** is a great spot to see dolphins, sea lions, and in winter, migrating southern right whales. It's also the perfect place to watch the sun go down.

A local landmark, **Murphy's Haystacks**, is not far from the turn-off to Baird Bay (see Sidetrack, p.149). The 'haystacks' are actually a hilltop outcrop of large granite boulders, with walkways between them. Local legend has it that a traveller mistook the rocks – which were on a farm owned by a Murphy – for hay, and the name stuck. It's a nice spot for a picnic.

In **Streaky Bay** (also famous for its oysters), pop into the Shell Roadhouse to take a look at the replica of the biggest white pointer shark ever caught by rod and reel – a very scary 5m long and weighing in at a whopping 1520kg. It was caught in the waters off Streaky Bay in 1990 and is enough to put you off swimming in the Southern Ocean for life.

From Streaky Bay continue north to **Ceduna** via Smoky Bay. Like just about everywhere else on the peninsula, both towns produce fabulous oysters. If you're not sick of them yet, make a beeline to the **Ceduna Oyster Barn**, opposite the service station on the Eyre Hwy on the northern edge of town where the road trains fill up before (and after) they hit the Nullarbor. At first glance it's not the most glamorous of spots for an alfresco lunch – a nondescript steel shed – but order a dozen freshly shucked oysters, some sushi or fish and chips, grab a piccolo of wine or a can of cold beer and head up on to the rooftop or the back verandah. They also serve curry and dumplings for those that don't like shellfish. Flash it's not, but who cares when you're dining out on some of the Eyre Peninsula's finest and it's cheap as chips. Get an extra dozen to take away.

Good for a rainy day

At **Mount Dutton Bay Woolshed**, enjoy a slice of delicious cheesecake or some homemade scones with jam and cream – aka a 'Duttonshear Tea' – and then check out the displays of the shearing, farming and fishing memorabilia in the heritage-listed woolshed, built in 1875. There's a gallery of local art on show as well.

SIDETRACK

Follow the signs to Baird Bay and the **Point Labatt** Australian sea lion colony, the only permanent breeding colony on mainland Australia – all other colonies occur on offshore islands. Your best chance to see them is between Sept and May. There is a viewing platform on the cliff-top where you can watch mothers teaching their pups to swim (you'll need binoculars if you want a really good view), or you can get really up close and personal by swimming with sea lions and dolphins on a tour with **Baird Bay Ocean Eco Experience** (bairdbay.com).

Opposite Driving along the beach in Coffin Bay National Park
Top Head of Bight *Bottom* Murphy's Haystacks

The Great Australian Bight

Opposite Southern right whale nursery, Head of Bight *Left* Black Springs, Coffin Bay National Park *Right* Eucla Telegraph Station

CEDUNA TO EUCLA (AND BEYOND)

There's been an assortment of old windmills on the outskirts of Penong, 73km west of Ceduna, for years, but the growing collection – all rescued and restored by local volunteers who call themselves the 'windmill warriors' – officially became the **Penong Windmill Museum** in late 2016. A highlight of the outdoor gallery, which currently stands at around 20 windmills, includes Bruce, a Comet wind pump thought to be the biggest windmill in the country and originally used to pump water to steam trains.

SIDETRACK

Take a short detour off the highway (signposted 46km west of Penong) to tranquil **Fowlers Bay**, a tiny fishing village by the sea with a general store, a few holiday shacks and not much else. It's a lovely spot to stretch the legs on the long jetty that juts into the ocean where, before road trains took over, the grain ships would load the wheat from the farms on the nearby Eyre Peninsula. Drop a fishing line over the edge and you may even be lucky enough to catch a feed.

West of Fowlers Bay the landscape starts to flatten out as you hit the **Nullarbor Plain**. Nullarbor is Latin for 'no trees' and many travellers, expecting to find an empty, featureless, windswept desert, are shocked to discover that it's covered in vegetation, a carpet of saltbush, bluebush, acacia and even the occasional mulga stretching from one horizon to the other. It is pretty flat though. There are no towns, just a few roadhouses that sell fuel, basics like frozen meat and bread, a few tins of food, long-life milk, snacks and burgers. It takes around three days to cross the Nullarbor. Most roadhouses (*see* p.151) also have campgrounds attached, motel rooms, and a couple even have a swimming pool.

The section of road between Head of Bight and the SA/WA border runs quite close to the coast, and there are half a dozen signposted tracks that lead to lookouts. Known as the **Bunda Cliffs**, these stunning walls of rock, some more than 65m high, stretch for more than 200km and are the longest line of sea cliffs in the world. It really is a breathtaking sight.

There's a quarantine station at the SA/WA border where you'll have to surrender all fresh fruit and vegetables, nuts and honey; if you're travelling in a van or camping and self-catering, you'll have to either rely on tinned food, or have a cook up the night before (cooked food is okay to take across the border) to get you through the next couple of nights because the next place where you'll be able to stock up, assuming you're continuing west at the end of this road trip, will be Norseman, around 710km away.

Built in 1887, the **Eucla Telegraph Station** was once one of the most important links in the overland telegraph line that kept the west in touch with the rest of the country. Back then Eucla, just west of the SA/WA border, was a bustling (if lonely) little town, but a rabbit plague in the 1890s saw the town abandoned and by 1927, the telegraph station was closed. Since then, large sand drifts have repeatedly covered and uncovered the stone buildings, and it's quite eerie wandering around the ruins, half buried in the dunes. They may soon be covered entirely, so see them while you still can.

Eucla really is in the middle of nowhere, and not the most obvious place to end a road trip, but beyond Eucla, the road moves away from the coastal edge of the Great Australian Bight. Most travellers, though, continue west across the remaining half of the Nullarbor, which officially ends at Norseman. Highlights along the way include the 90 Mile Straight – a 146.6km (91.1mi) stretch of road between Caiguna and Balladonia that doesn't have a single bend, the longest, straightest stretch of road in Australia – and the Balladonia Roadhouse, which has bits of a NASA space station called Skylab on display. In 1979 it become the focus of international attention when the space station crash-landed nearby after weeks of speculation about where it might end up (the scientists thought it was going to come to Earth in South Africa). It caused a bit of a fuss at the time. According to the locals, the Dundas Shire Council presented NASA with a littering fine, Canberra's American Ambassador visited to inspect any damage that may have been done, and President Jimmy Carter even rang the Balladonia Roadhouse to make his apologies. Who says the Nullarbor's boring!

☺ Kids' spot

At **Head of Bight**, the dip in the coastline 20km east of Nullarbor Roadhouse (around a 2hr drive west of Fowlers Bay, the turn-off is approximately 60km west of Yalata) there is a **whale-viewing platform** where during the whale season between June and Oct you can sometimes see up to 100 southern right whales and their calves lolling in the water at the foot of the cliffs beneath. The whales come here each year during winter from Antarctica to give birth and it's one of the best whale-watching places in the world. It's on private property, so there is an entrance fee, but it's worth it for the stunning views alone even if you don't see whales, and there is a nice shaded picnic area and a small cafe.

BEST BEDS

- **Baird Bay Apartments** The apartments have absolute waterfront views and lots of luxury touches, including a cappuccino machine. bairdbayoceaneocoapartments.com
- Set right on the water's edge, the historic **Streaky Bay Hotel** with motel-style rooms has sensational views and a menu full of local seafood, including King George whiting. streakybayhotel.com.au
- You don't have to tow a van or pitch a tent to enjoy the million-dollar views at **Venus Bay Beachfront Tourist Park**; the swish waterfront cabins are so close to the sea you feel like you're on a boat, and are great value to boot. venusbaybtp.com.au
- **Nullarbor roadhouses** Basic hotel, motel and caravan park accommodation is available at all roadhouses along the Nullarbor. The best choices are the **Nullarbor Hotel Motel** (184km east of the SA/WA border; (nullarborroadhouse.com.au) and the **Balladonia Hotel Motel** (balladoniahotelmotel.com.au). It pays to book during the busy winter season. Most roadhouses on the Nullarbor will allow pets on leashes in the caravan and camping areas; however, you should check before leaving home, as this may change.

VANLIFE

There are caravan parks in most coastal towns on the Eyre Peninsula. Beachside camping is available in both **Lincoln and Coffin Bay national parks** (see p.143). You can also camp overlooking the beach at **Wittelbee Conservation Park**, 10km south of Ceduna, via Decres Bay Rd. No camping is permitted in Nullarbor National Park. There are, however, designated camping areas at roadhouses and you can bush-camp at rest areas.

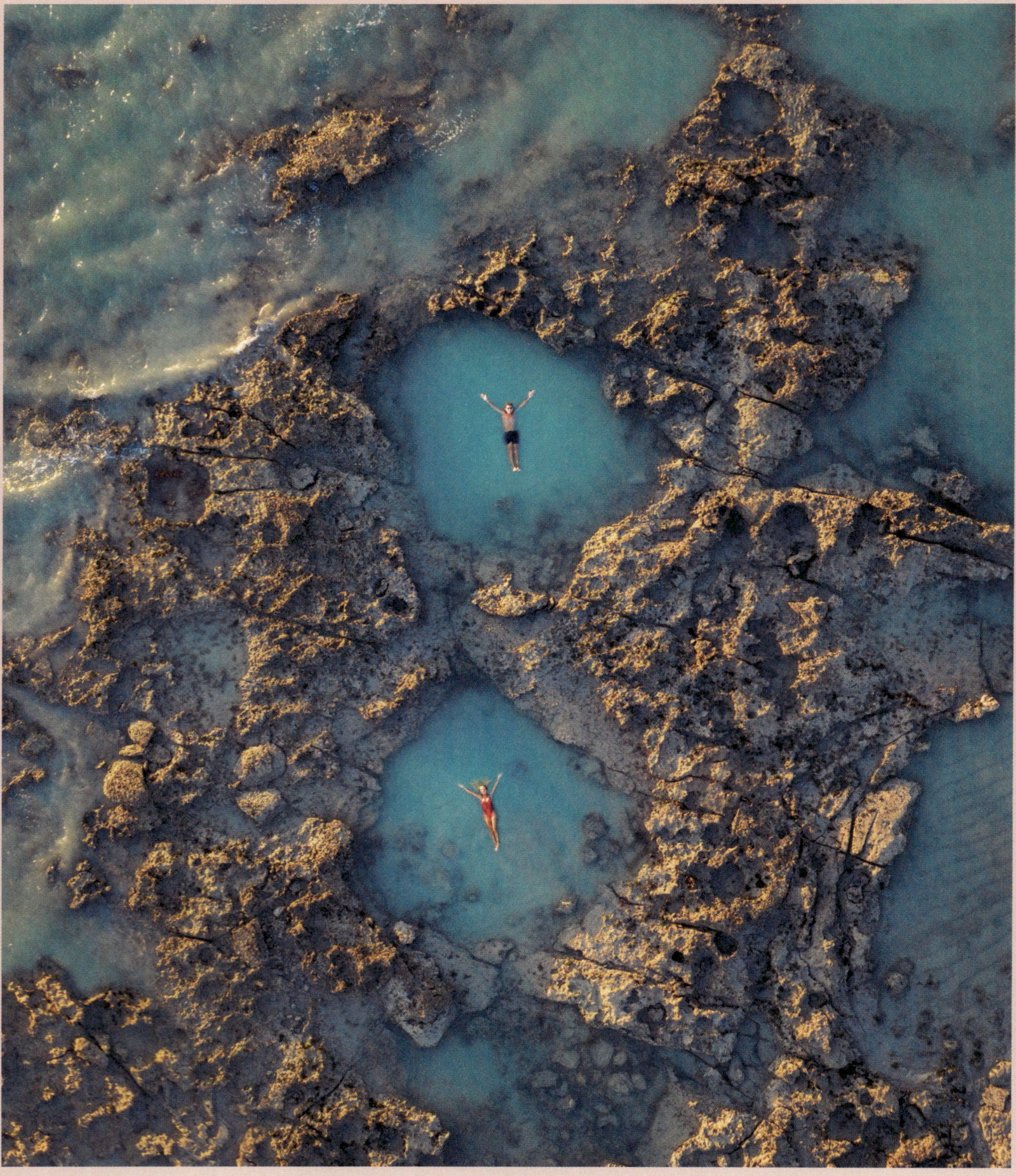

Western Australia

Where the desert meets the sea.

Western Australia

If it's your first time road tripping Australia's west coast, get ready to be blown away by the dazzling colours of the aquamarine sea and white sandy beaches.

Indian Ocean Drive

HOW LONG?
It's less than a 5hr drive from Perth/Boorloo to Geraldton, but it's worth spending a few days beachcombing along the way. Allow two to three days.

WHEN TO GO
It doesn't rain much in this region compared to the South West coast, but when it does, it's almost always during the winter months.

NEED TO KNOW
Between early July and late Nov the coastal plains burst into bloom with more than 800 species of native flowers and flowering shrubs. Get the latest wildflower news from a local website (wildflowercountry.com.au), which has a regularly updated wildflower hot spot page.

SNAPSHOT
The Indian Ocean Drive runs north along an extraordinarily beautiful coastline from Perth to Geraldton, through a string of seaside towns edged by powder-fine white-sand beaches lapped by turquoise-coloured water. Other reasons to go, if you still need some, include amazing wildflowers in spring and feasting on crayfish at bargain prices from local fish and chip shops.

Drive rating
Easy. Sealed roads.

Acknowledgement of Country
This is the Traditional Land of the Whadjuk, Juat, Amangu and Yamatji Peoples.

Distance planner
Perth to Geraldton: around 419km
- Perth to Cervantes: 197km
- Cervantes to Geraldton: 222km

More information
- Geraldton Visitor Centre, 24 Chapman Rd, Geraldton; (08) 9956 6670; visitgeraldton.com.au

Previous Floating in the rock pools near Broome's Gantheaume Point

PERTH/BOORLOO TO CERVANTES

Only a 20min drive west of the city centre, **Cottesloe Beach** is Perth's Bondi, lined with cafes, restaurants, bars – including the iconic Indiana Tea House at the edge of the sand – and surfwear stores. It's even host to an annual **Sculpture by the Sea** exhibition each Mar, just like the hugely popular one held between Bondi and Tamarama in Sydney each spring. With picture-perfect white sands it makes for a good starting point for this drive, because it's just one of half a dozen gorgeous beaches in Perth's northern outskirts. If Cottesloe is too busy for your liking, head north to **Scarborough**, **Trigg**, or if you'd prefer snorkelling to surfing, check out the natural lagoon of **Mettams Pool**.

If you haven't yet made it across to **Rottnest Island/Wadjemup** (see p.189) you can catch a fast ferry from Hillarys Boat Harbour.

The beautiful beaches continue as you head north. For a change of scene, head underground into the **Crystal Cave**, a richly decorated cave full of stalactites, stalagmites and helictites in **Yanchep National Park**, on the Traditional Land of the Whadjuk and Yued Peoples. You can book a guided tour through the WA Parks and Wildlife Service (exploreparks.dbca.wa.gov.au). There's also a raised boardwalk in the park where you can view koalas – even though they are not native to WA there has been a colony here since 1938, originally transferred from Perth Zoo.

Good for a rainy day

Be mesmerised by the diversity of marine life that exists in the waters of WA at **AQWA – The Aquarium of Western Australia** in Hillarys Boat Harbour. One of Australia's largest aquariums, it features only marine life found in WA waters, but with more than 12,000km of coastline to cover, there's plenty of variety, from the cold southern waters to the coral reefs and tropical seas of the far north. There are 45 exhibits, including one of the largest living coral reef exhibits in the world, a moving underwater tunnel, behind-the-scenes tours, snorkelling and diving with shark encounters, glass-bottom boat trips and lots of kids' activities too.

Head into the hills

New Norcia, Australia's only privately owned monastic town, attracts thousands of visitors each year, most of whom come to marvel at the traditional Spanish Mission-style architecture that rises from the surrounding parched grazing lands like a shimmering mirage, tour the abbey, and visit the museum and art gallery - one of the best religious art collections in Australia, it's full of paintings by Spanish and Italian masters, including a tapestry cartoon by Raphael. Others come to buy some of the delicious New Norcia bread, rich nut cakes and slightly sinful *pan chocolatti* that are cooked in a traditional wood-fired oven in the abbey bakery. The town was founded in 1846 by Spanish Benedictine monks, just 17 years after the establishment of Perth, with the aim to create a largely self-sufficient village based on agriculture. More than 175 years later it is still a working monastery with a handful of Benedictine monks in residence who adhere strictly to the abbey rules: prayer seven times a day; work or study in between; silence after 8pm. It's a beautiful place, but one that hides an evil past. For more than a century New Norcia ran a boarding school and 'orphanages' for Noongar and other First Nations children from all over WA - the majority forcibly removed from their families. The schools closed in 1974, and in 2017 the religious community was named as one of the country's worst historical offenders by the Royal Commission into Institutional Responses to Child Sexual Abuse. Survivors are still battling for justice.

Opposite Overlooking Jurien Bay *Right* Enjoying an overwater sunset on Perth's Cottesloe Beach

Lancelin, about an hour's drive up the road from Yanchep, is popular with surfers – Back Beach is celebrated for its big swells – windsurfers and sandboarders, who love the three-storey-high white powdery dunes. If you're keen to give it a go you can hire a sandboard at several spots around town.

This is also one of your first opportunities to try some of the crayfish – western rock lobster – that this section of the coast is famous for. You can buy them live straight off the boat from the fishers down at the Lancelin jetty for a whole lot less than you'd pay in a fancy restaurant, although the boats only bring in what's been pre-sold so to order online a day or two ahead (lancelin.com.au/product/live-lancelin-lobsters).

If you don't fancy cooking a live lobster, the **Lobster Shack** in Cervantes does lobster all sorts of ways for lunch, including chilli lobster fritters and a wickedly good lobster roll, as well as tours thorough their lobster processing plant.

There aren't many places in Australia where you can see the sea from the middle of the desert, but in the **Pinnacles Desert** near Cervantes you can. Thousands of huge limestone pillars rise out of a stark landscape of yellow sand in **Nambung National Park**. Some are jagged, sharp-edged columns, rising to a point; others are squat and rounded like a gravestone; some are little more than triangular-shaped boulders emerging from the dunes. In places they reach up to 3.5m tall. All of them are totally surreal. The towers formed as seashells were compacted and dissolved inside the surrounding dune system, which in turn eroded away leaving the crazy spikes that exist today. The 4km **Pinnacles Loop Drive** through the park is fine for 2WDs, but if you're towing you'll need to unhitch in the carpark at the visitor centre. Nambung is on the Traditional Land of the Yuat People. The pinnacles are more fragile than they look so resist the urge to climb on them, even if you think it would make a great selfie, and respect the Country of the Traditional Owners. Also worth seeing are the thrombolites (living fossils) at nearby **Lake Thetis**. Similar to the more well-known stromatolites of Hamelin Pool in Shark Bay (*see* p.166) this is one of the few places in the world where you can see them. They might just look like rocks, but they actually contain the oldest evidence of life on Earth. And if you're wondering what's the difference between thrombolites and stromatolites, the latter are formed in salt lakes by layers of cyanobacteria over millennia, while the thrombolites at Lake Thetis are clustered structures and much bigger. Both are very, very, very old.

Opposite top left Point Moore lighthouse, Geraldton *Opposite top right* Jurien Bay *Opposite bottom* Windmill and church in the ghost town of Greenough *Left* Pinnacles Desert, Nambung National Park

Indian Ocean Drive 159

CERVANTES TO GERALDTON

Another top spot for crayfishing – and fishing of all sorts from the beaches, jetty or offshore – **Jurien Bay** is also a great place to see some of the world's rarest sea lions. Found only in WA and SA, more than 20 per cent of WA's population of the endangered Australian sea lion live and breed in Jurien Bay Marine Park, and you can often see them on the beaches. If you want to get a closer look, tours are available with **Turquoise Safaris** (turquoisesafaris.com.au) where you can jump in the water and snorkel with them.

If you have a bike – or don't mind the longer walk – the 14km-long **Turquoise Way** is a car-free sealed cycling trail that stretches from the centre of town south along the coast to the mouth of the Hill River and offers one stunning view after another and more than 20 access points to beaches along the way, as well as several nice picnic spots near Dobbyn Park. If you don't feel like doing it all, the northern half of the trail is reasonably flat. There are no prizes for guessing how it got its name either, the colours are truly dazzling. You can hire bikes from **Jurien Bay Adventure Tours**: phone them on 1300 462 383.

The stunning vistas of stunning beaches just don't stop on this road trip, with more in store in at **Port Denison** and **Dongara** – head to Fishermans Memorial Lookout for sweeping views, and one of the three jetties on the marina for good fishing. The breezes here attract windsurfers and kitesurfers from around the world, especially in summer; **South Beach** is a good place to see them in action (or to join in the fun), and it's also a popular surfing spot. If you have a 4WD, you can drive on the beach here.

Don't miss the National Trust village of **Greenough**, 24km south of Geraldton, a collection of 11 restored buildings including a gaol, courthouse, police station, churches, and a school in what was once a vibrant country town of more than 1000 but became a (very solidly built) ghost town in the 1930s when wheat production in the area declined. And keep an eye out along the way for the surreal leaning trees, growing sideways thanks to the prevailing winds beside the road on the drive there.

At the **Museum of Geraldton** you can learn about the mutiny and massacre of the survivors of the *Batavia* shipwreck, which took place some 80km off this coast, in 1629. There is also a large gallery focusing on another equally famous maritime mystery, the disappearance of HMAS *Sydney* in 1941 after a battle with the German warship HSK *Kormoran*. The wreck of the *Sydney* was finally discovered off Dirk Hartog Island in 2008. A **memorial** to the crew has been built on Mount Scott overlooking Geraldton. The silver dome of seagulls represents the 645 lost sailors, and the southern wall displays ghostly photographs of the ships and the names of the crew, while a bronze statue of a woman gazes desperately out to sea as if awaiting news. Visit at sunset or in the early morning and you can't help but be moved by this striking piece of art.

Another work of art is the **St Francis Xavier Cathedral**, with its Californian Mission-style twin towers, and a Brunelleschi-ish cupola like the one in Florence, and a mix of Romanesque, French Renaissance, Eastern Orthodox and even Islamic design elements inside. It was designed by the famous architect-priest Monsignor John Cyril Hawes in 1915, who also built other remarkable chapels and churches in places such as Mullewa, Morawa and Perenjori, as well as in the Bahamas. Completed in 1938, it's one of the most original

HMAS *Sydney* Memorial, Geraldton

and unusual cathedrals in Australia and worth a look even if you don't usually care for churches.

Finish off your Indian Ocean Drive watching the sun slip into the sea at **Separation Point Lookout** or beneath the red and white striped lighthouse at **Point Moore**. Paired with a glass of bubbles – or whatever your drink of choice is – it's the perfect finish to one of the country's ultimate coastal road trips. But if you don't want it to end, keep driving to the Coral Coast (see p.163).

SIDETRACK

Ellendale Pool is a beautiful deep freshwater pool on the Greenough River encircled by tall sandstone cliffs near the ghost town of Greenough, around 47km east of Geraldton via Ellendale Rd. It's a popular location for picnics during the day, with good swimming in summer.

SIDETRACK

WA is renowned for its stunning wildflower displays, when inland areas explode into a riot of colour between July and Nov and roadsides are lined with flowers of all descriptions, including smokebush, black kangaroo paw, cats paw, scarlet feather flower, scholtzia, thryptomine, cowslip orchids, woody pear and banksia and wreath flower. See black and yellow varieties of kangaroo paw along the 2km nature trail through **Badgingarra National Park**, under an hour's drive inland from Jurien Bay. **Lesueur National Park**, just a 20min drive from Jurien Bay, is another good spot for variety. A couple of hours further north, if it's been a good season, you'll see carpets of everlastings in **Coalseam Conservation Park**.

Kids' spot

Kids of all ages love splashing about in the waterpark in the middle of the **Geraldton Foreshore**, and parents love the fact that it's free. There's a variety of fountains, a fenced toddler area and a playground. For those that like their fun on two wheels there's a Pump and Jump track in Spalding Park, and a 11km mountain-bike track that runs along the Chapman River.

BEST BEDS

- **Pinnacles Edge Resort** If you plan on seeing the Pinnacles at sunset or sunrise – the best times for photography – this low-key resort with a pool and self-catering apartments in the centre of Cervantes makes a good base. pinnaclesedgeresort.com.au
- **Broadwater Marina Resort** These quite spacious apartments overlook the Indian Ocean and are just a few minutes' walk from the restaurants and shops in the Geraldton CBD. mariner.broadwaters.com.au

VANLIFE

There are no camping facilities near the Pinnacles at Nambung National Park: the best caravan park option is the **RAC Cervantes Holiday Park**, which has grassy sites with beach access. **Cliff Head**, 38km south of Dongara, has three bush camping areas with toilets overlooking the sea. There are commercial caravan parks in most of the larger towns along the coast, and several in Geraldton, and you can also camp beside **Ellendale Pool**, east of Geraldton.

Western Australia

Reefs, gorges, cliffs, desert dunes, turquoise waters and sandy beaches, wild dolphins and whale sharks – you'll find it all on this drive.

Coral Coast

HOW LONG?
Allow at least a week, one way, because there is plenty to see and do along this stretch of the coast.

WHEN TO GO
Exmouth is dry and warm almost all year – perfect beach weather. Almost all the region's scarce rain falls during the winter months. Whale shark season is between Apr and early July. Wildflowers bloom from July to Nov and winter is the best time to see humpback whales.

LOCAL SECRET
The Cape Range is the only elevated limestone range on the north-western coast and has plateaus of up to 314m high, forming the spine of the North West Cape Peninsula and is around 10 million years old. If you can tear yourself away from the beach the 3km Mandu Mandu Gorge walk is steep in sections but worth it for the views, or take a scenic drive along Shothole Canyon Rd to a picnic area at the end of the canyon in Cape Range National Park.

SNAPSHOT
Outback red-desert dunes meet astonishingly turquoise sea on this long stretch of coastline known as the coral coast, between Geraldton and Exmouth, an ancient landscape of reefs, gorges, cliffs and startling rock formations. Ningaloo Reef is every bit as magnificent as Queensland's Great Barrier Reef, with the added advantage that it is one of the few places in the world where you can actually walk straight from the beach to the coral, as well as being home (Apr–early July) to the amazing whale shark.

Drive rating
Easy. Sealed roads but some long distances and remote sections.

Acknowledgement of Country
This is the Traditional Land of the Nhanda, Malgana, Jinigudera, Maya, Payungu, Thalanyji, Baiyungu and Yinigurdira Peoples.

Distance planner
Geraldton to Exmouth, via Monkey Mia: around 1140km
- Geraldton to Monkey Mia, via Kalbarri: 554km
- Monkey Mia to Coral Bay: 581km
- Coral Bay to Exmouth: 152km

More information
- Kalbarri Visitor Centre, 70 Grey St, Kalbarri; (08) 9937 1104; kalbarri.org.au
- Shark Bay World Heritage Discovery and Visitor Centre, 53 Knight Tce, Denham; 1300 367 072; sharkbayvisit.com.au
- Ningaloo Visitor Centre, 2 Truscott Cres, Exmouth; (08) 9949 3070; visitningaloo.com.au
- australiascoralcoast.com

Opposite Swimming with whale sharks is the ultimate wildlife encounter on Ningaloo Reef

GERALDTON TO KALBARRI

This coastal road trip starts where the Indian Ocean Drive (*see* p.155) ends, but don't be in a hurry to hit the road because there's plenty of good stuff to see and do in and around Geraldton, like diving into the extraordinary true crime story of the *Batavia* shipwreck, and the disappearance of HMAS *Sydney* in 1941 at the **Museum of Geraldton** (*see* p.160).

It is around a 2hr drive to Kalbarri but spear off Highway 1 at Northampton and follow the coastal route via Gregory and **Hutt Lagoon**, a pink salt lake. The rosy hue is the caroteinoid-producing algae and is pinkest on cloudless days when the sun is high – between 10am and 2pm.

If you're arriving in **Kalbarri** at sunset you're in for a treat. Along the coast, wind and wave erosion have exposed layers of coastal cliffs that rise more than 100m above the ocean. From Red Bluff, on the southern outskirts of town, the extensive views encompass colourful coastal limestone and sandstone ledges, which are at their best in the late afternoon as they glow in the setting sun. There are scenic lookouts signposted off the main road at Mushroom Rock, Rainbow Valley, Pot Alley and Eagle Gorge and you can walk between them on the **Mushroom Rock Nature Trail**, a leisurely 2hr-return walk.

Head into the hills

Kalbarri National Park is split into two sections: the coastal section is on the southern outskirts of the town of Kalbarri; the river section is to the north-east of the township. If you have a good head for heights step out onto **Kalbarri Skywalk**, two glass-floored lookout platforms cantilevered 17m and 25m beyond the rim of a gorge above the Murchison River 100m below. Less vertigo-inducing but just as Insta-worthy is the 1km-return (allow 45min) walk to **Nature's Window**, around 26km north-east of the town. It's part of a wider area of the park known as The Loop, where a short cliff-top walking trail runs above a loop of the Murchison River, leading to several lookouts along the way. Nature's Window is a natural rock arch that perfectly frames the upstream view and has become a must-have photo for travellers to the area. About 11km down the road, another star attraction is the **Z-Bend**, a Z-shaped gorge cut deep into the rock by the river.

Left Pink Lake near Geraldton *Right* Kalbarri Skywalk

Coral Coast 165

Kalbarri, a fishing settlement at the mouth of the Murchison River, was only formally settled in the 1950s. It's an ideal place to spend a few days in the winter sun, splashing in the shallows on the town's river beach, but it's the gorges and cliffs of the national park that surrounds the town that are the main attraction.

KALBARRI TO MONKEY MIA

Heading north from Kalbarri it is about a 3hr drive to get to **Hamelin Pool Marine Nature Reserve**, one of the few places in the world where you will find marine stromatolites: ancient 'living fossils'. Much more interesting than they look, these rocky lumps, seemingly strewn untidily around the beach, are actually constructed by microscopic living organisms – up to 3 billion of them per square metre – using sediment and other organic material. Some stromatolites are up to 1.5m high. Because they grow very slowly, a 1m-high stromatolite could be about 2000 years old. They are able to survive here because Hamelin Pool's water is twice as saline as seawater.

A few kilometres down the road is the remarkable **Shell Beach**, which is made up of millions of tiny coquina shells and is one of only two such places in the world. It stretches for approximately 110km and is up to 10m deep. When the first European settlers arrived in the area building materials were scarce, but they soon found that compacted coquina shells could be made into blocks. Several buildings still standing in Denham are built from these blocks.

The most westerly town in Australia, **Denham** began life as a pearling port (locals tell stories of streets kerbed with pearl shell, though that could be an urban myth), but is now better known for its prawn and crayfish industry. If you want to visit the most westerly point on the mainland head to Steep Point, 184km off the highway via Useless Loop Rd – to get there you'll need a 4WD.

You can find out about the Traditional Owners' enduring connections to the land, early exploration of the area, and the World Heritage status of the bay at the **Shark Bay World Heritage Discovery Centre** in Denham. It's a fascinating museum, with interactive displays and a replica of Hartog's Plate: the original is in the Rijksmuseum in the Netherlands.

Around 400 bottlenose dolphins live in the waters of **Shark Bay** near **Monkey Mia**, and most mornings several dolphins drift into the shallows to be hand-fed by scores of eager tourists, as they have been since 1964, when a woman from one of the nearby fishing camps befriended the dolphins and began regularly feeding them. It is one of the few places in Australia where dolphins visit daily, not seasonally, and unlike most dolphin encounters, costs nothing.

But the dolphins are not the only attraction of this World Heritage–listed marine park. Marine turtles are frequently seen in the bay and it is home to around 10,000 dugongs (around 10 per cent of the world's dugong population), who feed on Shark Bay's massive meadows of seagrass. **RAC Monkey Mia Dolphin Resort** (*see* p.169) runs afternoon sailing cruises to see them, as well as a range of other sailing trips, including sunset sails.

The nearby **Francois Peron National Park**, on the Traditional Land of the Malgana People, is also worth exploring. Here red pindan dunes spill into the sea, and the colours are extraordinary. It's also a great place to see sharks, rays, turtles, whales, dolphins, birds and other wildlife. Tracks are 4WD only, but day tours are available from Monkey Mia with **Wildsights** (monkeymiawildsights.com.au) or **Wula Gura Nyinda** (wulagura.com.au).

Opposite Feeding the dolphins at Monkey Mia
Left Nature's Window, Kalbarri National Park

SIDETRACK

Denham is opposite **Dirk Hartog Island/Wirruwana**, the first recorded place that Europeans visited on the Australian mainland. Dutch Skipper Dirk Hartog arrived on the *Eendracht* on 25 October 1616, announcing his arrival by nailing an inscribed pewter plate to a wooden post at the site now known as Cape Inscription. The island is accessible by 4WD barge from Steep Point and just 20 vehicles are allowed on the 80km-long island at any one time. All tracks on the island are sandy and 4WD only, but tours and boat transfers are available from Denham (*see* dirkhartogisland.com.au or sharkbaydive.com.au).

Kids' spot

You don't need to be able to swim to get up close to the marine life at the family-run **Ocean Park Aquarium**, 8km south of Denham in Shark Bay, and you don't even need to have any scuba diving experience to dive - cage free - with the sharks in the Aquarium Shark Dive Experience, although you will need to be over 14. Younger kids, and those of any age that don't fancy getting overly familiar with an apex predator can watch the sharks being fed, meet rescued sea turtles, and learn about the secret lives of clownfish and other creatures that live under the sea on a tour with the resident marine biologist. The on-site restaurant is also very good and has a cracker view.

MONKEY MIA TO EXMOUTH

It's a long haul from Monkey Mia to Exmouth, around 700km, so break the journey at **Carnarvon** with its interesting heritage buildings and space history.

The **Carnarvon Heritage Precinct** is a collection of historic buildings and museums near the One Mile Jetty (no prizes for guessing how long it is). Built in 1897, the wooden jetty was a major tourist attraction and popular fishing spot until it was damaged by cyclones and wild storms and closed in 2017. It's currently being rebuilt, but the new **One Mile Jetty Centre** has lots of displays about the jetty's history, as well as exhibits telling the story of the famous World War II battle between HMAS *Sydney* and the German warship *Kormoran* which took place off the coast nearby in 1941. After decades of searching, the two wrecks were finally discovered off Dirk Hartog Island/Wirruwana in 2008.

Australia's first live satellite television broadcast was transmitted from Carnarvon in 1966. The massive **OTC (Overseas Telecommunications Commission) dish** on the edge of town was Australia's first Earth station for satellite tracking and communications, and one of just eight in the world.

Carnarvon is also the fruit bowl of WA, and its main crop is bananas – more than half of WA's bananas are grown in the area and many of the local growers sell fruit and vegetables direct from their farms and offer plantation tours.

In **Coral Bay**, 238km further north, you can walk straight from the beach to the reef, which is great for novice snorkellers (but be aware of boats in the water). You can also take a glass-bottom boat tour over the coral.

Good for a rainy day

The **Carnarvon Space and Technology Museum** at the OTC Satellite Earth Station was officially opened by astronaut Buzz Aldrin (the second person to set foot on the moon) in 2012. There's lots of interactive exhibits, spacecraft equipment, displays that tell the story of Carnarvon's role in the space race, historic satellite broadcast footage and a full-size replica of the *Gemini* capsule.

Ningaloo Reef is one of the few places in the world where whale sharks routinely gather in large numbers close to the coast, coming here each year between Apr and early July to feed on abundant plankton. Despite their name, these massive but harmless fish are truly the gentle giants of the deep; they can measure up to 18m in length, with an adult whale shark weighing in at more than 15 tonnes and having a mouth more than 1m wide.

Ningaloo tours operate from both Coral Bay and Exmouth, and all employ spotter planes to help locate the huge fish. Because whale sharks swim near the surface, you don't have to scuba dive to see them, just snorkel. But you do have to be pretty fit. Despite their massive bulk, whale sharks are fast swimmers and a tour involves lots of clambering in and out of the boat and sprint-like swims to keep up with mighty fish. It's worth it, though: as you swim above or beside them, all else disappears and, even though there are a dozen or so other swimmers in the water with you, it feels like it's just you and the whale shark. Forget all those other '100 things to do before you die' lists. This is a special, awe-inspiring experience that everybody really should try and do at least once in their lives.

Exmouth began life as a pearling outpost before finally being settled in 1899, although it was not until the establishment of an American naval base in 1963 that the town really began to develop. These days, tourism is the town's main business.

If you get tired of the submarine wonderland, take a drive out to **Vlamingh Head Lighthouse** on the point north of Exmouth. The restored lighthouse was built in 1912 from local stone and is Australia's only kerosene burning lighthouse; it's open for tours. Just south of town is **Cape Range National Park** on the Traditional Land of the Baiyungu, Thalanyji and Yinigurdira Peoples. The Cape Range is the only elevated limestone range on the north-western coast of WA. The weathered limestone range has plateaus of up to 314m high, and forms the spine of the peninsula that stretches up towards North West Cape. It is around ten million years old, and lies just half an hour south of Exmouth. Take a scenic drive along **Shothole Canyon Rd** (not suitable for caravans) to a picnic area at the end of the canyon.

Chances are, however, you won't be able to tear yourself away from the beaches. And the good news is that this part of the coast is pretty much dry and warm almost all year – perfect swimming weather. What are you waiting for?

Opposite 4WD adventures on Dirk Hartog Island

BEST BEDS

- **Dirk Hartog Island Eco Lodge** Enjoy beautiful ocean views from your room in the historic shearers quarters at this family-run lodge. The owners, who used to farm sheep on the island, are the third generation to live there, and they also run 4WD and fishing tours in the surrounding national park. The family-style meals around the fire-pit are a highlight. dirkhartogisland.com
- **Kalbarri Palm Resort** The resort has comfortable motel-style rooms just a couple of blocks back from the river mouth and beach. palmresort.com.au
- **RAC Monkey Mia Dolphin Resort** All overnight visitors to Monkey Mia must stay here. Fortunately the resort has a range of accommodation from beachfront villas to family studio to backpacker dorms, powered caravan and tent sites, some also beachfront. The facilities include a swimming pool, hot tub and tennis court, internet cafe, barbecues, mini-mart and laundry. parksandresorts.rac.com.au/monkey-mia
- **Sal Salis Ningaloo Reef** This is one of the coast's top 'glamping' spots, where you can enjoy the outdoors in style surrounded by Cape Range National Park. The main camp building where you eat and drink has great views across the dunes to the sea beyond, and each of the five 'tents' has a supremely comfortable bed, a ceiling fan, solar-powered lights and an ensuite bathroom. salsalis.com.au
- **Mantarays Ningaloo Beach Resort** The resort is right on the beach in Exmouth's new marina development. Rooms range from one-bedroom studios to three-bedroom beachfront bungalows. mantaraysningalooresort.com.au

VANLIFE

There are no camping facilities within Kalbarri National Park, but a favourite with caravanners is pet-friendly **Murchison River Caravan Park**, which has shady sites opposite the beach in the heart of Kalbarri township. It's very popular during school holidays however, so you'll need to book. There are 11 beachside bush camping spots in **Cape Range National Park** near Exmouth, and they all get busy during winter so you'll need to book well ahead. There are powered sites at **RAC Monkey Mia Dolphin Resort** (see above). On **Dirk Hartog Island/Wirruwana**, you can camp overlooking the sea near the historic homestead or at one of the national park campgrounds. But elsewhere, aside from roadside rest areas, you'll be restricted to caravan parks, which you'll find in almost every town along this route: there are several good beachside ones in Coral Bay.

170

Take the road less travelled and you'll find incredible rock art and outback scenery on a monumental scale in one of Australia's least-visited regions.

Pilbara Coast

HOW LONG?
Everything is supersized in the Pilbara, including vast distances between towns and communities. Some of the highlights of this drive are inland from the coast, so allow at least a week for this trip.

WHEN TO GO
You really don't want to be in the Pilbara during summer. Marble Bar claims to hold the title of Australia's hottest town – for 161 consecutive days in 1924 the temperature never dropped below 100°F (37.8°C), a record that still stands. Summer daytime temperatures hovering close to 50°C are not unusual, made even hotter by the rocky landscape which absorbs and holds heat like an oven. Winter, on the other hand, is delightful with warm days and cold nights.

NEED TO KNOW
Until fairly recently sightings of saltwater crocodiles in the coastal waterways of the Pilbara were unusual, but several have been spotted in the past few years. Err on the side of caution, check with local authorities, and unless you know it's safe, stay out of the water.

SNAPSHOT
If you've never been to the Pilbara, prepare to be impressed. Often forgotten in the rush to get to or from the Kimberley, it's one of Australia's most underrated landscapes: grander, more expansive, more mountainous and much more magnificent than most people ever imagine. It really is the wild west.

Drive rating
Easy. Sealed roads with optional 4WD sections.

Acknowledgement of Country
This is the Traditional Land of the Nhuwala, Martuthunira, Ngarluma, Yaburarra, Kariyarra, Ngarla, Nyamal, Nyangumarda, Karajarri and Yawuru Peoples.

Distance planner
Onslow to Broome, without inland detours: around 1126km
- Onslow to Port Hedland: 522km
- Port Hedland to Broome: 604km

More information
- Karratha Tourism & Visitor Centre, De Witt Rd (formerly Karratha Rd), Karratha; (08) 9186 8055; karrathaiscalling.com.au
- Port Hedland Visitor Centre, 13 Wedge St, Port Hedland; (08) 9173 1711; visitporthedland.com.au
- destinationpilbara.com.au
- australiasnorthwest.com

ONSLOW TO PORT HEDLAND

This coastal road trip connects two of WA's most popular destinations, the Coral Coast south of Exmouth (see p.163) and the Kimberley (see p.179), but it – rather inexplicably to my mind – doesn't seem to register as highly on the road-tripping radar, aside from the lucky few doing The Big Lap on Highway 1. It's worth more than just a couple of overnight transit stops though, because this is a truly marvellous place, with the added bonus of having a lot less travellers around, so when you're there you almost feel like you've made your own discovery of somewhere special that no one else knows about – which is pretty priceless when it comes to travel experiences.

Part of the Highway 1 network that circumnavigates the country, the North West Coastal Hwy links Geraldton to Port Hedland. But for this road trip we're going to start in Onslow, 77km west of the whistlestop of Cane (not much more than a dot on the highway, really), around a 4.5hr drive north of Exmouth. One of the Pilbara's most historic towns, it was established in 1885, 18km away, at the mouth of the Ashburton River, as a port for the booming wool, gold and pearl trade, until repeated cyclones forced its abandonment in the mid 1920s and a new Onslow was built where you find it today. You can still see some interesting ruins of the old town, including the court house, hospital, gaol and cemetery, at the end of Old Onslow Rd.

Modern-day **Onslow** is one of the few places where you can see both sunrise and sunset from the beach: follow the signs to either **Sunrise Beach**, or **Sunset Beach**, depending on the time of day. If you're here when there's a full moon, you'll be treated to the 'Staircase to the Moon', a natural phenomenon seen only in northern WA when the reflections of the rising moon over the mudflats creates the illusion of an illuminated staircase. In Broome it attracts thousands of revellers (see p.182), but here in Onslow you'll probably share the experience with less than a handful of others.

Head north on Highway 1. **Peedamulla** is a working cattle station, first established in the 1880s, and now part of the Camping with Custodians program, where visitors are welcomed to camp on Aboriginal land, in this case, the Country of the Jundaru community. If you're here in mid July, you may be lucky enough to see the annual cattle muster. There's also a range of self-guided 4WD tracks you can follow. See the station's website (peedamulla.com.au) for more details and to book.

It's a long haul between towns in the Pilbara, and in many cases the most popular spots to stop and stay for a while aren't even towns. **Gnoorea Point**, also known as 40 Mile Beach, is a rustic camping area around 40min south of Karratha. Popular with grey nomads – and other lucky travellers with lots of time on their hands – who tend to find a spot and stay for the season, there is now a 28-day limit. There's not much shade, but it's ideal for those that like fishing and boating, and almost feels like a pop-up village in the middle of the dry season, albeit one with absolutely no facilities.

Good for a rainy day

Like Karratha, the nearby port of **Dampier** was also built in the late 1960s, and is prettier than Karratha, thanks to an attractive park-flanked foreshore, but it is still very much a working port. Bad weather days are very rare during the dry season, but the 3hr port tours that take you behind the scenes of the Rio Tinto mining operations are a good way to escape the elements and offer a close-up view of the iron ore ship-loading facilities and the Dampier salt mine: book at the Karratha Visitor Centre.

Kids' spot

Aside from the mining, Dampier's other claim to fame is Red Dog - the famous kelpie whose extensive travels across the Pilbara formed the basis of the 2011 hit film of the same name. There's a memorial to the much-loved canine on the way into town and a **Roaming with Red Dog trail** you can follow that leads to some of Red Dog's favourite spots around town; each site has a 'quest' or puzzle for kids (and adults) to solve.

Opposite Eighty Mile Beach between Port Hedland and Broome *Top* Exploring Karijini National Park *Bottom* Great Egret at De Grey River

Pilbara Coast

Cool off with a freshwater dip in **Miaree Pool**, a natural swimming hole on the Nullagine River, before tackling the last 30km to Karratha. Built in the late 1960s to service the nearby iron, petroleum and gas ventures, **Karratha** makes a good base to restock and rest, but most of the attractions are outside of the township.

Top of the list is one of the world's largest rock-art collections. On first glance **Ngajarli (Deep Gorge)** in **Murujuga National Park** on the Burrup Peninsula on Ngarda-Ngarli land (the collective term for the five Traditional Owner groups – the Ngarluma, Yindjibarndi, Yaburara, Mardudhunera and Wong-Goo-Tt-Oo Peoples) between Karratha and Dampier, may not be immediately apparent to those who aren't Traditional Owners. Look a little closer though, and you'll find almost every rock has a millennia-old petroglyph covering one face or another. It's estimated that there are more than one million engravings here (the highest concentration in the world apparently, and at the time of going to print was in the process of being considered for World Heritage listing), and once your eye becomes attuned to it, it is overwhelming. Head to **Hearson's Cove** (signposted off Burrup Rd) and keep an eye out for the gravel carpark a few hundred metres before the beach on the right. Follow the rocky walking track into the gorge. It will take a few minutes for your eyes to pick out the carvings – some of which are thought to be 20,000 years old – but once you've spotted the first few you soon see thousands and they feature everything from emus and boomerangs to thylacines (Tasmanian tigers), fish, humans and mythical beasts. Unfortunately there's not much interpretive signage, so joining a cultural tour with a Traditional Owner is a good idea if you want to know more: **Murujuga Aboriginal Corporation** (experiencemurujuga.com) or **Ngurrangga Tours** (ngurrangga.com.au).

Another remote beach that transforms into a pop-up van and trailer village during the dry season, **Cleaverville** between Karratha and Wickham is a good spot for boating (there is a natural boat ramp, but keep an eye on the tides, which can rise and fall by 5m) and fishing. **Point Samson**, home base for a commercial fishing fleet, is another good spot to cast a line; good catches include barramundi, mangrove jack and threadfin salmon.

If you're doing this road trip in late July or early Aug you might be surprised at what you find in the ghost town of **Cossack**. It's home to the annual Cossack Art Awards – the richest acquisitive art award in regional Australia – and attracts hundreds of entries competing for more than $80,000 in prize money, and thousands of people with a line-up of workshops and events. And if you like what you see, it's all for sale.

SIDETRACK

Millstream-Chichester National Park is a true oasis in the middle of a dry, spinifex-studded (but utterly magnificent) landscape and the last thing most people expect to find in the Pilbara; the lily-covered pools of Millstream encircled by Millstream Palms (*Livistona alfredii*), a relic of more tropical times, are so lush compared to the surrounding barren flat-topped hills and spreading plains. This little gem of a park about an hour's drive inland from Karratha has some fabulous wild swimming pools, like **Deep Reach Pool (Nhanggangunha)** on the Fortescue River, where wooden platforms provide easy access into the ink-black deep water. **Millstream Homestead**, built in 1920, was a pub between 1975 and 1986 - it's now home to a couple of interesting historic displays. There are half a dozen great walks in the park and a number of scenic drives that lead to spectacular lookouts, particularly in the northern section where the road winds through the **Chichester Range**, a line of weathered flat-topped mountains that frame the course of an ancient river, hiding deep gorges with permanent waterholes like **Python Pool**. You don't need to be told this is sacred country for the Yindjibarndi and Ngarluma Peoples - you can feel the power radiating from the landscape all around you.

Opposite top Pyramid Hill at Millstream-Chichester National Park
Opposite bottom Burrup Peninsula, Murujuga National Park

Pilbara Coast   175

PORT HEDLAND TO BROOME

Port Hedland's port is even bigger than Dampier's (*see p.173*): it handles more than 452 million tonnes of cargo – mostly iron ore, lithium and salt – each year, making it the world's largest bulk export port. A good place to watch the port in action is **Marapikurrinya Park**, and there's a **Port Interpretive Walk** along the Esplanade. You can also climb aboard the **Seafarers launch boat** for a harbour tour as they deliver supplies to crews onboard ships around the port: book at the visitor's centre in Port Hedland. And to snap a unique sunset photo, head out to **Redbank Bridge** to see the setting sun light up the salt mounds – it's guaranteed to get a few comments on your social media feeds.

Whoever did the naming – or at the very least the measuring – of **Eighty Mile Beach** obviously wasn't very good at counting, because Eighty Mile Beach is actually more like 137 miles – or in metric terms, 220km. It's the longest uninterrupted beach in WA and attracts thousands of migratory birds each summer. Turtles nest in the sand, dugongs graze the sea meadows and the waters teem with fish, much to the delight of anglers, and it's popular with beachcombers, who often find beautiful shells. Cable Beach, a couple of hours up the road in Broome, might get all the attention, but if you ask me, at ten times the size, this beach is even more impressive. Like everything else in the Pilbara, it's much bigger, bolder and brighter than you expect.

Head into the hills

It's a bit of a long drive - almost 350km one-way from Port Hedland - but if you've come all this way you'd be mad not to go a little further and tick Karijini off your bucket list. **Karijini National Park** is one of the Pilbara's must-see spots and on the Traditional Land of the Banyjima, Innawonga and Kurrama Peoples. There are half a dozen gorges here, and all of them are gorge-ous (sorry, couldn't resist!). But really, all bad puns aside, it is an amazing place. Plan to spend at least four days here, and even then you'll only scratch the surface. To see the best of the gorges you need to get down into them (and ultimately climb back up again), so you need good knees and a fair level of agility and fitness - some walks involve rock hopping and inching along rock ledges. The best time to visit is winter, when daytime temperatures are perfect for hiking but nights are freezing. Icy temperatures don't seem to deter the hardy swimmers at **Fortescue Falls** in **Dales Gorge**, one of the park's most popular spots, but note that hypothermia is an issue at some of the park's swimming spots during the cooler months. Staying dry can be tricky in some gorges, like the wonderful **Kalamina Gorge** where rock hopping back and forth across the river is the order of the day. And in places like **Weano Gorge**, where if you go all the way to the end of the gorge you'll be wading through water, you just have to accept you're going to get wet feet! Don't let that deter you though, these gorges are worth every bit of the effort. Check ahead at the visitor centre for swimming hole and walking track conditions and tips on staying safe in the park, as well as cultural information; note that the visitor centre is closed over summer.

BEST BEDS

- **Onslow Beach Resort** overlooks Beadon Bay, roughly halfway between Exmouth and Karratha, and has a waterfront restaurant, and a swimming pool. onslowbeachresort.com.au
- **Hedland Hotel** Ask for a room with a view when you book into this oceanfront hotel overlooking Cemetery Beach and you may be lucky enough to spy a nesting turtle or two. Facilities include a bar, bistro and swimming pool. hedlandhotel.com.au
- **Karijini Eco Retreat** Glamp it up at Karijini Eco Retreat, run by the Gumala Aboriginal Corporation - the hard-floored safari tents have a king-sized bed, ensuite with hot shower and private deck, perfect sunset drinks after a long day's walk or stargazing at night. There's also a restaurant on site. karijiniecoretreat.com.au

VANLIFE

The area known as **Three Mile** is on the Ashburton River 36km south of Onslow and has a long stretch of shady camping areas right on the riverbank. Like all bush camping areas, there are no facilities, but the view makes up for it. It's pet friendly and okay for 2WD: ask for directions at the visitor centre. **Gnoorea Point** is a handy spot to camp, a 40min drive south of Karratha (*see* p.173). There are two campgrounds in **Millstream-Chichester National Park**, both near the homestead. **Miliyana** has some good shade and a camp kitchen and is popular with caravanners and those with big rigs and generators. **Stargazers** has smaller individual sites, is generator-free and, as the name implies, perfect for stargazing. There are two campgrounds in **Karijini**: **Dales** and the privately-run **Karijini Eco Retreat** (*see* above). Dales, which has toilets but no showers, is much closer to most of the gorges. Station stays are a great option in the Pilbara, and **Pardoo Station**, a working cattle station, is at the southern end of 80 Mile Beach, between Port Hedland and Broome, with fishing, birdwatching and self-guided 4WD tours: pardoostation.com.au. You can also camp at **Cape Keraudren** and **Eighty Mile Beach Caravan Park**, which is on the beach, almost exactly halfway between Port Hedland and Broome, although it's very popular so book well ahead: summerstar.com.au.

Opposite Port Hedland

Western Australia

Remote, wild and ridiculously scenic, the Dampier Peninsula north of Broome is one of Australia's most undeveloped coastal wonderlands.

Kimberley Coast

HOW LONG?

It's only 220km from Broome to the northern tip of the Dampier Peninsula, but this is a road trip worth doing slowly because it's all about getting to know the country, people and culture in the beachside communities along the way. Trust me, no matter how long you spend here, you'll want to stay longer: allow at least a week.

WHEN TO GO

Best time to travel is May through to Oct – caravan parks can be very busy during winter school holidays. Some attractions are closed during the wet season between Nov and April.

NEED TO KNOW

Pick up everything you need in Broome, including alcohol, before exploring the Dampier Peninsula. Fuel is available at Beagle Bay, Djarindjin Roadhouse and Ardyaloon (closed on weekends) and both communities have small general stores if you run out of basics – you'll need to buy a permit at the community office to enter Ardyaloon.

Although the Kimberley floods every year during the wet season, in Jan 2023 the Kimberley was inundated by unusually high water levels. Although the worst of the flooding was several hundred kilometres inland, check road conditions and whether attractions are open before travelling to this region – national park authorities are a good resource, as are local visitor information centres.

SNAPSHOT

Most people have heard of the Dampier Peninsula, thanks to the fame of the Horizontal Falls, which are the most popular daytrip from Broome, and the successful campaign to save James Price Point – one of the world's largest humpback whale nurseries – from a gas plant (*see* p.183), but nothing prepares you for the dazzling colours of the landscape: blood red pindan soil and white sandy beaches washed by turquoise seas. It's a camper's paradise where tracks lead to free beachside camping spots and First Nations communities have opened up their waterfront land to visitors happy to camp in rustic surrounds. The Dampier is worth the time and bumpy roads it takes to get there.

Drive rating
Moderate. The main road on the Dampier Peninsula - the Cape Leveque Rd - is now a sealed all-weather road, but 4WD is still required to access many locations along the route which remain unsealed.

Acknowledgement of Country
This is the Traditional Land of the Yawuru, Jukun, Bardi, Nyunyul, Nimanburr and Jabirr Jabirr/Ngumbarl Peoples.

Distance planner
Broome to Ardyaloon: around 220km
- Broome to Beagle Bay: 129km
- Beagle Bay to Ardyaloon: 99km

More information
- Broome Visitor Centre, 1 Hamersley St, Broome; (08) 9195 2200; visitbroome.com.au
- australiasnorthwest.com

Opposite Iconic tin architecture in Broome

BROOME TO BEAGLE BAY

The Kimberley Coast is a wild and pristine place, beautiful thanks largely to its inaccessibility: roads are few and far between in the remote north-west, and much of the coastline is only accessible by sea or air, apart from the Dampier Peninsula, a special place where First Nations' culture and truly beautiful beaches combine to make it a unique place. And the good news is that, despite its remoteness, it's actually quite easy to get to if you fly into Broome and hire a car for a week or two.

But before you go, you'll want to spend a few days in **Broome**, known by the Traditional Owners as Rubibi, on Yawuru Country, which covers both the land and the waters. By day, the 23km expanse of **Cable Beach** – named after the telegraph cable laid between Broome and Java in 1889 – is quite lovely, but come sunset there is no better place to be, whether driving your 4WD on to the sand for a picnic dinner, sipping a cocktail at a beachside bar or swaying precariously on the back of a camel. But there's much more to this old pearling town on the seaward side of the Kimberley frontier.

Strung out along the shoreline of Roebuck Bay, the township of Broome began life as a pearling outpost in the 1880s and the frontier port boomed as the price of mother-of-pearl shell escalated. The lustre of the pearl shell lured thousands of immigrants to the town, and the population became a cosmopolitan mix of First Nations People, Malays, Chinese, Japanese, Filipinos and Europeans. Take a wander through the town centre and you'll see lots of evidence of the town's history, legacies of the industry's halcyon days before plastic made pearl shell buttons redundant. The unique corrugated-iron architecture, bustling **Chinatown** that was once full of gaming houses, pubs, eating houses and brothels, the **Japanese cemetery** – the largest in Australia – the restored pearl luggers and the remains of flying boats bombed during a Japanese air raid in 1942 that can be seen in Roebuck Bay during low tide, all testify to the town's tumultuous past. The industry may have changed, but it's still a pearl town. Take a guided tour of the museum and taste pearl meat at **Pearl Luggers**, visit a working pearl farm at **Willie Creek Pearls**, cruise into the sunset on a restored pearling lugger and resist the temptation to bend the credit card at a number of pearl jewellery showrooms in the town centre.

Watching 'stars under the stars' is the perfect way to enjoy Broome's balmy dry-season climate. **Sun Pictures**, in the middle of the main street, claims it is the world's oldest 'picture garden' – it's been showing films in its alfresco theatre since 1916. According to local legend, before the levee bank was built in 1974, moviegoers would lift their feet as the tide came in and some old timers will even try to convince you that you could catch a fish while watching the flicks.

Gantheaume Point, Broome

Kimberley Coast 181

If you are you are lucky enough to be on Broome's **Town Beach** during a full moon in the dry season you'll have a ringside seat at one of the Kimberley's most celebrated shows. The spectacular **'Staircase to the Moon'** is a natural phenomenon caused by the rising of a full moon reflecting off the tidal mud flats of Roebuck Bay. It's visible only for three nights each month between Mar and Oct, but well worth planning a trip around. As the huge blood-red sun slowly drops into the ocean, crowds of locals and tourists make their way to Town Beach. Buskers, fire dancers and local bands provide free entertainment, stalls offer weird and wonderful clothes, crafts, souvenirs and snacks and the beach begins to resemble a raucous but cheerful street party until suddenly, as the sky darkens and the moon begins to creep above the horizon, the crowd moves as one to the point for the best vantage spot – and silence descends. As the moon rises, its tangerine reflection builds a slow but steady staircase to heaven as the crowd cheers. The show only lasts a few minutes, but it's one of those unforgettable, uniquely Australian celebrations that lingers in the imagination much longer.

Kids' spot

Yes, it's touristy but is also one of the most memorable things you'll do in Broome, and your kids will love it as much as you do. Almost every visitor to Broome takes a **sunset camel ride along Cable Beach**, but because it is so popular it can feel a bit like a circus act with three different companies walking their camel trains along the beach and most of the visitor population there taking photos. Pre-sunset rides are a bit cheaper and shorter, so may be best for little kids, or go early in the morning and you (and your camels) will have the beach to yourself. Rides last around an hour.

Good for a rainy day

It's not what you'd expect to find in an outback frontier town, but Broome is home to what is reputed to be the largest quartz crystal Buddha in the world, a 3.5m-high pink Buddha hand-carved from Philippines crystal. You'll find it in the **Buddha Sanctuary** across the road from The Cable Beach Club. The Sanctuary - a gift to the town from the owners of the resort - is free if you just want to go and chill out or meditate and has daily yoga and tai chi classes.

Just south of Broome is **Gantheaume Point,** home to 130-million-year-old dinosaur footprints which can be seen at very low tides. If you miss the tides, it's still worth going just to see the red sandstone cliffs that meet the blue-green sea. Nearby, the **Broome Fishing Club** overlooking the jetty does great-value meals with a knockout water view. Don't leave town without sampling some mango beer (or one of the other eight locally brewed ales – the alcoholic ginger beer is very refreshing but dangerously drinkable) at **Matso's Brewery,** where bar snacks, burgers, steaks and fish and chips are served on the verandah of a historic former bank – and later trading store – built in 1910, or in the beer garden overlooking Roebuck Bay.

The Cape Leveque Rd that runs north from Broome through the middle of the Dampier Peninsula was once infamous for its corrugations, patches of deep bulldust and puddles that seemed deep enough for dolphins to frolic in after rain. It was sealed in late 2020, so it's a much easier trip these days, but the best bits are still at the end of often rough dirt roads and tracks. Because it's just the one main road – there are no roads on the eastern side of the peninsula to Derby or Hwy 1 – an added bonus is that you get to see it all again on the way back to Broome.

Head into the hills

Around a 2hr drive inland from Broome on a sealed road, **Derby**, on King Sound, is a much less touristy version of Broome - albeit without the white sandy beaches and pearl shops - and has a more authentic frontier feel about it. Wander along the impressive boab-lined streets, explore the historic buildings and check out the unusual horseshoe-shaped jetty, built to cope with the huge tidal ranges of up to 12m - the highest in the Southern Hemisphere. Join the locals fishing along the length or sit back and watch the sunset. Don't miss **Mowanjum Aboriginal Art & Culture Centre**, one of the best First Nations' culture centres in the Kimberley, where you'll find not only a fantastic collection of community-made art, but also a fascinating museum that will give you one of the best insights in to Wandjina Wunggurr history and traditions.

Derby is also a good base for scenic flights over the magnificent **Buccaneer Archipelago**, a beautiful area consisting of some 800 to 1000 rocky islands surrounded by turquoise water, part of a drowned coastline. A highlight is flying over the famous **Horizontal Waterfall** in Talbot Bay, caused by the differential created when the tide flows between narrow island gaps. Accessible only by boat or plane, the falls are a very popular and heavily promoted daytrip from Broome, on the bucket-list of many travellers. However, think twice before you sign up for a zodiac or speed boat ride through the logic-defying rapids. The Traditional Owners, the Dambimangari People, call the Horizontal Falls Garaangaddim and request that visitors only negotiate the falls by boat during a neap tide (calm water time) as they believe the rushing tide is the Woongudd creator snake.

Cable Beach, Broome

Kimberley Coast

SIDETRACK

Quondong Point is a picturesque free camp overlooking a curve of deserted white sand just off the Manari Rd, not far from the start of the Cape Leveque Rd, around 50km north of Broome. It's a popular place to camp: there are half a dozen free campsites overlooking the water but there are no facilities so you'll need to be self-sufficient. Some people do swim here, but there are saltwater crocodiles in the area. Nearby is **James Price Point**. A sacred place known as Walmadany to the Jabirr Jabirr and Goolarabooloo People, it's where Marella, a creator being, left his footprints here. This beautiful headland with its striking red cliffs and cyan seas was set to be transformed into a LNG gas terminal, but was saved thanks to a huge community campaign that attracted rock stars and conservation groups. It's also home to one of the largest collections of dinosaur tracks in the world - 21 different types of dinosaur tracks on a 25km-long stretch - including the world's largest single print, a whopping 1.7m long.

The tiny community of **Beagle Bay** – on Nyul-Nyul Country 180km north of Broome – is home to one of the most remote churches in the country. It was established in the 1890s by Trappist monks as a mission for First Nations children from across the north-west who had been stolen from their families, as per the government policy at the time. Beagle Bay is now a self-governing community, so you'll need to get an entry permit from the community centre when you arrive in the township. And while from the outside the white-washed, bell-towered, tin-roofed bush church doesn't look all that impressive, step inside and you'll be dazzled by a lustrous interior of silvery pearls and shells. Built in the last days of the 19th century by French monks out of sheets of tin, the original **Sacred Heart Church** was blown away by a cyclone. The community scoured the beaches for shells and handmade more than 60,000 bricks from white clay, rebuilding the church in 1918 using shell-lime to hold it all together. Once done, they decorated the ceiling with shells to represent stars, the walls with tribal symbols made from pearl and plaster frescos of fish inlaid with gleaming shells. The masterpiece is a luminous grand altar made entirely from mother-of-pearl that glows silver in the sunlight that streams through the shell-framed windows overlooking the sea. There's nothing quite like it anywhere else in the country.

BEAGLE BAY TO CAPE LEVEQUE

One of several small family-based First Nations communities on the peninsula that have opened up their land for camping, **Middle Lagoon** is a beautiful spot on a grassy headland between two glorious beaches that are, according to the Traditional Owners, safe for swimming (*see* Best beds section).

Lombadina is another community that welcomes travellers. Like at Beagle Bay, you'll need to call into the community office on arrival to buy a day pass before visiting the beach or walking around the village, and you'll also need to plan ahead because the community is closed to visitors on weekends. Tours range from guided culture and history community tours to mud crabbing adventures, whale watching, bush tucker, fishing, kayaking and ancient footprint tours which include swimming opportunities.

If you've ever wondered what pearl meat tastes like, call into **Cygnet Bay Pearl Farm**. Home to the world's largest South Sea pearl, there are regular tours of the pearl farm which has been run by the same family since 1946, as well as pearl-grading classes and sessions on the traditional Bardi Jawi art of riji shell carving and a hard-to-resist range of gorgeous pearl jewellery for sale, but another reason to come here is the restaurant. The Pearl Meat Tasting Plate has pearl meat prepared half a dozen ways, or try some pearl meat and seafood pasta, but there are also bistro classics such as local barramundi, burgers, chicken and squid. There's even a gin made with pearl oyster botanicals, distilled with juniper berries, Burdekin plum, lemon myrtle, mint and oyster mantle. The restaurant is open Apr to Nov, and you can also stay at the farm (*see* Best beds section).

Ardyaloon (One Arm Point) is the northernmost community on the Dampier Peninsula. You'll need a community day pass, available from the community office, which includes access to the beaches as well as a guided tour of the trochus shell hatchery, set up in 1988 to ensure the sustainability of the sought-after sea snails with conical shells shaped like a pearly witch's hat; they have been harvested by the community here since the early 1900s. You'll also learn about Bardi Jawi culture, meet the resident sea turtle and see tidal whirlpools produced by one of the highest tides in the world.

The picture-perfect beaches may be the Dampier Peninsula's drawcard, but it's the cultural connections you'll make in the communities along the way that makes this place so memorable.

BEST BEDS

- **Cable Beach Club Resort & Spa** The only resort in Broome located on Cable Beach, this is still the best place in town to stay - and watch the sun go down with a cocktail in hand. cablebeachclub.com
- **Nature's Hideaway at Middle Lagoon** You can camp overlooking the beach or opt for one of the rustic cabins: linen is provided but the bathrooms are shared with the campers and the walls are made of insect screens, but what they lack in luxury they make up for with stunning water views. middlelagoon.com.au
- **Cygnet Bay Pearl Farm** This working pearl farm has a mix of accommodation options, from simple cabins to very comfortable glamping and the opulent Master Pearlers Private Retreat. There's a restaurant and swimming pool, as well as a host of tours. cygnetbaypearlfarm.com.au

VANLIFE

There are half a dozen caravan parks in Broome, and during the middle of the holiday season, in July, they can all be full to capacity. The **Broome Caravan Park** has a large overflow section - a big grassy paddock at the back of the park - but you can almost always find a spot there, even if you haven't booked ahead. It has a fabulous resort-style pool with a 25m lap pool and bathroom and laundry facilities that manage to cope with the crowds. You can bush camp overlooking the sea at **Quondong Point**, **James Price Point** and **Coulomb Point**. You can also camp in the community-run campground at **Middle Lagoon** and at **Cygnet Bay Pearl Farm**.

Opposite Coulomb Point *Above* Pearl shell altar, Sacred Heart Church, Beagle Bay

Western Australia

The Margaret River area is famous for its wine – but it's also got some of the world's best surf breaks, beautiful uncrowded beaches, caves, forests, whales and coastal walking trails.

Cape to Cape

HOW LONG?
Perfect for a long weekend, although with food and scenery this good you might be tempted to stay a little longer.

WHEN TO GO
Summer is normally dry and warm, although tempered by sea breezes. Almost all the region's rain falls during the winter months, but winter is also the best time to see whales.

LOCAL SECRET
If you like food and wine you'll love this part of WA – local specialities, other than wine, include olives and olive oils, truffles, apples, oysters, chocolate and cheese – free gourmet food guides are available at visitor centres. **Margaret River Farmers Market** is every Sat morning at the TAFE grounds just south of the township on the Bussell Hwy.

SNAPSHOT
The Margaret River wine region is more or less in the middle of Caves Rd, a 110km scenic drive that stretches from Cape Naturaliste in the north to Cape Leeuwin, the most south-westerly point in Australia where two of the world's greatest oceans, the Southern and the Indian, meet. In between is a succession of wave-washed beaches, rocky headlands, sea cliffs and vast forests of karri – one of the world's tallest trees – which you can explore on Boranup Dr.

Drive rating
Easy. Mostly sealed roads.

Acknowledgement of Country
This is the Traditional Land of the Whadjuk, Pinjarup, Wardandi and Pibelmen Boodja Peoples.

Distance planner
Perth to Cape Leeuwin, via Margaret River: 355km
- Perth to Margaret River: 270km
- Margaret River to Augusta: 51km

More information
- Margaret River Visitor Centre, 100 Bussell Hwy, Margaret River; (08) 9780 5911; margaretriver.com

PERTH/BOORLOO TO MARGARET RIVER

Perth to Margaret River is around a 3hr drive, but there's plenty of reasons to take your time.

Make your first port of call the port of **Fremantle**. On the mouth of the Swan River just 20km south of Perth, Fremantle – aka Freo – has a thriving cafe culture, popular markets, boutique shopping, museums, art galleries and a relaxed coastal vibe. It's also one of the oldest European settlements in WA and one of the best-preserved 19th-century seaports anywhere. More than 150 buildings are classified by the National Trust, including the oldest public building in WA, a 12-sided tower at the end of High St on Arthur Head that was built as a gaol in 1831. Called the **Round House**, it's open daily and entry is free.

Fremantle's favourite son is Bon Scott, lead singer of AC/DC from 1974 until his death in 1980. Although born in Scotland, Scott lived in Fremantle as a teenager and even spent some time as a guest in Fremantle Prison. His gravesite in **Fremantle cemetery** is visited by thousands of Acca Dacca fans each year and was given a heritage listing in 2006. In 2008 a life-size bronze statue of a singing Scott standing on an amplifier in trademark skin-tight jeans was erected at Fremantle Fishing Boat Harbour. The **Fishing Boat Harbour** is also the place to go for super-fresh seafood – try **Cicerello's**, it's been serving up fish and chips since 1903. Check out the aquariums while you're there: the 50 different species of fish were all collected in Fremantle waters (don't worry, they are for show, not for eating!).

SIDETRACK

Called Wadjemup by the Whadjuk Noongar People, no trip to Perth is complete without a trip out to Rotto: **Rottnest Island/Wadjemup**, the favourite holiday destination for many westcoasters. It's 18km off the coast from Perth, and an easy half-hour ferry ride from Fremantle. A visit to the **Wadjemup Museum** is a good way to start your time on the island to understand the island's dark history as a prison for Noongar People from the mainland - many of the historic buildings on the island, including some that are now luxury hotels, were built by convict labour. The Wadjemup Project is assessing how to memorialise the Burial Ground and prison buildings.

While renowned for superb snorkelling, diving, surfing, fishing, boating and swimming in crystal bays, it's the wildlife that is the main attraction of the island, because the one photo everyone wants is a selfie with a quokka. These incredibly cute, naturally inquisitive animals that always appear to be smiling are actually small wallabies, about the size of a domestic cat. There are 12,000 quokkas on Rotto, so you are pretty much guaranteed to see some, particularly in the morning or late afternoon. Getting a selfie is a little harder: for best results you'll need to be at quokka level, belly down on the ground - but don't feed or touch them. Rotto is car free, so the best way to get around is on a bus tour, or to hire a bike on arrival.

Good for a rainy day

Built by convicts in the 1850s and home to the state's worst criminals until 1991, **Fremantle Prison** (fremantleprison.com.au) is WA's only World Heritage-listed building. There are a range of tours available where you can learn all about the various successful and unsuccessful escape attempts, including the fascinating story of six Irish Fenians (Irish Republicans), who managed not only to get out of gaol, but sail away in a waiting ship, the *Catalpa*, to the USA and a hero's welcome in 1876. Some tours include an underground tunnels and submerged passageways (by boat) and there's a rather spooky nighttime torchlight tour.

Opposite Sunset at Bathers Bay, Fremantle *Right* Rottnest Island/Wadjemup

Continue south from Fremantle past a series of beautiful white-sand beaches to **Rockingham**, where you can swim with sea lions, dive with dolphins, kayak with seals at Seal Island or hang out with penguins at Penguin Island. You'll find more beautiful beaches in **Bunbury**, as well as lots of great street and public art and **Bunbury Regional Art Gallery**, WA's largest regional art gallery, and another chance to get up close and personal with wild dolphins in **Koombana Bay** as well.

Stretch your legs in **Busselton**, where you can walk the 2km heritage-listed wooden jetty – the longest timber-piled jetty in the Southern Hemisphere. If you don't want to walk, there's a miniature train.

Although you can continue to follow the coast south from Busselton, head inland to Margaret River on the Bussell Hwy instead, and base yourself in or near the township as you explore the area: allow at least one day for the south, and one for the north.

😊 Kids' spot

You don't have to know how to swim to go underwater at Busselton. At the **Underwater Observatory** at the end of **Busselton Jetty** you can take a guided tour and descend 8m below the surface to an observation chamber where you can gaze out at vividly coloured corals, sponges, fish and other sea creatures. It's one of just six underwater observatories in the world and the piles have created a vast artificial reef (snorkelling tours are also available). In summer school holidays, if you time your visit right, kids may well spot a mermaid or go online (busseltonjetty.com.au) for times and tours.

MARGARET RIVER TO CAPE NATURALISTE AND CAPE LEEUWIN

Think Margaret River and most people automatically think 'great wine'. And rightly so. The **Margaret River region**, a wild knob of land jutting into the sea off the bottom corner of WA, crowned in the north by Cape Naturaliste and Cape Leeuwin in the south, is home to some of the finest white wines produced in Australia (and plenty of terrific reds). The region produces less than 3 per cent of Australia's overall wine – but more than 25 per cent of the country's premium wine, so it's definitely quality over quantity. But it also has some great art galleries, beautiful scenery, wildflowers and deserted beaches.

Before being known as a gourmet food and wine destination, Margaret River was a chilled-out surfing town with a hippy culture and you can still find traces of its surfie past at any number of surf shops and surf breaks in the area. Much of the coastline is protected as part of **Leeuwin–Naturaliste National Park**, which stretches 120km from Bunker Bay in the north to Augusta in the south; the park is on the Traditional Land of the Wadandi People. Even if you don't surf, finding a nice spot to sit and watch the experts carve up some truly impressive waves is a fabulous way to spend some time. Famous breaks with big waves (and easy-to-get-to good vantage points) include the **Margaret River Main Break** at Surfers Point between the Margaret River mouth and Prevelly, **Injidup Beach**, **Cowaramup Bay** near Gracetown, **Smiths Beach** and **Yallingup**, although locals will tell you there are more than 75 breaks between the capes. You may even be lucky enough to see dolphins riding the waves as well.

The best way to explore the region is along **Caves Rd**, a 110km scenic drive that stretches from cape to cape. The township of Margaret River is roughly in the middle.

Opposite top left A quokka on Rottnest Island/Wadjemup *Opposite top right* South Mole Lighthouse, Fremantle *Opposite bottom left* Margaret River vines *Opposite bottom right* Fremantle Round House *Above* Yallingup Beach

Cape to Cape 191

You can also walk it: the **Cape to Cape** trail is a 140km trail between the two capes with beautiful coastal scenery and wildflowers from Aug to Nov. If you don't fancy doing the whole thing you can join the track at various spots along the way and just do a couple of hours.

In the north, Caves Rd begins at Cape Naturaliste. Take a tour of the **Cape Naturaliste Lighthouse** or walk around the headland to enjoy views of the coastline and, depending on the time of year, possibly spot some migrating whales. Thousands of whales – humpbacks, southern rights and even the rare and endangered blue whale, the world's largest animal – journey along the South West coast on their way to and from the warm breeding grounds of the Kimberley coast and the Antarctic, often sheltering in the bays to rest with their calves. Best time to see them is during the winter months through to early spring – May to Sept – and the best time of day is usually around midday.

Not long after **Gracetown** – a lovely spot for a stroll along the rocks and white-sand beach lapped by turquoise water – the road cuts through the heart of the main wine-producing area. There are around 50 wineries clumped together in a stretch of around 15km.

Take a detour off Caves Rd to wind your way through the **Boranup Karri Forest** on Boranup Dr. Although the forest was burnt by bushfires in late 2021, it has already started to regenerate. Stop to take a short walk through the grand 190m-high trees, some off the world's tallest. You can embrace the Japanese philosophy of shinrin yoku – forest bathing – here!

The official collective noun for rays is a 'fever', so try not to get too feverish counting the smooth stingrays, black stingrays and eagle rays at **Hamelin Bay**. With wing spans of up to a metre across, these massive but very graceful creatures congregate in the shallows on the beach near the old jetty and can be seen most days, although you have a better chance during the summer months. They are not aggressive but can stab you if you inadvertently step on one half buried in the sand, so it pays to keep well out of reach: the venomous barb is at the base of the tail.

Continue south past barely there beachside communities as you head towards **Cape Leeuwin**, the most south-westerly tip of Australia. The **lighthouse** here has watched over the point where the Indian and Southern oceans meet since 1895. It's a good place to watch whales off the shore and during spring masses of beautiful wildflowers dot the windswept headland.

Head into the hills

The limestone ridge of Leeuwin-Naturaliste National Park also hides a series of caves, many of which are open to the public. You can explore **Calgardup, Giants and Mammoth caves** on your own (you'll need a torch), or join a tour – the most popular are **Jewel Cave** just north of Augusta – home to one of the longest straw stalactites to be found in any tourist cave – and **Lake Cave** near Margaret River, which has some beautiful reflections, and the richly decorated **Ngilgi Cave**, just north of Yallingup. Book tours at the visitor centre in Margaret River.

Above Busselton Jetty

SIDETRACK

Two of the most popular cellar doors are just a few minutes south of Margaret River township, on Stevens Rd. **Leeuwin Estate Winery** is set in bushland and constructed of natural timber, wrought iron and long sweeping curves of corrugated iron; like many of the wineries in Margaret River, it also has an art gallery. Practically next door is **Voyager Estate**, with its faux Cape Dutch architecture and extensive formal gardens. Both wineries have excellent restaurants and offer a range of winery and tasting tours at their cellar doors.

BEST BEDS

- **Cape Lodge** This award-winning country estate hotel near Yallingup is the perfect combination of luxury accommodation and gourmet food. It's not cheap, but worth the splurge, especially if you're a foodie. capelodge.com.au
- **Grand Mecure Basildene Manor** This boutique manor house hotel with beautiful gardens is about a 5min drive from Margaret River. basildenemanor.com.au
- **Margarets Beach Resort** A range of well-appointed studios and apartments overlooking Gnarabup Beach 10km from the township of Margaret River. margaretsbeachresort.com.au

VANLIFE

You'll find a good range of commercial caravan parks scattered in and around Margaret River and the larger coastal towns like Busselton and Augusta. If you're looking for something a little wilder, you can camp in the middle of the forest at **Boranup campground** or at **Conto** near the beach in Leeuwin-Naturaliste National Park; both have toilets, barbecues, tables, water and individual sites in the bush. The **Point Road campground** at the northern end of Boranup Drive is 4WD only. Book these three campgrounds through WA Parks and Wildlife Service (exploreparks.dbca.wa.gov.au).

Western Australia

Get back to nature on WA's wild and wonderful southern coast between Albany and Esperance, where the tall forests meet the sea.

The South West Edge

HOW LONG?
Allow a week, one way.

WHEN TO GO
Summer is normally dry and warm, although tempered by sea breezes. Almost all the region's rain falls during the winter months, but winter is the best time to see whales. For wildflowers, visit in spring: the peak flowering time is Aug to Nov.

NEED TO KNOW
Fallen trees may sometimes block roads in the national parks of the South West, so allow plenty of time for drives in case you find yourself needing to backtrack.

SNAPSHOT
The southern edge of WA is a striking stretch of largely undeveloped and often rugged coastline bordered by towering old-growth jarrah and karri forests. Known as the Great Southern, the area includes the scenic Stirling Ranges, wineries and the historic town of Albany, the oldest European settlement in WA. Further east, the beautiful turquoise coastline continues to Esperance and Cape Arid at the western end of the Great Australian Bight.

Drive rating
Easy. Mostly sealed roads with optional 4WD sections.

Acknowledgement of Country
This is the Traditional Land of the Bibbulman, Menang, Goreng, Ngatjumay and Wudjari Peoples.

Distance planner
Augusta to Cape Arid National Park: around 955km
- Augusta to Albany: 364km
- Albany to Esperance: 474km
- Esperance to Cape Arid National Park: 156km
- Esperance to Perth (direct): 715km

More information
- Albany Visitor Centre, 221 York St, Albany; (08) 6820 3700; amazingalbany.com.au
- Esperance Visitor Centre, in the Historic Museum Village, cnr Dempster and Kemp sts, Esperance; 1300 664 455; visitesperance.com

Opposite Wildflowers carpet the landscape of the south west in spring

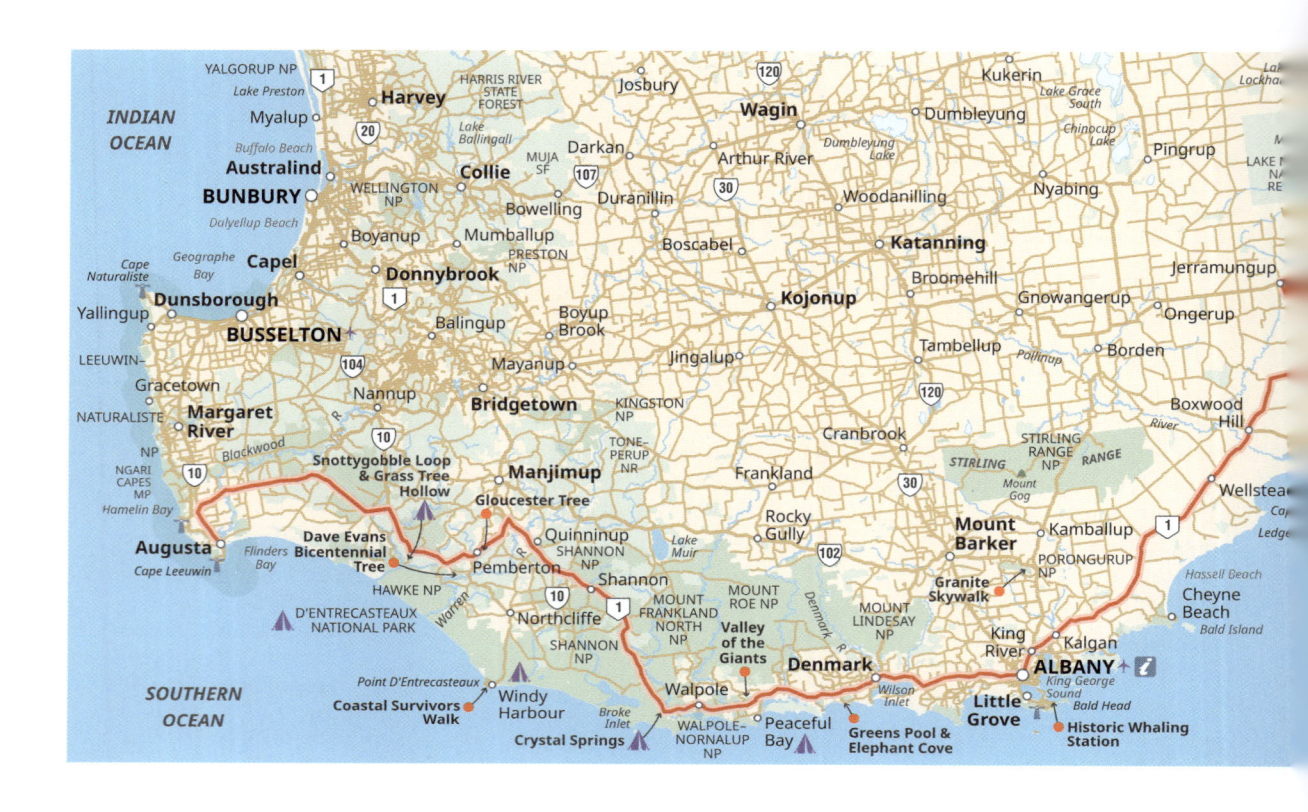

AUGUSTA TO ALBANY

Head east from Augusta, not far from where two of the world's greatest oceans converge (see the Cape to Cape road trip, p.187) to Pemberton. This is big-tree country, and the state's most famous tree, the **Gloucester Tree**, is 3km from Pemberton in **Gloucester National Park** on the Traditional Land of the Bibbulman People. This 61m-high giant karri made a great lookout to help spot forest fires in the 1930s and '40s. Back then you had to get to the top the hard way, using special boots and a belt, but these days there's a spiral of iron spikes embedded in the trunk. Be warned though: it's harder (and scarier) than it looks, and less than a quarter of all those who try to climb the tree make it to the top.

There's an even bigger giant in **Warren National Park**, also the Traditional Land of the Bibbulman People, around a 15min drive south-west of Pemberton. The **Dave Evans Bicentennial Tree**, another colossal karri, is a whopping 75m high, and you can climb that one too, if you're game.

Both trees are part of the **Karri Forest Explorer Drive**, an 86km loop drive from Pemberton. It's largely unsealed, and there are some steep sections, like the descriptively named Heartbreak Trail (not suitable for caravans or motorhomes), a one-way side-trip loop above and beside the Warren River.

Follow the South Western Hwy to Walpole and the **Valley of the Giants**, a forest of towering karri and tingle trees in **Walpole–Nornalup National Park**, on the Traditional Land of the Menang People. Some of the trees, particularly the red tingle, are as high as 75m, with a base circumference of 20m. The best way to really get to grips with just how big these majestic trees are is on the **Tree Top Walk**, which leads you along a 600m steel-truss treetop walkway up and over a deep red tingle gully. Below, a boardwalk winds through a grove of tingle trees known as the Ancient Empire, some of which are 400 years old. Some of the buttressed trees are split or hollowed out at the base, forming huge woody arches and tunnels that you can walk through.

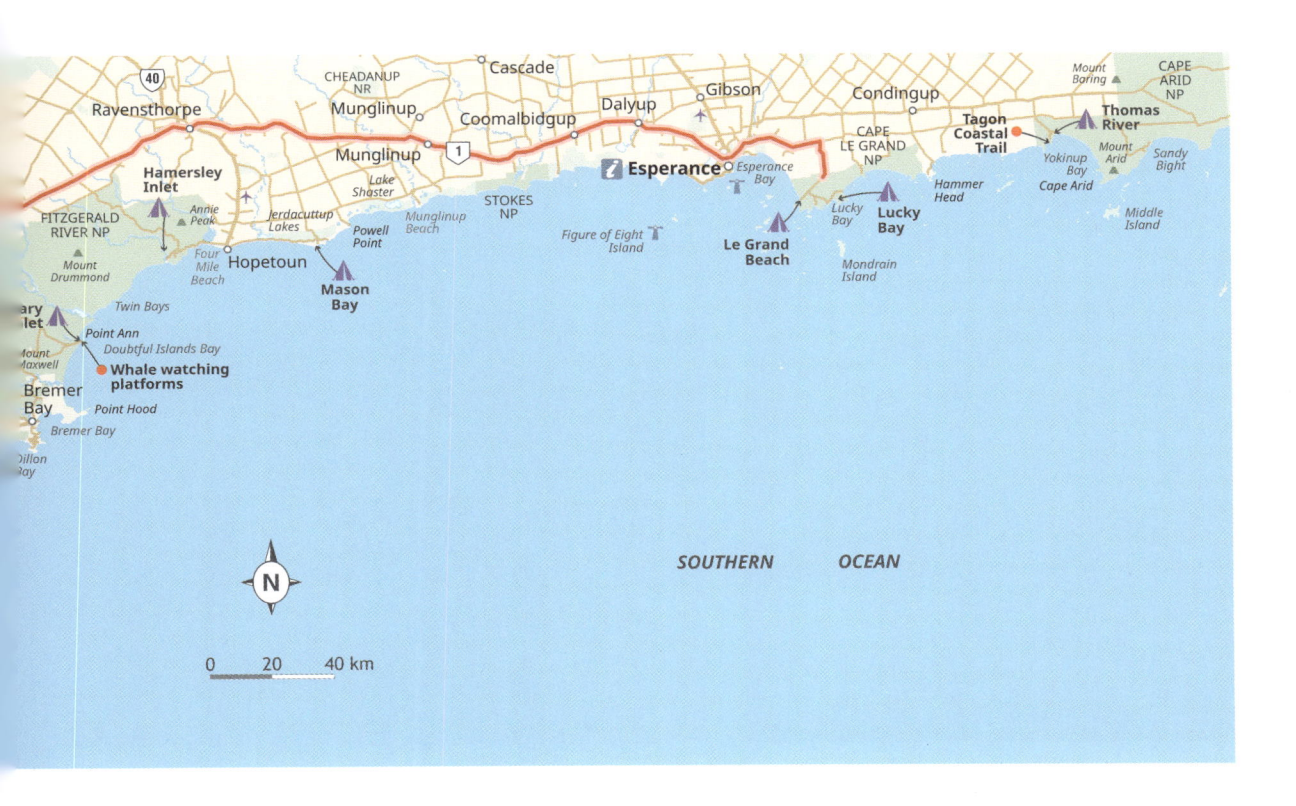

Valley of the Giants Tree Top Walk

The South West Edge   197

Western Australia

198

SIDETRACK

If you've got a 4WD, spend some time exploring **D'Entrecasteaux National Park** whose Traditional Owners are the Bibbulman and Menang Peoples. Pronounced *don-truh-cast-oh*, with the stress on the *oh*, it is named in honour of French explorer Bruni D'Entrecasteaux, who charted this coastline on a scientific expedition in 1792. The park is a 130km-long narrow coastal strip featuring sand dunes, volcanic rock columns and string of beaches. If you're looking for a rugged and remote coastal park where you can get away from it all, this is the one for you. It is popular with anglers, who come here to fish from the rocks, beaches and riverbanks, and off-roaders, who like to tackle the sand dunes and sandy tracks. If you don't have a 4WD though, don't despair, because you can follow the sealed road to the community of **Windy Harbour**, an enclave of around 200 or so cottages surrounded by national park, built around the time of the Great Depression in the 1930s. Most people come for the fishing, but there's also some scenic coastal walking trails: a favourite is the 2.8km **Coastal Survivors Walk** along the cliff-tops to Point D'Entrecasteaux.

Opposite top left National ANZAC Centre, Albany *Opposite top right* Cormorants in Denmark *Opposite bottom left* Albany's Historic Whaling Station *Opposite bottom right* Qualup Bell *Top* Lucky Bay

From the Valley of the Giants it will take around 90min to drive to Albany, but chances are you'll get sidetracked by one of the numerous roads that lead to the sea along the way. The beaches of WA's southern coast are truly spectacular, with dazzling white sand so fine it squeaks.

A good spot to base yourself for a day or two en route is the charming township of **Denmark** beside the Denmark River on the shores of Wilson Inlet. It has a higher-than-average proportion of artists and alternative lifestylers, which gives it a relaxed – some may call it hippy – vibe. Denmark is also perfectly positioned to explore the scenic backroads that wind through vine-clad valleys and fabulous forests of tingle and karri. There's also plenty of walking options along coastal trails – don't miss **Greens Pool** and **Elephant Cove** in nearby **William Bay National Park**, both are magical spots to swim in summer, and **Ocean Beach** at the mouth of Wilson Inlet, where several tracks lead off to sensational lookouts. The Traditional Owners of William Bay National Park are the Menang People.

Albany is a pretty town on King George Sound with a fascinating history. Established in 1827 as a far-flung military outpost of NSW by a party of 21 soldiers and 23 convicts who arrived on the *Amity*, it is the oldest town in WA. It was also the last place to stop commercial whaling on mainland Australia and when operations ceased at the whaling station in November 1978 the doors were simply locked with all the equipment left in situ, producing a unique time capsule and the only complete whaling station in the world that is open to visitors. Join a guided tour of the **Historic Whaling Station** to learn about the history of whaling and also conservation, and climb aboard the last whalechaser boat in Australia. Albany was also the final departure point for the first ANZAC troops on their way to the battlefields of World War I and the **National ANZAC Centre** is both a moving memorial and fascinating museum that retells the story of the ANZACs and the conflict they fought in.

Good for a rainy day

You can easily spend a couple of hours at the free **Museum of the Great Southern** in Albany. Star attraction is the replica of the Brig *Amity*, but before you walk the gangplank take a deep dive into the stories of the Menang People, who have lived in the South West for more than 50,000 years, to gain a deeper understanding of the enduring web of connections between Country and culture. Other displays range from meteorites to lighthouses and local history. The museum also hosts a variety of travelling exhibitions, with everything from dinosaurs to whales and other creatures from the sea.

Head into the hills

One of few truly rugged mountain ranges in the west, the **Stirling Range** is one of only a small number of areas in WA that is high enough, and cold enough, to receive dustings of snow in winter - sometimes as much as 5cm on the highest peaks. Around an hour's drive north-east of Albany, it's also one of the world's most important areas for wildflowers, with 1500 species (many of which grow nowhere else) packed within its boundaries. You'll see flowers all year round, but they are most spectacular in spring. The 42km-long **Stirling Range Rd** is a very scenic unsealed road that cuts through the heart of the range, linking up with the sealed Chester Pass Rd. Stop on the way to marvel at the view from the **Granite Skywalk in Porongurup National Park**, a suspended walkway on the top of a huge granite outcrop called Castle Rock: you'll need a good head for heights as the 2km walk through the karri forest to get there from the picnic area includes climbing a 6m-high ladder, but the views stretch all the way to Albany on the coast. Porongurup National Park is on the Traditional Land of the Menang People.

ALBANY TO ESPERANCE

Follow the South Coast Hwy – Highway 1 – from Albany east towards Esperance. It's about a 5hr drive but will take a lot longer with the many scenic stops and detours: last time we drove this section it took us several days.

Take a 60km detour off the South Coast Hwy to **Bremer Bay**. This little seaside town is a gem of a place that developers seem to have overlooked. Heaven knows why, as it's surrounded by stunning beaches with rolling surf, great expanses of sand dunes and views that stretch forever. But I won't tell if you won't. If you're here in summer – Jan and Feb – you'll be treated to one of nature's most thrilling spectacles: a killer whale feeding frenzy. Every year hundreds of orcas (killer whales) congregate in the deep waters of the submarine Bremer Canyon around a 1hr boat ride from Bremer Bay to hunt and feast, mostly on giant squid. There are several tours available: try **Whale Watch Western Australia** (whalewatchwesternaustralia.com) or **Naturaliste Charters** (whales-australia.com.au).

You can either backtrack from Bremer Bay to link up with the highway again, or meander your way east on unsealed local roads to **Point Ann** in **Fitzgerald River National Park,** on the Traditional Land of the Goreng, Menang and Wudjari Peoples. Every year, thousands of whales – humpbacks, southern rights and even the rare and endangered blue whale – journey along the South West coast on their way to and from the warm breeding grounds of the Kimberley coast and the Antarctic, often sheltering in the bays to rest, and the calm waters of the bay at Point Ann are just one of two places in Australia, where southern right whales come to calve in large numbers (the other is Head of Bight on the Nullarbor in SA; see p.151). There are two whale watching platforms on the headlands. The best time to see whales is during the winter months through to early spring – May to Sept – and the best time of day is usually around midday. The road is not suitable for caravans or large motorhomes, and to explore further in the national park you'll need to drive north on Pabelup Dr and Quiss Rd back up to the South Coast Hwy.

Fitzgerald River National Park is one of the most diverse botanical regions in the world. More than 1800 beautiful and bizarre species of flowering plants thrive here, nearly 20 per cent of the state's plant species. You can't miss the brightly coloured royal hakea that towers above the surrounding plains or the pretty qualup bell, which is not found anywhere else. Other highlights of this large tract of coastal wilderness include deserted beaches with 4WD access, inland lakes and rivers, and cliffs full of sea-sponge fossils.

Top The seaside town of Bremer Bay

SIDETRACK

Hamersley Dr is a scenic unsealed drive bisecting the eastern section of Fitzgerald River National Park. It's signposted off the South Coast Hwy (take the West River Rd) and you'll end up at the coast not far from Hopetoun, and the beaches here (West Beach, Mileys Beach, Barrens Beach and Four Mile Beach) are all good fishing spots and whale watching points: Barrens is best for swimming, although all these beaches are unpatrolled, so check conditions (beachsafe.org.au) and be careful. Allow at least an hour for the 57km drive, longer if you like photographing wildflowers along the way. The road is fine for 2WD but not suitable for caravans or large motorhomes. If you don't fancy tackling the dirt road in the national park you can also get to Hopetoun on a sealed road from Ravensthorpe.

Once back on the highway at Ravensthorpe – around a 30min drive from Hopetoun – it will take around 2hr to get to **Esperance,** one of the most popular holiday towns on the south coast. The **Museum Village** is a collection of historical buildings relocated from various locations in and around Esperance, now housing art, craft and design shops. Don't miss the **Esperance Museum** which includes bits of the American Space Station Skylab which famously crashed to Earth in 1979, spreading debris around Esperance and across the Nullarbor. But it's the beaches that are the main attraction in Esperance. Take a drive around the aptly named **Great Ocean Drive** on the outskirts of town, which traces the sweeping curves of the coastline and offers views every bit as impressive as those on that other great ocean drive in Victoria, without the crumbling rock stacks of course – or the traffic. With dazzling white sand lapped by turquoise water, the beaches are so implausibly picture perfect they look like they could be photoshopped.

Left Scarlet banksia, Stirling Ranges *Right* Point Ann, Fitzgerald River National Park

Head out to **Cape Le Grand National Park**, on the Traditional Land of the Wudjari People. The park is around 50km south-east of Esperance by sealed roads, to see whether **Lucky Bay** really is the whitest beach in Australia – similar claims are made for Whitehaven Beach in Queensland's Whitsundays and Hyams Beach in Jervis Bay in NSW, but the locals here are quick to remind you that it's been 'scientifically proven' by the National Committee on Soil and Terrain. Best way to settle the argument is to see it for yourself, but don't forget your sunglasses, because it is definitely dazzling. There are some excellent bay-to-bay walking trails along the cliff-tops, where sea eagles soar above carpets of brightly coloured banksias and other wildflowers that are in full bloom during late winter and early spring.

Personally, I think the scientists that made the call about Lucky Bay should check out **Cape Arid National Park**, on the Traditional Land of the Ngatjumay and Wudjari Peoples, around 75km to the east. Sand can't possibly come any whiter than this – the water really couldn't be much bluer either – especially on the **Tagon Coastal Trail**, a gorgeous 4hr beach-to-beach-to-beach walk that starts near the Thomas River campground.

There is also a network of sandy 4WD tracks that criss-cross the park, although they are quite rough. If you're up for a bit of an adventure, a highlight is the remote settlement of **Israelite Bay**. Once home to around 150 people, all that's left are the ruins of an old post office and telegraph station built in 1895, as well as the remains of a few old cottages and some historic graves. It's a stunning section of coastline, part of a chain of national parks and reserves that stretches from Esperance almost all the way to the SA border and includes the 90m-high **Baxter Cliffs**. You'll need a high-clearance 4WD to get to Israelite Bay, but the sheltered bush camping area has good access to the beach (keep an eye on the tides if driving and watch out for boggy sections of soft sand) and a jetty for fishing: check road conditions before travelling by calling Esperance District Parks and Wildlife Office on (08) 9083 2100, as the track was temporarily closed at the time of going to print.

There used to be a track that led northward through the park from the coast past Israelite Bay and Mount Ragged to link up with Highway 1 near Balladonia at the western end of the Nullarbor, but it too has been closed to through traffic for a couple of years, so the only option is to head back to Esperance. From there you can head north for 200km or so to Norseman and hook up with the Eyre Hwy, which runs east across the Nullarbor, or continue north to pick up the Great Eastern Hwy and circle back to Perth.

Kids' spot

Even the hardest-to-please kids will find something fun at **Adventureland Park** in Esperance, including an 18-hole mini golf course, a giant swing, flying fox, a bike track with lots of humps, bumps and berms, playground, slides and miniature railway. You'll find it on the Esplanade, near the Taylor St jetty, not far from the equally popular skate park.

BEST BEDS

- **Beach House at Bayside** This small boutique hotel - there are only eight rooms - is a luxurious bolthole just a few minutes' walk from Middleton Bay on King George Sound near Albany. thebeachhouseatbayside.com.au
- **Bremer Bay Beaches Resort Tourist Park** The resort offers comfortable spa cabins (and caravan and campsites) and is within easy walking distance of beautiful beaches. bremerbaybeaches.com.au
- **The Jetty Resort** This family-run hotel in Esperance has motel rooms, family rooms and two-bedroom apartments. It's opposite the beach and some rooms have ocean views. thejettyresort.com.au

VANLIFE

There's a variety of campgrounds to choose from, including sheltered seaside spots and magical camps deep in enchanted forests. There are a number of campsites scattered throughout **D'Entrecasteaux National Park**, but you'll need a 4WD to access the coastal ones, apart from the camping ground at **Windy Harbour** and beneath the peppermints at **Crystal Springs**, both of which are accessible to 2WD vehicles. In neighbouring **Hawke National Park** there are campgrounds at **Snottygobble Loop** and **Grass Tree Hollow**. Not far from the Valley of the Giants, there is a good, if a little rustic, caravan park at **Peaceful Bay**, which has large grassy powered sites just behind the beach. In **Fitzgerald River National Park**, **St Mary Inlet** is a sheltered site behind the sand dunes near Point Ann, and **Hamersley Inlet** is a lovely lakeside camping spot. **Mason Bay**, 34km east of Hopetoun is a real gem: it's pretty basic - there's a long-drop toilet and that's about it - but it's in a lovely sheltered spot beside a beautiful white-sand beach. In **Cape Le Grand National Park** there are two beachside campgrounds, both with solar-powered hot showers: **Lucky Bay** has a boat ramp and large (unpowered) caravan sites with a great view overlooking the beach, while **Le Grand Beach** has small sites tucked behind a dune. There are five campgrounds in **Cape Arid National Park**: **Thomas River** is the most popular with hilltop sites surrounded by bird-attracting banksias overlooking the bay. Book national park campgrounds through WA Parks and Wildlife Service (exploreparks.dbca.wa.gov.au).

The South West Edge

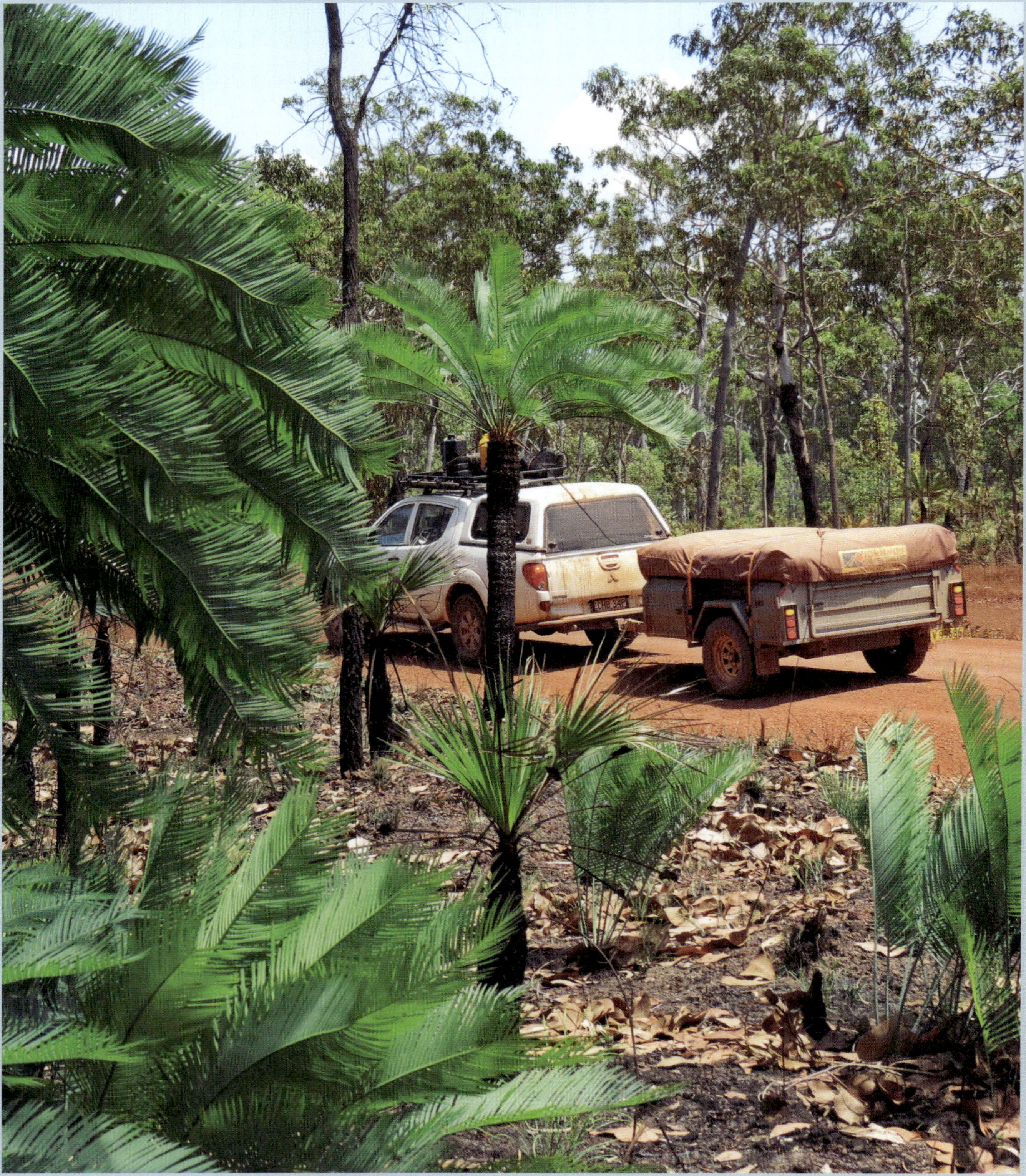

Northern Territory

Wild, remote and rich in culture.

ARAFURA SEA
Banubanu Beach Retreat
Gutjangan
Bremer Island
Gayngaru Wetlands (Town Lagoon)
Gäluru (East Woody)
Middle Beach
Wirrwawuy (Cape Wirawawoi)
Manyimi
Gove Boat Club
Lombuy (Crocodile Creek)
Wargarpunda Point
Gadalathami (Town Beach)
Gove Peninsula Surf Life Saving Club
Nhulunbuy
Dundas Point
Inverell Bay
Gove Harbour
Gunyangara
Nhulun (Roy Marika Lookout)
Gumuniya (Buffalo Creek)
Banambarrnga (Rainbow Cliff)
Drimmie Head
Melville Bay
Yirrkala
Miles Island
ARNHEM LAND ABORIGINAL LAND TRUST
Gangurimurru Beach
Rocky Bay
GOVE AIRPORT
Rocky Point
24
Giddy
Baringura (Little Bondi)
Wathawuy (Latram River)
Manangaymi (Scout Camp)
Ngumuy (Turtle Beach)
Wathawuy (Goanna Lagoon)
Garanhan (Macassan Beach)
Binydjarrnga (Daliwuy Bay)
Wanuwuy (Cape Arnhem)
Binydjarrnga (Daliwuy Bay)
Wanuwuy (Cape Arnhem)
River
GOVE PENINSULA
Lurrpukurru (Cape Arnhem)
Guwatjurumurru (Giddy River)
GULF OF CARPENTARIA
Ganami (Wonga Creek)
Gapuru (Memorial Park)
Ck
Wonga
Lurrupukurru (Oyster Beach)
Mount Harold
Port Bradshaw
Cato
24
River
Gwapilina Point
N
To Katherine
Binanangoi Point
ARNHEM LAND ABORIGINAL LAND TRUST
0 4 8 km

East Arnhem Land really is a special place to explore pristine beaches and experience First Nations culture.

Gove Peninsula

HOW LONG?
You can fly to Nhulunbuy from Darwin/Garramilla or Cairns and hire a vehicle, but if you drive in from Katherine it's a two-day trip each way; once you're here, allow at least a week or two to really explore this spectacular area.

WHEN TO GO
Roads across Arnhem Land are only accessible in the dry season and impassable during the wet season, Nov–Apr. Be aware that creek levels rise quickly after rain which may cause road closures no matter what time of year.

NEED TO KNOW
You need two permits to visit East Arnhem Land. One to travel the Central Arnhem Rd from Northern Land Council (NLC, nlc.org.au) and another from Dhimurru (dhimurru.com.au) to access the 15 beaches and recreation areas on the peninsula – even as a day visitor. Allow 10 days for the NLC permit, but the Dhimurru one is issued immediately. If you are planning to buy takeaway alcohol in East Arnhem Land you'll need to apply for a liquor permit (eastarnhemland.com.au/plan/liquor-permit).

There are quite a few reasons why hardly anyone drives to East Arnhem Land, but none of them really make sense. Granted, it takes two days to drive the corrugated dirt road from Katherine to Nhulunbuy. Heavy duty off-road caravans are allowed on the Central Arnhem Rd but are only allowed to stay in the township of Nhulunbuy.

SNAPSHOT
Declared an Aboriginal Reserve in 1931 and granted to the First Nations clans of Arnhem Land, this is a unique, unforgettable experience. The beaches of the Gove Peninsula, where the Gulf of Carpentaria meets the Arafura Sea, are truly stunning. Turtle tracks lace the sand, dugongs and dolphins cruise by, the fish practically leap onto your hook and you almost always have the entire stretch of paradise to yourself. The beaches would be perfect if only it were safe enough to swim – these waters are home to saltwater crocodiles and sharks year-round and deadly stingers during the wet season. Pitching a tent with a waterfront view – from a safe distance though, is still pretty special, even if you can't get wet.

Drive rating
Challenging: 4WD only. The Central Arnhem Rd is deeply corrugated in parts and has several creek and river crossings. Many of the beach access roads and tracks are rocky with deep sandy sections. You'll need to know how to let your tyres down and have recovery ramps, a shovel and the appropriate kit.

Acknowledgement of Country
This is the Traditional Land of the Yolŋu People.

Distance planner
Katherine to Wanuway via Nhulunbuy: 814km
- Katherine to Nhulunbuy: 728km
- Nhulunbuy to Wanuway (Cape Arnhem), via the coast: 86km

More information
- Nhulunbuy Visitor Information Centre, Westal St, Nhulunbuy; 1800 512 460; eastarnhemland.com.au

Previous Central Arnhem Road

KATHERINE TO NHULUNBUY

When you meet a local on the Central Arnhem Rd between Katherine and East Arnhem Land they always ask if you're 'going in or coming out?'. But it's not just the isolation that sets this place apart. First Nations People have lived on this continent for more than 60,000 years and north-east Arnhem Land, thanks to its remoteness, long-time status as a protected Aboriginal Reserve and the Yolŋu People's freehold title, which means they can control – through the permit system – who enters their land, has experienced less impact to Traditional cultural practices compared with other parts of Australia. Home to the annual Garma Festival – one of the biggest First Nations cultural events in the country – ceremony is interwoven into all aspects of life in this part of the world. As you explore the peninsula, you'll often come across areas that are closed due to cultural reasons and Traditional hunting is still practised in many communities.

The turn-off to the Central Arnhem Rd is 50km south of Katherine. **Mainoru Outstation Store**, around 200km along the road, is the only place to get fuel between Katherine and Nhulunbuy, and the only designated overnight spot on the Central Arnhem Rd (*see* p.213) – free camping on the side of the road is not allowed. From there, it will take the best part of a full day to get to Nhulunbuy.

SIDETRACK

Bremer Island is a speck of land less than 8km long and little more than 3km wide, around a 45min boat ride or 15min flight from Nhulunbuy. It's a staggeringly beautiful place, lapped by water so clear it's almost invisible and encircled by white sandy beaches laced with a filigree of sea turtle tracks. Aside from the half-dozen or so houses in the Yolŋu community of Gutjangan, **Banubanu Beach Retreat** (*see* p.213) is the only other building on the island.

Given that Bremer Island is surrounded by some of the country's most unfished waters and the retreat has its own boat available for fishing trips, seafood – more often than not caught by the guests that day – features strongly on the menu and is prepared by the resident chef. Bread and desserts are all made on the premises and canapés and sparkling wine are served each evening on the sunset viewing deck down by the beach.

With no wi-fi or mobile phone coverage, it's a beautiful spot to chill out and relax but it's the Yolŋu culture that sets this place apart from your standard tropical island paradise experience. Bremer Island is a Registered Sacred Site, and the island is the homeland of members of the Yunupingu clan. Traditional hunting and gathering is still a very important part of life on the island and the locals are happy for Banubanu guests – and the Banubanu chef – to tag along.

Opposite top left Cycads on the Central Arnhem Rd *Opposite top right* Catch of the day on Bremer Island *Opposite bottom left* Yirrkala *Opposite bottom right* Wild buffalo *Above* Track to Yarrapay (Rocky Point)

Gove Peninsula 209

Once there, you'll find all the services you need, such as accommodation, cafes, a pizza shop, a tavern, fuel, a pharmacy and a supermarket, although sometimes fresh food can be hard to get if the supply barge has been held up by rough weather. **Gove Boat Club**, overlooking Melville Bay about 12km from the town centre, has one of the town's best restaurants and is a great place for a sundowner while soaking in the views.

But it's the wild, deserted and completely undeveloped beaches that are the real lure. Take a drive out to **Lombuy (Crocodile Creek)**, and work your way east back to the town, via **Gäluru (East Woody)**, **Middle Beach**, **Wirrawuy**, the lookout at **Nhulun**, **Gadalathami** (Town Beach: the Surf Life Saving Club here is open on Fri nights and a great spot for a sunset drink with coastline views) and **Gumuniya (Buffalo Creek)**. All, apart from Lombuy, are accessible via sealed roads. They are all day-use areas only but are covered in your Visitor Access Permit from Dhimurru (*see* p.207). Also worth a look are the **Gayŋaru Wetlands (Town Lagoon)**, just behind Gadalathami, where a 3km trail winds around the edge of the wetlands to viewing platforms and a bird hide.

NHULUNBUY TO WANUWAY (CAPE ARNHEM)

There is no one coastal road or track that links the beaches highlighted on this road trip – you'll need to zig-zag back and forth from the main road as you head south. There's no commercial accommodation available beyond the township of Nhulunbuy on the peninsula either, so you'll need to be set up with all the gear you need to camp and have a set of recovery ramps and a shovel to get you out of trouble if you get stuck in the sand on some of the access tracks. But it's worth it, because the campsites scattered around the peninsula are some of the most spectacular in the country. They are almost all either right on the beach or overlooking one, and so few people travel up here that more often than not you'll have the whole beach to yourself.

As you head south the first campsite you'll find is **Baṉambarrŋa (Rainbow Cliffs)**, a truly magical place to set up camp on the edge of a small cliff overlooking a rocky beach. Photographers will love capturing the colours of the cliffs from the beach below as they glow in the late afternoon light and watch the sun slide into the water at the end of the day. Baṉambarrŋa is just across the water from Nhulunbuy so it has good phone coverage but the sandflies can be murderous, so cover up and wear good repellent. There are no facilities and the access road is pretty rough, but it's a short drive into Nhulunbuy for supplies and fresh water when you need them and makes for a great base to explore the other beaches, rivers and tracks on daytrips.

Good for a rainy day

A must-see whatever the weather, allow plenty of time to visit the township of **Yirrkala**, just a few kilometres south of Nhulunbuy. It was established as a mission in 1935, and some of the most important expressions of Yolŋu art and culture have come from here, such as the **Yirrkala Church Panels** - painted in 1963 they were the first time that Land Rights were documented in this way and they led to the famous bark petition that is now in Parliament House in Canberra/Ngambri/Ngunnawal. The Yirrkala Church Panels are now on display at the **Buku-Larrŋggay Mulka Centre** at Yirrkala, along with a fantastic collection of painted barks, sculptures, weaving, film and music recordings. East Arnhem Land is the home of the didgeridoo - known to the Yolŋu People as the yiḏaki - and the Yolŋu are masters at making them and playing them. This is also an excellent place to buy high-quality locally made art directly from the local First Nations community.

Opposite The expansive landscape of Central Arnhem Land
Above Bremer Island

Gove Peninsula

Almost every camping area covered by the Dhimurru general permit has spectacular views, but if you really want to camp right on the beach head to **Bariṉura**, aka Little Bondi. You need to be careful manoeuvring your vehicle in the soft sand, but there are toilets and fireplaces, and if you want to wake up to a million-dollar view this is the place for you. A walking trail links this beach to Numuy (Turtle Beach), Garanhan (Macassan Beach) and Binydjarrŋa (Daliwuy Bay).

Garanhan, approximately 40km south of Nhulunbuy, is also known as Macassan Beach because of the fascinating 'stone pictures' – made by arranging rocks on the ground – telling the stories of the annual visits of the Macassan from Indonesia who visited the peninsula collecting trepang (sea cucumber) and turtle shell in the days before European settlement. The arrangements of stones show sections of the Macassan boats and details how the traders boiled the trepang in huge cauldrons.

The most developed of all the beachside campgrounds on the Gove Peninsula, **Binydjarrŋa (Daliwuy Bay)** has toilets and a boat launching area (but not much else), and if you prefer camping with others, this is your best bet, although neighbours are not guaranteed. It's a popular fishing spot, particularly with locals who harvest shellfish along the shoreline and in rockpools. Deeper water catches include red emperor, Spanish mackerel and coral trout.

Because it's a place of significant cultural importance for the Yolŋu People with more than 50 sacred sites is **Wanuwuy (Cape Arnhem)**, on the far-eastern tip of the Gove Peninsula – you'll need to apply for a special permit to visit, apply online (dhimurru.com.au) at least a day ahead, but it's worth it for the beautiful long white sandy beach flanked by extensive dunes, some up to 60m high, rocky escarpments and mangroves. Like everywhere else on the peninsula, it's a bit of a challenging soft sandy track to get there, but that's half the fun – just make sure you have recovery gear as your chances of meeting other people on the track or the beach (there's a maximum of just 10 vehicle permits per day) are quite slim. You can camp here, either at **Wanuway** on the northern end, or at **Lurrpukurra** at the southern end. You may be only 50km, as the crow flies, from Nhulunbuy, but as far as adventure travel goes, it doesn't get much better than this.

Head into the hills

Gapuru (Memorial Park), around 65km south-west of Nhulunbuy off the Central Arnhem Rd, is a beautiful spot beside a chain of shallow freshwater rockpools, linked by clear streams and small rapids. You need a camping permit from Dhimurru to visit, even if you only want to visit during the day, but it's exclusive, which means you're guaranteed to have it all to yourself. Locals do occasionally swim here, but the official advice is that crocodiles inhabit all waterways on the peninsula, so if you do, it's at your own risk.

BEST BEDS

- **Mainoru Outstation Store** Set beside a small bend of the Mainoru River beside the store, there is basic accommodation with both ensuite and shared bathrooms, as well as a grassy bush campground with rustic hot showers and plenty of shade. Evening meals are available in the licensed restaurant if you book 24 hours in advance. mainoruoutstationstore.com.au
- **Walkabout Lodge** Opposite Gadalathami (Town Beach) in the centre of Nhulunbuy the lodge has motel-style units, a tavern, licensed restaurant, swimming pool and a camping area. walkaboutlodge.com.au
- At **Banubanu Beach Retreat** on Bremer Island, there are six beachfront glamping bungalows overlooking the Arafura Sea - each with ensuite, deck and outdoor shower. There's no hot water, but you don't need it - it's so warm up here that cooling off under a cold shower is exactly what you want. banubanu.com

VANLIFE

There are powered campsites, showers and laundry facilities in the **Manyimi Campground** at Gove Boat Club, and at **Walkabout Lodge**, also in Nhulunbuy; these are the only places where caravans can park. Other camping areas not covered above include **Wathawuy (Goanna Lagoon and Latram River)**, **Mananaymi (Scout Camp)**, **Guwatjurumurru (Giddy River)**, **Ganami (Wonga Creek)** and **Gapuru (Memorial Park)**: they are all inland campsites, rather than coastal, but all are on watercourses. Camping permits and bookings can be booked online through Dhimurru via dhimurru.com.au

Numuy (Turtle Beach)

Gove Peninsula

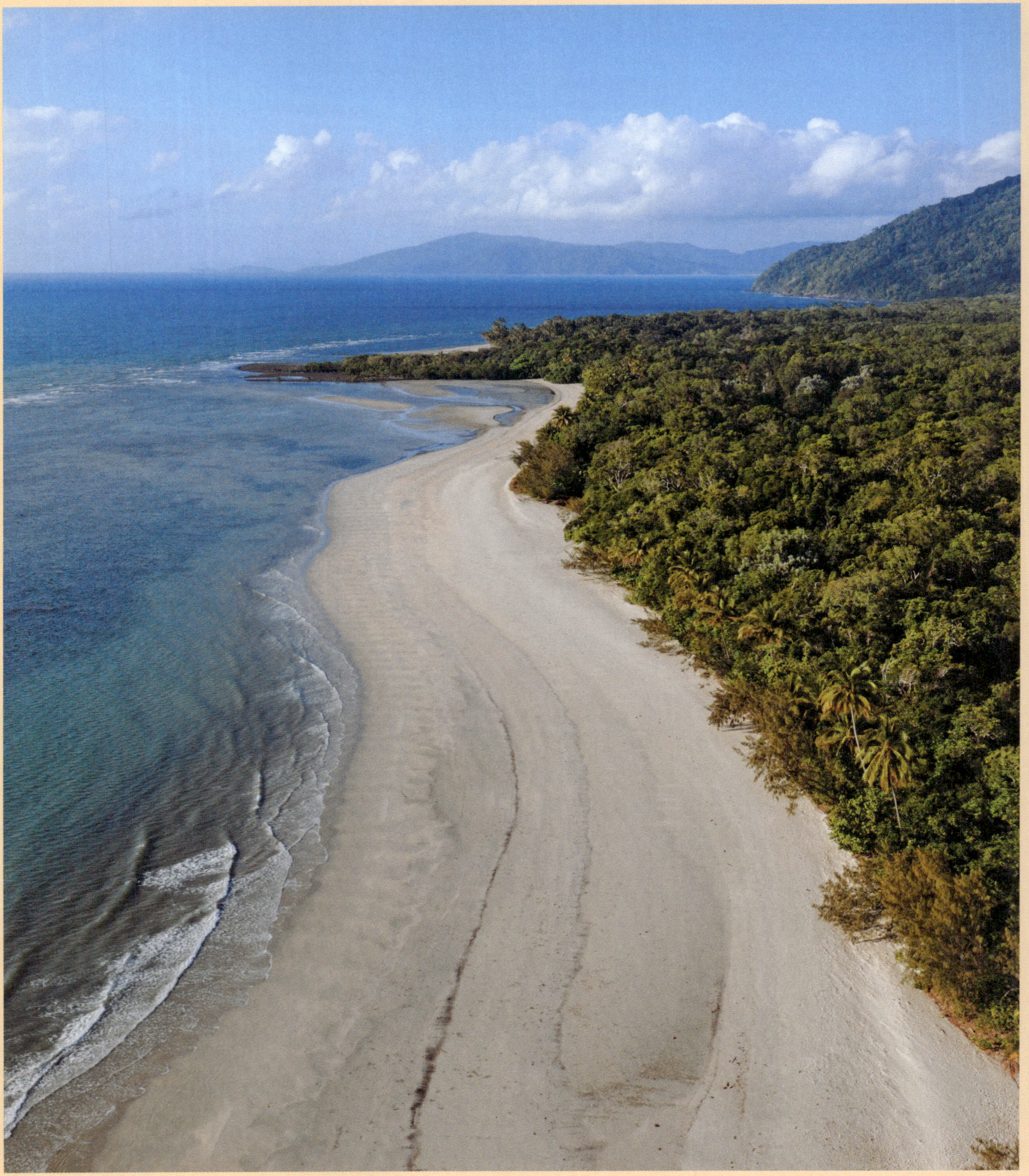

Queensland

*Sandy highways, island getaways
and underwater wonders.*

Boreen Point
GREAT SANDY NP
Noosa Heads
NOOSA NP
Sunshine Beach
Marcus Beach
Peregian Beach
Coolum Beach
Mount Coolum
MOUNT COOLUM NP
MAROOCHYDORE
MOOLOOLABA
SEA LIFE Sunshine Coast
CALOUNDRA
Australia Zoo
Coochin Creek
Bribie Island
BRIBIE ISLAND NP & RECREATION AREA
BONGAREE
Cape Moreton
Bulwer
GHEEBULUM KUNUNGAI (MORETON ISLAND) NP
Mount Tempest
Beachmere
Deception Bay
MORETON BAY MP
Redcliffe
Tangalooma
Moreton Bay (Quandamooka)
Mulgumpin/Moreton Is
Toompani Beach
Brighton
Mud Island (Bungumba)
Kooringal
Amity Point
Flinders Beach
Wynnum
Point Lookout
Cleveland
Blue Lake Beach
Ferry
Dunwich
Main Beach
Redland Bay
Minjerribah/ North Stradbroke Is
NAREE BUDJONG DJARA NP
CORAL SEA
SUNSHINE COAST
GOLD COAST
N
0 10 20 km
Jacobs Well
Dreamworld
Sanctuary Cove
Oxenford
Movie World, Wet'n'Wild Water World, Australian Outback Spectacular & Paradise Country
Helensvale
Sea World
Main Beach
Surfers Paradise
Burleigh Heads
Currumbin
Coolangatta
Tweed Heads
Banora Point
Kingscliff
Bogangar
Hastings Point
Chinderah
Tumbulgum
Murwillumbah
WOLLUMBIN NP
Uki
Lake Baroombah
Manumbar
WRATTENS NP
Cooran
Pomona
Gallangowan
AMAMOOR SF
A3
ELGIN VALE SF
YABBA FR
Imbil
Cooroy
Tewantin
Noosaville
Mount Gibbarnee
Lake Borumba
IMBIL STATE FOREST
Mary
Eumundi
51
MOUNT STANLEY FR
JIMNA RANGE
BLACKALL RA
Yandina
EAST NANANGO SF
Kenilworth
Bli Bli
Mount Monsildale
Jimna
Mapleton Falls
Mapleton
Brisbane
SQUIRREL CREEK SF
CONONDALE NP
JIMNA SF
NAMBOUR
Big Pineapple
Avoca Vale
Conondale
Montville
BUDERIM
Mount Spencer
Yednia
Maleny
Blackbutt
Linville
Mary Cairncross Scenic Reserve
6
Benarkin
Moore
Landsborough
BELLTHORPE NP
Beerwah
Emu Ck
Kilcoy
Harlin
85
Glass House Mountains
River
Woodford
Toogoolawah
DEER RESERVE NP
Lake Somerset
Elimbah
Wamuran
Caboonbah
CABOOLTURE
Lake Cressbrook
Crossdale
58
Esk
Mount Sim Jue
D'AGUILAR NP
Burpengary
A17
Mount Hallen
Lake Wivenhoe
Dundas
Lake Samsonvale
M1
Coominya
Strathpine
22
Aspley
LOCKYER NATIONAL PARK
Lowood
A3
Fernvale
Gatton
A17
BRISBANE/ MEANJIN
Grantham
A2
Pine Mountain
Lone Pine Koala Sanctuary
Mount Gravatt
Laidley
Marburg
Archerfield
Rosewood
IPSWICH
Slacks Creek
Ingoldsby
A15
A5
M6
Purga
Mutdapilly
Bremer
Peak Crossing
Logan
Beenleigh
Warrill View
Rosevale
Flinders Peak
Jimboomba
95
M1
MAIN RANGE NATIONAL PARK
Tamborine Rainforest Skywalk
Palm Grove, Witches Falls, The Knoll
Zamia Grove & Curtis Falls
Kalbar
Tamborine
Aratula
90
North Tamborine
GONDWANA RAINFORESTS OF AUSTRALIA WHA
Boonah
TAMBORINE NP
Mount Tamborine
Mount Sugarloaf
Beaudesert
Mount Alford
Canungra
NERANG
Croftby
93
Kooralbyn
13
SARABAH RA
Mudgeeraba
MAIN RANGE NP
Maroon
Rathdowney
Mount Alexander
Bally Mountain
Killarney
MOUNT BARNEY NP
QLD
LAMINGTON NP
Springbrook
KOREELAH NATIONAL PARK
Lamington
O'Reilly's Rainforest Retreat
RA
Mount Lindesay
Woodenbong
MCPHERSON RA
MCPHERSON
Legume
TOOLOOM NP
BORDER RANGES NP
NSW
M1
Urbenville
Mulli Mulli
Grevillia

Glorious beaches and islands, holiday towns and hinterland villages, and an average of more of than 300 days of sunshine per year, what's not to love about that?

Gold and Sunshine coasts

HOW LONG?
You could drive this stretch of the coastline easily in a couple of hours or so, but stretch it out over a couple of days – or longer if you have the time – because this is beach holiday heaven.

WHEN TO GO
Summer is temperate, with the ranges being much cooler than the coast, but the area is prone to rain and thunderstorms in summer and can be quite humid. Winter is more likely to be dry and sunny. Most of the coastal towns along this route are busy during school holidays, so book accommodation or campsites ahead, especially in summer.

LOCAL SECRET
Eating out in Noosa can be an expensive proposition, but **Noosa Heads Surf Life Saving Club**, at the eastern end of Hastings St, offers affordable meals and million-dollar views over the beach, and is a great spot for lunch, particularly if you can get a table on the deck.

SNAPSHOT
The coastline of south-east Queensland has been attracting sunlovers, surfers and beachgoers for generations, and while holiday trends may come and go, the Gold Coast has never lost its glitzy glamour – although many of its mid-century hotels and attractions are now retro hip – nor the Sunshine Coast its beachy allure. Join in the holiday buzz with the crowds or chill out in a quiet spot away from it all – perhaps in the Sunshine Coast's beautiful hinterland villages. There's a slice of coastal cool here for everyone.

Drive rating
Easy. Mostly sealed roads with some optional 4WD beach driving.

Acknowledgement of Country
This is the Traditional Land of the Bundjalung, Yuggera, Quandamooka and Gubbi Gubbi Peoples.

Distance planner
Coolangatta to Noosa Heads: around 250km, not including a trip across to North Stradbroke/Minjerribah.
- Coolangatta to Brisbane (Cleveland): 98km
- Amity Point to the southern end of Minjerribah/North Stradbroke: roughly 60km
- Brisbane to Noosa Heads via Coolum Beach: 145km

More information
- Surfers Paradise Visitor Information and Booking Centre, 2 Cavill Ave (Cavill Mall), Surfers Paradise, 1300 309 440; destinationgoldcoast.com
- Redlands Coast Visitor Information Centre, Raby Bay Harbour Precinct, Shore St, Cleveland; 1300 667 386; visit.brisbane.qld.au; stradbrokeisland.com
- Glass House Mountains Visitor and Interpretive Centre, Bruce Pde, cnr Reed St, Settler's Rotary Park, Glass House Mountains; 1300 847 481; visitsunshinecoast.com
- Noosa Visitor Information Centre, 61 Hastings St, Noosa Heads; 1300 066 672; visitnoosa.com.au

Previous Myall Beach, Cape Tribulation

COOLANGATTA TO BRISBANE

So well known it hardly needs an introduction, the **Gold Coast** has been drawing holidaymakers of all persuasions to its sunny shore for more than 100 years with its combination of surf, shopping, restaurants, bars, nightclubs, affordable accommodation and family-friendly attractions.

Surfers Paradise, known as Surfers, is its unofficial centre, but the Gold Coast is actually a city – the sixth largest in the country and largest non-capital – with an urban sprawl that stretches roughly 70km from Coolangatta on the NSW border north to the outskirts of Brisbane/Meanjin. If you like more nature, less razzle dazzle, you'll probably prefer the southern end of the Gold Coast strip, around **Burleigh Heads**. If your kids are insisting you visit the theme parks (*see* p.219), they're mostly at the northern end, near Oxenford.

Originally known as Elston, Surfers was little more than a collection of beach shacks and weekenders until 1933 when a local hotelier, Jim Cavill, pushed for the area to be renamed after his hotel. According to the history books the original name was going to be 'Sea Glint'.

Nowhere in Australia does high-rise quite like Surfers, so take a trip up to the top of one of the world's tallest residential towers, **Q1** (it was the world's tallest when built in 2005, but at the time of going to print it had slipped down to number 13 on the list), for a bird's-eye view. The Skypoint Observation Deck is on levels 77 and 78 and on a good day you can see from Brisbane to Byron Bay. The elevator, which takes you from ground to level 77 in 42.7 seconds is one of the fastest in the world. If you've really got a good head for heights you can suit up, head outside and climb to the spire.

Beyond the high-rise strip is a canal system longer than those of both Amsterdam and Venice combined, and there are dozens of **river and canal cruises** to choose from.

Opposite Tamborine Rainforest Skywalk *Below* Surfers Paradise

Head into the hills

Just a 1hr drive from Brisbane, and half an hour from the Gold Coast, is an altogether different world: mountains, rainforest, valleys, wide plains and World Heritage-listed wilderness - the green behind the gold, an area known as the Scenic Rim. **Tamborine Mountain** is about a 45min drive from Surfers Paradise via the Nerang-Broadbeach/Beaudesert-Nerang Rd (State Rd 90). The air up here is cooler and the views from the plateau are fantastic, but the drive is steep, winding and narrow. Stop and explore the villages of Tamborine Mountain - shoppers should head for Gallery Walk on Long Road, a string of galleries, craft shops, antique stores, cafes and eateries.

Queensland's first national park was established at Witches Falls in 1908, and since then additional reserves of subtropical rainforest on the Tamborine Plateau have been added to it, making up what is now known as **Tamborine National Park**. There are 22km of graded walking tracks, with most walks taking less than half a day and almost all easily reached from Tamborine Mountain township. Most are either wheelchair accessible or graded as easy, so they are also great for kids and families with strollers. **Palm Grove**, **Witches Falls** and **The Knoll** have spectacular views, and **Zamia Grove** has ancient cycads, relics of plants that flourished 150 million years ago. There are also lovely waterfalls and rockpools throughout the park, including **Curtis Falls**, one of the prettiest - and most popular - waterfalls on the mountain, an easy 1.5km-return walk from the carpark on Dapsang Dr at Eagle Heights.

Tamborine Rainforest Skywalk is a privately owned steel canopy walk with a 40m-long cantilevered bridge suspended 30m above the forest floor. It's a great way to get a bird's-eye view of the rainforest and is suitable for wheelchairs and strollers.

If you'd like to really give your hiking boots a workout, head still further south to **Lamington National Park**. This World Heritage-listed park has more than 160km of walking tracks. Highlights include several of the 150 waterfalls and stands of 15,000-year-old Antarctic beech trees. There is also a tree-top canopy walk: it might seem a little tame by today's standards but 25 years ago it was the first of its kind in Australia. It's at **O'Reilly's Rainforest Retreat** in the Green Mountain section of the park. There are two entrances to Lamington: the Green Mountains entrance is 115km south of Brisbane via Canungra, or 70km from Surfers via Nerang and Canungra, while Binna Burra is 107km from Brisbane/Meanjin via Canungra, and 55km from the Gold Coast. Both routes are fully sealed, but the road to Green Mountains is too steep and winding for RVs, caravans or camper trailers. The 21.4km Border Track walking trail links the two sections.

Kids' spot

Chances are your kids already know all about the Gold Coast theme parks - **Warner Bros. Movie World**, **Sea World**, **Wet'n'Wild**, **Dreamworld** and **Paradise Country** farm are the big hitters but there is a raft of other smaller ones - and they won't let you get away with a visit to this corner of world without some serious ride time. Take heart, there's some great stuff for you to enjoy as well. The **Australian Outback Spectacular** is an exciting dinner show extravaganza, where the arena thunders with the hooves of Australian stockhorses as stunt riders and stockmen play out a story of life on a cattle station. There's lots of trick riding, breathtaking high-tech sound and light effects, and even a mustering helicopter that dives into the arena driving a herd of cattle.

Gold and Sunshine coasts

MINJERRIBAH/NORTH STRADBROKE

The world's second largest sand island (K'gari is the biggest, *see* p.225), **Minjerribah/North Stradbroke** is affectionately known as Straddie by the locals who all believe they live in paradise, and they are probably right. Even though it's only a 45min ferry trip (book ahead at stradbrokeferries.com.au) from Cleveland in the outer suburbs of Brisbane/Meanjin, and close enough that you can see the high-rise towers of the Gold Coast on the horizon, it feels a world away – this is a place where old-school holidays rule and it's all about family-friendly fun in the sun. It's not cheap to get there with a caravan or camper trailer – a three-day trip can cost several hundred dollars if you take the ferry during peak times – but it's a special place worth the splurge, particularly if you go out of holiday season when the ferry is much cheaper and you'll pretty much have the place to yourself, aside from the resident koalas that you'll often see roaming around the streets (and even in the hotel beer gardens).

The island is holiday heaven with good surf, sensational beaches, great fishing, dolphins, whales and sea turtles, fun 4WD tracks, beautiful freshwater lakes perfect for swimming, and a lovely coastal boardwalk that ends at an ice-cream shop in the middle of a cafe strip in the township of **Point Lookout**.

Not all roads on the island are 4WD, but if you have one you'll be able to access the beachside campgrounds and drive along **Main Beach** from the north to the south of the island. There are several good beachfront caravan parks if you don't want to drive on the sand: try Amity Point or Adder Rock, and lots of holiday rentals that you can get to in a 2WD car.

BRISBANE/MEANJIN TO NOOSA HEADS

Brisbane might be Australia's third largest city, but it has a surprising amount of ways you can go wild, especially with animals. Queensland is one of the few states that allow you to hold or cuddle a koala, and the best place to do it is at **Lone Pine Koala Sanctuary**, the world's first and largest koala sanctuary, home to more than 130 koalas and a host of other native wildlife. It's an easy 12km drive from the city centre, or ditch the car for the day and take a **Mirimar Cruise** from the Cultural Centre Pontoon (out the front of the State Library) at 10am daily. The whole cruise takes approximately 1.5.hr.

From Brisbane, head north on the M1 (Bruce Hwy), past the craggy peaks of the **Glass House Mountains**, and take the turn-off to **Caloundra**. From here you can snake your way up the Sunshine Coast,, past countless seaside holiday towns, towards **Mooloolaba** and **Maroochydore**. All offer sun, sand, surf and plenty of family-friendly things to see and do, without all the frenetic razzle dazzle of the Gold Coast. If you enjoy seafood, you'll love this part of the Sunny Coast. Locals like to boast that more seafood is caught by boats operating out of Mooloolaba than at any other port on the eastern seaboard of Australia and that more game fish are tagged and released by boats based in Mooloolaba than in Cairns.

The glorious beaches continue as you keep heading north, past the volcanic dome of Mount Coolum and the resort towns of **Coolum Beach**, **Peregian Beach**, **Marcus Beach** and **Sunshine Beach**, all the way to Noosa Heads, at the mouth of the Noosa River.

Spend some time in **Noosa** browsing the boutiques or watching the passing parade from one of the sidewalk cafes along Hastings St (Noosa's main street), then take a walk through **Noosa National Park** (at the eastern end of Hastings St) to the headland. If you're lucky, you may see koalas along the way. A great bargain is the all-day ticket on the wooden ferry that plies the waterways between Hastings St, Noosaville and Tewantin. Take the 90min-return trip, or hop on and off as often as you like.

Opposite top left Cooroy Mountain *Opposite top right* Strangler Cairn in Conondale National Park *Opposite bottom left* Point Lookout, North Stradbroke/Minjerribah *Opposite bottom right* Koala on Straddie

Gold and Sunshine coasts 221

SIDETRACK

Another popular daytrip from Brisbane/Meanjin is out to **Mulgumpin/Moreton Island** - the least developed of the large sand islands in Moreton Bay/Quandamooka and number three in the world's largest sand islands list - where you can hand-feed wild dolphins at **Tangalooma Island Resort** (*see* Best beds). Each evening the dolphins, varying in numbers from five to nine, swim into the shallow well-lit area adjacent to the resort jetty to be hand-fed their favourite fish. Full daytrips are available that return to the city after the dolphins have been fed. Hard-to-impress teenagers (and grown-ups) will also love sand tobogganing. For the real thrill seeker, the big sandhills reach up to 80m in height and speeds have been clocked up to 50km/h,, while for the not-so-daring and the kids, the small sandhills and The Desert are perfect for giving this fun sport a try. Sand tobogganing boards are available to hire on the island and are included in many of the guided tours. Book tours at tangalooma.com.

Kids' spot

Brisbane is also home to Australia's only artificial inland city beach. **Streets Beach**, in the South Bank Parklands, holds three mega litres of water or approximately three Olympic size swimming pools and is surrounded by 4000 cubic metres of sand. Perfect for littlies, there are no waves or dangerous rips like on coastal beaches and it's patrolled by professional lifeguards. There's also lots of open space to run in, and three playgrounds to slide and swing and climb on.

Head into the hills

A 20min drive west of Noosa is **Eumundi**, where every Sat and Wed morning crowds flock to the markets to browse a huge array of local produce, art and crafts. If you are not in town on market day, there are several good art galleries and craft studios to browse in the main street. From Eumundi drive south to **Nambour** (snap a selfie at the iconic **Big Pineapple**) and then cut west to **Mapleton** along the spine of the Blackall Range to **Montville** and **Maleny** for great views of the coast and hinterland and good shopping. Take the short loop drive out of Maleny along Mountain View Rd for more views and a boardwalk stroll through **Mary Cairncross Scenic Reserve**, a 53ha rainforest reserve. Wind your way down the mountains along the **Maleny–Kenilworth Rd** via Conondale and cross the beautiful **Obi Obi Valley** to negotiate the steep, mountain-hugging ascent back up the range (not suitable for caravans) to Mapleton, stopping at **Mapleton Falls** to look out over the waterfall or step out on the 1hr circuit walk.

Sunshine Beach, Noosa National Park

Good for a rainy day

Kids (and adults) love watching the crocodile shows and other Australian wildlife at **Australia Zoo** in Beerwah. Alternatively, introduce them to the wonders of the deep at Mooloolaba's **SEA LIFE Sunshine Coast**, where they can be kissed by seals, handle sea stars and sea cucumbers, watch a variety of shows and presentations, or walk through the shark-tunnel aquarium that houses more than eight species of shark. If you are game, you can even dive with the sharks, as well as swim with seals or become a seal trainer for the day. You can also go behind the scenes to see the turtle hospital and learn about rescuing, caring for and feeding marine creatures.

BEST BEDS

- The **JW Marriott Gold Coast Resort & Spa** is a hit with families who love the snorkel-friendly saltwater lagoon with its waterfall, lava tube waterslide, sandy beaches and tropical fish. marriott.com.au
- There are plenty of tours that return to Brisbane after the wild dolphin feeding on Mulgumpin/Moreton Island but if you don't fancy a 75min trip back to the city after dark you can stay at **Tangalooma Island Resort**, which is comfortable rather than flash. Not all room rates include dolphin feeding, so check before booking. tangalooma.com
- **Oceans Mooloolaba** has luxury two- and three-bedroom suites and is on the Esplanade opposite the beach, so most have great views. oceansmooloolaba.com.au
- Wedged between a splendidly empty surf beach and the tranquil Maroochy River, **Novotel Sunshine Coast Resort** is set amidst lush tropical gardens surrounding a private lagoon. But as hard to beat as the location is, it's the resort's huge range of activities that include an 18-hole championship golf course, over-water spa and adventure water sports that make it a hit with everyone. novotelsunshinecoast.com.au
- **Noosa Hill Resort** The large self-contained apartments here have fantastic views and it's an easy 5min downhill walk to Hastings St - although the walk home up the hill is steep. noosahillresort.com.au

VANLIFE

If you're looking for the ultimate beachfront camping spot head to **Flinders Beach** on Minjerribah/North Stradbroke, although make sure you check the tide chart first, because the only way to get there is via the beach, which disappears at high tide. Campsites are right on the edge of the sand, there's lots of shade and outside of holiday season there's plenty of room to move. Look up into the trees and you'll probably spot a koala or three. If you would prefer an even more remote camp head to **Main Beach**, where individual campsites are tucked away in the dunes but there are no facilities at all, and access is cut during high tide. For more information on campgrounds, 4WD permits and to book sites, see minjerribahcamping.com.au. Another great camping spot is **Coochin Creek**, 9km east of Beerwah, which has tent and caravan sites, wheelchair-accessible toilets and a boat ramp, so it's a good spot for those that like fishing and messing about in boats. Elsewhere on the coast you'll find caravan parks in most coastal towns. It gets busy in summer and you'll need to book ahead during those times; bookings are essential for all campgrounds in Queensland national parks year-round. See parks.des.qld.gov.au/camping/bookings.

Gold and Sunshine coasts

Queensland

One of the longest beach drives in the world, and about as close as you can get to the sea in four wheels without getting wet.

Great Beach Drive

HOW LONG?

With scenery this special, this is not a road trip you want to rush. You can do the Noosa to Rainbow Beach section in half a day but to do the full Great Beach Drive all the way to top of K'gari, you really need between three and five days.

WHEN TO GO

Summer is the most popular time to do this trip, and the beach can get busy on sunny weekends. On the Great Beach Drive it's the tide, not traffic tailbacks you have to worry about – the notorious Mudlo Rocks just south of Rainbow Beach township is infamous for wrecking an average of 40 4WDs each year, their drivers left stranded by a combination of soft sand and rapidly rising seawater. Whale watching season is June through to Nov, but the best time to see them is Aug, Sept and Oct, when they are heading back south to Antarctica with their calves.

NEED TO KNOW

Permits to drive on Rainbow Beach and K'gari are required and must be bought online before driving from Queensland Parks and forests (parks.des.qld.gov.au/management/managed-areas/recreation/vehicle-permits) or call 13 74 68.

The Kingfisher Bay Ferry departs from the Kingfisher Bay Resort (50min), the Fraser Venture Barge departs from Wanggoolba Creek on the western side of the island (30min). Both arrive at River Heads on the mainland, 20min south of Hervey Bay. For ferry times see Sealink (fraserislandferry.com.au) or call 1800 227 437.

Dingoes can be a threat to young children on K'gari, so if you are camping with kids under the age of 16 camp only in fenced campgrounds.

SNAPSHOT

The Great Beach Drive between Noosa's north shore, Rainbow Beach and beyond to K'gari trumps all other coastal highways when it comes to scenic seaside drives because this road is actually on the beach. Throw in one of Australia's most spectacular World Heritage–listed wilderness areas – the rainforest and beautiful freshwater lakes and streams of K'gari – as well as one of the country's best whale watching spots and you have all the reasons you need to hit the road – or beach, in this case.

Drive rating
Moderate to challenging. Mostly 4WD-only beach driving.

Acknowledgement of Country
This is the Traditional Land of the Gubbi Gubbi and Butchulla Peoples.

Distance planner
The Great Beach Drive stretches approximately 225km from the north shore of Noosa to the northern tip of K'gari (via the barge at Inskip Point).
- Noosa to Rainbow Beach and Inskip Point via the beach: roughly 85km
- Hook Point to Sandy Cape on K'gari: roughly 138km

More information
- Noosa Visitor Information Centre, 61 Hastings St, Noosa Heads; 1300 066 672; visitnoosa.com.au; visitsunshinecoast.com
- Hervey Bay Visitor Information Centre, 227 Maryborough-Hervey Bay Rd, Hervey Bay; 1800 811 728; visitfrasercoast.com

Opposite Driving along Rainbow Beach

NOOSA TO RAINBOW BEACH

The fun begins almost as soon as you drive off the little ferry at Tewantin near Noosa Heads (135km north of Brisbane/Meanjin). This is the time and place to air down your tyres – reducing the pressure to around 20psi will give you a lot more traction when driving in sand – because the street turns to sand just up the road.

There's no line markings or overtaking lanes, in fact there's not even a track, but it is actually a designated road. All the usual road rules apply, including speed limits: 80km/h on the beach, 50km/h along beach camping areas, but drive to the conditions. There are a whole lot of other hazards that you normally don't have to worry about too much on a normal highway, like kids building sandcastles and teenagers sunbaking in the middle of the road and vehicles parked pretty much anywhere their owners feel like it. But don't let any of this put you off. This is a great on-the-beach drive for first timers – it's challenging enough to be exciting but as long as you travel at low tide and keep your air pressure low you're not too likely to get into trouble, and if you do there will be plenty of people around to help you out. The only really tricky bits are the sometimes soft and bumpy sand ramps that lead on and off the beach. If you've never driven on sand before, and are feeling nervous, there are lots of places you can sign up for some lessons before you go: search online for '4WD Sand Driving Courses'.

Teewah Beach, part of the Cooloola Recreation Area in Great Sandy National Park, extends some 50 or so sandy wave-washed kilometres to Double Island Point. It's a bit of an uphill walk, but the views from the lookout beside the **iron lighthouse**, built in 1884, are worth the slog, particularly in winter when you may just be treated to a spectacular show of breaching, blowing, head slapping and spyhopping from passing **humpback whales**.

Other highlights include a large tidal lake and **Rainbow Beach**'s famous, although slightly-misnamed, coloured sands – they are actually sandy cliffs coloured by iron oxides in, if you believe the locals, 72 different shades of red, yellow, orange, ochre and rust.

To get to the township of Rainbow Beach, leave the beach at Freshwater camping area and wind your way along the sandy rollercoaster track over the vegetated dunes through the rainforest, past stands of satinay (turpentine), kauri, strangler figs and dense pockets of piccabeen palms.

Don't miss a walk across **Carlo Sandblow**, a massive slow-moving sand dune that towers over Rainbow Beach and is one of the largest piles of wind-blown sand on the Queensland coast. With views of Rainbow Beach and the coloured sands in one direction, across to K'gari and west to Tin Can Bay in the other, it's hard to imagine a better spot to watch the sun go down – or come up, depending on the time of day you get there.

Stopping for a swim along the Great Beach Drive

Great Beach Drive

Queensland

228

RAINBOW BEACH TO K'GARI

The Great Beach Drive continues north along Rainbow Beach to **Inskip Point**, where you can catch the **Manta Ray** barge for a 10min trip across to K'gari for yet more sand-under-the-wheels motoring. Book ahead online (mantarayfraserislandbarge.com.au) or call (07) 5486 3935.

Smothered in rainforest that shelters beautiful freshwater lakes and streams so clear that the water is practically invisible, and encircled by beautiful crowd-free stretches of white sandy beach, getting back to nature is easy on **K'gari** as almost all of the island is national park.

At 123km long and 22km wide, it's officially the largest sand island in the world. There are no roads, just a network of sandy 4WD tracks and the famous **Seventy Five Mile Beach** which runs the length of the island's eastern coast and does double duty as the island's main highway during low tide.

Beyond the beach, exploring the island by 4WD, and visiting magical spots such as **Pile Valley** and the **Valley of the Giants**, home to some of the world's tallest rainforest trees, is a great adventure. These sandy tracks that criss-cross the island can be a little more challenging than the relatively smooth run along the beach, and you'll need a high-clearance 4WD – all-wheel drive vehicles are not suitable. Most of the inland tracks are wide enough for just one vehicle, so you will need to pull over frequently to let oncoming traffic pass – those downhill should give way. Go mid-week for less traffic. If you'd rather let someone else worry about the driving, there are plenty of 4WD tours available.

A highlight of most people's time on the island, though, is floating in water so clear that it's practically invisible. One of the most popular sites is **Lake McKenzie (Boorangoora)**, an almost perfectly circular perched lake – which means it's fed only by rainwater – ringed with dazzling white sand. Gin-clear when you're floating in it, implausibly bright blue from a distance, it's the type of place that you'd swear is a photoshopped fake until you've seen it in real life. Swimming here is divine and it's the perfect spot for a leisurely picnic lunch. Other top spots to get wet include **Lake Wabby** (the deepest lake on the island) at the advancing edge of the **Hammerstone Sandblow** and **Eli Creek**, a crystal-clear freshwater creek that winds through the rainforest – walk the boardwalk then float down with the current to the beach. The wreck of the *Maheno* lies slowly deteriorating on the water's edge just a few kilometres further up the beach. The trans-Tasman liner, bound for a Japanese wrecking yard, was driven ashore during a cyclone in 1935.

Good for a rainy day

Perfect for a bad weather day, the **Tastes of Australia** program at **Kingfisher Bay Resort** includes a Bush Tucker Talk and Taste Experience with the resort's chef and a ranger. You'll learn how to identify and cook with native ingredients – many grown on K'gari – and even better, get to taste some, before tucking into some very swish bush tucker at Kingfisher Bay's fine-dining restaurant.

Opposite top Wreck of the *Maheno*, K'gari *Opposite bottom* Boorangoora (Lake McKenzie), K'gari *Above* Rainbow Beach

Great Beach Drive 229

Keep going along the beach until you get to **Waddy Point** headland at the northern tip of Ocean Beach, where you'll be greeted with great views of beach and ocean and you can often see sea turtles, sharks and stingrays in the water below. **Champagne Pools**, where the surf crashes over a series of rock walls into calm but bubbly rockpools below the headland, is another popular swimming spot.

Stretch your legs on one of the walking trails. The big one is the 90km multi-day **Fraser Island Great Walk**, but if that sounds a little hardcore, there are dozens of day walks – a **circuit of Lake Mackenzie (Boorangoora)** or the hike across the sand dunes from **Lake Wabby to Ocean Beach** are two of the best – as well as easy 2hr strolls to lookouts and along the beach to historic ruins that start not far from Kingfisher Bay Resort. Or join one of the resort's ranger-guided bush tucker or local history walks.

You'll also see plenty of wildlife. Famous for its whales – humpbacks stop in Hervey Bay for a rest on their annual migration from Antarctica, taking advantage of the calm waters in the shelter provided by the island – you can get very close to them during winter-time **whale watching tours**.

Head down to the jetty at sunset and you might be lucky enough to see turtles, dugongs or dolphins. There are more than 354 recorded species of birds on the island, as well as large populations of wallabies, possums and gliders. The dingo population is regarded as the most pure strain of dingoes remaining in eastern Australia – you'll often glimpse them on the beach but stay well away (*see* p.225).

Kids' spot

K'gari is a great spot for a family holiday. The calm waters of the Great Sandy Strait can be good for older children to canoe, swim and play; there are 'learn to fish' clinics, Segway adventure tours, free tennis courts and for the little ones a playground with climbing frames, swings and slides. **Kingfisher Bay Resort** (*see* p.231) also has four large saltwater swimming pools. But it's the **Junior Eco Ranger** activities that most kids love: activities include bush art, guided nature walks, orienteering, rope courses and canoeing. Night-time activities include spotlighting for animals, stargazing, campfires with damper making, storytelling and singalongs.

SIDETRACK

The action might have happened in Cherry Tree Lane in London, but Mary Poppins was actually from Maryborough, 34km south of Hervey Bay. PL Travers, the creator of the famous children's books, was born here (as Helen Lyndon Goff) in 1899, and she is quoted as saying that 'Mary Poppins is the story of my life'. Local legend has it that Travers was inspired by an old-fashioned Maryborough local who carried an umbrella with a bird's head carved into the handle. There's a life-sized statue of the famous nanny outside the old bank - now a museum called **Story Bank** - where the author's father was bank manager, on the corner of Richmond and Wharf sts. The annual **Mary Poppins Festival** is held in Maryborough during the June/July school holidays with the Great Nanny Race, Chimney Sweep Challenge, costume competitions and a parade. Maryborough's also a good spot for a toilet break: check out the ornately decorated **Cistern Chapel in the City Hall**, complete with chandeliers and a golden 'throne', it's got to be Australia's flashiest loo.

BEST BEDS

- Perched high on the hill beside Carlo Sandblow most of the apartments at **Rainbow Ocean Palms Resort** have spectacular views across Rainbow Beach and beyond to K'gari. rainbowoceanpalms.com.au
- Best spot to stay on K'gari is **Kingfisher Bay Resort**, which has a four-star hotel, self-contained villas, fine dining, a range of tours, and a Wilderness Lodge for backpackers. kingfisherbay.com

VANLIFE

As far as beach camps go they don't get much better than the campsites spread out along **Teewah Beach**, where you can camp in the dunes with absolute ocean views. There are no facilities so you'll need a portable toilet - but you can camp on any site you like within a 15km stretch of beach. There's also a more formal camping area behind the beach near pretty **Freshwater Lake**. There are coin-operated hot showers, flushing toilets and free gas barbecues. **Inskip Peninsula Recreation Area** has several campgrounds right on the beach and offers good fishing and sheltered swimming on both sides of the peninsula. Facilities are basic though, with toilets but no showers. There are dozens of campgrounds on **K'gari**, the bigger ones have water and toilets and most have gas barbecues, as well as informal camping areas with no facilities behind the dunes on **Eastern Beach** and **Western Beach**. Book well ahead in summer; bookings are essential for all campgrounds in Queensland national parks, whatever the time of year. See parks.des.qld.gov.au/camping/bookings.

Opposite Campfire pitstop at Inskip Point *Left* Double Island Point Lighthouse, Rainbow Beach *Right* Humpback whale, Hervey Bay

Great Beach Drive

Glen Geddes
Canoona
Yaamba
Milman
Fitzroy
The Caves
Farnborough
BYFIELD NP
Sandy Point
North Keppel Island
Yeppoon
Mulambin
Kinka
Great Keppel Is (Wop-pa)
Emu Park
Koorana Crocodile Farm
Ridgelands
Parkhurst
ROCKHAMPTON
Tungamull
Joskeleigh
Gracemere
Rockhampton Botanic Gardens & Zoo
Keppel Bay
Cape Keppel
Stanwell
Midgee
Cattle Point
Cape Capricorn
Bouldercombe
Port Alma
Mount Morgan
Bajool
Marmor
Mount Barney
CURTIS ISLAND NP
Curtis Island
GELOBERA SF
Raglan
Ambrose
Southend
Mount Alma
Mount Pleasant
ULAM RANGE SF
Mount Larcom
Yarwun
GLADSTONE
Cedric Mountain
Boyne Island
Tannum Sands
DON RIVER SF
Mount Gerard
Mount Redshirt
Calliope
CALLIOPE
Benaraby
Rodds Bay
RODDS PENINSULA
Bustard Head
Bustard Bay
Jambin
DAN DAN NP
Barmundu
Awoonga Reservoir
Turkey Beach
Argoon
Callide
Mount Fane
Mount Seaview
RANGE
CASTLE TOWER NP
Seventeen Seventy
Lookouts
JOSEPH BANKS (ROUND HILL HEAD) CP
Biloela
Creek
KROOMBIT TOPS NP
Boyne
Bororen
Miriam Vale
EURIMBULA NP
Agnes Water
DEEPWATER NP
Thangool
Mount Cave
Nagoorin
BULBURIN NP
DAWES NP
Ubobo
Red Rock walking trail
Middle Rock
Wreck Rock
DAWES
Baffle
Dawes
Blue Mountain
BELMONT SF
DAWES NP
Builyan
Many Peaks
Lowmead
GREVILLEA SF
CANIA GORGE NP
BULBURIN NP
Ck
LITTABELLA NP
Mount Shaw
Moonford
Mungungo
Kalpowar
Mount Molangul
WARRO NP
Rosedale
Lake Monduran
MONTOUR SF
Bancroft
Yandaran
Moore Park
Bundaberg Rum Distillery & Bundaberg Barrel
COOMINGLAH STATE FOREST
Monto
BURNETT
Mount Gaeta
LITTABELLA NP
Flagstone Creek
Burnett Heads
Mon Repos Turtle Centre
Nogo
Mulgildie
Bucca
Bargara
BUNDABERG
K'GARI (FRASER ISLAND) WHA
Sandy Cape
River
Wuruma Reservoir
Burnett
BANIA NATIONAL PARK
RANGE
Elliott Heads
Coonarr
Rooney Point
BORANIA STATE FOREST
Abercorn
Gin Gin
Wallaville
BINGERA NP
BURRUM COAST NP
Platypus Bay
CALROSSIE STATE FOREST
Cynthia
NOUR NOUR NP
Mount Perry
Woodgate
Hervey Bay
K'gari/ Fraser Island
Orchid Beach
Ceratodus
Apple Tree Creek
Booyal
Goodwood
Burrum Heads
Port of Maryborough
Eidsvold
NOUR NOUR NP
Childers
Buxton
Quaggy Mountain
Grosvenor
GOOD NIGHT SCRUB NP
Toogoom
GREAT SANDY NP
YERILLA STATE FOREST
HERVEY BAY
Binjour
Dallarnil
WONGI STATE FOREST
Howard
Torbanlea
Lake Lenthall
Happy Valley
Byrnestown
River Heads
Kingfisher Bay Resort
Mundubbera
Biggenden
WONGI NP
Mount Narayen
River
Gayndah
Coalstoun Lakes
Brooweena
Mungar
MARYBOROUGH
Eurong
Aramara
Maaroom
GREAT BARRIER REEF
TROPIC OF CAPRICORN
GREAT BARRIER REEF MARINE PARK
GREAT BARRIER REEF WORLD HERITAGE AREA
Lady Musgrave Island
Lady Elliot Island
CORAL SEA
N
0 20 40 km
A1
A3
58
60
69
16
12
3
52
73
75
86
57

Once-in-a-lifetime wildlife encounters with whales, turtles and manta rays are just the beginning on this road trip at the southern end of the Great Barrier Reef.

Capricorn Coast

HOW LONG?
Allow four to five days to really explore the coastal towns and do some island hopping.

WHEN TO GO
Any time of the year is a good time to visit the area, although the best swimming weather on the southern beaches is during the summer months, which is also turtle nesting time. The northern section is best in winter, when days are dry and the water is stinger free; it's also the best time to see whales in Hervey Bay.

NEED TO KNOW
All beaches north of the towns of Seventeen Seventy and Agnes Waters have deadly and very painful marine stingers – box and Irukandji jellyfish – during the summer months. Swim only in netted areas or wear a stinger suit.

SNAPSHOT
One of the world's most significant turtle and humpback whale breeding grounds, the coastal stretch between Hervey Bay and the Tropic of Capricorn is rather underrated, which means you can find some fantastic beachside spots often overlooked by other travellers, especially in the coastal national parks.

Drive rating
Easy. Mostly sealed roads with optional 4WD sections.

Acknowledgement of Country
This is the Traditional Land of the Darumbal, Bailai, Gooreng Gooreng, Gurang, Taribelang, Wakka Wakka and Butchulla Peoples.

Distance planner
Hervey Bay to Yeppoon: around 575km. Hervey Bay is a 3.5hr drive north of Brisbane.
- Hervey Bay to Bundaberg via Bargara: 125km
- Bundaberg to Seventeen Seventy: 129km
- Seventeen Seventy to Yeppoon via Emu Park: 299km

More information
- Hervey Bay Visitor Information Centre, 227 Maryborough-Hervey Bay Rd, Hervey Bay; 1800 811 728; visitfrasercoast.com
- Bundaberg Visitor Information Centre, 36 Avenue St, Bundaberg; 1300 722 099; bundabergregion.org
- Explore Rockhampton Centre, 176 Gladstone Rd, Rockhampton; (07) 4936 8000; explorerockhampton.com.au

HERVEY BAY TO BUNDABERG VIA BARGARA

This drive cheats a little as it's not purely coastal. Although much of the driving is on the A1 – aka the Bruce Hwy – which runs parallel to the coast but seldom features water views, it links some of central Queensland's best seaside destinations, which qualifies it as one of the country's ultimate coastal road trips.

More than 14km of calm beaches with water warm enough for swimming for most of the year and plenty of tour options makes the starting point, **Hervey Bay** (say *Harvey*, not *Hervey*), a favourite family holiday spot. It's lovely in summer, but even better in winter, because it's one of the best places to see humpback whales: they stop here on their annual migration from Antarctica taking advantage of the calm waters in the shelter provided by K'gari and you can get very close to them on whale watching tours – there are almost a dozen whale watching operators who run cruises in the bay during the whale watching season, June through to Nov. Best time to see them is Aug, Sept and Oct, when they are heading back south to Antarctica with their newborn calves. They stop in Hervey Bay for a rest, and the whales are quite active with lots of spectacular displays of breaching, tail flapping and pectoral slapping. For details of whale watching tours, search online (visitfrasercoast.com).

From Hervey Bay, head north on the highway towards Bundaberg, but don't go all the way. If you've got a 4WD, **Burrum Coast National Park** offers crowd-free coastal camping, with lots of opportunities for fishing, boating and walking. If you'd rather stay on bitumen, opt for Bargara instead, 15min to the east of Bundy, which is what the locals call Bundaberg.

SIDETRACK

Hervey Bay is the main gateway to World Heritage-listed **K'gari** and there are several day tours available that take in the highlights. You can also take a passenger ferry and stay overnight at Kingfisher Bay Resort, leaving your car at the resort's mainland reception at River Heads (a 20min drive south of Hervey Bay), or, if you have a high-clearance 4WD and are confident driving in sand, take it across on the ferry or barge and explore the island at your own pace. See the Great Beach Drive road trip (p.225) for more details.

Strung out along the promenade of Nielsen Beach, **Bargara** lies at the very southern tip of the Great Barrier Reef. Even though Bargara is about as classic beach holiday territory as you'll find anywhere, it lacks the crowds, bling and bluster of the Gold and Sunshine coasts, which means it's a brilliant place to learn to surf as not only is the water delightfully warm almost all year round, but you're not battling other more territorial surfers for your waves. There are several surf schools in town.

It's not only would-be surfers who find the waters in this part of the world irresistible. Just a few minutes from town, at another gloriously beautiful beach, is the Mon Repos turtle rookery, the largest number of nesting loggerhead turtles on mainland eastern Australia, and the star attraction of the **Mon Repos Conservation Park**. Between Nov and Mar you can watch one of nature's most fascinating spectacles: the annual onshore pilgrimage of sea turtles as they come ashore to lay their eggs, and the subsequent hatching of young sea turtles eight weeks later and their return to the sea. The best time to see turtles laying eggs is after dark from mid Nov to Feb. Hatchlings usually leave their nests to begin their journey to the sea at night from mid Jan until late Mar. If you visit in Jan you might be lucky enough to see both adults and hatchlings.

During the turtle season public access to the beach is restricted after 6pm and the only way to see the turtles is to join a guided tour with one of the rangers, who will take you out onto the beach to visit nesting and hatching sites. It's very popular, so you'll need to book ahead at the Bundaberg Visitor Information Centre, and be prepared for a late night – the turtles don't always arrive on the beach right on time so sometimes you'll need to wait a few hours at the **Turtle Centre** nearby (there are turtle displays, ranger talks and video presentations to help you while away the time, snacks for sale and bathrooms facilities) and the tours often don't finish until around midnight – the earlier you book, the more likely you'll be one of the first groups to go out onto the beach. There's also a bit of walking through soft sand by torchlight involved, so wear comfortable shoes, bring a small torch (not a mobile phone torch, they are too bright – it needs to be 100 lumens or less, if in doubt, ask one of the staff at the Turtle Centre if your torch is suitable), a jumper and raincoat (no umbrellas are allowed on the beach). Find out more online (bundabergregion.org/turtles).

Ocean views near 1770

Back in **Bundaberg** you can wander around the impressive historic buildings in the centre of town or cool off in the shade of the **Botanic Gardens** in North Bundaberg. **Hinkler House** within the Botanic Gardens was originally built in Southampton, England, and was home for a while to one of Australia's greatest pioneer aviators, Squadron Leader Bert Hinkler. Born in Bundaberg in 1892, Hinkler flew solo from England to Australia in 1928 in a small plane, *Ibis*, which he designed and built in the backyard of his English house. The house was relocated to Bundaberg and now houses the museum, along with the **Hinkler Hall of Aviation** with six aircraft on display, flight simulators and a host of other exhibits.

The **Bundaberg Railway Museum** is on the site of Bundaberg's first railway station. It was built in 1881 as an outlet for the Mount Perry railway that brought copper from the mines, and now houses a wide variety of railway items in the old station buildings as well as outdoor displays.

Good for a rainy day

No visit to Bundy is complete without a tour of the **Bundaberg Rum Distillery**. The 1hr tours depart on the hour between 10am and 3pm weekdays or between 10am and 2pm on weekends and follow the rum production process from the sugar mill to the bottling line. You can also blend your own rum. You will need to wear fully enclosed shoes to join the tour. Book ahead (bundabergrum.com.au).

Drivers and kids will probably prefer the self-guided tour of the holograms and interactive displays at the nearby **Bundaberg Barrel**, home of naturally brewed Bundaberg Ginger Beer. At least here you can taste as much of the 14 different drinks on offer as you want without worrying about your blood alcohol levels.

SIDETRACK

Swimming with manta rays that have a wingspan of more than 7m might be a once-in-a-lifetime thrill, but it's an everyday thing on **Lady Elliot Island**, home to more than 450 of these gentle giants of the deep that don't have a stinging barb, or even any sharp teeth. Best time to swim with them is during winter, from June through to Sept. If you miss them, you'll usually see turtles on the island and in the lagoon year-round. Lady Elliot is 80km north-east of Bundaberg and is the southernmost coral cay on the Great Barrier Reef. Daytrips are available as well as overnight stays.

Lady Musgrave Island is another great daytrip option, especially for novice snorkellers and divers, as the surrounding ring of reef provides a barrier against outside currents in the lagoon, and forms a refuge for turtles. Swim with turtle tours are available year-round, and there's also an underwater observatory and glass-bottom boat tours for those that don't want to get wet. You can also camp on the island, for the ultimate coastal back-to-nature escape. Lady Musgrave Cruises (ladymusgraveexperience.com.au) can organise the transfers to and from the island.

Opposite top **Yeppoon Lagoon** *Opposite bottom* **Wreck Rock Beach, Deepwater National Park** *Left* **Swim with turtles on Lady Elliot Island**

Capricorn Coast

Lady Elliot Island

BUNDABERG TO 1770

From Bundaberg it's a 90min drive up the Bruce Hwy to **1770**, the only town in Australia to have a number instead of a name – officially it's called Seventeen Seventy, but locals all spell it 1770. The inspiration for the town's unusual name came from James Cook, who came ashore here in May 1770. If you like places where there's little more to do than throw out a fishing line, take long walks on deserted beaches, watch the sun set or simply settle in under a shady tree to read a good book, then 1770 is the place for you.

Surrounded on three sides by the Coral Sea, 1770 is one of the few places on the east coast of mainland Australia where you can see both the sun rise and set over water. Best place to watch it go down is on the deck of the Tree Bar at the **1770 Beach Hotel** on Captain Cook Dr. 1770 is twinned with nearby **Agnes Water**, which is where you'll find the small collection of shops and a supermarket.

Depending on which way you are travelling, this is either your first – or last – chance to surf: 1770 has the northernmost surf beach in Queensland. The rocky headland north of 1770 is part of **Joseph Banks (Round Hill Head) Conservation Park**, named after the botanist who collected 33 plant species here in 1770, and the lookout walk provides magnificent views north across Eurimbula National Park to Bustard Head and Rodds Peninsula. Another good walk is the 2hr **Red Rock walking trail** along the coast south of town. If you're lucky you may see turtles – they nest on the beaches in summer and hatch in autumn.

1770 TO YEPPOON

Rockhampton is around a 2.5hr drive north of 1770 – but break up the journey in **Gladstone**. Most famous for its coal mining, gas plant and huge port facilities, there are actually some nice coastal communities in and around the city. Head to **Tannum Sands**, **Boyne Island** on the south side or, if you have a 4WD, catch the vehicle ferry over to **Curtis Island**, where you can explore the dunes, rainforest and beaches; it's a haven for birdwatchers and fishers.

Just a few kilometres north of the Tropic of Capricorn – you can't miss the spire on the side of the road, it makes a great photo stop – **Rockhampton** (Rocky) is Australia's beef capital; more than two million cattle graze the surrounding countryside and giant fibreglass bulls seem to decorate almost every roundabout, park and awning in the city. The city is also full of elegant historic buildings with 30 listed as historically significant, and you'll find most of these as you wander down Quay St, opposite the river.

Attractions include **Rockhampton Art Gallery**, home to an amazing Australian art collection, and the **Rockhampton Botanic Gardens and Zoo**, a beautiful tropical garden with excellent specimens of palms, cycads and ferns, some more than 100 years old.

Head east of the city for 45km to Emu Park and wind your way up the coast to the charming seaside village of **Yeppoon**. It's the type of place where street signs warn you to watch out for osprey chicks learning to fly in roadside trees and the beach is the centre of the town. Stretch your legs along the esplanade and cool off in the **Yeppoon Lagoon** – a free swimming pool – or the nearby aquatic playground called **Keppel Kraken**, also free.

You can catch the ferry from Yeppoon to **Wop-pa/Great Keppel Island** from the Keppel Bay Marina in Rosslyn Bay. The famous former resort where everyone 'got wrecked' in the 1980s is in a dilapidated state, but the 17 beaches are still beautiful – you can snorkel right off the beach – and there are plenty of walking tracks to explore.

Or take a drive out to **Byfield National Park**. This park tends to fly a little under the radar of many travellers, but it's a fabulous mix of sand dunes, rainforests, creeks, mountains, wetlands and coastal views.

With the islands and coral cays of the southern end of the Great Barrier Reef within day-tripping distance of coastal towns, this road trip is a great way to escape the everyday.

Kids' spot

If you're travelling with kids a visit to the **Koorana Crocodile Farm** should be high on your list, although it's just as interesting for adults. It's a commercial crocodile farm home to more than 3000 crocs with guided tours that focus on croc behaviour and conservation and include the chance to snap a selfie cradling a baby crocodile. Depending on the time of year you can watch staff collect crocodile eggs from the nests. Between Feb and May you can see crocodile hatchings.

BEST BEDS

- **Oaks Hervey Bay Resort and Spa** is opposite the pier on Urangan Beach and has a range of one-, two- and three-bedroom suites, most with views towards K'gari. Facilities include two heated pools, a day spa and restaurant. oakshotels.com
- **Pavillions on 1770** has a range of one-, two- and three-bedroom luxury apartments opposite the beach halfway between Agnes Water and 1770. The complex features a heated plunge pool, 25m lap pool, heated children's wading pool and barbecue facilities. pavillionson1770.com.au
- All the apartments at **Salt** have an ocean view, and it's in a great location opposite the foreshore in Yeppoon. saltyeppoon.com.au

VANLIFE

Just about every town along this stretch has a caravan park, but if I had to pick a favourite it would be **1770 Camping Ground** (1770campingground.com.au). Facilities are basic, but the sites are right on the beach and it's an easy stroll to the heart of the village. Deepwater National Park, just south of 1770, has two great camping areas just behind the dunes at **Wreck Rock** and **Middle Rock**. Both are 4WD only. Burrum Coast National Park (see p.234) is a good option for camping without the crowds but you'll also need a 4WD here. You can camp on **Lady Musgrave Island**, but you'll need to be totally self-sufficient with a fuel stove and all your food and drinking water. Bush camping on **Curtis Island** is 4WD only, although there is a campground in the little town of Southend,, which is fine for conventional vehicles and campervans. The **Riverside Tourist Park** (riversiderockhampton.com.au) in Rockhampton isn't fancy, but it's right beside the Fitzroy River and just a short walk across the bridge from the city centre. The unpowered sites are only metres from the water - watch the city light up from your camp. It's also a good spot to try your luck catching a barramundi. For truly remote camping, head to **Byfield National Park**. Bookings are essential for all campgrounds in Queensland national parks. See parks.des.qld.gov.au/camping/bookings.

Queensland

240

The beautiful islands of the Whitsundays beckon, but there are just as many wonders to see onshore on this road trip along the Whitsunday Coast.

Whitsunday Coast

HOW LONG?

Allow three or more days to really explore the coastal towns and do some island hopping.

WHEN TO GO

Best time to visit is between Apr and Oct; summer is cyclone season. Swimming is not recommended between Oct and May as box jellyfish and the Irukandji jellyfish are prevalent in the waters, although stinger suits are available. From May to Sept the Whitsundays are an important calving ground for migrating humpback whales.

NEED TO KNOW

Summertime stingers aren't the only danger lurking in the tropical waters of the Whitsundays: this is also saltwater crocodile territory. Although crocodile sightings in the ocean around the Whitsunday Islands are rare, they are found in creeks, rivers and estuaries. Be crocwise and obey all warning signs. If in doubt, keep away from the water's edge.

LOCAL SECRET

The large number of sheltered bays and coves make the Whitsundays an ideal place for bareboating – hiring a boat without a skipper or crew. You don't need a boat licence, but if you're not comfortable sailing yourself, you can pay extra for a sailing guide or a skipper or opt for a catamaran or cruiser. They come stocked with everything you need, including bed linen, cooking equipment and often kayaks, paddle boards and snorkelling gear, too. You can provision the boat yourself or have it done so you're ready to set sail.

SNAPSHOT

The stretch of coast from Mackay to Townsville is a chain of unspoiled bays and beautiful beaches, bordered by emerald fields of sugar cane and highland national parks with waterfalls and tropical rainforest. But for most travellers the real attractions are the beautiful Whitsunday Islands, famous worldwide for their white beaches and aquamarine seas, and, of course, the underwater wonders of the Great Barrier Reef.

Drive rating
Easy. Mostly sealed roads.

Acknowledgement of Country
This is the Traditional Land of the Yuwibara, Giya, Juru, Bindal, Gugu-Badhun, Nywaigi and Wulgurukaba Peoples.

Distance planner
Mackay to Townsville: around 425km
- Mackay to Airlie Beach: 152km
- Airlie Beach to Townsville: 272km

More information
- Mackay Region Visitor Information Centre, Sarina Field of Dreams, Bruce Hwy, Sarina; (07) 4837 1228; mackayisaac.com
- Whitsundays Visitor Information Centre, 12505 Bruce Hwy, Proserpine; (07) 4945 3967; tourismwhitsundays.com.au
- Townsville Visitor Information Centre, Bulletin Square, Flinders St, Townsville, (07) 4721 3660; townsvillenorthqueensland.com.au

Opposite Hill Inlet, Whitsunday Island

MACKAY TO AIRLIE BEACH, VIA SARINA

Technically this coastal road trip kicks off in Mackay (the 'ay' rhymes with eye), but if you haven't already been there it's worth backtracking a little to **Sarina**, half an hour's drive south on the Bruce Hwy. If you ask the locals, they'll tell you that everything is bigger and better in Queensland, and in Sarina, that includes not just the hats but also the cane toads. The biggest of them all – around 1m high and just as wide – squats proudly between parked cars in the centre of the main street. Known as Buffy (short for her scientific name *Bufo marinus*), she's often decorated with scarves and streamers, and is a popular spot for a selfie. It's one of Australia's lesser-known (and, it has to be said, less attractive) 'Big Things'!

Ugly giant feral invaders aside, Sarina is a sweet place to spend time in, quite literally. The surrounding area produces more than 25 per cent of all Australia's sugar and the countryside is a sea of undulating green sugar cane. During harvest time (late Oct/early Nov), you'll see lots of cute little trains laden with cane as you drive through the patchwork of cane fields and past sugar mills.

Good for a rainy day

To find out what goes on behind the scenes at all these sugar mills that you're driving past, take a tour of the **Sarina Sugar Shed**. Huddled beneath the shadow of the much bigger Plane Creek Mill, this working miniature sugar-processing mill is the only one of its kind in Australia and gives a great insight into how the sweet crystals are extracted from the strappy lengths of cane. It's a fun and informative tour, with lots of tasting along the way, although most of it is pretty awful stuff until you get to the final product, and luckily the last tasting is of the range of sweet (and very alcoholic) liqueurs. If you're still craving a sugar hit, they also make great fudge. Book a tour (sarinasugarshed.com.au).

Whitehaven Beach, Whitsunday Island

Whitsunday Coast 243

A pretty city, **Mackay** has a distinctly tropical feel to it with lots of swaying palm trees and colourful flowers brightening the town's wide streets. There are lots of heritage-listed buildings, some of Queensland's finest Art Deco architecture, a great range of cafes and eateries, a large built **swimming lagoon** and **children's water playpark** and there is a very pleasant boardwalk beside the blue Pioneer River. The **Mackay Botanic Gardens** are another good place to escape the heat. Built around a chain of ponds they are alive with birdlife, particularly in the early morning and late afternoon. Mackay fishermen catch about half of Queensland's fish exports, so there's plenty of fresh fish on offer and the marina is next to sandy **Harbour Beach** and home to the **Pine Islet Lighthouse**, one of the only working kerosene lighthouses left in the world.

The beaches of **Cape Hillsborough National Park** (50km north of Mackay), and on the Traditional Land of the Yuibera People, are famous for their beachcombing kangaroos that can often be seen paddling at the water's edge early in the morning or late in the afternoon. It's a beautiful park with a dramatic coastline of rock-strewn sandy beaches, hoop pine-dotted hillsides plunging towards the sea, subtropical rainforest, mangrove-fringed wetlands and also a fantastic beachside camping area.

Until recently **Airlie Beach** was backpacker central, known for its budget accommodation and an all-night party vibe. There's still plenty of cheap and cheerful options, but in the past couple of years it has smartened up and now has a range of more upmarket places to eat and stay. One of the best things about Airlie Beach is that you don't have to go far, or spend any money, to get wet in style. Between the palm-fringed beach and the main street you'll find a massive built **lagoon** where you can swim stinger-free year-round. There are lifeguards on duty during daylight hours, a kids'

pool and the surrounding parkland has lots of shade and free barbecues. It's just like having your own five-star resort pool, but it's free. In the heart of town, the 850m **Airlie Creek walking track** takes you through the rainforest to a hilltop lookout. If you're lucky, you might even get a glimpse of the endangered Proserpine rock wallaby along the way.

Most people use Airlie Beach as a base to explore the **Whitsundays**, 74 islands in the heart of the Great Barrier Reef. It's picture-postcard stuff: think swaying palm trees and white sandy beaches, uninhabited islands, warm azure waters teeming with tropical fish and coral and you've got the idea.

The Whitsundays are a sailor's paradise, with a number of sailing tours, including bareboat charters (be your own skipper, *see* p.241), based at Airlie Beach – most head out to **Whitehaven Beach**, a popular contender for having the world's whitest sands (the detail is in scientific analysis, but it is gorgeous).

Head into the hills

Broken River in Eungella National Park (pronounced *yun-galah*) in the Mackay Highlands is probably the best place on the planet to see platypus in the wild. There are several viewing platforms strung out along the river near the picnic area - go early in the morning or late in the afternoon and you'll more than likely see half a dozen of the elusive monotremes. The park is split into two sections, above and below the ranges. Up the top are lots of rainforest walks and a lookout called **Sky Window** overlooking the cane-filled Pioneer Valley (the view is almost as good from the garden terrace of the historic Eungella Chalet - perfect for a post-walk beer on a hot day). The national park is a place where the Traditional Lands of three Traditional Owner groups meet: the Yuwibara, Widi and Barada Barna Peoples. Down below is **Finch Hatton Gorge**, which features two swimming holes fed by waterfalls. The only way in is by foot (both walks take around 2hr-return and the rocks are pretty slippery) but once you get there, it's downhill all the way back. Eungella is around 80km west of Mackay and the road up the Clarke Range is very steep, and not really suitable for large caravans. The Finch Hatton Gorge access road involves crossing several low-level causeways, so take care after rain.

SIDETRACK

It can be difficult to tear yourself away from the magical water and beautiful islands, but there's some magnificent rainforest to explore south of Airlie Beach. A highlight is swimming in the crystal-clear cool water below **Cedar Creek Falls** at the edge of **Conway National Park** - the Traditional Land of the Birri-Gubba Peoples. Here a 12m-high waterfall cascades into a beautiful plunge pool and long-necked turtles poke their heads above the surface to check you out as they float by.

Opposite top left Finch Hatton Gorge in Eungella National Park
Opposite top right Bowen's Big Mango *Opposite bottom left* Sugar cane in the Pioneer Valley west of Mackay *Opposite bottom right* The Museum of Underwater Art (MOUA), Townsville

Whitsunday Coast 245

Driving around Yunbenun/Magnetic Island

AIRLIE BEACH TO TOWNSVILLE

Around a 1hr drive north of Airlie Beach, the town of **Bowen** is famed for its mangoes – you can't miss the **Big Mango** on the edge of town, and it's admittedly much more photogenic than Sarina's big cane toad (*see* p.242).

Much quieter than Airlie, but just as beautiful, Bowen was transformed into 'Bowenwood' during the filming of Baz Luhrmann's epic film, *Australia* (2008), movie magic turning it into World War II Darwin for the bombing scenes. Many of the existing buildings featured in the film, including **Customs House** and the **Grandview Hotel**, embellished somewhat to resemble a typical 1930s hotel. Today though, the main attractions are the eight **palm-fringed beaches** all within a 10min drive, and a **coral reef** that you can explore straight from the shore. Head up to the top of **Flagstaff Hill** for great views too, or cool the kids down in the free waterpark on the beachfront.

It's around a 2hr drive to **Townsville**, home to one of the country's best beach promenades. Known as **The Strand**, the 2.5km stretch of inner-city beachfront is lined with restaurants, cafes, parks, playgrounds, swimming enclosures, and picnic and barbecue areas. On any given morning it's the place to be. Massive fig trees provide welcome shade, as do the palm trees that lean over the beach. Kids splash and squeal in the free, fun waterparks and dog walkers trot by along the walking path through the park. Under the shade of sail cloth slung over a wharf, hopeful anglers watch the tide come in, hoping for some fresh fish to take home, while on the horizon, the blue-grey silhouette of Yunbenun/Magnetic Island (*see* p.247) beckons.

Climb **Castle Hill** for views of the city (night-time views are spectacular) and then, if you can resist the lure of the beach or the shade of The Strand, head to **Reef HQ**, the world's largest coral reef aquarium and only living coral reef in captivity – which means you can actually explore the Great Barrier Reef while safely on land. At the time of going to print the aquarium was closed for redevelopment and is expected to reopen, bigger and even better, in 2026.

If you're a diver, you'll want to explore the **SS Yongala**, one of North Queensland's most famous shipwrecks. When *Yongala* foundered during a cyclone in Mar 1911 it sank without trace, and the wreck was not discovered until 1958. Certified divers with a minimum level of six logged dives can dive the real wreck of the *SS Yongala*, which is around

48 nautical miles south-east of Townsville, and considered to be one of the best wreck dives in the world.

Another must-see sunken attraction is **The Museum of Underwater Art (MOUA)**, a series of underwater sculptures created by artist Jason deCaires Taylor. You can see one of them, *Ocean Siren*, which changes colour according to the water temperature, rising out of the sea beside the Strand Jetty. Go online (moua.com.au) for details of local dive operators who run trips to the art sites.

Just next door to Reef HQ is the **Museum of Tropical Queensland** which has three levels of interactive exhibits on a variety of subjects, including life in the tropics, weird and wonderful creatures from the deep and a tropical science centre. The main exhibit, though, is another shipwreck – the *HMS Pandora*. The British Admiralty sent *HMS Pandora* in pursuit of the *HMS Bounty* and her mutinous crew in 1790. On her return voyage, having captured 14 of the mutineers in Tahiti, the Pandora struck the Great Barrier Reef and sank. The wreck was discovered in 1977 and has been carefully excavated, with the artefacts on show at the museum, as well as a life-size replica of the ship's bow. The story of the mutineers, their capture and subsequent fight for survival after the wrecking is fascinating.

For more things nautical, the **Maritime Museum of Townsville** across the river in Palmer St houses a collection of regional and Australian maritime history. Or if you prefer a land-based view of things, head for the **Palmetum**, where you'll find Australia's largest collection of palm species in this botanical garden featuring just one family of plants – the palms. The collection contains around 300 species, many rare and threatened in their natural habitat.

SIDETRACK

Jump aboard the car ferry to **Yunbenun/Magnetic Island**. Surrounded by marine park waters and fringing reefs, just over half of the island is a national park. Features include rocky granite headlands dotted with hoop pines, sandy bays and pockets of rainforest. You can snorkel to coral and wrecks direct from the beach and there is a network of walking tracks. The most popular is the 4km **Forts Walk**, a bit of a steep slog, but the view from the historic World War II forts is worth the effort. You've also got a good chance of seeing koalas and rock wallabies.

BEST BEDS

- **Mantra Mackay** Balcony suites overlooking the Mackay Marina. mantrahotels.com/mantra-mackay
- If you're keen to see platypus at Broken River, your best bet is early in the morning and late in the evening, so consider staying overnight. **Broken River Mountain Resort** offers comfortable motel-style cabins within easy walking distance of the platypus viewing areas, as well as a pool and licensed restaurant. brokenrivermr.com.au
- Midway between the centre of Airlie Beach township and the marina, **Coral Sea Marina Resort** is in a great spot, and has excellent views of the Whitsunday Passage. coralsearesort.com
- A terrific spot to stay if you are travelling with kids, the **BIG4 Adventure Whitsunday Resort** is a sprawling holiday park with a range of cabin options as well as caravan sites, set in lush tropical gardens near Airlie Beach (it's around 4km from town). Facilities that kids will love include a lagoon-style swimming pool (the largest resort pool in the Whitsundays), waterslide park with 13 slides, giant jumping pillow, pedal karts, full-size tennis court, mini-golf, adventure playground, basketball, volleyball, badminton, bocce and table tennis, and even an animal petting park. A special activity schedule is organised every school holidays, including outdoor movies, family barbecue night and a country music show. adventurewhitsunday.com.au
- A classic motel, Townsville's **Beach House Motel** is right on The Strand. beachhousemotel.com.au

VANLIFE

Many of the caravan parks on this stretch of coast have resort-style facilities, but if you'd like to get a little closer to nature, the campsites at **Smalleys Beach** in Cape Hillsborough National Park all have fabulous views, but it can be very popular so book well ahead. The beach, as inviting as it looks, is not recommended for swimming thanks to local crocs and summer stingers, but it's a beautiful place for walking and wildlife watching. Bring insect repellent as the sandflies can sometimes be intense. Mackay Regional Council operates camping reserves at **Seaforth**, **Ball Bay** and **St Helen's Beach**, and you can also camp on several of the Whitsunday Islands, including **Whitehaven Beach**, although you'll need to arrange your own boat transfer from Airlie Beach or Shute Harbour. See parks.des.qld.gov.au for more information, and for bookings for all national park campgrounds in Queensland.

Mount Mulligan
HANN TABLELAND NP
Koah
Clifton Beach
Trinity Bay
Smithfield
Kuranda
Lake Mitchell
Barron R
Port of Cairns
Green Is
Kingsborough
Biboohra
CAIRNS/GIMUY
DINDEN NP
Fitzroy Is
Mareeba
Arringunna Mountain
Lake Morris
Edmonton
Tabacum
LITTLE MULGRAVE NP
Dimbulah
Walkamin
Gordonvale
Aloomba
Mutchilba
Lake Tinaroo
Tinaroo Falls
Kairi
Fishery Falls
Emu
Tolga
Tinaburra
Deeral
Russell Is
CORAL SEA
GREAT BARRIER REEF
Atherton
WOOROONOORAN NP
Petford
Yungaburra
Babinda Boulders
Watsonville
Malanda
Babinda
Herberton
Bartle Frere South Peak
Bramston Beach
Josephine Falls
Irvinebank
Kalunga
Miriwinni
ELLA BAY NP
Three Mile Mountain
Millaa Millaa Falls
Zillie Falls
Ella Bay
Flying Fish Point
Ellinjaa Falls
Tumoulin
Millaa Millaa
Innisfail
Mount Garnet
Millstream Falls
Etty Bay
Ravenshoe
Mourilyan
South Johnstone
Innot Hot Springs
TULLY FALLS NP
Mungalli Falls
Mena Creek
Paronella Park
Mamu Tropical Skywalk
Cowley Beach
Tully Gorge Lookout
Cardstone
Silkwood
GREAT BARRIER REEF WORLD HERITAGE AREA
King Reef
El Arish
Kurrimine Beach
Koombooloomba Dam
Bingil Bay
Dreaming Trail
Mission Beach
KOOMBOOLOOMBA NATIONAL PARK
Herbert
Tully
CARDWELL
Wongaling Beach
TULLY GORGE NP
South Mission Beach
Dunk Is
Euramo
Kennedy Bay
Tully Heads
Kennedy Bay walking track
Mount Sharples
Mount Jones
KIRRAMA NP
Bilyana
GIRRAMAY NP
Rockingham Bay
Goold Is
RA
WET TROPICS OF QUEENSLAND WHA
Kennedy
Cardwell
Shepherd Bay
KINRARA NATIONAL PARK
Walters Plains Lake
GIRRINGUN CP
GIRRINGUN NATIONAL PARK
Cardwell Spa Pool
Attie Creek Falls
Cardwell Lookout
Ramsay Bay
Mount Graham
Hinchinbrook Is/Munamudanamy
Mount Bowen
HINCHINBROOK ISLAND NP
Wallaman Falls
Abergowrie
Thorsborne Trail
George Point
Burdekin
Lannercost
Lucinda
Palm Islands
GREAT BARRIER REEF MARINE PARK
Pelorus Is (North Palm Is) (Yanooa)
Trebonne
Halifax
ORPHEUS ISLAND NP
Ingham
Taylors Beach
Orpheus Is (Goolboddi)
Black Mountain
Toobanna
Ironstone Mountain
Forrest Beach
Great Palm Island
Great Palm Is
Michael Creek
Bambaroo
Greenvale
Mount Grey
Jourama Falls
Mount Dora
Mutarnee
Christmas Creek
Paluma
Balgal Beach
PALUMA RA
Rollingstone
Rattlesnake Is
Halifax Bay
Yunbenun/ Magnetic Is
Horseshoe Bay
PALUMA RANGE NATIONAL PARK
Mount Halifax
Jalloonda
Nelly Bay
Mount Nokomis
Bluewater
Pallarenda
Cape Cleveland
Cleveland Bay
BOWLING GREEN BAY NP
Clarke
Mount Cudmore
Blue Water Springs Roadhouse
Star
Mount Cataract
Garbutt
TOWNSVILLE
Thuringowa
Bowling Green Bay
Cape Bowling Green
N
0 10 20 km

Plunge-worthy swimming spots surrounded by lush rainforest and deserted sandy beaches. This under-the-radar road trip overdelivers with some of the biggest, widest and highest natural attractions in the country.

Great Green Way

HOW LONG?
It's less than a 5hr drive between Townsville and Cairns but take your time and spend three or four days.

WHEN TO GO
Best time to visit is between Apr and Oct when temperatures are warm but not uncomfortably humid; summer is very hot and wet. The cooler months are also the best time to get wet, as swimming in the ocean is not recommended between Oct and May as box jellyfish and the Irukandji jellyfish are prevalent in the waters.

NEED TO KNOW
There's plenty of places to swim on this road trip, but before you take the plunge make sure it's safe to do so, because this is saltwater crocodile country. Read and obey all crocodile warning signs and if in doubt, stay away from the water's edge and out of the water.

SNAPSHOT
Warm up and chill out getting back to nature on the beaches and in the rainforest of tropical north Queensland between Townsville and Cairns. This road trip has an abundance of waterfalls, wild swimming pools, coral reefs and tropical islands to explore. Keep your swimwear handy because you'll be wearing it a lot.

Drive rating
Easy. Sealed roads.

Acknowledgement of Country
This is the Traditional Land of the Gugu-Badhun, Wulgurukaba, Nywaigi, Warrgamay, Djirbalngan, Gimuy-walubara, Yidinji, Bandjin and Girramay Peoples.

Distance planner
Townsville to Cairns: around 350km, plus detours
- Townsville to Mission Beach: 232km
- Mission Beach to Cairns: 146km

More information
- Townsville Visitor Information Centre, Bulletin Square, Flinders St, Townsville; (07) 4721 3660; townsvillenorthqueensland.com.au
- Mission Beach Visitor Information Centre, 55 Porter Prom, Mission Beach; (07) 4068 7099; missionbeachtourism.com
- Cardwell Visitor and Heritage Centre, 51-53 Victoria St, Cardwell; (07) 4066 2412; cassowarycoasttourism.com.au
- tropicalnorthqueensland.org.au

TOWNSVILLE TO MISSION BEACH

You don't have to drive very far from the city centre of Townsville before you find a string of gloriously empty beaches. Townsville's northern beaches tend to be overlooked by many travellers, so chances are you'll be sharing them with just a handful of locals. As tempting as it is to linger longer here, there's plenty more special spots to come on this tropical coastal road trip, so point the car north.

Driving though this lush landscape it doesn't take long to realise why this drive has been nicknamed the Great Green Way by tourism marketing departments, as it's the gateway to the **Wet Tropics World Heritage Area**. Known as Munan Gumburu to the Nywaigi People – which translates to misty mountain – the **Paluma Range** is home to beautiful rainforests and some truly delightful swimming holes and waterfalls and, yes, plenty of atmospheric tendrils of mist drifting through the forested folds. Stretch your legs at **Jourama Falls**, signposted off the Bruce Hwy 91km north of Townsville, in Paluma Range National Park. The 1hr-return walk has a bit of uphill, but rewards with great views of the multi-tiered falls from the lookout, and it's a great swimming spot – but check conditions first with Parks Queensland as it can become dangerous after rain with slippery rocks and submerged objects; there have been fatalities here.

Not to be outdone on the bigger, higher, longer stakes, the coastal town of **Lucinda**, north-east of Ingham, has the longest jetty in the Southern Hemisphere, almost 6km long. It's a working service jetty for the sugar terminal, so off-limits to walkers, but there's a fishing jetty nearby that's almost as good as having your own boat – regulars often land northern bluefin tuna, Spanish mackerel and queenfish.

Don't leave Cardwell without a dip in the photogenic **Cardwell Spa Pool**, a natural but unusually blue swimming hole. It's 26km from town, on the very scenic **Cardwell Forest Drive**. Other highlights along the way include **Attie Creek Falls** and the views over Rockingham Bay and across to Hinchinbrook Island from **Cardwell Lookout**.

The stretch of coast between Cardwell and Innisfail known as the **Cassowary Coast** and **Mission Beach** – which is actually four villages linked by a 14km stretch of golden sand – is one of the best places to see the notoriously shy cassowary in the wild. One of Australia's largest flightless birds – it's our heaviest bird, but the emu is a tad taller – there are thought to be around 100 adult cassowaries living in and around Mission Beach, quite a lot given it's estimated that the entire wild population, which are found only in north-east Australia and New Guinea, is less than 4000. Weighing in at 60kg and up to 2m tall, they have brilliant blue necks and bright red

Opposite South Mission Beach *Left* Wallaman Falls *Right* Paronella Park

wattles, but despite their size they can be very hard to spot in the forest – thanks to their camouflage. You will see plenty of warning signs on the roads around town asking motorists to slow down – road accidents are the greatest single cause of southern cassowary death. There are a few hot spots around town where you have a better-than-average chance of seeing a cassowary, including the **South Mission Beach Transfer Station** (i.e. the tip – not the usual place to be in a travel book), the 3km-long rainforest **Dreaming Trail on El Arish Mission Beach Rd** and at the back of the **South Mission** caravan park across the road from the beach.

Hire a tinnie and explore nearby **Dunk Island** or enjoy a swim – there's a netted stinger enclosure on the beach opposite the caravan park. **South Mission Beach** is ideal for long strolls or hit the 7km **Kennedy Bay walking track** – it's very scenic but you need to check the tides before you go, otherwise you'll end up wading half of it when the beach disappears at high tide. And keep your eyes peeled for cassowaries along the way.

Head into the hills

The highest permanent single-drop waterfall in the country, **Wallaman Falls** is 50km west of Ingham in Girringun National Park and plunges 268m though a rainbow-decorated mist. You can camp here, and there are two short walks along the creek and to the base of the falls, where you may just see platypus, water dragons or saw-shelled turtles.

Good for a rainy day

Tully is famous (or infamous, depending on your point of view) as the wettest place in Australia: most years it gets around 4m of rain, but the record is 7.9m, exactly the same height as the Golden Gumboot, Tully's monument to rainy days. Adorned with a giant green tree frog, you can climb a spiral staircase to the viewing platform at the top of the boot. All that rain makes for good river rapids, and the nearby Tully River is a popular place for white water rafting and guided tubing tours.

SIDETRACK

Hinchinbrook Island/Munamudanamy dominates the view as you continue north to Cardwell. Australia's largest island national park, it's a wildly beautiful place that the Bandjin and Girramay Peoples call Munamudanamy, with cloud-shrouded peaks, rainforest and white sandy beaches, fringing reefs and prolific wildlife. It's home to one of Queensland's epic coastal walks, the four-day **Thorsborne Trail**. Stretching for 32km along the east coast of the island from Ramsay Bay to George Point, you need to be fit and well-equipped , as well as organised enough to book well ahead as only 40 walkers are allowed on the trail at any one time. There are no hotels on the island, but you can camp. If that sounds a bit too challenging, you can also explore the island on daytrip tours from Cardwell and Lucinda. Water taxis and a ferry are also available from both towns (visithinchinbrook.com.au; absolutenorthcharters.com.au).

Great Green Way

MISSION BEACH TO CAIRNS

There are plenty of rainforest-fringed beaches to explore – most are so undeveloped you feel like you're the first to discover them – on the next section of coast between Mission Beach and Innisfail, although you'll need to detour off the highway to get there. **Kurrimine Beach** is one of the closest to the Great Barrier Reef; if you're here at low tide (check ahead) you'll be able to walk out to **King Reef**, so don't forget to bring reef shoes. And bring a fishing line, because this is seriously good fishing territory. There's not much at **Cowley Beach** apart from a kiosk and caravan park, which is part of its charm, and **Etty Bay** is another good spot to see cassowaries as they often come out of the rainforest onto the beach, sometimes with their chicks. The best time to see them is early in the morning or late in the afternoon.

By now the endless fields of sugar cane on either side of the road will be a familiar sight, and many of the towns along the coast have sugar mills and large sugar loading facilities. The **Australian Sugar Heritage Centre** in Mourilyan, just south of Innisfail, will take you through the process of turning the strappy green cane into sweet crystals, and also chronicles the history of Australia's second largest export crop (after wheat), with displays that include old tractors, farm implements and even a train. It also examines some of the industry's past use of indentured labour and illegal kidnapping – known as blackbirding – of South Pacific Islanders.

If you're a lover of architecture – or even just a fan of the jazz age and the fashions of the Roaring Twenties – you'll love **Innisfail**. Practically destroyed by a cyclone in 1918 most of the town was rebuilt in the Art Deco style and it has the highest concentration of Art Deco buildings and facades in the country. One of the most impressive is the **Johnstone Shire Hall**, complete with parapets, which runs regular free half-hour tours on Fri mornings. If you miss those you can download a free walking tour with the Tropical Deco App.

It's just over a 1hr drive from Innisfail to Cairns, but factor in some extra time for a swim at **Babinda Boulders** – a beautiful freshwater swimming pool encircled by giant granite rocks – and **Josephine Falls**, in the shadow of Queensland's highest peak, Bartle Frere, in Wooroonooran National Park. Cooler than you'd expect in such a warm place, it's a refreshing way to finish a very tropical road trip.

Kids' spot

It's not just kids who are mesmerised by the magical ruins of a real-life Spanish castle in the rainforest at **Paronella Park**, north of Innisfail. Built by hand by a Catalonian cane cutter, José Paronella, as a gift for his wife, when it opened to the public in 1935 it featured a grand staircase and even grander ballroom with a suspended disco ball made with more than 1270 mirrors (decades before disco was even invented), a movie theatre, refreshment rooms, tea gardens, a waterfall, extensive gardens with more than 7000 planted trees, and the first hydro-electricity plant in north Queensland. It was a popular spot for dances, parties and celebrations. Since then, fire, floods and several cyclones have wreaked havoc on the extraordinary creation, but new owners have brought the pleasure gardens back to life, and now offer both day and night tours, wildlife, turtle and fish feeding, as well as accommodation and camping grounds.

Head into the hills

You've seen the highest waterfall in the country at Wallaman (see p.251), now see the widest: **Millstream Falls**, 3km from Ravenshoe in the Atherton Tablelands. The falls, which spill over an old basalt lava flow, are best seen during the wet season when they are at their most spectacular. It's not the town's only claim to fame - at 930m above sea level, Ravenshoe is Queensland's highest town and who can resist having a drink in Queensland's 'top' pub - the **Ravenshoe Hotel** is the highest in the state. Ravenshoe is surrounded by cool, misty rainforest, aptly called the Misty Mountains, and there's a network of wilderness walking tracks, although they really are wild - some of the tracks are quite hard to find and overgrown. Follow the scenic Tully Falls Rd from Ravenshoe to the spectacular **Tully Gorge Lookout**. The falls only run in a big wet season, but the walls of rock and rainforest which plunge 300m down to the Tully River are still an awe-inspiring sight. Get there via the **Waterfall Circuit** from Innisfail, which includes Mungalli Falls, Ellinjaa Falls, Zillie Falls and Millaa Millaa Falls (another splendid swimming spot). If you have a head for heights, the **Mamu Tropical Skywalk**, around a 15min drive out of Innisfail on the way to the falls, has elevated walkways, a cantilevered viewing platform and an observation tower.

BEST BEDS

- Opposite the beach and more of a holiday resort than a caravan park, **Tasman Holiday Parks - South Mission Beach** is a great spot to stay with kids: there's a large playground, swimming pool with a waterslide and splash park, tennis, basketball, outdoor movie nights, bicycles - hire fat-wheeled bikes and cycle the beach - and a games room. You can also hire boogie boards, cricket sets, bocce, racquets and board games. There's a range of accommodation options, from two-bedroom cabins with a spa bath, to cute little one-roomed beach shacks that don't have a bathroom but do have stunning views across to Dunk Island, and powered caravan sites surrounded by beautiful tropical gardens and a large shady camping area at the back. The holiday park borders a cassowary conservation zone and if you're lucky you may even have one wander through your camp. tasmanholidayparks.com
- **Novotel Cairns Oasis Resort** In a great location close to the centre of Cairns, the resort has one of the largest swimming pools in town. novotelcairnsresort.com.au

VANLIFE

There's no shortage of great places to park a van or pitch a tent in this part of Queensland. You'll find caravan parks in almost every town, often overlooking the beach; favourites include the parks at **South Mission Beach**, **Etty Bay**, **Kurrimine Beach** and **Cowley Beach**. Top spots if you want to go a little wilder and immerse yourself in the rainforest include beside Waterview creek at **Jourama Falls** in Paluma Range National Park, at **Babinda Boulders**, and **Paronella Park**. You can also camp at a dozen beachside camping areas on **Hinchinbrook Island/Munamudanamy**, but you'll need to be self-sufficient and BYO everything. See parks.des.qld.gov.au for bookings for all national park campgrounds in Queensland.

Top Cardwell Spa Pool

Queensland

The rainforest meets the sea on this journey between Cairns and Cooktown, the only place on the planet where two World Heritage–listed areas (the Wet Tropics and the Great Barrier Reef) sit side by side.

Great Barrier Reef Drive

HOW LONG?

If you just drive straight from Cairns to Cooktown, it will take less than a day, but there's plenty to see and do in both Port Douglas and Cape Tribulation (Cape Trib) so give yourself four or five days.

WHEN TO GO

Summer is very wet, humid and stormy. Winter is warm and sunny with little rain. The cooler months are also the best time to get wet, as swimming in the ocean is not recommended between Oct and May as box jellyfish and the Irukandji jellyfish are prevalent in the waters.

NEED TO KNOW

Most of the unsealed roads in Far North Queensland become impassable after rain. Check road conditions before travelling (qldtraffic.qld.gov.au) or call 13 19 40. This is also crocodile country, so be crocwise, obey all warning signs, and if in doubt, stay away from the water's edge.

SNAPSHOT

There are two main reasons that thousands of visitors head to tropical north Queensland each year – the rainforest and the Great Barrier Reef – and you can explore them both on this drive from Cairns to Cooktown, one of the country's most scenic coastal drives.

Drive rating
Moderate. Sealed roads with unsealed 4WD section with some creek crossings.

Acknowledgement of Country
This is the Traditional Land of the Gimuy-walubarra yidi, Yirrganydji, Ang Gnarra, Kuku Yalanji and Guugu Yimithirr Peoples.

Distance planner
Cairns to Cooktown via Bloomfield Track: around 242km
- Cairns to Port Douglas: 67km
- Port Douglas to Cape Tribulation: 84km
- Cape Tribulation to Cooktown: 102km
- Optional sidetracks: Cooktown to Laura: 159km; Atherton Tablelands loop: 175km

More information
- Atherton Tablelands Information Centre, cnr Main St and Silo Rd, Atherton; 1300 366 361
- Cooktown Visitor Information Centre, Walker St, Cooktown; (07) 4069 5763; cooktownandcapeyork.com
- Mareeba Visitor Information Centre, 345 Byrnes St, Mareeba; (07) 4092 5674; mareebaheritagecentre.com.au
- tropicalnorthqueensland.org.au

Opposite Thala Beach Nature Reserve

CAIRNS TO CAPE TRIBULATION

With so many great things to see and do in and around **Cairns** – reef trips, rainforest skyways, heritage train trips, island hopping, shopping, visiting museums, art galleries and the aquarium, eating out or even just lazing around the free swimming lagoon on the promenade – it can be tempting to spend your whole holiday in Cairns, but this coastal road trip is not one you want to miss.

Officially called the Captain Cook Highway, but branded as the Great Barrier Reef Drive, the 67km stretch of curvy bitumen that runs north of Cairns to Port Douglas is one of the most picturesque roads in the country, proving that it doesn't have to be a long road trip to be a great one. It hugs the coast almost the entire way, one eye-stretching sea view unfurling after another and there are plenty of places to pull over and admire the scenery along the way, including **Rex Lookout**, around 56km north of Cairns, which looks out over Trinity Bay.

Mossman Gorge is a beautiful boulder-strewn river gorge in dense rainforest 20km north of Port Douglas and is a must-see spot in the Wet Tropics. The **Mossman Gorge Cultural Centre** is an Indigenous ecotourism development that offers easy access to the gorge, with shuttles departing every 10min from the carpark, as well as a cafe, Indigenous art gallery and gift shop. There are two Ngadiku Dreamtime Walks on Kuku Yalanji land, run by First Nations guides. The walks start with a Traditional 'smoking' ceremony that cleanses and wards off bad spirits before meandering through the rainforest, and takes in Traditional huts or humpies, a swim in a waterhole and, at the end, bush tea and damper. You can also do self-guided walks, which include a shuttle service from the Mossman Gorge Cultural Centre.

☺ Kids' spot

Port Douglas has plenty of eating choices on its main thoroughfare, Macrossan St, but its best breakfast is served on the southern edge of town: it's the daily 'Breakfast with the Birds' at the **Wildlife Habitat** wildlife centre, where you can also swim with a 4.5m saltie in a purpose-built underwater viewing space, meet kangaroos and snap a selfie with a koala, as well as special hands-on activities for 'junior keepers'.

Cairns Esplanade Lagoon

Great Barrier Reef Drive 257

The rainforest meets the sea at **Cape Tribulation** in the Daintree rainforest, believed to be the oldest rainforest in the world, 64km north of Mossman. The road to the cape is sealed, but you'll need to take the ferry across the Daintree River. There are four wheelchair-accessible boardwalks through the rainforest and mangroves, all of which include interpretation boards; these are a great way to explore the wet forests and swamps without getting your feet wet. The Dubuji and Kulki boardwalks lead out to beautiful **Myall Beach**. Swimming is not recommended, however, as saltwater crocodiles live in the park's creeks and nearby coastal waters; take on a **Daintree River Cruise** (daintreerivercruisecentre.com.au) you're pretty much guaranteed to see several crocs. The roads here are narrow and winding, not recommended for caravans and may be closed after heavy rain.

Opposite top left Boyd's forest dragon *Opposite top right* Grassy Hill Lighthouse, Cooktown *Opposite bottom left* Shell ginger, Cooktown Botanic Gardens *Opposite bottom right* Azure kingfisher *Above* Jindalba Boardwalk, Daintree National Park

Head into the hills

A cool daytrip from Cairns is to drive straight up into the mountains on the Kennedy Hwy, via a series of tight, twisting switchback turns through the World Heritage-listed rainforest up to **Kuranda** and **Mareeba**, where the country opens out into fields of sugar cane, paddocks of macadamia and mango trees, and orchards laden with strange-looking fruit. This is also coffee country: almost all of Australia's coffee is grown in the Mareeba area. **Skybury** coffee plantation has a terrific cafe - taste some of their delicious own-grown coffee on the deck, which has views that seem to stretch forever, or learn about how the coffee is roasted at **Coffee Works** in Mareeba.

The sleepy township of **Atherton** is 33km south of Mareeba. One hundred years ago, this little town had a flourishing Chinatown that had sprung up during the 19th-century gold rushes. Today, the only sign of this once thriving community of more than 1100 is the small timber and iron **Hou Wang Temple**, built in 1903, that somehow managed to survive while all around it buildings were demolished and carted away for scrap. It's now protected by the National Trust and houses a very good museum crammed with innovative, interactive displays and artefacts. Free guided tours run on demand and are well worth the hour or so it takes to explore the old Chinatown area and the interior of the temple, which is still fitted out with the original elaborate carvings, bell and metal vessels brought from China last century.

Head back to Cairns via the heritage town of **Yungaburra**. It's the largest National Trust village in Queensland and is full of lovely old wooden buildings and the **Curtain Fig Tree**, a massive fig with aerial roots that drop more than 15m to the forest floor, in the national park of the same name. All up, it's around a 175km loop from Cairns.

CABE TRIBULATION TO COOKTOWN

You'll need a 4WD to tackle the **Bloomfield Track** up to Cooktown (if you are in a conventional car or camper you can still go to Cooktown via the sealed, inland route, aka the Mulligan Hwy, via Lakeland and Mount Molloy, but you'll need to backtrack down to Shannonvale, between Mossman and Port Douglas).

This is the controversial road that was blazed through the Daintree rainforest back in the 1980s, provoking protests, blockades and several arrests, and ultimately led to the Daintree being proclaimed a World Heritage Site, despite opposition by the Queensland Government at the time.

Great Barrier Reef Drive 259

Today, the Bloomfield Track makes for an exciting trip, with lots of creek crossings, steep climbs and plenty of opportunity to get stuck if it has been wet. A highlight is **Wujal Wujal (Bloomfield Falls)**, which are at their best after rain or very early in the dry season, when a thundering torrent spills over a basin-like cliff into the river. They are on Kuku Yalanji land, and guided cultural tours are available through Wujal Wujal Aboriginal Shire Council (wujalwujalcouncil.qld.gov.au/visit). You've also got a good chance of seeing cassowaries foraging beside the road or darting into the rainforest as you drive past.

The Bloomfield Track hooks up with the sealed Mulligan Hwy around 25km south of Cooktown, but just before you reach the intersection you'll find the **Lions Den Hotel** – you can't miss it, it's the only thing there! Built in 1875 at the height of the gold rush, this historic hotel knocked together with scraps of wood and iron is full of quirky decorations and walls adorned with visitors' signatures. They serve a very good burger.

A sleepy, half-forgotten type of place yet to burst onto the tourist trail, **Cooktown** still has a last-frontier feel to it. It's also the only place in Australia where Captain Cook and his crew spent an extended period of time ashore. Back in 1770, Cook's ship, the *Endeavour*, ran afoul of the Great Barrier Reef, seriously damaging its hull near the place now known as Cape Tribulation. It was sink or swim, and Cook needed to find safe waters, fast, so he sailed his damaged vessel into the closest river he could find and set up camp at what is now known as Cooktown for seven weeks while he repaired his ship. Cook's landing site on the banks of the Endeavour River in the centre of town is marked with a plaque and statue commemorating him.

Take a stroll though the beautiful **Botanic Gardens** in Walker St – established in 1878 they are one of the oldest in the state. The **historic cemetery** (Boundary St) is also good for a wander: informative plaques recount the history and stories of some of the people buried here, as well as a large shrine to the many Chinese people who died here during the Palmer River gold rush of the 1870s.

The developers haven't yet found the road to Cooktown, but they will. Go now before everyone else does.

SIDETRACK

Renowned worldwide, the **Quinkan Galleries**, a collection of rock paintings, is located near the tiny township of Laura (also known for its biennial Laura Quinkan Indigenous Dance Festival). Around 60km north-west of Lakeland, the Quinkan Galleries include artworks painted 15,000-40,000 years ago. One of the most accessible sites is at Split Rock, just a few kilometres east of town. There are three galleries here, connected by a boardwalk, that encompass paintings of flying foxes and the bizarre, spiteful, tall spirits with knobbly knees and bent limbs, the Quinkans. There's not a lot of interpretive information at the site, so it helps if you call into the **Quinkan and Regional Cultural Centre** first. It's an excellent information centre cum museum, with all sorts of artefacts, films and recorded oral histories, but opening hours vary so call first to check: (07) 4060 2239. To see rock-art sites, organise a guided tour via **Ang-Gnarra Corporation** (anggnarra.org.au). Combine a Quinkan rock-art tour and overnight camping with **Jarramali Tours** (jarramalirockarttours.com.au): you can tag along in your own 4WD or let someone else do the driving for you if you are in a 2WD. The road to Laura is sealed.

Opposite Cherry Tree Bay, Cooktown *Above* Cooktown Museum

Good for a rainy day

Housed in an historic convent, it looks small from the outside but the **Cooktown Museum** is worth a few hours of your time. Here you'll find a large collection of Guugu Yimithirr - the Traditional Owners of the land around Cooktown - artefacts and learn about the first recorded interactions between the Guugu Yimithirr People and Cook. Also on display is the original anchor and canon from *HMB Endeavour*, salvaged in the 1970s, and exhibits relating to the 19th-century Queensland gold rush.

BEST BEDS

- **Thala Beach Nature Reserve** Perched atop a privately owned headland near Oak Beach on the only beachfront nature reserve between Cairns and Port Douglas, this eco-friendly lodge has its own 2km stretch of secluded beach exclusive for the use of Thala guests and is flanked by the Wet Tropics rainforest. You can choose between bungalows and suites, all furnished in an elegant tropical style and set in the rainforest with views. All accommodation sleeps two, except for the Kingfisher Suite bungalow that sleeps four people. thalabeach.com.au
- **Silky Oaks Lodge** The lodge offers luxury treehouse or riverside accommodation at the edge of Mossman Gorge in the Daintree Rainforest. All suites feature spa baths and verandah hammocks and the complex includes the Healing Waters Spa. silkyoakslodge.com.au
- **Cape Trib Beach House** Immerse yourself in the rainforest in one of the cute cabins beside Cape Tribulation Beach. Facilities include a swimming pool and deckside restaurant and bar. capetribbeach.com.au
- **Sovereign Resort Hotel** The best place to stay in Cooktown is this hotel in the middle of the main street. It has large air-conditioned rooms, a resort-style swimming pool set in tropical gardens and a good balcony restaurant. sovereignresort.com.au

VANLIFE

You can camp at **Noah Beach**, around 8km south of Cape Tribulation. The small sites are unsuitable for caravans or larger campervans, however. The camping area is closed in the wet season and after heavy rains. **Cape Trib Camping** (capetribcamping.com.au) offers lots of room with powered and unpowered sites in a big grassy area beside Myall Beach surrounded by rainforest and coconut trees - facilities include a handy coconut spike to husk the unlimited supply of free coconuts. Caravanners can choose from a range of caravan parks in and around Cairns, Port Douglas and Cooktown.

Great Barrier Reef Drive

PACIFIC OCEAN
Point Vincent
Point Howe
Duncombe Bay
The Hilli Goat
Captain Cook Lookout
Captain Cook Monument
Moo-oo Stone
Green Pool Stone
Cathedral Rock
Anson Point
Anson Bay
Bird Rock
Mount Bates
NORFOLK ISLAND NATIONAL PARK
SELWYN RESERVE
Jacobs Rock
Mount Pitt Lookout
Mount Pitt
Puppy's Point
NORFOLK ISLAND
Cockpit Waterfall & lookout
Botanic Gardens
CASCADE RESERVE
Cascade Bay
Cascade Pier
BURNT PINE
St Barnabas Chapel
NORFOLK ISLAND AIRPORT
HEADSTONE RESERVE
Headstone Point
Moreton Bay fig trees
The Bounty Centre Toy Shop
Chimney Hill
Fletcher's Mutiny Cyclorama
Two Chimneys Wines
Steels Point
Rocky Point
All Saints Church & museum
HUNDRED ACRES RESERVE
Sirius Museum
TWO CHIMNEYS RESERVE
The Pier Store Museum
BALL BAY RESERVE
POINT ROSS RESERVE
No 10 Quality Row Museum
Bucks Point
Point Blackbourne
Crystal Pool
Bumboras Beach
Ball Bay
Kingston
Point Ross
Slaughter Bay
Emily Bay
Collins Head
Cemetery Bay
Kingston & Arthur's Vale Historic Area
Norfolk Island Golf Club
NORFOLK ISLAND NP
Nepean Island
N
0
1
2 km
PACIFIC OCEAN
Hard Balli Stone
Dar Stool Inlet
Cow Bay
Red Stone
West End Point
Dar Moo-oo Bay
NORFOLK ISLAND NP
Phillip Island
East End Point
Dar Tomato Bay
Spin Bay
Juvenile Point
Whales Hump
Garnet Point

Norfolk Island is part of Australia, but has its own language, stamps, mobile phone network and even its own Commonwealth Games team. It is a fascinating place like no other.

Norfolk Island, South Pacific

HOW LONG?

Time moves slowly on this speck of land in the middle of the Pacific Ocean, so do as the locals do and be 'hilli'. It technically means lazy, but I think it's more readily interpreted as 'relax and take your time'. A week on the island would be perfect.

WHEN TO GO

Norfolk Island is a subtropical island, with delightfully mild temperatures and good swimming weather most of the year. Summer seldom gets above 30°C, and it rarely drops below 12°C, even in the middle of winter.

NEED TO KNOW

The maximum speed limit on the island is 50km/h (40km/h in the town centre and 30km/h in Kingston) and all animals, including feral chooks, ducks and cows, which roam free on the island, have right of way; it's more or less mandatory to acknowledge every passing vehicle with a 'Norfolk wave'. Even though it's a domestic flight to get to Norfolk, flights depart from the international airport in Sydney (2.5hr flight time) or Brisbane (2hr flight time), so you'll need photographic ID, preferably a passport. Flights are also available from Auckland. Many accommodation providers include car hire in the room rate, so it's worth checking when you book.

Burnt Pine is the commercial hub of the island and where you'll find cafes, shops, supermarkets and just about anything else you might need during your stay.

SNAPSHOT

Roughly halfway between Australia and New Zealand, Norfolk Island – made notorious as a brutal convict settlement before being gifted to the descendants of *HMS Bounty* mutineers in 1856 – may only be 35sqkm, but there are more than 120km of roads on the island. Driving them will take longer than you think – waiting for an obstinate cow to move off the road is a common occurrence. There is lots to distract you on your way round, with UNESCO World Heritage–listed convict ruins, fascinating museums and stunning beaches at the top of the list.

Drive rating
Easy. Sealed roads with some gravel roads that can become impassable after rain.

History of the island
Norfolk Island was uninhabited when settled by the British in 1788, although archaeological evidence shows that the island was inhabited by Polynesian seafarers between the 13th and 15th centuries - the reasons for the abandonment of the settlement are still unknown.

Distance planner
A loose lap of the island, including detours: around 40km.
- Kingston to Captain Cook Lookout, via Anson Bay: 16km
- Burnt Pine to Kingston (direct): 4km
- Burnt Pine to Kingston via Cascade and Two Chimneys Reserve: 16km

More information
- Norfolk Island Visitor Information Centre, Bicentennial Complex, Taylors Rd; +6723 22 147 (1800 214 603 to call from Australia); norfolkisland.com.au

KINGSTON TO CAPTAIN COOK LOOKOUT

It's difficult to get lost on Norfolk, and where you start – and finish – each day depends on where you're staying. So for this road trip we're suggesting you make your own way around the island, using this itinerary – a clockwise circuit of the island starting and finishing in historic Kingston – just as a rough guide.

But before you hit the road, you'll need to practise your Norf'k. Although everyone you meet will speak English, it's fun to try and learn a few words of this lilting language. A mix of Tahitian and 18th-century English, it's one of the rarest in the world with less than 1000 locals (but around half the island's population) speaking the local dialect. Among the words you'll hear all the time are 'watawieh yourle' (hello, how are you?), 'kushu' (good, thank you and 'dar-de-way' (that's the way).

Norfolk Islanders are an incredibly friendly bunch. Everybody waves to everybody, although it does mean tourists can be easy to spot – while locals deliver a nonchalant salute of one or two fingers raised from the steering wheel, enthusiastic visitors tend to wave with their whole hand, giving up their 'come from away' status straight away.

So friendly is the island that it's the only place in the world where the telephone book lists people under their nicknames (one can only wonder how Diddles, Pinky, Book, Bing, Slugs, Pumpkin and Lettuce Leaf got their names), although that's probably because so many people on the island share the same surnames of Christian, Quintal and McCoy, all direct descendants of the island's first permanent settlers who arrived from Pitcairn Island in 1856. Norfolk Islanders are immensely proud of their history and it's one of the major attractions for travellers to the island.

It might look like an island paradise, but Norfolk Island was the original hell hole. Established as a convict colony just six weeks after the First Fleet landed in Sydney/Warrang, it was meant to be a place 'of the extremist punishment, short of death' for the worst convicts from NSW and Van Diemen's Land (Tasmania). Actually, it was a convict colony twice: the first settlement was abandoned in 1814; then a second one was established in 1825, until it, too, was abandoned in 1855.

The following year, Queen Victoria granted Norfolk Island to the descendants of one of the most famous naval mutinies in modern history, the *HMS Bounty* led by Fletcher Christian. The mutineers had settled on Pitcairn Island with their Tahitian wives in 1789, but with a growing population the tiny island could no longer support the community, so in 1856, 194 of the mutineers' descendants (40 men and 47 women, 54 boys and 53 girls) made the 5954km, five-week journey to Norfolk Island, arriving on 8 June.

You can wander around the beautiful stone buildings of Kingston, built during the convict settlement. **Kingston and Arthur's Vale Historic Area** is one of the best-preserved Georgian settlements in the Southern Hemisphere, the oldest of the 11 convict sites across Australia, and given World Heritage Status by UNESCO in 2010. Some buildings are still private homes, others are ruins, four are museums, and a few have been repurposed, such as the Commissariat Store that's now the **All Saints Church** and home to regular church services, including the annual Thanksgiving service, when the church is decorated with ears of corn and other fruit and vegetables and long, slow hymns are sung: these hymns are among the slowest in the world, the same slow pace that the whalers used to match the rhythm of their rowing. It was these American whalers that began the tradition of celebrating Thanksgiving on Norfolk Island in the 19th century, the only place in Australia to traditionally do so, although unlike the United States, Norfolk celebrates Thanksgiving on the last Wednesday in November, rather than on the fourth Thursday. Even if you're not a regular churchgoer, it's worth attending a service here during Sunday evensong to hear the Pitcairn hymns. Downstairs is **The Pier Store Museum** that has artefacts from the *Bounty*. The **Sirius Museum** is dedicated to the items salvaged from the *Sirius*, the British ship that led the First Fleet. The actual wreck site is nearby, in Slaughter Bay.

But it's after dark when the history of Norfolk Island really comes alive. It's the most haunted place in Australia, according to Richard Davies, author of the *Ghost Guide to Australia*, with more ghosts per square kilometre than any

Opposite Quality Row, Kingston *Top* Norfolk Pines *Bottom* World Heritage Site ruins

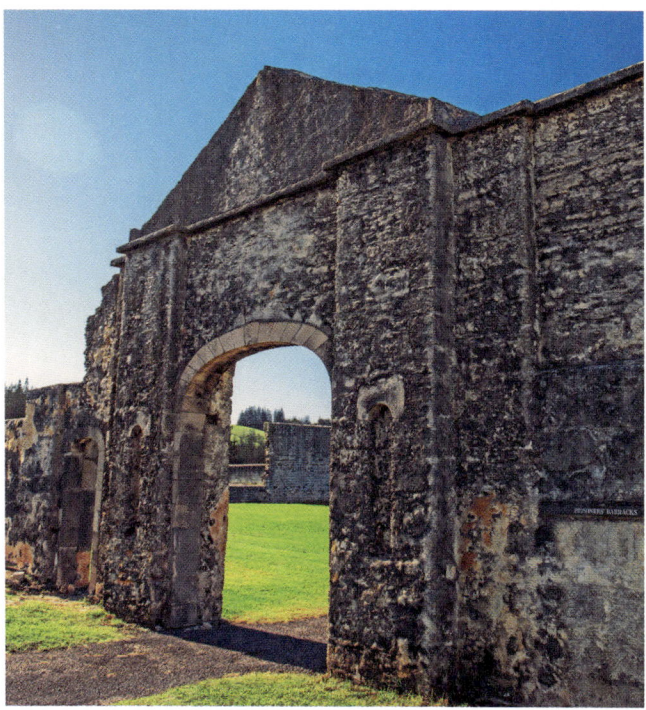

Norfolk Island, South Pacific   265

other state or territory. You can hear some of the ghost stories at the **Ghost Tour Dinner**, which begins with a three-course dinner in one of the old stone houses on **Quality Row** in the heart of Kingston and includes a spooky lantern-lit stroll through the cemetery and past the convict ruins and old gaol hospital. As with all the tours on the island, you'll need to book ahead via the visitor information centre or online (norfolkisland.com.au).

Good for a rainy day

Worth seeing even if the sun is shining, **Fletcher's Mutiny Cyclorama** is a huge 360-degree panoramic depiction of the voyage of the *Bounty* to Tahiti, the mutiny and the settlement of Norfolk Island. It's big, so allow at least half an hour to see it all.

The one-hour **Sound and Light Tour** is a bus trip through time back to the days of the convict settlement with clever light and sound effects and a cast of actors bringing the blood-curdling past alive. Also worth doing is the 1hr-long **Trial of the 15** – a courtroom drama staged in the old courtroom. Kids (and a few of the adults) really get into the spirit of things as they hiss and boo the villains and cheer the good guys.

Other evening options include an **Island Fish Fry** with local dancers showing off their Tahitian dancing skills, a **Mutiny on the Bounty Show**, progressive dinners at island homes – local specialities to try include banana pilhi (a savoury slice made with green bananas), coconut bread and mudda (green banana dumplings in coconut milk) – and even a dress-up night where you can pretend to be a convict for the evening, although with much more singing and dancing than the original convicts would have enjoyed, no doubt.

From Kingston wind your way up the western side of the island. None of the beaches on the island are ever crowded, but if you really want a secluded spot head to **Bumboras Beach** – aka Bumby – and explore the rockpools. Just up the road is another fabulous rockpool, called **Crystal Pool**, that even has its own coral reef, although it can be a bit of a challenge getting there on the sometimes steep and slippery hiking track that includes some rope work: you'll need reef shoes for walking across the rocks. The road is impassable after rain, so check with the visitor information centre before heading out.

Other highlights on this stretch of road include the majestic avenue of enormous 200-year-old Moreton Bay fig trees opposite Hundred Acres Reserve, where a walking track leads to **Rocky Point** and you can watch the seabirds swoop and soar from the cliff-tops. **St Barnabas Chapel** has some beautiful stained-glass windows and an impressive vaulted ceiling reminiscent of a ship (shut the door behind you or the church will end up full of birds), and **Puppy's Point**, near Anson Bay, is a popular spot to unpack a picnic while watching the sunset as the mutton birds come home to roost. If you're a surfer you'll love **Anson Bay**. It's also a good picnic spot – pick up supplies from some of the honesty box roadside produce stalls along the way or call into **The Hilli Goat** for a farm tour and cheese tasting, and check out the gallery of pottery while you're there. Whatever you do, don't leave without trying the goat's cheese cheesecake – it's delicious.

In terms of perfect picnic spots though, they don't get much better than at **Captain Cook Monument**. Overlooking Duncombe Bay on the northern coast the lookout marks the spot where Captain Cook landed in 1774, and has free barbecues, picnic tables and a sensational view. If you're lucky you may even see some red-tailed tropicbirds.

Norfolk Island's rocky coastline

BURNT PINE TO KINGSTON

Highlights in the south-east half of the island include the **Botanic Gardens**, a wonderful collection of plants endemic to the island. It's now part of the national park, but it was originally a private garden, the passion project of a local, Mrs Pat Moore, who set about collecting and preserving as many of the island's unique plants as she could.

The north-east coast is the quieter side of the island, and chances are you'll be the only ones admiring the view from the lookout at the top of **Cockpit Waterfall**, where the water rushes beneath your feet to tumble over the cliff-edge.

Cascade Bay is the site of the old whaling station that was once the most lucrative industry on the island, although nothing remains today. The pier here is one of just two on the island (the other is in Kingston). There is no safe harbour on Norfolk and all cargo is unloaded by tender and hoisted up onto the pier by crane, which can be quite an exciting thing to watch when the sea is rough.

Ball Bay Reserve is another rocky beauty spot, as is the nearby **Two Chimneys Reserve**, worth the detour just to visit the island's only winery, **Two Chimneys Wines**, which does a great lunch platter and some very nice whites, best sipped on the verandah of the cellar door overlooking the vines.

If you're a golfer you'll love teeing off at **Norfolk Island Golf Club**, the world's only golf course located within a World Heritage Site, it's just east of Kingston. Every hole on the nine-hole links course has a stunning view, although beware the notorious fourth (and 13th), where the green is tucked into a rock face. Even the clubhouse is historic – built by convicts in 1843 it was the home of the Stipendiary Magistrate.

Make sure you have your swimming gear handy because it's almost impossible to resist taking a dip at the island's best swimming beach, the beautiful **Emily Bay Lagoon**. Unlike many of the island's other beaches, Emily Bay features a beautiful stretch of sand rather than volcanic rock. The water is crystal clear and protected by a reef so it's virtually waveless, and it's a fabulous spot to snorkel with lots of coral and colourful fish to see. If you're lucky you may see the resident turtle: there was once so many here that the bay was called Turtle Bay before being renamed in 1831. Emily Bay is the ideal place to relax with a good book on the beach and be mesmerised by the sheer beauty of the place. After all, as they say on Norfolk Island, you're in 'Da Bass Side Orn Earth' (the best place on Earth).

Head into the hills

Take a drive up to the top of **Mount Pitt** in Norfolk Island National Park. The views from the top take in almost the whole island, but if you were expecting the classic South Pacific Island vista of swaying palms and coconut trees, think again. Here the soaring Norfolk Pine is the predominant tree on the island, along with giant tree ferns – some of the tallest in the world. You can also forget the beachfront high-rises of many holiday islands – no building on Norfolk is allowed to be higher than the iconic pines. For more great views follow the 500m trail that links the island's two highest points, Mount Pitt and Mount Bates; come back at night to the lookout at Mount Pitt for some sensational stargazing. Being hundreds of kilometres form the nearest landmass, there's next to no light pollution and in 2019 Norfolk Island was declared a Gold Level Dark Sky Town by the Australian Dark Sky Register, and the night skies really are quite extraordinary.

Kids' spot

Burnt Pine has the world's cheapest LEGO, thanks to the island's duty-free and GST-free status. So if your kids are LEGO pros – or you know some kids that are – **The Bounty Centre Toy Shop** (57 Taylors Rd) is the place to stock up.

SIDETRACK

Phillip Island is a tiny pile of basalt that rises from the ocean floor around 6km south of Norfolk Island and a unique place for birdwatching. It's a bit of an adventure to get there – there are no wharves or landing platforms. Our skipper simply edged the boat as close to the jumble of slippery seaweed-covered rocks at the bottom of the cliff as he could, and we jumped ashore from the bow of the boat, trying our best to time our leap of faith with a receding wave before quickly scrambling up the cliffs. But you'll soon leave all the sea-going drama behind as you trek across the plateau, enthralled by the density of birdlife and how unafraid and unaccustomed to humans they are. There are whale birds in their thousands, black noddys nesting in every available branch and large masked boobys – many with fluffy chicks – on every rock ledge. Even if you're not a birdwatcher, the birdlife on this island will bowl you over, quite literally. Ask at the visitor centre for details of tours.

BEST BEDS

- **Tintoela** Choose from one of two cottages or share the six-bedroom island-style homestead with friends or family. Located near Cascade Bay on the north-west side of the island, a car, local mobile phone and even stand-up paddle boards are included as part of the deal. tintoela.com
- **Endeavour Lodge** Enjoy million-dollar ocean views from the cliff-top apartments in the south-east corner of the island, not far from Kingston historic site. Discounted rental cars are available. endeavour.nf
- **Coast** A collection of cottages, apartments and beach houses surrounded by 30 acres of gardens, with a swimming pool and day spa. There are bikes, golf clubs, snorkelling gear, fishing rods and a hire car included for use, or walk the resort's trail to the convict ruins. coastnorfolkisland.com

VANLIFE

There's no camping on Norfolk Island.

Opposite Masked booby, Philip Island *Right* Kayaking Norfolk's wild north coast

Norfolk Island, South Pacific   269

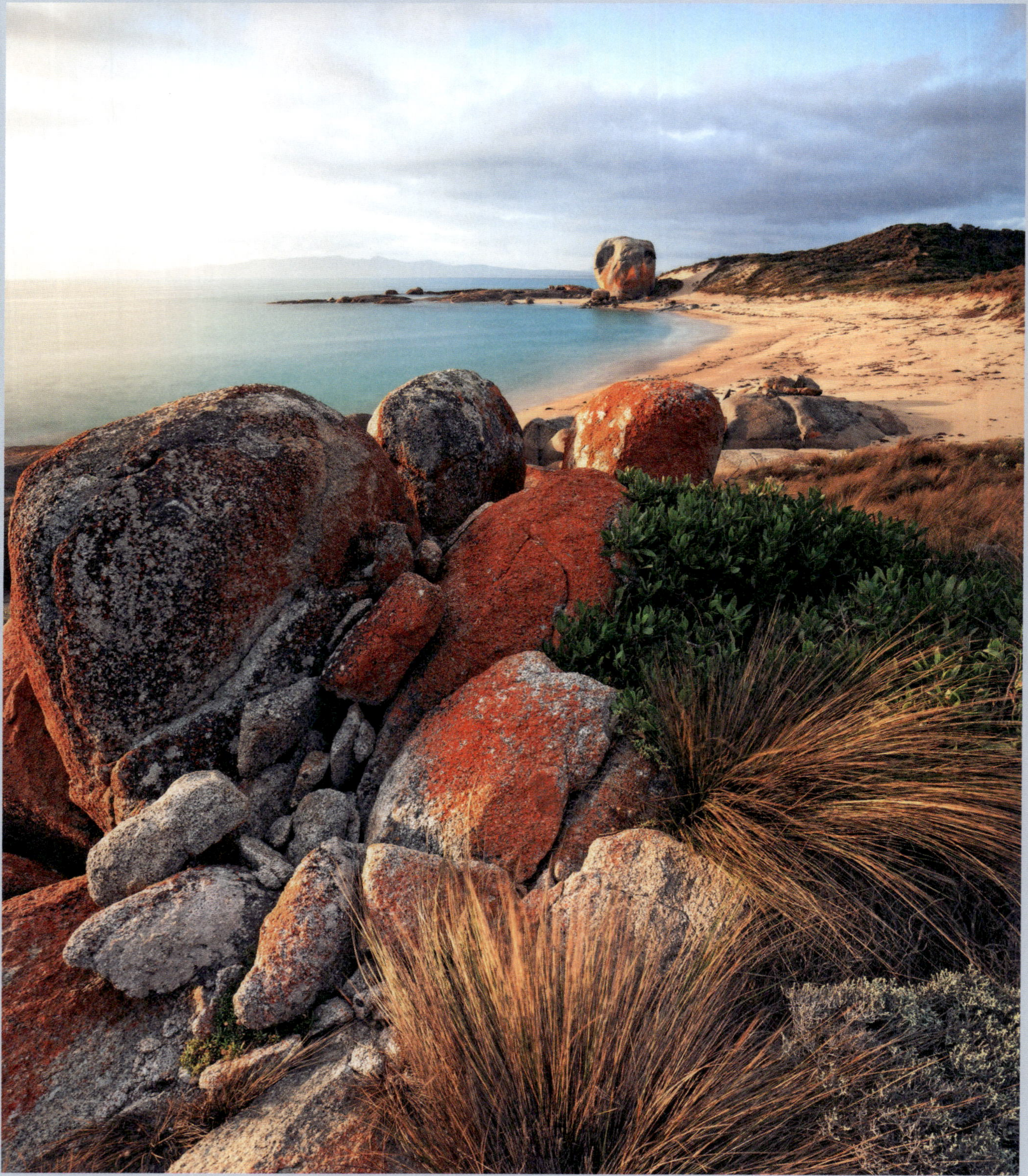

Tasmania

Untamed wilderness and gourmet food.

HOBART/nipaluna
Huonville
Kingston
Margate
Taroona
Blackmans Bay
Lauderdale
Rokeby
Seven Mile Beach
Midway Point
Cambridge
Lindisfarne
Rosny Park
Sandy Bay
Fern Tree
Neika
Mountain River
Crabtree
Lucaston
Grove
Longley
Leslie Vale
Sandfly
Kaoota
Ranelagh
Judbury
Glen Huon
Lonnavale
Collinsvale
Glenorchy
Home Hill Winery
The Apple Shed
Huon Valley Caravan Park
Wooden Boat Centre
Franklin
Castle Forbes Bay
Shipwrights Point Regatta Ground
Port Huon
Geeveston
Cairns Bay
Waterloo
Surges Bay
Glendevie
Woodstock
Pelverata
Cradoc
Glaziers Bay
Cygnet
Lymington
Nicholls Rivulet
Hartzview Vineyard
Gardners Bay
Grandvewe Cheeses
Garden Island Creek
Verona Sands
Police Point
Surveyors Bay
Francistown
Dover
Raminea
Strathblane
Port Esperance
Hastings
Thermal Springs
Lune River
Ida Bay
Southport
Lady Bay
Newdegate Cave
Leprena
Moss Glen
Catamaran
Cockle Creek
Whale sculpture
South Cape Bay Walk
Lookout
Tahune Forest Reserve
Tahune AirWalk & Huon Pine boardwalk
Arve River Nature Walk
Howden
Tinderbox
Dennes Point
Snug
Coningham
Oyster Cove
Kettering
Killora
Barnes Bay
Woodbridge
Birchs Bay
Flowerpoint
Middleton
Gordon
Simpsons Bay
Alonnah
Lunawanna
Adventure Bay
Cookville
Fluted Cape Walk
Bligh Museum of Pacific Exploration
Truganini Lookout
Jetty Beach
Cape Bruny Lighthouse
Opossum Bay
South Arm
Sandford
Cremorne
Clifton Beach
Shot Tower
SOUTHERN OCEAN
Storm Bay
Adventure Bay
BRUNY ISLAND
SOUTHWEST NATIONAL PARK
TASMANIAN WILDERNESS WORLD HERITAGE AREA
HARTZ MOUNTAINS NP
SOUTH BRUNY NP
A6
B68
C619
C632
C638
C636
B66
B33
0 5 10 km
N

Fabulous food and wine and edge-of-the-world scenery await as you follow the road as far south as you can go on four wheels.

The deep south

HOW LONG?
You could easily do this drive, without the side trips, as a daytrip from Hobart/nipaluna. If you'd like to explore Bruny Island, add on a couple of extra days.

WHEN TO GO
Tasmania's south can often be windswept and lashed with rain, but that's part of its wild and woolly charm. Spring is a lovely time to explore the Huon Valley, when fruit trees are smothered in white and pink blossoms. Roads can be icy during winter.

NEED TO KNOW
There are no shops at Cockle Creek and apart from a general store that sells just the basics in Adventure Bay, there's no supermarket on Bruny Island. There are, however, plenty of farm gate stalls and producers who sell direct scattered all over the Huon Valley and on Bruny Island. Pick up a free copy of the **Tasmanian Fruits Farm Gate Guide**. Produced by Fruit Growers Tasmania, it details more than 40 farms and growers that welcome visitors or who have farm gate market stalls. It's available at visitor information centres or online (fruitgrowerstas.com.au). If you're in or near Cygnet on the first or third Sun of the month, visit the markets in the Town Hall on Mary St for a great array of local produce.

SNAPSHOT
There's nowhere quite like Tasmania's deep south, a beguiling mix of remote wilderness and fertile farmlands that produces some extraordinarily good food and wine. Few can resist the siren call of driving to the end of the road, as far south as cars can go – Tasmania's southernmost edge is closer to the Antarctic ice shelf than it is to Cairns, and staring out across a storm-lashed sea knowing there is nothing between you and the South Pole but rolling waves is exhilarating.

Drive rating
Moderate. Mostly sealed roads but with some gravel roads.

Acknowledgement of Country
This is the Traditional Land of the Melukerdee, Nuenonne and Lyluequonny Peoples.

Distance planner
Hobart to Cockle Creek via the coast: around 190km
- Hobart to Huonville, via Cygnet: 90km
- Huonville to Cockle Creek: 94km
- Bruny Island side trip, tip to tip: 60km

More information
- Geeveston Town Hall Visitor Centre, 15 Church St, Geeveston; (03) 6297 1120; huonvalleytas.com
- The Gateway and Visitor Information Centre, 3959 Bruny Island Main Rd, Alonnah: (03) 6293 1148; brunyisland.com
- discovertasmania.com.au

Previous Castle Rock on Flinders Island

HOBART TO HUONVILLE, VIA CYGNET

The Huon Valley is the fruit bowl of Tasmania – almost all of the state's apples and stone fruits are grown in this region and when the orchards are in blossom in early spring it's a spectacularly pretty area to drive around. The main town, **Huonville**, is an easy half-hour drive south of Hobart via the Huon Hwy, but like almost all the road trips in this book it's much more fun if you take the longer way to get there.

Head south out of Hobart on the Channel Hwy (B68), through Sandy Bay and past the city's tallest building, the iconic circular tower – actually it's a dodecagonal prism – of Wrest Point Casino, Australia's first legal gambling den, and follow the coast to another famous round tower, just beyond the suburb of Taroona. Known as the **Shot Tower**, if you've ever wondered how they got those old-fashioned bullets so round, this the place to find out. Climb the 58m-high tower – built in 1870 it is the only remaining circular sandstone shot tower left in the world – to see how the lead was dropped to form perfectly round shot (lead bullets), plus you'll get great views of the River Derwent Estuary. Head through the southern suburb of Kingston, then the coastal hamlets of Margate, Snug, Oyster Cove and Kettering.

Opposite Craypots at Dover *Below* The Neck, Bruny Island

SIDETRACK

It only takes 20min to cross the D'Entrecasteaux Channel to **Bruny Island** on the car ferry from Kettering with **Sealink** (brunyislandferry.com.au), but once you're there, it's worth spending a day or two to explore this beautiful place. An island clinging to the edge of an island clinging to the edge of the world, Bruny really is on the very edge of nowhere, despite being less than an hour from Hobart. It's wild, lonely, beautiful and remote.

Bruny Island is really two islands, joined by a narrow sandy isthmus called **The Neck**. There's 180 or so steps to climb, and a viewing platform at the bottom of the steps where you can see little penguins come back to their burrows at dusk. Climb the steps for great views of the long curve of white sandy beaches that stretch south on both sides. **The Truganini Lookout** here has a small memorial plaque commemorating the life of Truganini, a strong and resilient Nuenonne woman who lived on Bruny Island, known as lunawanna-alonnah to the Nuenonne People, in the 19th century. Truganini endured horrific circumstances during her life - many of her family were murdered during the Black War, her Traditional way of life was irreparably impacted and, despite her pleas for a respectful burial, upon her passing her body was exhumed and put on display at the Tasmanian Museum for almost 50 years. During the height of the Black War, Truganini agreed to act as a guide to the controversial George Augustus Robinson - who was tasked with resettling First Nations People - in the hope of putting an end to the violence and murder of her people.

At the southern end of Adventure Bay, the 2.5hr **Fluted Cape** walk offers dramatic coastal scenery, and drive to the southernmost point of the island and climb the hill to **Cape Bruny Lighthouse** for views across the cliffs to the southern edge of Australia. Built in 1838, it's the third oldest in lighthouse Australia.

Bruny is the Traditional Land of the Nuenonne People, once home to Truganini (*see* above), and to her father, Mangana, who was the chief when both Furneaux and Cook arrived. The first European to chart the island was Abel Tasman in 1642, and the first to actually set foot on it was Tobias Furneaux in 1773, who named Adventure Bay after his ship, but one of its most famous visitors was William Bligh. In 1788 and then again in 1792 and 1809, Bligh anchored in Adventure Bay; the first time in the *Bounty* (before the famous mutiny), the final time while virtually a prisoner aboard his ship, the *Porpoise*, awaiting trial after he was deposed as Governor of NSW during the rum rebellion. Legend has it that Bligh planted the first apple tree in Australia during that first visit in 1788, perhaps a hint of Tasmania's later moniker as the 'Apple Isle'. Learn all about it at the **Bligh Museum of Pacific Exploration** in Adventure Bay.

Bruny is home to one of the largest colonies of the endangered forty-spotted pardalote, as well as penguins and shearwaters, rare white wallabies, seals, dolphins and whales in season, and the 3hr wildlife cruise from Adventure Bay with **Bruny Island Cruises** (brunycruises.com.au) is one of the most popular things to do on the island. It's also the best way to see some of Australia's highest and most dramatic sea cliffs and the cruise takes you past sea caves and tall rock stacks.

Bruny is also home to some very good cheesemakers, oyster growers, meat smokers, wine and whisky makers.

From Kettering and Woodbridge's **Peppermint Bay**, more grand views unfurl as you follow the Channel Hwy around the curve of the peninsula, especially at **Grandvewe Cheeses** (grandvewe.com.au), an organic sheep dairy in Birchs Bay. Their handmade sheep cheeses are delicious, but their unique claim to fame is that they also produce a range of spirits, including sheep whey vodka. Guided tasting tours, of both cheese and spirits, are available, as well as classes in gin and butter-making: book online.

The bustling town of **Cygnet** is a popular place to stop and shop with a main street lined with boutiques, craft shops and quite a few cafes, although it's the surrounding orchards that are the real drawcard here. As you head north along the river towards Huonville, you'll find dozens of shed-door stalls where you can buy apples (and other fruits in season), but if you really want to learn about the apple industry take a little detour and visit the little museum at **The Apple Shed** at Willie Smith's Cider House in Grove (just a few kilometres north of Huonville heading back up towards Hobart) and try some of the organic (alcoholic) apple cider. But there's much more than just apples grown in this fertile valley – as well as a booming cider industry other produce to look out for include saffron, all types of berries, organic meat and mushrooms.

There are several wineries open to the public for tastings and cellar door sales in the Huon Valley – favourites include **Home Hill** at Ranelagh for its restaurant serving local produce – try the Huon Valley mushrooms if they are on the menu – and **Hartzview** at Nicholls Rivulet (between Woodbridge and Cygnet) for its spiced apple and honey liqueur mead.

HUONVILLE TO COCKLE CREEK

Once you've got to Huonville – the commercial hub of the valley – turn around and head 10min south, this time along the western bank of the Huon River, towards the township of **Franklin**. You don't have to be a boatie to appreciate the craftmanship on show at the **Wooden Boat Centre** here. A showcase for traditional boat-building skills, you can watch students and masters at work and learn about wooden boats – their history, construction, use and the tools that shape them and all the unique names and terms.

Geeveston, a small timber-getting town on the edge of the Southern Forests, will be familiar to fans of the TV show *Rosehaven*, which was filmed here. The Town Hall Visitor Centre has a small forestry museum and interpretive centre with displays on woodworking, forest management and timber.

Opposite Huon Valley Apple Museum *Left* Amongst the treetops on Tahune AirWalk

It also includes a woodwork gallery and craft shop, and is worth a visit. Take a late afternoon stroll on the **Platypus Walk** in the adjacent Heritage Park and you may be lucky enough to spot one of the elusive monotremes. If you're here in winter, this is also a good place to see the **Aurora Australis**, aka the Southern Lights, although there are countless good vantage points in southern Tasmania, all you need are clear dark skies; for forecasts see, head online (sws.bom.gov.au/Aurora).

It's around a 2hr drive from Hobart to **Cockle Creek** – the last section, from Lune River, is loose gravel and a bit rough, but fine for most 2WDs. Once there, check out the bronze sculpture of a southern right whale and read about the history of whaling in Recherche Bay – during the 1830s there were four whaling stations here. Cockle Creek is as far south as you can go by road in Australia – any further and you'll have to do it on foot, a sensational 2hr (each way) walk to a cliff-top lookout at South Cape Bay overlooking the southernmost point on mainland Tasmania. A trip worth celebrating, however far south you end up.

Kids' spot

From Geeveston it's a lovely 29km winding drive though the Arve Forest on a sealed road (watch for logging trucks) to **Tahune Forest Reserve**, where you can wander above the treetops on the **Tahune AirWalk**, a 600m elevated treetop walk that leads out over the canopy of the wet eucalypt forest to a cantilever 50m above the ground for stunning views of the Huon and Picton rivers; a bonus is that it's wheelchair- and stroller-friendly. For a thrill, older kids can try a cable-controlled hang-gliding adventure. If you don't have a head for heights, there are several lookouts and short walks leading off the Arve Forest Drive. The 10min riverside loop at the **Arve River Streamside Reserve** is one of the best short walks in the country, as is the 20min Huon Pine boardwalk underneath the AirWalk. Family-friendly rafting and kayaking trips are available on the Picton River. AirWalk is open daily but closes during severe winds.

Good for a rainy day

Discover a subterranean wonderland on a guided tour of **Newdegate Cave** at **Hastings Caves State Reserve**. Richly decorated with large flowstones, stalactites, columns, shawls, straws, and stalagmites, it's an unusual dolomite (rather than limestone) cave - but be warned: there are 240 stairs to negotiate. Soothe sore knees afterwards with a soak in the **Thermal Springs** surrounded by forest and ferns. The caves and springs are 6km west of Lune River; 26km north of Cockle Creek. Book ahead by phone: (03) 6298 3209.

BEST BEDS

- **The Old Bank B&B** in Cygnet has three charming rooms, one with ensuite, the other two with their own private bathrooms. A full English breakfast is served in the sun-soaked conservatory and in winter, the sitting room is a great place to curl up with a book beside the open fire. cygnetoldbank.com.au
- Perched in the treetops 70m above the beach on the very northern tip of Bruny Island, the three-bedroom **Bruny Shore** has fantastic ocean views. There are large wraparound decks, a fully equipped kitchen and views from every room, including the main bathroom. brunyshore.com.au

VANLIFE

Shipwrights Point Regatta Ground - 17km south of Huonville - overlooks the Huon River. There's a boat ramp, flushing toilets and a public jetty - perfect for dangling a fishing line - and a playground for kids, a shelter and barbecue. Sites are unpowered and undesignated but there's a caretaker on site. If you're travelling with kids, the **Huon Valley Caravan Park** (huonvalleycaravanpark.com.au) at Huonville combines camping and farm stay activities along with Tassie devil feeding sessions. You can also camp in the **Tahune Forest Reserve** and at **Jetty Beach** in South Bruny National Park, near Cape Bruny. There are three grassy camping areas at **Cockle Creek**, all pretty basic with pit-toilets and not much else (BYO water).

The deep south

HOBART/ nipaluna
Richmond
Orielton
Pawleena
Nugent
Grasstree Hill
Wattle Hill
Penna
Sorell
Midway Point
Forcett
Lewisham
Otago
Risdon Vale
Risdon
Moonah
Lindisfarne
Cambridge
New Town
Rosny Park
Howrah
Rokeby
Seven Mile Beach
Dodges Ferry
Park Beach
Carlton
Primrose Sands
Sandy Bay
Lauderdale
Taroona
Sandford
Cremorne
Opossum Bay
Clifton Beach
Blackmans Bay
South Arm
Tinderbox
Dennes Point
Killora
Barnes Bay
Kellevie
Bream Creek
Marion Bay
Copping
Connellys Marsh
Dunalley
Murdunna
Teralina/ Eaglehawk Neck
Tasman Bay Lookout
Tessellated Pavement
Penzance
Doo Town
Tasman Blowhole
Tasman Arch
Devils Kitchen
Waterfall Bay Lookout
Taranna
Premaydena
Koonya
Tasmanian Devil Unzoo
Nubeena
Oakwood
White Beach
Highcroft
Port Arthur
Port Arthur Historic Site
Stormlea
Cape Raoul Walk
Remarkable Cave & Maingon Bay Lookout
Fortescue Bay
Cape Hauy Track
Three Capes Track
Lime Bay
Coal Mines Historic Site
Gwandalan
Saltwater River
AUSTRALIAN CONVICT SITES WHA
Frederick Henry Bay
Norfolk Bay
Storm Bay
Marion Bay
Maingon Bay
TASMAN SEA
BRUNY ISLAND
MARIA ISLAND
FORESTIER PENINSULA
TURRAKANA/ TASMAN PENINSULA
TASMAN NP
HOBART AIRPORT
SOUTH ARM MARINE CA
0 3 6 km
N

Stunning coastal rock formations, towering sea cliffs, world-class seafood and World Heritage–listed historical convict sites.

Turrakana/Tasman Peninsula

HOW LONG?
Two to three days is ideal, including a full day at the UNESCO World Heritage–listed Port Arthur Historic Site.

WHEN TO GO
Avoid winter as this is when the most rain falls and the roads can be icy.

LOCAL SECRET
For a sea level look at some of the peninsula's most dramatic sections of coastline, including the highest sea cliffs in the Southern Hemisphere, join a sightseeing and wildlife watching Tasman Island Cruise with **Pennicott Wilderness Journeys** (pennicottjourneys.com.au). The 3hr cruises depart daily from Port Arthur and should be booked online ahead of time.

SNAPSHOT
An easy day drive from Hobart/nipaluna, Port Arthur Historic Site is one of Tasmania's most popular tourist attractions. But beyond convict ruins so atmospheric that you can almost hear the clanking of the chains, you'll also find beautiful beaches and a coastline riddled with dramatic rock formations, extraordinary rock pillars, sea stacks and sea caves.

Drive rating
Easy. Mostly sealed roads.

Acknowledgement of Country
This is the Traditional Land of the Paredarerme Pungenna People.

Distance planner
The return loop from Hobart to Port Arthur is 235km
- Hobart to Port Arthur: 91km
- Port Arthur to Lime Bay via Nubeena: 32km
- Lime Bay to Teralina/Eaglehawk Neck: 35km

More information
- Port Arthur Visitor Centre, 6973 Arthur Hwy; (03) 6251 2310; portarthur.org.au
- discovertasmania.com.au
- tasmanunlocked.com.au

HOBART/NIPALUNA TO PORT ARTHUR

From Hobart/nipaluna, head north out past the airport to Sorell and then cut across to Dunalley – if you're hungry stop at the **Dunalley Fish Market** to pick up some fresh fish and chips and eat it at one of the riverside picnic tables – and then follow the Arthur Hwy. Port Arthur might only be a 90min drive from Hobart, but there is practically a full day's worth of things to see and do along the way, so resist the temptation to rush.

The rocky coastline of Turrakana/Tasman Peninsula is truly spectacular. The **Tasman Bay Lookout** (sometimes called Pirates Bay Lookout) gives a taste of the sensational scenery to come. Like many places in this part of Tasmania there's a swashbuckling story behind the European name, and the pirates of this bay were six escaped convicts who stole a schooner in Hobart called the *Sunflower* in 1822 and tried to sail back to England: they were eventually recaptured on the south coast of NSW.

Follow the road down to the bay, where you'll find the **Tessellated Pavement**, a photogenic expanse of rock fractured by earth movements that resembles giant tiles.

Known as Teralina to the Paredarerme Pungenna People, **Teralina/Eaglehawk Neck**, a narrow isthmus of land only a few hundred metres wide, is the reason nearby Port Arthur was chosen as the site for a prison in 1830: the tiny strip of land was easily patrolled, few people could swim, the surrounding bush was dense and inhospitable and, if all else failed, a line of snarling dogs roused the soldiers if anyone tried to get by. The **Officers Quarters**, built in 1832 and reputed to be the oldest wooden military building remaining in Australia, has been restored as a museum.

Hugging the shores of Norfolk Bay the road winds its way to Taranna, and south towards Port Arthur.

Added to the UNESCO World Heritage list in 2010, **Port Arthur Historic Site** (portarthur.org.au) is one of Australia's most significant – and most notorious – convict settlement sites. Established in 1833 as a 'place of terror' for repeat offenders, you'll need a minimum of half a day, preferably a full day or even longer (tickets are valid for two days) to explore the 40ha site. More than just a gaol, it was, at its height in the 1850s, an industrial village with shipworks, a flour mill, a timber mill, and shoemaking, smithing and brick-making operations. It was abandoned as a prison in 1877, then largely destroyed by bushfires in 1895 and 1897 and what remains today is a mixture of intact buildings, atmospheric ruins and re-created gardens.

More than 12,500 convicts called the settlement home while it was operational, and it became known as 'Hell on Earth', thanks largely to a cruel experiment in penal reform whereby silence and solitary confinement replaced physical punishment as a means of rehabilitation; in reality it just sent most of the prisoners mad.

Take the time to visit the interactive museum in at the Port Arthur Visitor Centre to gain a deeper understanding of what life was like for the convicts – before and after transportation to the colony – and join a **guided walking tour** for an overview of the site before exploring on your own. Buildings worth seeing include the ruined penitentiary and church, the cruciform-shaped separate prison, and the furnished museum houses. Other tours include the **Isle of the Dead cemetery** and a cruise to **Point Puer** – the prison home to more than 3000 boys ranging in age from nine to 18 between 1834 and 1849 – as well as guided garden and archaeological tours and special behind-the-scenes access. There are also lots of interactive activities for kids, including a free activity book, and a range of ticket passes available but all must be pre-booked before arrival (portarthur.org.au).

Probably not a great one to do with easily scared littlies, but one tour not to miss if you're not easily spooked is the **night-time ghost tour**. Led by guides dressed in black and carrying glass lanterns, you learn about the most documented ghost sightings and unexplained happenings in many of the houses and cells. Almost all the guides will enthral you with their own on-site encounters with the supernatural. If you didn't believe in ghosts when you arrived you probably will by the time you leave.

SIDETRACK

Fortescue Bay Rd is an unsealed – but pretty – road that winds through the forest in Tasman National Park to the bay, where you'll find one of the most dramatic half-day hikes in Tassie. The **Cape Hauy Track**, which starts at the Fortescue Bay camping area, is a magnificent 4hr-return walk that delivers wonderful views of cliffs and rock formations, although be warned: there are hundreds of steps. It's part of the celebrated four-day **Three Capes Track** that also includes Cape Pillar and the towering 300m-high dolerite sea cliffs, the highest in the Southern Hemisphere. If walking's not your thing, you can also see them on a Tasman Island Cruise (*see* p.279).

Opposite Cape Hauy, Tasman National Park *Above* Government Gardens, Port Arthur Historic Site

Good for a rainy day

Love Me Doo, Doodle Doo, Much-A-Doo, Gunnadoo, Doo Come In, Just Doo It ... everyone gets a giggle out of the names of all the cottages in **Doo Town**, just past Teralina/Eaglehawk Neck, all of which end (or start) with 'doo'. And a bonus is you can see it all without leaving the car if you happen to be there when the weather is unkind. Legend has it that the tradition began in 1935, although the reasons why have been lost in the mists of time. While you're there, treat yourself to some fish and chips or an ice-cream from the **Doo-lishus** caravan, usually parked near the blowhole during summer months.

SIDETRACK

On the southern side of Teralina/Eaglehawk Neck, in Tasman National Park, you'll find the **Tasman Blowhole**, the ruins of once-huge sea caves at Tasman Arch and the Devils Kitchen, a 60m-deep cleft carved into a cliff by an often furious sea that, according to local legend, looks a bit like a big cauldron on the boil when seen from above on a rough day. All are easily accessible by car. Also worth the short drive (or the 90min walk from Tasman Arch) is the lookout at **Waterfall Bay**. Particularly impressive after rain, the waterfall plunges 100m over the cliff-edge into the sea.

SIDETRACK

Remarkable Cave is a sea cave 6km from Port Arthur, where you'll get great views to Cape Raoul from the lookout above the beach. You can climb down the 115 steps to the sand to explore the aptly named cave (but you'll also have to climb 115 back up!).

Penitentiary ruins, Port Arthur Historic Site

PORT ARTHUR TO TARANNA VIA LIME BAY

There's another World Heritage convict site a half-hour drive away from Port Arthur on the shores of Norfolk Bay near Lime Bay (35km via the B37 and Saltwater River Rd) called the **Coal Mines Historic Site**. Port Arthur's prisoners were sent to the coal mines here as punishment, where around 600 of them at any given time were forced to work, and live, underground – a doubly cruel punishment, given the natural beauty of the place. You can no longer see the underground workings of the mines, but the houses, barracks, offices and cells are still there, now mostly roofless ruins. There are three short walks around the settlement, mine shaft and to the convict quarry. The site is free to enter, and not nearly as well-known as Port Arthur, and more often than not you'll be the only person there.

Continue on from the Coal Mines to **Lime Bay State Reserve**, which has several sheltered swimming beaches, including a fabulous waterfront campground (see Best beds), before looping back towards Taranna and then Teralina/Eaglehawk Neck, reconnecting with the Tasman Hwy (A3) at Sorell.

As you drive though this beautiful and often serene landscape, it's hard to imagine what the convicts who were incarcerated here almost 200 years ago would make of the stream of travellers and happy holidaymakers who flock here today.

Kids' spot

If you thought your kids were ferocious eaters, wait until you see a group of Tasmanian devils in a feeding frenzy at **Tasmanian Devil Unzoo**. There are presentations throughout the day but this is an 'unzoo', so it's not about captive animals putting on a show for entertainment, but observing wild animals in their native habitat. One experience is going nose-to-nose with a devil inside the bubble-like devil den (humans are inside the ground-level Perspex dome, devils are outside roaming free, and it makes you wonder exactly who's gawking at who). You can also join a guided 'Devil Tracker Adventure' in a 4WD to scientific monitoring stations hidden in the forest. The wild population of devils has been decimated in recent years by a mysterious facial cancer - it's been estimated that between 80 and 90 per cent of the wild population has been wiped out - and entry fees help fund much-needed research and the park's breeding program.

SIDETRACK

If you'd like a closer look at **Cape Raoul**, turn off the Nubeena Rd before you get to the township and drive to the end of Stormlea Rd. From there it's a 14km walk but worth every step if you're up for it; it takes around 5hr return, although there is a shorter 1hr option that will take you as far as the lookout. The famous monster waves of **Shipstern Bluff** are just off the coast of the cape, where fearless surfers are towed out to ride the gigantic storm-swollen 5m swells.

BEST BEDS

- In terms of location the **Port Arthur Motor Inn** is difficult to top, because this older-style motel is actually in the grounds of the historic site, although the rooms are a bit tired and in need of a makeover. portarthur-inn.com.au
- **Stewarts Bay Lodge** These bayfront cabins are just a 15min walk from the Port Arthur ruins. All of the 40 cabins have well-equipped kitchens but there is also a restaurant on site. stewartsbaylodge.com.au
- **NRMA Port Arthur Holiday Park** has a range of good-value cabins and glamping-style safari tents with ensuites, surrounded by bush on the shores of Stewarts Bay, and is also within walking distance of the Port Arthur Historic Site. Kids love the playground, go-karts and pump track (BYO bikes) and free activities in school holidays. nrmaparksandresorts.com.au/port-arthur

VANLIFE

One of the best-kept beachside camping secrets in Australia is at beautiful **Lime Bay** near the Coal Mines Historic Site – shady campsites with million-dollar water views. There are also basic camping facilities and unpowered caravan sites at **Fortescue Bay** in Tasman National Park, and lovely grassy waterfront caravan and camping sites within walking distance to Port Arthur at **NRMA Port Arthur Holiday Park**.

Tasmania

Tasmania's East Coast is home to some of the most beautiful coastal scenery in the state. You'll find glorious views unfolding around practically every bend.

East Coast

HOW LONG?
Allow at least four or five days to drive from Hobart/nipaluna to Freycinet National Park and up the coast to the Bay of Fires/larapuna.

WHEN TO GO
Most rain falls during the winter months. The roads can be icy during winter, but that's also the best time to see whales. For swimming, go in summer, although Freycinet National Park can be very busy during holiday periods.

NEED TO KNOW
No dogs are allowed in national parks, including the carpark at the beginning of the Wineglass Bay walk. If you are planning on spending more than one or two days in national parks, a National Parks Pass will save you money: for most travellers the eight-week holiday pass, which covers all parks, offers the best value. You can buy a parks pass at national park visitor centres and most Tasmanian visitor information centres, or online (parks.tas.gov.au).

LOCAL SECRET
Don't leave Tassie without sampling one of its most famous delicacies, a Tasmanian scallop pie. Those in the know (St Helens locals) will tell you that the 'Best Tasmanian Scallop Pie in the World' is found at **St Helens Bakery**, which is guaranteed to have at least six scallops in every pie (if they have sold out, the chain bakery opposite, Banjo's, does a pretty good one too).

SNAPSHOT
Tasmania's eastern seaboard is a spectacularly scenic coastline: a long, ragged strip of peninsulas, islands, channels and often deserted beaches, flanked by rugged mountains enclosing gorges, waterfalls and forests and punctuated with quaint historic villages full of convict-built houses and pockets of lush rainforest, as well as the much-photographed Wineglass Bay in Freycinet National Park, a practically perfect curve of white sand that is guaranteed to take your breath away. An added bonus is that nowhere is very far from anywhere in Tasmania, which means you have plenty of time to get out there and explore.

Drive rating
Easy. Mostly sealed roads with some winding sections.

Acknowledgement of Country
This is the Traditional Lands of the Oyster Bay Nation, paredarerme, tyerrernotepanner, puthikwilayti and pyemmairrener Peoples.

Distance planner
Hobart to Ansons Bay: around 300km
- Hobart to Coles Bay: 193km
- Coles Bay to Bay of Fires/larapuna: 139km

More information
- Tasmanian Travel and Information Centre, 20 Davey St, Hobart; (03) 6238 4222; hobarttravelcentre.com.au
- discovertasmania.com.au

Opposite Coles Bay, The Hazards and Wineglass Bay, Freycinet National Park

HOBART/NIPALUNA TO FREYCINET

From Hobart, head north out past the airport to Sorell, where, if you have a couple of spare days at your disposal, you can take a detour and explore the spectacular coastline on the Turrakana/Tasman Peninsula road trip, including the World Heritage–listed convict site of Port Arthur (*see* p.279).

But if you are intent on heading to the magnificent beaches of the East Coast – and who could blame you – it's a pretty drive north on the A3 along descriptively named signposted sections of road, such as the climb up Bust-Me-Gall Hill and the descent of Break-Me-Neck Hill, and across the valley floor, following the river, to the holiday town of **Orford**, from where the road, carved into the mountainside above the Prosser River, winds its way to the coast. Take a break at **Triabunna** and watch the fishers unload their catch or carry out their deckside chores.

Between Triabunna and Swansea, the cliff-hugging road meanders beside deserted beaches and offers magnificent coastal views across Great Oyster Bay to the rocky peaks of the Freycinet Peninsula.

Keep an eye out for the **Spiky Bridge** (about 7.5km south of Swansea). It was built by convicts in 1843, but no one really knows why it's lined with rocky spikes. Legend has it the convicts wanted to annoy the overseer by sticking the stones in the wrong way; others will tell you it's to stop cows falling off the bridge. Nearby, **Spiky Beach** is one of those spots that most people miss, but it's a beautiful sandy cove with some gorgeous rockpools.

Below Stopping to enjoy the view at The Gardens, Bay of Fires/larapuna

East Coast 287

Opposite left Tasmania's famous Wineglass Bay *Opposite right* Orange-lichen rocks of The Hazards, Coles Bay *Above* The Maria Island Walk

From Swansea, continue north to Cranbrook, then take the turn-off to Coles Bay and **Freycinet National Park**, one of Tasmania's most popular parks. The distinctive pink granite peaks of **The Hazards** dominate the scenery as you drive along the edge of the bay to the tiny town of **Coles Bay**, a collection of holiday houses clinging to the shoreline. Call into the **Freycinet Marine Farm** on Coles Bay Rd on the way for freshly shucked oysters on the deck, as well as local scallops, salmon and rock lobster. You can also pull on a pair of waders and join an oyster farm tour where you get to eat oysters straight from the rack while standing in the sea, washed down with a glass of local riesling.

There are many secluded beaches in the national park, but the one everyone wants to see is **Wineglass Bay**, a perfect semicircle of white sand washed by teal blue waters, instantly recognisable from hundreds of postcards, posters and tourist brochures. The 1hr walk up to the lookout over Wineglass Bay is worth the steep climb. What's more, while you'll see lots of people on the trek, if you continue down to the beach (2hr return), you're just as likely to have it to yourself, as most daytrippers don't get that far.

Take a drive up to the lighthouse at **Cape Tourville** for good sunset views and whale and dolphin watching in season, or spend a few hours on one of several longer walks in the park. Also popular is sea kayaking, snorkelling and diving in the bull kelp beds at **Sleepy Bay**, surfing at **Friendly Beaches**, rock climbing, abseiling and mountain biking.

Good for a rainy day

Tassie, with its cool climate, is famous for its berries with many small producers making delicious jams, spreads, sauces and even wines from the fruit. Call into **Kate's Berry Farm** (katesberryfarm.com) on the southern outskirts of Swansea for a Devonshire Tea or ice-cream made with one of the thick homemade jams of strawberry, raspberry, Himalayan wildberries, youngberries or wild blackberry, and even some berry wine. The views from here are spectacular.

SIDETRACK

There are several wineries along this stretch of coast: visit the **East Coast Wine Trail** (winetasmania.com.au) for cellar door opening times.

SIDETRACK

You'll need to leave your car at Triabunna, but a trip out to **Maria Island** is worth the time. The ferry crossing takes around 20min, and ferries depart regularly throughout the day in summer, less frequently in winter (encountermaria.com.au). The World Heritage-listed convict ruins of **Darlington**, near the ferry wharf, are easily explored on foot, and you can explore the rest of the island, which is 20km long and 13km wide, by bike: if you don't have your own you can hire one when you book your ferry crossing.

Called wukaluwikiwayna by the puthikwilayti People, Maria Island became a penal colony in 1825. The colony was soon infamous for the high number of escapes - one unlucky group drifted across the channel on a raft only to walk ashore into the arms of two lost policemen - but it was known among convicts as a place of relative comfort. By 1832, the convict settlement had been abandoned in favour of Port Arthur (see p.281) and after a second incarnation as a convict probation station between 1842 and 1850, it was eventually taken over by a flamboyant Italian entrepreneur, Diego Bernacchi, who planted grapes, cultivated silkworms and established a cement works. But none of these enterprises survived the Great Depression and by the 1930s the island was home to just a handful of farmers, though many of the original convict buildings still stand to this day.

The entire island is now national park and it's steep and mountainous in the interior, and ringed by stretches of white sandy beaches and limestone cliffs. The island is home to a staggering amount of wildlife, including possums, wallabies, pademelons, echidnas, kangaroos and wombats, Tasmanian devils, muttonbirds and the endangered forty-spotted pardalote, one of the smallest and rarest birds in Australia.

The **Painted Cliffs** - beautifully patterned sandstone cliffs - are an easy 90min-return walk from the ferry wharf. Alternatively, you can head off in the other direction to some spectacular cliffs along the northern shore of the island, which contain thousands of marine fossils. If you're up for a challenge, there's a strenuous 4-5hr-return climb to the summit of the mountain known as **Bishop and Clerk**. It entails lots of rock-hopping and scrambling over large boulders, but provides amazing views from the top.

There are no shops on Maria Island so you need to take everything with you. Most people visit as a daytrip, but you can stay at the Penitentiary in bunkhouse-style accommodation or camp at Darlington (see p.291).

FREYCINET NATIONAL PARK TO BAY OF FIRES/ LARAPUNA

Retrace the drive back to the A3 and head for **Bicheno**. Part of the East Coast Whale Trail, there are several good whale watching vantage spots with information boards along the 3km-long coastal walkway that curves around the town. The best time to see whales is between May and Nov. Bicheno's also a great place to see little penguins as they waddle ashore to their burrows at dusk; you can see them on the beaches near the **Blowhole** (worth a visit when there are good swells to see the sea water erupt from a sea cave below), **Redbill Beach** and even **Waubs Beach** in the centre of town, or take a tour to a private rookery (bichenopenguintours.com.au).

From Bicheno, continue north. Dubbed the Surf Coast for its reliable swell year-round, you'll find plenty of great surfing – and fishing – beaches all along this next section of the trip. If you have no luck catching your own, **St Helens**, a pretty holiday and fishing town on the edge of narrow Georges Bay, is the 'game-fishing capital of Tasmania'. St Helens is a great place to pick up super fresh seafood.

North of St Helens in **Bay of Fires Conservation Area** is an area known as **The Gardens**, named by Lady Jane Franklin, the wife of Governor John Franklin, who spent some time in the region in the 1840s. It offers sweeping views of a crowd-free stretch of teal blue sea rimmed with long curves of powdery white sand, lots of rockpools to explore and the very photogenic and rather ubiquitous orange-lichen-covered boulders to climb over and around and paddle between. Because it's a conservation park, rather than a national park, you can even bring your dog.

Kids' spot

Introduce the kids to some adorable baby devils - called joeys - at **East Coast Natureworld** (natureworld.com.au) in Bicheno. There's also echidna feeding encounters and hands-on sessions with wombats and sugar gliders. The night-time **Devils in the Dark tour** - for those over age six - is your chance to watch Tasmanian devils devour a carcass up close from the comfort of a wildlife shelter (with Tassie wine and cheese on offer for the adults). Book online.

Bay of Fires Conservation Park stretches north to **Ansons Bay**, around 15km away, but to get there you either have to walk along the beaches or take the unsealed 52km inland road. It continues to **Mount William National Park**, which boasts exactly the same type of scenery but has more established campgrounds and toilet facilities, although you have to pay the normal national park entry and camping fees. At the southern end of the national park is historic **Eddystone Point Lighthouse**, a striking pink granite tower on a point that juts out into the sea. From the northern end of the park at Musselroe Bay, you can see across to the Bass Strait islands.

For reasons we can't fathom, this part of the world is not only heart-achingly beautiful, it's also, for the most part, completely deserted. Only in Tasmania can you find somewhere this close to paradise and have it all to yourself.

Opposite Wineglass Bay *Below* Gourmet goodies at Kate's Berry Farm

Head into the hills

For a change of scenery head inland to **Douglas-Apsley National Park**, just north of Bicheno. **Apsley Waterhole** is just a 10min walk from the carpark off Rosedale Rd, and if you explore further you'll find deep river gorges, waterfalls, swimming holes and a dolerite-capped plateau crisscrossed by walking tracks.

Around a half-hour drive further north the very pretty but steep and winding road up the range through the rainforest to **St Marys** via **Elephant Pass** is popular with motorcyclists and caravanners, so the going can be slow sometimes.

BEST BEDS

- **Edge of the Bay** The luxury suites set on the beachfront have dazzling views across the bay to the pink granite peaks of the Hazards on the Freycinet Peninsula. There's a licensed restaurant, and the Coles Bay cafes are just a 20min walk up the beach. edgeofthebay.com.au
- **Freycinet Lodge** You're right in the middle of the national park here, and many of the cabins have water views. There are a range of tours on offer, as well as special packages. freycinetlodge.com.au
- **Tranquility Bay of Fires** This modern three-bedroom beach house between Binnalong Bay and the Bay of Fires/larapuna has spectacular views. destinationbayoffires.com/tranquility-bay-of-fires

VANLIFE

Most of the towns along this route have caravan parks. You can camp on **Maria Island** at Darlington without booking but you pay before you board the ferry to the island at Triabunna; take everything with you. Camping at **Freycinet** is by the beach with beautiful views and there are plenty of shady sites to choose from, including powered sites for campervans and caravans; the park is very popular, however, so it's best to book ahead (parks.tas.gov.au). There is also good camping at **Friendly Beaches** close to the border of the park. In the southern section of **Bay of Fires Conservation Area** there are six free camping areas, most overlooking the beach; facilities are basic and include pit-toilets but there's no water or firewood. In **Mount William National Park** there are several sheltered camping areas at **Stumpys Bay** in the north of the park; there are also campsites at the far northern end of the park, just before **Musselroe Bay**, and at the end of the beachside road from Eddystone Point to Deep Creek, in the southern section of the park.

Tasmania

The scenic Bass Hwy follows the coast from Devonport in the east to the charming village of Stanley in the west. Kennaook/Cape Grim on the far-western tip has the world's cleanest air and at tiny Boat Harbour you'll find one of the country's most glorious beaches.

The north-west

HOW LONG?
Allow two to three days, one way.

WHEN TO GO
Summer is mild and winter tends to be the wettest season, but anytime is a good time to do this road trip. The best time to see little penguins is between Nov and Mar; Table Cape Tulip Farm (*see* p.294) and other flowering gardens are most spectacular in spring.

NEED TO KNOW
The *Spirit of Tasmania* has two car ferries that cross Bass Strait between Geelong in Victoria and Devonport, in both directions. The journey takes around ten hours and departs from both ports in the evening, arriving early the following morning; during peak holiday time (mid Dec to mid Mar and during Easter) there is also a daytime sailing. Onboard accommodation ranges from airline-style reclining seats to private cabins with an ensuite, including two-berth and four-berth cabins, which you can book for exclusive use or opt to share with other passengers. You can also take your caravan, and pets. Book ahead online (spiritoftasmania.com.au).

LOCAL SECRET
Providore 24, housed in a cute little 1830s cottage in Stanley, is the place to go hunting and gathering everything you need to fill a picnic hamper with Tasmanian produce, from pickled octopus to cheese and gin made from gorse flowers and leatherwood honey, as well as artisan bread, local preserves and lots of sweet treats.

SNAPSHOT
Most road trippers who drive off the *Spirit of Tasmania* ferry when it docks in Devonport tend to either head south, to Cradle Mountain, or east to Launceston, Freycinet or Hobart/nipaluna. But go west, along the Bass Coast, and not only will you leave the crowds behind, but you'll uncover a beautiful coastline punctuated with stunning natural attractions, including the famous Nut at Stanley, and the extraordinary forest wilderness of takayna/Tarkine.

Drive rating
Easy. Mostly sealed roads.

Acknowledgement of Country
This is the Traditional Land of the Tommeginne and Peerapper Peoples.

Distance planner
Devonport to Arthur River: around 200km
- Devonport to Stanley: 126km
- Stanley to Arthur River: 82km

More information
- Stanley Information Centre, 10 Church St, Stanley; 1300 138 229; stanleyandtarkine.com.au
- Devonport Information Centre, 145 Rooke St, Devonport; (03) 6420 2900; visitdevonport.com.au
- northwesttasmania.com.au

Opposite The Nut, Stanley

DEVONPORT TO STANLEY

Starting in Devonport, follow National Highway 1 – the Bass Hwy – west along the coastline, detouring off it at Ulverstone to take the Penguin Rd to the seaside township of **Penguin**; you'll know you're there when you spot the 3m-high cement penguin opposite the post office in the main street, or the rubbish bins festooned with penguins, or the penguin-themed murals that decorate many of the walls in and around town. There are no prizes for guessing what the town's main attraction is, and if you want to see the little penguins that give the town its name, head to one of the beaches around sunset, between Nov and Mar, where you've got a better-than-average chance of seeing them come waddling up out of the sea after a day spent hunting food in the water.

Once infamous for its heavy industry and associated smells, particularly from the large pulp and paper mill which closed in 2010, **Burnie** has shaken off its industrial past and is now a pleasant seaside town, with some fabulous Art Deco architecture and a waterfront boardwalk, as well as another chance to see little penguins at the **Little Penguin Observation Centre**, on the foreshore. **Fern Glade Platypus Reserve** is a good spot to see platypus at dawn and dusk. Garden lovers will enjoy a stroll around **Emu Valley Rhododendron Garden**, home to more than 24,000 plants. Peak flowering time is in spring (mid Sept to mid Nov), but it's also spectacular in autumn.

Make **Wynyard** your next stop (home to Burnie Airport if you've flown in). If you're here in spring (Sept and Oct), drive out to Table Cape and visit **Table Cape Tulip Farm** to wander through rows and rows of stunning blooms, all the by-product of the farm's main business: growing the bulbs. The farm covers most of the flat-topped circular headland, and if you're lucky enough to be flying over it the patchwork of brilliant red, yellow, pink and purple flowers is a breathtaking sight. But if you miss the spring display it's still worth driving out to **Table Cape Lookout**, perched above the ocean just a few kilometres from town. The cape is actually a volcanic plug which rises to about 190m above sea level, capped with **Table Cape Lighthouse**, built in 1888. The views along the coast in both directions are mesmerising.

Fossil Bluff is nearby. Created by an ancient tidewater glacier, you can see fossilised shells caught in the rocks on the beach at low tide, as well as quartz, jasper and agates on the beach.

Boat Harbour, a tiny collection of beach houses adorning the dune behind the white sandy beach, is just 15km down the road. It's the type of place you can easily base yourself for a week of sun, sand and sea, even if the water tends to be a little on the cold (read freezing) side.

It's a lovely half-hour drive from Boat Harbour to your next port of call, **Stanley**. Most well-known for the distinctive 152m-high flat-topped circular headland called **The Nut** that looms above the town, Stanley is a pretty fishing community crammed with picturesque historic buildings. The Nut is actually the stump of a volcano, and it's a steep climb to the top (or take the chair lift) where there's a 40min circular track with great coastal and ocean views.

☺ Kids' spot

Two attractions in Devonport that will appeal to both kids and grown-ups are the **Don River Railway** - a 30min ride back in time on a restored steam train along with a museum and workshop displaying old locomotives and carriages - and the **Bass Strait Maritime Museum**, where you can 'Take the Helm' and guide a steamship into the Mersey River or through the heads of Port Phillip Bay in the *SS Woniora* Simulator Experience.

Lookout near Arthur River

There are 30,000 shearwaters (mutton birds) that nest on The Nut and when they all take off to go out to sea at once, it's an amazing sight. Rug up and head to the viewing platform on **Godfreys Beach** to watch little penguins as they toddle out of the sea and back to their burrows at the foot of The Nut (Nov to Mar), or take a cruise aboard the *Sylvia C* to check out the colony of Australian fur seals that 'haul out' at a tiny speck of an island called **Bull Rock**, around 600m offshore.

Stanley's most famous son is Tasmania's only prime minister, 'Honest Joe' Lyons, born here in 1879. The cottage he grew up in – **Lyons Cottage** – is furnished as it was when he lived there and has a collection of photographs and memorabilia that relate to both him and his equally famous wife, Dame Enid Lyons, the first woman elected to the federal House of Representatives.

For more history take a drive up the hill to tour **Highfield Historic Site**, a beautiful Regency-era home that was originally built for Edward Curr, chief agent of the Van Diemen's Land Company not long after the company first established Stanley as the base for its sheep-raising enterprise in 1826. The sensational views across to The Nut and Bass Strait are worth it – even if historic houses aren't quite your thing.

The north-west

Good for a rainy day

If you've come to Tassie keen to taste some of the whisky the island has recently become world famous for, you won't be disappointed if you call into **Hellyers Road Distillery** (don't be misled by the name, it's on Old Surrey Rd) for a guided behind-the-scenes Whisky Walk. Book online (hellyersroaddistillery.com.au).

SIDETRACK

Popular with hikers who come here to walk the coastal walking tracks, which range from short easy strolls to longer full-day walks, **Rocky Cape National Park** has secluded beaches, sea caves and rock pools to discover, including the lighthouse on the headland known as pinmatik/Rocky Cape. Many of the rocky shelters and caves contain middens and other culturally significant items sacred to palawa People, who ask that you do not enter the caves.

A favourite trail is the one that starts near the boat ramp at **Sisters Beach**, where you can climb the heath-covered hills to an extensive stand of banksias with spectacularly large cylindrical flowers, as well as see caves set dramatically above the rocky shore and breathtaking views. It takes around an hour return, and there are picnic facilities at Sisters Beach.

Opposite Emu Valley Rhododendron Garden, Burnie *Below* Looking out over Stanley from The Nut

STANLEY TO ARTHUR RIVER

From Stanley it's a beautiful drive up and over endless windswept and heath-covered dunes, past picturesque stone cottages with streamers of thick kelp drying on the clotheslines and lush green paddocks (the grass-fed beef produced here is renowned for its flavour and tenderness) to the tiny township of Arthur River on the west coast.

At Arthur River you can take a 14km cruise up one of the few rivers in Tasmania that hasn't been dammed and whose banks have never been logged. Book ahead with **Arthur River Cruises** (arthurrivercruises.com.au). Even in bad weather (and it often is), it's a serene journey into an untouched wilderness, where sea eagles and kingfishers swoop and reflections dance in the light (when the sun shines). Cruises include lunch at a clearing in the old-growth forest, deep in the takayna/Tarkine wilderness area.

Finish your trip at the **Edge of the World**. Aptly named, it is a wild and desolate place where the river spills into the sea and monstrous waves crash up against a rocky shore and the wind is so strong it almost blows you off your feet. They have a saying in these parts: 'If the wind stops blowing the cows would fall over'. It's easy to see why. Take a deep breath while you're there, because this is officially some of the cleanest air in the world – air pollution levels at nearby Kennaook/Cape Grim are the lowest on the planet. With nothing but the Southern Ocean between you and the tip of South America, it really does feel like you're standing at the edge of the world.

Head into the hills

You can also explore the takayna/Tarkine, Australia's largest temperate rainforest and the second largest in the world - on land. The **Tarkine Drive** is a sealed 130km loop from Stanley to Arthur River and back via Sumac and Trowutta (although some of the attractions are accessed via short gravel sections). Highlights include sinkholes, lakes lookouts, historic wooden bridges and the Trowutta Arch - formed when a cave between sinkholes collapsed - riverside picnic areas, walking trails and truly sublime rainforest. For those with the right vehicle, the **Arthur-Pieman Conservation Area** is a favourite destination for four-wheel-drivers, especially those keen to tackle the challenging **Sandy Cape Track**. Check tides before driving on the beach and carry recovery gear. You'll need to get a Recreational Driver Pass from the ranger station (or online at parks.tas.gov.au) before you hit the tracks - the pass includes detailed maps.

BEST BEDS

- There are lots of houses to rent for accommodation in the holiday towns of Penguin, Boat Harbour, Sisters Beach and Stanley. stayz.com.au or airbnb.com.au
- **Ship Inn Stanley** Beautifully renovated historic inn (built in 1849 by the grandfather of former Prime Minister Joseph Lyons) on the waterfront beneath The Nut at Stanley. shipinnstanley.com.au

VANLIFE

Most of the towns along this route have caravan parks, and many are right beside the beach. You can also camp at **Preservation Bay** near Penguin, and there are two campgrounds **in Peggs Beach Conservation Area**, east of Stanley. **Montagu Campground**, a council-run camping reserve 20km from Smithton, has great views to Robbins Island, although facilities are pretty basic. There are three campgrounds at Arthur River in **Arthur-Pieman Conservation Area** - **Manuka**, **Prickly Wattle** and **Peppermint** - all operated by National Parks, but because it's a Conservation Area, there's no park entry fee (although you'll still need to book), you can camp with your dog, and you don't need a 4WD to reach the campgrounds. See parks.tas.gov.au for camping information.

TASMAN
SEA
BASS
STRAIT
BANKS
STRAIT
0 5 10 km
N
Craggy Island
Inner Sister Island
SISTER ISLANDS CA
Outer Sister Island
North East River
Stanley Point
Holloway Point
Blyth Point
Blyth Bay
Quoin Hill
Palana
North East River
Limestone Bay
NORTH EAST RIVER GR
Mount Killiecrankie
B85
Killiecrankie Bay
Mount Blyth
Foochow Beach
Boat Harbour Beach
Killiecrankie
Cape Frankland
MOUNT TANNER NRA
Mount Boyes
Hogans Lagoon
Mount Tanner
Leeka
WINGAROO NATURE RESERVE
Fergusons Lagoon
FOOCHOW CONSERVATION AREA
Roydon Is
North Pasco Is
Pine Scrub
Foochow Inlet
Pasco Group
Tanners Bay
Foochow Beach
South Pasco Is
Castle Rock
FLINDERS ISLAND
Marshall Bay
Lughrata
Patriarch Inlet
Babel Island
Allports Beach
Furneaux Museum
Swimming Beach
Cat Is
Settlement Point Viewing Platform
Port Davies
Emita
Memana
PATRIARCHS CA
Sellars Point
C801
Furneaux Lookout
Middle Patriarch
Prime Seal Island
Wybalenna
Walkers Lookout
Patriarch Wildlife Sanctuary
Lillies Bay
Survey Hill
South Patriarch
Sellars Lagoon
PRIME SEAL ISLAND CA
Sawyers Beach
DARLING RA
Planter Beach
Blue Rocks
C803
DARLING RANGE CA
Arthur Bay
SELLARS LAGOON GR
Safe Passage
Chalky Island
Flinders Island Golf Club
Long Point
Lackrana
Low Islets
Mount Hauland
Cameron Inlet
Whitemark
North Chain Lagoon
Furneaux
C803
Parrys Bay
Big Green Island
B85
Ranga
South Chain Lagoon
East Kangaroo Island
Adelaide Bay bird hide
LOGAN LAGOON CA
C805
Fotheringate Beach
Strzelecki Peaks
Logan Lagoon
Trousers Point
STRZELECKI NP
Vinegar Hill
Yellow Beach
Loccota
Trousers Point Beach
Mount Belstead
Adelaide Bay
Lady Barron
Chappell Islands
Mount Chappell Island
Unavale Vineyard
Cooma
Great Dog Is
Goose Is
Anderson Island
Franklin Sound
Vansittart Island
Badger Island
Tin Kettle Island
VANSITTART ISLAND CA
CHAPPELL ISLANDS NR
Puncheon Point
Neds Point
Riddles Bay
Deep Bay
Long Island
Group
Cape Barren Island
Big Stony Hill
Mount Munro
Double Peak
Phils Hill
Harleys Point
Sir John Cape
truwana/Cape Barren Island
Thirsty Lagoon
River Point
Mount Kerferd
Hogans Hill
Cape Barren
Dyas Bay
Battery Bay
Kent Bay
Preservation Island
Armstrong Channel
Kangaroo Bay
Seal Point
Jamiesons Bay
Home Hill
Cone Point
Foam Point
Clarke Island
Forsyth Island
Passage Island
Spike Bay
Green Hill
Lookout Head
Moriarty Point
South Head

With its spine of steep granite mountains, necklace of more than 100 glorious white sand beaches and a population of less than 1000 people, you're almost always guaranteed to find an empty beach here.

Flinders Island

HOW LONG?
At roughly 80km long, it doesn't take long to drive the length of the island, but it will take much longer than you expect as you won't be able to resist the urge to get out of the car to check out one beautiful beach after another. Aim to spend three or four days, or even a week.

WHEN TO GO
Despite its location straddling the 40th parallel in the middle of one of the most storm-wracked stretches of water, Flinders Island is a surprisingly balmy place – even if it does get a little windy on occasion. As the locals like to boast, it's much warmer than Melbourne in the winter. But don't expect tropical; summer temperatures peak in the low 20s, and be prepared for showers year-round.

NEED TO KNOW
Most people get to Flinders Island by air, from Launceston, Hobart or Melbourne: see Sharp Airlines (sharpairlines.com.au). Car and campervan hire is available, but arrange this before you arrive, as cars are limited on the island: ficr.com.au or flindersislandcp.com.au. If you really want to bring your own vehicle across, Bass Strait Freight make one round trip each week between Bridport on Tasmania's north-east coast and Lady Barron Port (bassstraitfreight.com.au) If you are arriving on the island on a Sun you'll find most shops and restaurants are closed, so arrange for your accommodation to have some provisions brought in for you in advance.

SNAPSHOT
Flinders Island, in the middle of Bass Strait off Tasmania's north-east coast, is home to some of the most beautiful fine white-sand beaches in the country. The largest of the Furneaux Group – 52 islands that once formed a land bridge between Tasmania and mainland Australia – it's part of the same dramatic rocky mountain range that forms Wilsons Promontory in Victoria and the Hazard mountains of Freycinet Peninsula on Tassie's East Coast. It's about as far away from your typical island paradise as you can possibly get, but if you want to play castaways there's no better place.

Drive rating
Easy. Mostly sealed with some gravel roads.

Acknowledgement of Country
This is the Traditional Land of the palawa People of the trawulwai Nation.

Distance planner
Lady Barron to North East River, via Whitemark: around 80km
- Whitemark to Lady Barron, via Trousers Point: 48km
- Whitemark to North East River: 51km

More information
- Flinders Island Visitor Information Centre, 9 Patrick St, Whitemark; (03) 6259 5001; visitflindersisland.com.au

WHITEMARK TO LADY BARRON

Forget about battling it out for towel space on the crowded beaches of Bondi, Byron and Cottesloe. You're pretty much guaranteed to find a deserted beach on Flinders Island, even in the middle of the summer. After all, the locals have a golden rule when it comes to sharing their sandy shores: 'if you find a beach with someone on it, find another one'.

There's really only one major road on the island – the B85 – and it runs tip to toe on the western side. **Whitemark**, the island's main (only, really) town (imagine a pub, supermarket, newsagent, cafe and bakery and you've pictured the whole town) is roughly in the middle, and where the airport and car rental pick up is, so we've split this road trip up into two sections: one in the north, the other in the south. There is accommodation available all over the island, but you could also base yourself in the middle at Whitemark, and head out on daytrips from there.

Time moves slowly on Flinders, and it doesn't seem to take very long at all before you've slowed down to match the pace of the locals, who always wave as you drive past, and usually stop for a chat when picking up supplies in Whitemark. By your third morning you'll probably find yourself on a first-name basis with most folk you pass, so be prepared that a quick outing to get a morning coffee may well turn into a 45min walk as people stop to ask you how you've been getting on and what you've been doing during your stay: it's that kind of place.

The island's most famous beach, **Trousers Point**, is close to the southern end of the island, via Lady Barron Rd (B85) and Trousers Point Rd.

There's a bit of a mystery as to how this dazzling beach got its name: legend has it that a shipless Richard Burgess washed up here without his pants in the 1870s; another tale credits the name to the discovery on the beach of a box of trousers from a different shipwreck in 1875. Either way, with its curve of white sand lapped by the palest of turquoise water bookended by the ubiquitous orange-lichen-covered boulders that seem an essential ingredient of every beach on the island, it's one of the most photographed spots on Flinders. It's also home to one of the best walks on the island, a 1hr loop along the rocky coastline to **Fotheringate Beach** and back. Or if you're feeling really energetic, climb to the summit of the **Strzelecki Peaks**. The 3km walk to the summit is not an easy one (it takes about four to five hours return), but if you make it to the top without the weather closing in, the 360-degree views of the island and surrounding waters are spectacular.

Backtrack to the B85 and head to the port of **Lady Barron**. Call in on the way to **Unavale Vineyard** (unavale.com.au), a lovely little boutique winery hidden away in the bush that produces some great tasting handcrafted organic wine. They also welcome visitors helping out with various vineyard activities, so check out their website to see what's happening during your visit if you want to get involved.

There's no town centre to speak of in **Lady Barron**, even though there are just as many people living here as in 'town' (Whitemark). It's also the island's main port. The **Furneaux Tavern** offers good food with knock-out views over Franklin Sound, and often has spontaneous live music when the locals get together for a play-a-long and sing some songs. If you're keen to catch a fish, this is the place to ask the locals what's biting where: good catches include snapper, salmon, flathead and kingfish. Nearby **Yellow Beach** is great for a walk and barbecue, especially if you've managed to catch your own dinner (or bought some crayfish from a local).

Flinders is home to more than 200 species of birds, including the giant wandering albatross and huge pacific gulls, eagles and endangered forty-spotted pardalote, as well as Cape Barren geese; the **Adelaide Bay bird hide** on the coast road is a good place to watch them.

If you're a golfer, the nine-hole golf course at **Flinders Island Golf Club**, just south of Whitemark, has only ever been parred once in its 40-year history. Could have something to do with the distracting ocean views – or maybe it's those challenging sea breezes. If you think you can break the record (or fancy a round), the club welcomes visitors, and they are happy to lend you a set of clubs if you call ahead: (03) 6359 2070.

Head into the hills

An alternative way to get back to Whitemark from Lady Barron is to take the inland route, following the Lackrana Rd to Memana and then heading west to Whitemark, along the Darling Range. Both the **Furneaux and Walkers lookouts** offer wonderful views.

Opposite Sawyers Beach *Above* Lady Barron, Flinders Island

Kids' spot

Run by volunteers, the **Patriarch Wildlife Sanctuary** at Lackrana between two of the three granite mountains known as Middle and South Patriarch is a conservation habitat for wombats, wallabies, pademelons, echidna and Cape Barren geese. It's a good place for kids to meet some of these animals in the wild – they roam free but will come quite close. It's off Lees Rd, east of Memana – the road in is a bit rough, but fine for 2WD if you take it slow.

SIDETRACK

The nearby islands, including **truwana/Cape Barren Island**, are home to millions of short-tailed shearwaters (mutton birds) and during the summer and autumn months – Nov to May – you can join a sunset cruise from the Lady Barron jetty to see the spectacular spectacle of the birds returning to the rookery to feed their chicks. Book the ferry at flindersislandtravel.com.au.

WHITEMARK TO NORTH EAST RIVER

The beaches of the north are just as spectacular as those in the south, and just as deserted. Around a 10min drive north of Whitemark towards Emita you'll find **Sawyers Beach**, a near perfect combination of white sand and gin-clear water, with three shady picnic areas and lots of boulders to clamber over and snorkel around, and good paddling for little kids in the many sheltered sections near the northern end.

In 1834, 135 palawa People from across mainland Tasmania and the Furneaux Islands were forcibly moved onto Flinders Island to be 'Civilised and Christianised' at a place called **Wybalenna**. Almost all died in a matter of years as a result of European causes. All that is left of the ill-fated settlement that lasted less than 15 years is the chapel and a few European graves; palawa People were buried in unmarked graves. In 1995 the land was returned to the Tasmanian Aboriginal Community, and it's now a protected historic monument and sacred burial site. A visit to the chapel is a brutal reminder of a very dark time in Australia's history.

Just a few kilometres past Wybalenna at Port Davies is another good spot to watch thousands of mutton birds return to their burrows, at the **Settlement Point Viewing Platform**. Breeding season starts in Sept, but the best time to see them is at dusk between Nov and Apr; if you're here in late Jan you may see chicks as well. There's also a good 90min-return coastal walk from Allports Beach to **Castle Rock**, a very photogenic, very big boulder on Marshall Bay.

At the top of the island, **Palana** looks big on the map, but is little more than a clutch of beach houses overlooking a spectacular stretch of sand, perfect for long solitary strolls. It was originally set up as a radar station in World War II, and some of the old shacks are still there. From here, follow the road to North East River on the northernmost tip of the island for fabulous views across to the offshore islands known as The Sisters. Spend some time exploring the tidal estuaries, rockpools, granite bluffs and lichen-covered rocks. Wild and windswept, pounded by surf, it's highly unlikely you'll see anyone else, let alone another set of footprints.

Head into the hills

On the way to Palana take the turn-off to West End Rd and wind your way up to the top of **Mount Tanner** for a fantastic view of Killiecrankie Bay and Roydon Island.

SIDETRACK

Between Marshall Bay near Emita and Palana in the north there are several roads that spear off to the coast to fabulous beaches. If you only stop at one, make it the close-to-perfect crescent of white sand lapped by sapphire water at **Killiecrankie**, 25km north of Emita. In summer you'll often see cray boats tethered to the rocks and wooden holding pens bobbing in the water, full of crayfish, but it's not the scenery or seafood that's the attraction. If you are lucky enough to spy a local here, ask them to point you in the direction of **Diamond Creek** (about 2km along the beach), where you can try your luck looking for the locally famous Killiecrankie 'diamonds'. You'll need a shovel and sieve. They are actually topaz - the ones found on the island are usually clear, ice blue or pink gold - but they look so much like diamonds you'd have to be an expert to tell the difference and the shops (both of them) in Whitemark sell these beautiful stones. If you don't find a gem, you may be lucky enough to see a paper nautilus shell. According to local legend, these paper-thin shells made by an argonaut - a type of octopus - wash up on the western beaches of the island in largish numbers every seven years, but as with all rare finds, you have to be in the right place at the right time. And as tempting as it may be to take one of the beautiful shells home, take a photo instead.

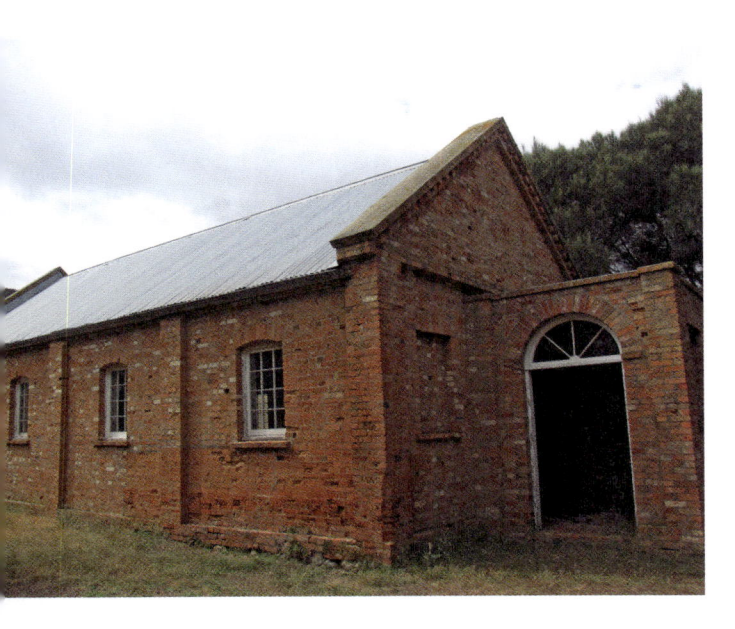

Good for a rainy day

You can find out a bit more about the brutal and tragic events that happened at Wybalenna and during the Black Wars at the **Furneaux Museum** (furneauxmuseum.org.au). You can easily spend an hour or two wandering around the exhibits. The collection of exquisite palawa shell necklaces, many donated by the owner of Bowman's General Store in Whitemark where they had been traded for supplies over the years, is outstanding. Other artefacts include the anchor of the *Sydney Cove*, wrecked on Preservation Island in 1797 more than 12 months before Bass Strait was even discovered by Europeans. The story of the epic journey of some of the survivors by sea and land back to Sydney to mount a rescue mission is fascinating, as is the subsequent settlement of the Furneaux Group of islands by sealers. Other exhibitions focus on mutton-birding, an important traditional industry in the islands that is still carried out today, as well as local history preserved in hundreds of photo albums and extensive displays of natural history specimens. Opening hours vary, so check before travelling.

BEST BEDS

- **Island Quarters** These smart spacious one-bedroom apartments in Whitemark with all mod cons, including kitchen and laundry, are the ideal base from which to explore the island. islandquarters.com.au
- **Palana Beach House** has stunning ocean views and is just metres from the beach at the northern tip of the island. There are two bedrooms in a separate wing, a double bed in the main section of the open-plan house and a fully equipped kitchen, TV and open fireplace for cold nights. flindersislandbeach.com
- The motel-style units at the **Furneaux Tavern** are in a good spot to explore the south of the island. furneauxtavern.com.au

VANLIFE

You need to be self-sufficient when it comes to recharging devices and cooking if you want to camp on Flinders, as there are no powered camping spots and there's a total fire ban in all campsites and reserves, although there are lots of free barbecues. There are some spectacular beachside camping spots though, including **Yellow Beach, Killiecrankie, North East River, Allports Beach** near Emita and at **Trousers Point** in Strzelecki National Park. For more info see flinders.tas.gov.au/camping-on-flinders-island.

Opposite North East River *Left* Wybalenna Chapel

BASS
STRAIT
Cape Wickham Lighthouse
Cape Wickham
Victoria Cove
Wickham Hill
Cape Farewell
Cape Wickham Golf Links
Disappointment Bay
Rocky Point
White Beach
Lake Flannigan
B25
LAVINIA STATE RESERVE
Boulder Point
Phoques Bay
Lake Martha Lavinia
Lavinia Beach
Egg Lagoon
Pennys Lagoon
New Year Is
Yellow Rock Beach
Lavinia Point
Christmas Is
Cooper Bluff
Shannon wreck
Quarantine Bay
LAVINIA STATE RESERVE
Whistler Point
Yambacoona
Duck Bay
N
0
3
6 km
Reekara
Nine Mile Beach
COUNSEL HILL CA
PORKY BEACH CA
KING ISLAND
LAVINIA STATE RESERVE
Counsel Hill
Pass River Bay
B25
Unlucky Bay
Sea Elephant
Cowper Point
Porky Beach
Loorana
SEA ELEPHANT CA
Councillor Island
King Island Dairy
Ocean Dunes Golf Course
KING ISLAND AIRPORT
Elephant
ELDORADO CA
Sea Elephant Bay
C202
King Island Arts & Cultural Centre
King Island Distillery
Sea
Fraser Beach
The Boathouse
Currie
Naracoopa
Currie Lighthouse
Fraser Bluff
B25
C203
King Island Museum
Kelp Industries
Pegarah
Parenna
King Island Golf Course
Millers Bay
Mary Hill
CITY OF MELBOURNE BAY CA
C201
C202
CATARAQUI POINT CA
B25
Yarra Creek
Lymwood
City of Melbourne Bay
KENTFORD FOREST CA
Gentle Annie
BASS
STRAIT
Fitzmaurice Bay
Grassy
Bold Head
Cataraqui Point
Pearshape
SEAL ROCKS CA
COLLIERS SWAMP CA
Mount Stanley
Grassy Bay
Copperhead Trail
Sandblow Point
Seal Rocks Lookout
Seal Rocks
SEAL ROCKS STATE RESERVE
Big Lake
Colliers Beach
RED HUT POINT CA
Calcified Forest
Surprise Bay
Black Point
Seal Bay
STOKES POINT CA
Stokes Point Lighthouse
Stokes Point

Walk the beaches and along the cliff-tops and throw your diet to the wind, because the food on King Island is seriously good.

King Island

HOW LONG?

You could see the island in two days, but you'd be rushing – allow at least four: there are more than 480km of roads that crisscross the island to explore.

WHEN TO GO

Be prepared for all sorts of weather on King Island, every day. Summer temperatures hover around 20°C, but it can be wet, cold and windy at any time of the year. Winter tends to be wetter, but relatively mild compared to Melbourne or Hobart.

NEED TO KNOW

The best way to road trip on King Island is to fly from Melbourne, Launceston or Burnie, and hire a car, but cars are limited, so arrange it before you go. See kingisland.org.au for information on both flights and car hire. You can ship your vehicle across from Tasmania with Bass Island Lines (bassislandline.com.au). It's not a passenger ferry, so you'll still need to fly to the island, and vehicles can take anywhere from four days to two weeks to be delivered, depending on the shipping schedule (and weather). There is no public transport on the island, so you'll need to arrange a lift with a local to pick up your car.

SNAPSHOT

When most people think of King Island they think of its famous cheese and melt-in-the-mouth beef. But there's much more to this island in the western waters of Bass Strait than just its gourmet produce. Beautiful beaches, towering lighthouses and a fascinating history of shipwrecks are just some of its attractions.

Drive rating
Easy. Mostly sealed roads with some minor gravel roads.

Acknowledgement of Country
This is the Traditional Land of the palawa People.

Distance planner
Stokes Point to Cape Wickham, without detours: around 82km
- Currie to Grassy, via Stokes Point: 66km
- Currie to Cape Wickham: 46km

More information
- King Island Tourism, 5 George St, Currie; 1800 645 014; kingisland.org.au

CURRIE TO GRASSY, VIA STOKES POINT

Nowhere is very far from anywhere on King Island, and since the airport is at Currie – the main township on the island – we've spilt this road trip into two halves in either direction of Currie, one to the southern tip of the island, the other to the north.

There's plenty to see and do in **Currie**, though, before you hit the road. Make your first stop the **lighthouse**, one of the few in Australia that was turned off (in 1989), only to be recommissioned in 1995. Made of wrought- and cast-iron, it was shipped over from England in 312 bits and was first lit in 1880. You can climb the 20m spiral staircase inside on a guided tour – the views are amazing. The volunteers at the **museum** next door, in the former lighthouse keeper's cottage, will be able to let you know when the next tour is scheduled. The museum is packed with interesting displays on the island's history and hundreds of shipwreck relics brought up from the bottom of the sea.

Clinging to the rocks beneath the lighthouse at the edge of the harbour is King Island's best restaurant, **The Boathouse**. Be warned though, it's strictly BYO – BYO drinks and BYO food! You'll also need to cook it yourself and wash the dishes, but it really is one the best places on the island to eat. Sourcing ingredients is easy – pop into the butcher for some grass-fed beef, call into the **King Island Dairy** (see p.311) for some wickedly rich cheese and buy a crayfish on the wharf, or pick up a ready-made hamper of local produce from the supermarket, **Foodworks** in Currie – order hampers and crayfish (mid Nov to mid Jan) a day ahead – or a famous crayfish pie from the bakery. There's also island-made tipples (gin, whisky and limoncello) from **King Island Distillery** and keep an eye out for bottled Cloud Juice (pure delicious rainwater). The colourful art-filled space of The Boathouse has indoor and outdoor tables, floor-to-ceiling harbour views, cutlery, crockery, glassware and all the cooking equipment you need. With ingredients this good, you don't need to be a Michelin-starred chef to whip up a good meal. All you really need to do is heat up the barbecue, crack a few shells, unwrap the cheese and open the wine. Dining is free as long as you clean up after yourself – and drop a few dollars in the donation box.

King Island is a trusting kind of place. When I picked up my hire car at the airport I was told to leave the keys in the ignition when I dropped it off, someone would be around in a day or two to pick up the car. On a 64km-long and 24km-wide island in the middle of the ocean a stolen car is going to be pretty easy to spot, I guess.

Pop into the **King Island Arts & Cultural Centre** while you're harbourside for a chat with local artists and makers and to browse the changing array of locally made art and craft.

As you follow South Rd down to the southern tip of the island, there are several roads leading off to secluded bays and beaches on the west coast. Many are littered with massive piles of stormcast bull kelp that has been washed up on the beaches. These are harvested by the locals and then brought to the **Kelp Industries** plant on the outskirts of Currie (Netherby Rd), where the kelp is hung to air dry on racks before being ground up and shipped overseas for processing. Pop into the free visitor's centre to learn more about the process.

Opposite Colliers Beach on the south coast of the island
Above Naracoopa's historic wharf

SIDETRACK

Most of King Island is gently undulating, but on the southern tip of the island you'll find a long line of towering cliffs at **Seal Rocks**. Plunging more than 60m into a furious sea, the views are dramatic but despite the name there are no seals. If you're lucky though, you may spot a few little penguins nesting underneath the boardwalk to the lookout. The 90min-return **Copperhead Trail** follows the line of cliffs north from the lookout, passing Cataraqui Point, site of Australia's worst maritime civil disaster when 400 people drowned during the wreck of the *Cataraqui* in 1845.

Kids' spot

On the drive back to the South Rd turn off to see the **Calcified Forest**, where the stumpy remains of a 7000-year-old forest have been preserved by the lime-laden sand in an array of weird shapes and sizes. There's an easy 30min walk through the 'forest' with a viewing platform around the halfway mark.

Unlike the island's more celebrated lighthouses in Currie and in the north, the one at **Stokes Point**, on the very southern tip of the island, is a little underwhelming: a modern, squat, unmanned beacon. The views make up for it though, as it feels like you are standing at the edge of the world, especially if the wind is blowing (and it usually is!).

Retrace your steps to **Pearshape** (named after a nearby lagoon shaped like, well, a pear) and cut across to **Grassy** on the east coast of the island. If you're a surfer, **Colliers Beach** off Red Hut Rd is one of the island's renowned surf spots. Once a thriving scheelite mining village (the mine closed in 1990), Grassy is now little more than a quiet collection of holiday cottages with sea-forever views. It also has the island's only deep-water shipping port; this is where the island's supplies are brought in every Sun morning, weather permitting. Head out to the breakwall on the harbour at dusk to watch the little penguins return to their burrows after a day at sea. For more local produce book a table at **Wild Harvest Restaurant** (wildharvestkingisland.com.au), a fine diner with fabulous views and a hyper-seasonal paddock-to-plate, ocean-to-table focus when it comes to food.

SIDETRACK

King Island's third 'village', **Naracoopa**, is just a few houses strung out along a rocky beach on the shores of Sea Elephant Bay about a third of the way up the east coast. When the bay was first sighted by the French in 1802, naturalist Francois Peron observed that 'The whole of this bay, when we landed, was covered with sea elephants'. Sadly, just three years later, not one elephant seal was left, thanks to the work of English sealers. Today, though, it is a nice place for beachcombing and the 200m-long historic wooden wharf is a great place to drop a fishing line into the sea; if you're lucky you may just hook a salmon or some squid. Nearby is Sea Elephant River, the island's largest. It's a good spot for birdwatching.

Opposite top The Boathouse, Currie *Opposite bottom* Cape Wickham Lighthouse *Top* Currie Harbour *Middle* Outdoor dining at the Boatshed, Currie *Bottom* Wreck of the *Shannon* on Yellow Rock Beach

King Island 309

CURRIE TO CAPE WICKHAM

For some visitors, an ultimate coastal road trip is all about fairways rather than freeways. Two of Australia's most highly rated links courses are on the island, **Ocean Dunes**, just north of Currie, and **Cape Wickham**, and packages are available that play both. There's also a nine-hole course in the heart of Currie.

Porky Beach is another surfing hot spot, and just like in the south, North Rd has lots of side roads that lead to wild, deserted beaches. Many are named for the ship that was wrecked there. Hundreds of ships – and more than 1000 lives – have been lost in the waters around King Island, and there's no escaping the legacy of the wrecks on the island. The maritime trail, **Shipwrecks and Safe Havens**, tells the stories of the shipwrecks on interpretation boards at some of the sites, and you can download more details at kingisland.org.au/maritime-trails.

Pick up a unique King Island keepsake at **King Island Kelp Craft** in the Reekara Community Complex Top Shop, where all manner of items from toys to jewellery are made from bull kelp, which dries like leather (and no, it doesn't smell).

On **Yellow Rock Beach** the rusting remains of the *Shannon*, a paddlesteamer that was driven ashore by wild weather in 1906, are exposed at low tide just metres from the shore. Of all the known shipwrecks in the waters around the island this is the only one you can see without getting wet. It's around a 20min walk from the carpark over the hill and along the beach.

At 48m high, the lighthouse at **Cape Wickham** on the northernmost point of the island is the tallest in the Southern Hemisphere. It was built in 1861 and marks the western entrance of the Bass Strait. Enjoy the panoramic vistas at the lighthouse, then wander across the point to **Victoria Cove**, a lovely little curve of white sandy beach. Even if you're not a golfer, it's worth making a reservation at the clubhouse at **Cape Wickham Golf Links** (capewickham.com.au), just to drink in the incredible views.

Make a detour on the way back to Currie to one of the most beautiful spots on the island – **Pennys Lagoon** is an unusual perched freshwater lake (a perched lake is one that is above the groundwater table). It's a good place for a swim, a walk around the lake and a picnic or cook-up on one of the free barbecues.

Nearby is **Lavinia Beach**, a popular shell-hunting spot and the island's most well-known surfing spot, its famed northernmost break on the bucket-list of many surfers and a favourite with surfing legends like Kelly Slater. It, too, was named for a ship that struck a reef here in 1871. There's a legend that shipwrecks are to thank for the rich pastures that produce the island's delicious beef and cheese – apparently the result of grass seeds in straw mattresses that washed ashore.

Whatever the reason, the lush grasses certainly produce milk sweet enough that you don't need sugar in your tea, milkshakes good enough to convince you to turn teetotal and yoghurts and creams so decadent they'll transport you straight to heaven – and with their high fat content, that's probably exactly what they will do if you eat too much. Luckily, there's plenty of unspoilt beaches on the island where you can walk off the indulgence.

SIDETRACK

Don't worry about being disappointed when you get to **Disappointment Bay**, a short 4min detour off the Cape Wickham Rd, because there's not much to be disappointed about with this beautiful north-facing bay, ideal for swimming, surfing and generally just lazing about. It gets its rather misleading name from the *Neva*, a ship carrying female convicts and children, which sank here in 1835 with the loss of 224 lives; it's Tasmania's second worst shipwreck.

Good for a rainy day

No visit to King Island is complete without a visit to the legendary **King Island Dairy** (kingislanddairy.com.au), a 5min drive north of Currie on the North Rd. The lush pastures of the island produce an unusually rich milk that in turn makes wickedly good cheese. Although you can buy King Island Dairy cheeses in supermarkets and food stores around the country, you'll find a much bigger range here in the cheese store at Loorana, including cheesy desserts. You can also watch a video on the history of the dairy that was founded in 1901, learn about the cheese-making process and taste the range of cheeses - you'll recognise the names on the labels from your road trip as they are all named after island localities - and stock up on picnic and breakfast supplies. It's not open every day, so check the website before you go.

BEST BEDS

- **Blencathra Coastal Spa Getaway** Boasting one of Currie's best views from the expansive deck, this two-storey three-bedroom holiday house not far from the harbour is an easy walk into town. airbnb.com.au/rooms/23620260
- **Boomerang by the Sea** Motel-style units in Currie overlooking the King Island Golf Course with an on-site restaurant serving 270-degree views along with the food. boomerangbythesea.com
- **Ocean Views** This simple but comfortable two-bedroom house in the heart of Grassy village also has sweeping ocean views and a hot tub big enough for four that also has great views - when the fog lifts! kingislandaccommodation.com

VANLIFE

There are no 'official' camping grounds or campsites on King Island, but camping is popular with locals and there are some truly spectacular coastal spots. Best way to find them would be to ask a friendly islander - or check out hipcamp.com, as some landowners are opening up their properties to campers; always check first with the landowner that it is okay before you pitch a tent.

Opposite Drying kelp *Left* King Island is known for its delicious cheese *Right* King Island's famous cows

INDEX

42 Mile Crossing, Coorong National Park SA 129
75 Mile Beach Qld 229
80 Mile Beach WA 176, 177
90 Mile Straight SA 151
1770 Qld 238, 239
1770 Beach Hotel Qld 238
1770 Camping Ground Qld 239

A

A Maze'N Things, Phillip Island Vic. 79
Aboriginal art, culture and heritage
   Bataluk Coastal Trail Vic. 102
   Beowa National Park NSW 55
   Booderee National Park JBT 46-7
   Bournda National Park NSW 54
   Budj Bim Cultural Landscape, Heywood Vic. 74
   Buku-Larrnggay Mulka Centre, Yirrkala NT 211
   Crossing Country Tour, Yolgnu Homelands NT 213
   Dark Point Aboriginal Place, Myall Lakes National Park NSW 5
   Kimberley Coast WA 183, 184-5
   Krowathunkoolong Keeping Place, Bairnsdale Vic. 102
   Laura Qld 261
   Mimosa Rocks National Park NSW 52
   Mossman Gorge Cultural Centre Qld 256
   Mowanjum Aboriginal Art & Culture Centre, Derby WA 183
   Murujuga National Park WA 174
   Quinkan Galleries, Laura Qld 261
   Quinkan and Regional Cultural Centre, Laura Qld 261
   Royal National Park NSW 40
   The Truganini Lookout, Bruny Island Tas. 25
   Towee Hill Wildlife Reserve Vic. 73
   Worimi Conservation Lands NSW 15
   Wujal Wujal Aboriginal Shire Council Qld 260
   Wybalenna, Flinders Island Tas. 302
Adelaide/Tarndanya SA 109, 110, 117, 129, 131, 132
Adelaide Bay bird hide, Flinders Island Tas. 301
Adjahdura People 131
Admirals Arch, Flinders Chase National Park SA 120
Adventure Bay Tas. 273, 275
Adventureland Park, Esperance WA 203

Agnes Water Qld 238
Aireys Inlet Vic. 64
Airlie Beach Qld 241, 244, 246, 247
Airlie Beach lagoon Qld 244
Airlie Creek walking track, Airlie Beach Qld 244
Alba Thermal Springs and Spa, Fingal Vic. 87
Albany WA 195, 199-200, 203
All Saints Church, Kingston, Norfolk Island 265
Allports Beach, Flinders Island Tas. 302, 303
Alonnah Tas. 273
Alstonville NSW 33, 35
Amangu People 155
American River SA 121
Amity Point Qld 217
Anchorage Hotel, Victor Harbor 115
Anderson Vic. 91, 92
Anderson Inlet Vic. 92
Ang Gnarra People 255
Anglesea Vic. 64, 67
Anglesea Riverside Motel Vic. 67
Angourie Point NSW 28
Anson Bay, Norfolk Island 263, 267
Ansons Bay Tas. 285, 291
Antarctic Journey, Phillip Island Vic. 77, 80
Antechamber Bay SA 118, 121
Apollo Bay Vic. 61, 65, 66, 67
Apple Shed, The, Grove Tas. 276
Apsley Waterhole, Douglas-Apsley National Park Tas. 291
Aquifer Tours, Mount Gambier SA 124
AQWA – The Aquarium of Western Australia, Hillarys Boat Harbour WA 157
Aragunnu campground, Mimosa Rocks National Park NSW 57
Arakoon NSW 21
Arakoon National Park NSW 17, 21
Arakwal People 31
Ardrossan SA 132
Ardyaloon (One Arm Point) WA 179, 185
Armstrong Oysters, Laurieton NSW 18
Arnhem Land NT 207
Arno Bay SA 141
Artfusion Gallery, Anderson Vic. 78
Arthur Pieman Conservation Area Tas. 297
Arthur River Tas. 297
Arthur River Cruises Tas. 297
Arve River Streamside Reserve, Geeveston Tas. 277
Ashcombe Maze and Lavender Gardens, Shoreham Vic. 89
Atherton Qld 255, 258

Atherton Tablelands Qld 252, 255, 258
Attic Creek Falls, Cardwell Qld 250
Augusta WA 187, 190, 192, 193, 196
Aurora Australis 277
Aurora Ozone Hotel, Kingscote SA 121
Australia Zoo, Beerwah Qld 222
Australian Motorcycle Grand Prix, Phillip Island Vic. 77, 80
Australian Motorlife Museum, Kembla Grange NSW 42
Australian National Goanna Pulling Championships, Woolo NSW 28
Australian National Surfing Museum, Torquay Vic. 64
Australian Outback Spectacular, Gold Coast Qld 219
Australian Reptile Park, Somersby NSW 12
Australian Sugar Heritage Centre, Mourilyan Qld 252
Avoca NSW 10
Avoca Lake NSW 10
Awabakal People 3, 9

B

Babinda Boulders Qld 252, 253
Badgingarra National Park WA 161
Bago Vineyars, Wauchope NSW 19
Bailai People 233
Baird Bay SA 148, 149, 151
Baird Bay Apartments SA 151
Baird Bay Ocean Eco Experience SA 149
Bairnsdale Vic. 99, 102
Baiyungu People 163, 169
Ball Bay Qld 247
Ball Bay Reserve, Norfolk Island 268
Balladonia SA WA 151
Balladonia Hotel Motel SA 151
Balladonia Roadhouse WA 151
Ballina NSW 31, 32, 35
Balnarring Vic. 89
Banambarrna (Rainbow Cliff) NT 211
Bandjalang People 32
Bandjin People 249, 251
Bangalow NSW 35
Banubanu Beach Retreat, Bremer Island NT 208, 213
Banyjima People 177
Barada Barna People 244
Barunguba (Montague Island) NSW 48
Bardi People 179, 185
Bargara Qld 234, 235
Barinjura NT 212
Barngarla People 117, 139, 145

Barwon Heads Vic. 90
Barwon Heads Bluff Vic. 86
Bass Coast Tas. 293
Bass Coast Vic. 91-7
Bass Coast Rail Trail Vic. 92
Bass Strait Maritime Museum, Devonport Tas. 295
Bataluk Coastal Trail Vic. 102
Batemans Bay NSW 45, 47
Bather's Way, Newcastle NSW 12
Bay of Fires Conservation Park Tas. 285, 290-1
Bay of Islands Coastal Park Vic. 66
Beach House at Bayside, Albany WA 203
Beach House Hotel, Port Macquarie NSW 19
Beach House Motel, Townsville Qld 247
Beach Huts Middleton SA 115
beach run (4WD), Beachport to Robe SA 126
Beachport Conservation Park SA 129
Beachport SA 124, 125, 126, 129
Beachport Southern Ocean Tourist Park SA 129
Beagle Bay WA 179, 184-5
Bear Gully, Cape Liptrap Coastal Park Vic. 97
Beaumaris Vic. 84
Beech Forest Vic. 65
Beerwah Qld 222, 223
Bega NSW 51, 54
Bega Cheese Factory NSW 54
Bellarine Peninsula Vic. 83, 86, 89
Bellingen NSW 27
Bells Beach Vic. 64
Belmore NSW 20
Beowa National Park NSW 55, 57
Bermagui NSW 51, 52
Berry 39, 43
Berry Bay SA 135
Berry Beach, Phillip Island Vic. 80
Berry Donut Van at Berry Service Station NSW 39
Beyond the Great Ocean Road Vic. 69-75
Bibbulman People 195, 196, 199
Bicheno Tas. 290
Bidawal People 51, 99
Big Banana, Coffs Harbour NSW 27
Big Buzz Fun Park, Forster NSW 7
Big Cane Toad, Sarina Qld 242
Big Lobster, Kingston SE 128
Big Mango, Bowen Qld 246
Big Pineapple, Nambour Qld 222
Big Prawn, Ballina NSW 35
Big Yangie, Coffin Bay National Park SA 143
BIG4 Adventure Whitsunday Resort, Airlie Beach Qld 247
Billabong Koala Wildife Park, Port Macquarie NSW 19
Bindal People 241
Bindjali People 123

Binna Burra Qld 219
Binydjarrnga (Daliwuy Bay) NT 212
Birchs Bay Tas. 276
bird watching see wildlife-watching
Biripi Country 3
Birks Harbour SA 129
Birpal People 17
Birregurra Vic. 65
Bishop and Clerk, Maria Island Tas. 289
Bittangabee Bay NSW 57
Black Rocks Campground, Ten Mile Beach NSW 32, 37
Black Springs, Coffin Bay National Park SA 143, 148
Blencathra Coastal Spa Gateway, Currie, King Island Tas. 311
Bligh Museum of Pacific Exploration, Adventure Bay, Bruny Island Tas. 275
Bloomfield Track Qld 255, 258-60
Blowhole, Bicheno Tas. 290
Blue Dolphin Holiday Resort, Yamba NSW 29
Blue Lake, Mount Gambier SA 123, 124
Blue Pool, Bermagui NSW 52
Blue Pool, Yamba NSW 28
Boat Harbour Tas. 293, 294, 297
Boat Harbour Beach, Deep Creek National Park SA 112
Boat Harbour Beach Haven Tas. 297
Boathouse Resort, Tea Gardens NSW 7
Boathouse, The, Birks Harbour SA 129
Boathouse, The, Currie, King Island Tas. 306
boating/sailing
    Anderson Inlet Vic. 92
    Batemans Bay NSW 47
    Burrum Coast National Park Qld 234
    Cleaverville WA 174
    Cooyong National Park SA 128
    Gnoorea Point WA 173
    Jervis Bay JBT 46
    Mallacoota Vic. 104
    Metung Vic. 103
    Paynesville Vic. 103
    Whitsundays coast Qld 241
Bogey Hole, Newcastle Beach NSW 12
Bollywood Beach market, Woolgoolga NSW 28
Bombah Point NSW 5, 6, 7
Booderee Botanic Gardens JBT 46
Booderee National Park JBT 46-7, 49
Boomerang by the Sea, Currie, King Island Tas. 311
Boon Wurrung/Bunurong People 77, 78, 83, 91
Booti Booti National Park NSW 6
Boranup WA 192, 193
Boranup campground WA 193
Boranup Karri Forest WA 192
Border Ranges National Park NSW 36

Boston Bay Wines, Port Lincoln SA 142
Botanic Gardens, Bundaberg Qld 236
Botanic Gardens, Burnt Pine, Norfolk Island 268
Botanic Gardens, Cooktown Qld 260
Botanic Gardens, Mackay Qld 244
Bouddi National Park NSW 10
Bounty Centre Toy Shop, The, Burnt Pine, Norfolk Island 268
Bournda National Park NSW 54, 57
Bowen Qld 246
Bowman Scenic Drive, Beachport SA 124
Bowraville NSW 26
Boyd's Tower, Beowa National Park NSW 55, 57
Brae, Birregurra Vic. 65
Braidwood NSW 47
Break-Me-Gall Hill Tas. 286
Break-Me-Neck Hill Tas. 286
Bremer Bay WA 200
Bremer Bay Beaches Resort Tourist Park WA 203
Bremer Island NT 208, 213
Bridgewater Bay Cafe, Cape Bridgewater Vic. 69
Bridgewater blowholes, Cape Bridgewater Vic. 75
Bridport Tas. 299
Brighton Vic. 84
Brighton Beach Vic. 84
Brisbane/Meanjin Qld 217, 220
Bristol Point, Booderee National Park JBT 49
Broadwater Marina Resort, Geraldton WA 161
Brogo Dam NSW 54
Brogo Wilderness Canoes NSW 52
Broken River, Eungella National Park Qld 244
Broken River Mountain Resort, Eungella National Park Qld 247
Broome WA 171, 172, 177, 179, 180-2, 184, 185
Broome Caravan Park WA 185
Broome Fishing Club WA 184
Brooms Head NSW 23, 28
Broulee NSW 47
Brown's Beach SA 121
Brunswick Heads NSW 31, 36, 37
Bruny Island Tas. 273, 275
Bruny Shore, Bruny Island Tas. 277
Buccaneer Archipelago WA 183
Buddha Sanctuary, Broome WA 182
Budj Bim Cultural Landscape, Heywood Vic. 74
Buku-Larrnggay Mulka Centre, Yirrkala NT 211
Bulahdelah NSW 3, 5
Bulbararing Lagoon NSW 10
Bull Rock, Stanley 295
Bulli Tops NSW 39

Index 313

Bulls Cruisers, Paynesville Vic. 103
Bumboras Beach, Norfolk Island 267
Bunbury WA 190
Bunbury Regional Art Gallery WA 190
Bunda Cliffs SA 150
Bundaberg Qld 233, 234, 236, 238
Bundaberg Barrel Qld 236
Bundaberg Railway Museum Qld 236
Bundaberg Rum Distillery Qld 236
Bundadung Trails, Tathra NSW 52
Bundjalung Nation 31, 32, 33
Bundjalung National Park NSW 32, 37
Bundjalung People 217
Bunganditj/Boandik People 123
Bungendore NSW 47
Bungendore Wood Works NSW 47
Bungwahl NSW 7
Bunker Bay WA 190
Bunurong Coastal Drive Vic. 92
Burleigh Heads Qld 218
Burnie Tas. 294
Burnt Pine, Norfolk Island 263, 268
Burrum Coast National Park Qld 234
Burrup Peninsula WA 174
Busselton WA 190, 193
Butchulla People 225, 233
Byfield National Park Qld 239
Byron and beyond NSW 31-7
Byron Bay NSW 31, 35-6

C
Cabarita NSW 36
Cable Beach WA 180, 182
Cable Beach Club Resort & Spa WA 185
Cable Tram, Portland Vic. 74
Caiguna WA 151
Cairns Qld 207, 249, 252, 253, 255, 256, 258, 261
Calcified Forest, King Island Tas. 307
Calgardup Cave, Margaret River region WA 192
Caloundra Qld 220
Camden Haven NSW 18
camel ride, Cable Beach WA 182
Canberra ACT 46, 47
Cane WA 174
Canondale Qld 222
Canunda National Park SA 125, 129
Canungra Qld 219
Cape Arid National Park WA 195, 203
Cape Barren Island Tas. 301
Cape Borda SA 117, 121
Cape Bridgewater Vic. 69, 75
Cape Bruny Lighthouse, Bruny Island Tas. 275
Cape Byron Lighthouse, Byron Bay NSW 35
Cape Conran Vic. 104, 105
Cape Conran Nature Trail Vic. 104

Cape du Couedic SA 117, 120
Cape Gantheaume Wilderness Area SA 121
Cape Hauy walking trail Tas. 281
Cape Hillsborough National Park Qld 244, 247
Cape Jervis SA 109, 110, 113, 117
Cape Keraudren WA 177
Cape Le Grand National Park WA 203
Cape Leeuwin WA 187, 190, 192
Cape Leeuwin Lighthouse WA 192
Cape Leveque Road WA 179, 183, 184
Cape Liptrap Vic. 96
Cape Liptrap Coastal Park Vic. 96, 97
Cape Lodge, Yallingup WA 193
Cape Naturaliste Lighthouse WA 192
Cape Naturaliste WA 187, 190, 192
Cape Nelson Vic. 75
Cape Nelson Lighthouse Vic. 75
Cape Otway Lighthouse Vic. 66
Cape Paterson Vic. 91, 92, 97
Cape Patton Lookout, Wongarra Vic. 65
Cape Pillar Tas. 281
Cape Range WA 163, 169
Cape Range National Park WA 163, 169
Cape Raoul Tas. 282, 283
Cape Schanck Lighthouse Reserve Vic. 87
Cape Schanck Vic. 83, 87, 89
Cape to Cape trail WA 192
Cape to Cape WA 187-93
Cape Tourville Tas. 288
Cape Trib Beach House Qld 261
Cape Trib Camping Qld 261
Cape Tribulation Qld 255, 258, 261
Cape Wickham, King Island Tas. 305, 310
Cape Wickham Golf Links, King Island Tas. 310
Cape Wickham Lighthouse, King Island Tas. 310
Cape Willoughby SA 117, 118, 121
Cape Willoughby lighthouse SA 118
Cape Woolamai Vic. 77, 80
Capricorn Coast Qld 233-9
Captain Cook Lookout, Copacabana NSW 10
Captain Cook Lookout, Norfolk Island 263
Captain Cook Monument, Norfolk Island 267
Captains Cove Resort, Paynesville Vic. 105
Carcase Rock, Lincoln National Park SA 143
Cardwell Qld 249, 250, 251
Cardwell Forest Drive Qld 250
Cardwell Spa Pool Qld 150
Carlo Sandblow, Rainbow Beach Qld 226
Carnarvon WA 168
Carnarvon Heritage Precinct WA 168
Carnarvon Space and Technology Museum WA 168
Carpe Conran Coastal Park Vic. 104
Carrickalinga SA 110
Cascade Bay, Norfolk Island 263, 268, 269

Cassowary Coast Qld 250
Castle Cove Lookout, Glenaire Vic. 66
Castle Hill, Townsville Qld 246
Castle Rock, Flinders Island Tas. 302
Cave Beach, Booderee National Park JBT 49
Cave Garden, Mount Gambier SA 124
Caves Road, Cape to Cape WA 190, 192
Ceduna SA 142, 145, 149, 150
Ceduna Oyster Bar SA 149
Celia Rosser Gallery, Fish Creek Vic. 96
Central Arnhem Road NT 207, 208, 213
Central Coast to Nelson Bay NSW 9-15
Central Mangrove NSW 12
Central Tilba 49
Cervates WA 155, 158, 161
Champagne Pools, K'gari Qld 230
Chelsea Vic. 84
Chichester Range WA 174
Chinatown, Broome WA 180
Chris's Beacon Point Villas, Apollo Bay Vic. 67
Churchill Island Vic. 77, 78
Churchill Island Heritage Farm Vic. 78
Cicerello's, Fremantle WA 88
Cistern Chapel in the City Hall, Maryborough Qld 231
Clarence River NSW 32
Clarence River Fishermans' Co-op, Yamba NSW 23
Cleaverville WA 174
Cleft Island Vic. 97
Cleveland Qld 217, 220
Cliff Head WA 161
Clifford's Honey Farm, Haines SA 119
Clifftop at Tathra Beach NSW 57
Clifton NSW 40
Coal Mines Historic Site, Lime Bay Tas. 283
Coalcliff NSW 40
Coalseam Conservation Park WA 161
Coaramup Bay WA 190
Coast Norfolk Island 269
Coast Resort Merimbula NSW 57
Coastal Survivors Walk, D'Entrecasteaux National Park WA 199
Cobbler Hill, Deep Creek National Park SA 115
Cockle Creek Tas. 273, 277
Cockle Train SA 115, 129
Cockpit Waterfall, Norfolk Island 268
Coffee Works, Mareeba Qld 258
Coffin Bay SA 148
Coffin Bay National Park SA 139, 143, 148, 151
Coffs Coast to Yamba NSW 23-9
Coffs Harbour NSW 23, 26-8, 29
Coles Bay Tas. 285, 288, 291
Colliers Beach, King Island Tas. 308

314

Comboyne NSW 19
Conto, Leeuwin-Naturaliste National Park WA 193
convict settlements
　Coal Mines Historic Site Tas. 283
　Darlington, Maria Island Tas. 289
　Kingston, Norfolk Island 265
　Port Arthur Historic Site Tas. 281
Coochin Creek Qld 223
Cooktown Museum Qld 261
Cooktown Qld 255, 258, 260, 261
Coolangatta Qld 217, 218
Coolangatta Estate, Coolangatta NSW 43
Cooloola Recreation Area, Great Sandy National Park Qld 226
Coolum Beach Qld 217, 220
Coonawarra SA 125
Coorong National Park SA 128
Copacabana NSW 10
Copper Coast SA 136
Copperhead Trail, King Island Tas. 307
Coral Bay WA 163, 168, 169
Coral Coast WA 163-9
Coral Sea Qld 238, 241-61
Coral Sea Marina Resort, Airlie Beach Qld 247
Corindi Beach NSW 28
Corny Point SA 135
Corringle Slips, Marlo Vic. 105
Cosmopolitan Hotel, Taylors Arm NSW 24
Cossack WA 174
Cottesloe Beach WA 156
Coulomb Point WA 185
Cowell SA 139, 140
Cowes Vic. 69, 77, 78, 80
Cowley Beach Qld 252, 253
Cradle Mountain Tas. 293
Cranbrook Tas. 288
Crescent Head NSW 17, 20
Crescent Head Holiday Park NSW 21
Croajingolong National Park Vic. 104, 105
Crooked River NSW 43
Crossing Country Tour, Yolngu Homelands NT 213
Crown Plaza Terrigal Pacific, Terrigal NSW 15
Crystal Cave, Yanchep National Park WA 156
Crystal Pool, Norfolk Island 267
Crystal Springs, D'Entrecasteaux National Park WA 203
Cumberland River Holiday Park, Lorne Vic. 67
Currie, King Island Tas. 305, 306, 310, 311
Currie Lighthouse, King Island Tas. 306
Curryfest, Woolgoolga NSW 28
Curtis Falls, Tamborine National Park Qld 219
Curtis Island Qld 239
Customs House, Bowen Qld 246

Customs House, Robe SA 126
cycling
　Bass Coast Rail Trail Vic. 92
　East Gippsland Rail Trail Vic. 103
　Gippsland Lakes Discovery Trail Vic. 103
　Goolwa SA 115
　Turquoise Way, Jurian Bay WA 160
Cygnet Tas. 273, 276, 277
Cygnet Bay Pearl Farm WA 185

D
Daintree Rainforest Qld 258-60, 261
Daintree River Cruise Qld 256
Dales Campground, Karijini National Park WA 177
Dales Gorge, Karijini National Park WA 177
Daly Head SA 135
Dambimangari People 183
Dampier WA 173
Dampier Peninsula WA 179, 184, 185
Dangar Falls, Dorrigo NSW 27
d'Arenberg Cube, McLaren Vale SA 110
Dark Point Aboriginal Place, Myall Lakes National Park NSW 5
Darlington Tas. 289, 291
Darumbal People 233
Darwin NT 207
Dave Evans Bicentennial Tree, Warren National Park WA 196
Davidson Whaling Station, Beowa National Park NSW 55
Deen Maar (Lady Julia Percy Island) Vic. 74
Deep Blue Hotel and Hot Springs, Warrnambool Vic. 67, 73
Deep Creek Cove, Deep Creek National Park SA 113
Deep Creek National Park SA 113, 115
Deep Creek Waterfall, Deep Creek National Park SA 113
Deep Reach Pool (Nhanggangunha), Millstream- Chichester National Park WA 174
deep south, The Tas. 273-7
Deepwater National Park Qld 239
Denham WA 166, 167
Denmark WA 199
Dennington Vic. 70
D'Entrecasteaux Channel Tas. 275
D'Entrecasteaux National Park WA 199, 203
Depot Beach, Murramarang National Park NSW 49
Derby WA 183
D'Estrees Bay, Cape Gantheaume Wilderness Area SA 121
Devils Kitchen, Tasman National Park Tas. 281
Devonport Tas. 293, 294, 295
Dhalliwanggu-Lake Sunday SA 135

Dharawal People 39
Dhilba Guuranda-Innes National Park SA 134-5, 137
Dhimurru Permit (East Arnhem Land) NT 207, 210, 212, 213
Dhurga People NSW 51, 54
Diamond Creek, Flinders Island Tas. 303
Dirawong Reserve, Evans Head NSW 33
Dirk Hartog Island/Wirruwana WA 167, 169
Dirk Hartog Island Eco Lodge WA 169
Disappointment Bay, King Island Tas. 310
Discovery Bay Coastal Park Vic. 75
diving
　Avoca Beach NSW 10-12
　Edithburgh SA 134
　Jervis Bay NSW 46
　Lady Musgrave Island Qld 236
　Museum of Underwater Art (MOUA), John Brewer Reef Qld 247
　Second Valley SA 112
　Sleepy Bay Tas. 288
　Solitary Islands Marine Park NSW 27
　SS Yongala Qld 246-7
Djirbalngan People 249
Dolphin Beach SA 135
Dolphin Marine Conservation Park, Coffs Harbour NSW 27
Don River Railway, Devonport Tas. 295
Dongara WA 160, 161
Donington Cottage, Lincoln National Park SA 143
Doo Town Tas. 281
Doo-lishus, Doo Town Tas. 281
Dooragan National Park NSW 18
Dorrigo NSW 27
Dorrigo National Park NSW 27
Dorsal Boutique Hotel, Forster NSW 7
Double Island Point Lighthouse Qld 226
Douglas-Apsley National Park Tas. 291
Dreamworld, Gold Coast Qld 219
Dromana Vic. 85, 89
Dunalley Tas. 280
Dunalley Fish Market Tas. 280
Dunbogan Boatshed NSW 18
Dunbogan NSW 18
Duncombe Bay, Norfolk Island 267
Dunes Walk, Croajingolong National Park Vic. 105
Dunghutti People 17, 23
Dunk Island Qld 251
Dunoon NSW 35

E
Eagle Point Vic. 102
Eaglehawk Neck/Teralina Tas. 279, 280
East Arnhem Land NT 207, 208, 211
East Cape Vic. 104
East Coast Tas. 284-91

East Coast Natureworld, Bicheno Tas. 290
East Coast Wine Trail Tas. 288
East Gippsland Vic. 99–105
East Gippsland Rail Trail Vic. 103
East Yeerung Track Vic. 104
Eastern Beach, K'gari Qld 231
Eastern Maar People 61
Eastern View Vic. 61, 64
Eddystone Point Lighthouse Tas. 291
Eden NSW 51, 55
Eden Killer Whale Museum NSW 55
Edge of the Bay, Coles Bay Tas. 291
Edge of the World Tas. 297
Edithburgh SA 131, 132, 134
Edithburgh Caravan Park SA 137
Eighty Mile Beach WA 176, 177
Eighty Mile Beach Caravan Park WA 177
El Paso Motor Inn, Port Macquarie NSW 21
Elements of Byron, Byron Bay NSW 37
Elephant Cove, William Bay National Park WA 199
Elephant Pass Tas. 291
Eli Creek, K'gari Qld 229
Elizabeth Beach NSW 3
Ellenborough Falls, Elands NSW 19
Ellendale Pool, Greenough WA 161
Ellinjaa Falls Qld 252
Elliston SA 148
Emily Bay Lagoon, Norfolk Island 268
Emita, Flinders Island Tas. 303
Emu Bay SA 121
Emu Park Qld 239
Emu Ridge Eucalyptus Distillery, Macgillivray SA 119
Emu Valley Rhododendron Garden, Burnie Tas. 294
Encounter Bikeway, Goolwa SA 115
Endeavour Lodge, Kingston, Norfolk Island 269
Engelbrecht Cave, Mount Gambier SA 125
Engineers and Managers Lodges, Inneston SA 137
Erskine Falls, Lorne Vic. 65
Esk River NSW 32
Esperance WA 195, 200, 202
Esperance Museum WA 202
Ethel Beach, Dhilba Guuranda-Innes National Park SA 134
Ettalong Beach NSW 9, 10, 15
Etty Bay Qld 252, 253
Eucla WA 145, 151
Eucla Telegraph Station WA 151
Eumundi Qld 222
Eungella National Park Qld 244
Eurimbula National Park Qld 238
Eurobodalla NSW 45
Evans Head NSW 33, 37
Evans Head Holiday Park NSW 37

Evans Head Living Museum NSW 33
Ewingsdale NSW 35
Exmouth WA 163, 168, 169, 172
Eyre Peninsula SA 139–43, 145

F
Fairhaven Vic. 61, 89
Farm at Byron, Ewingsdale NSW 35
Farm Shed Museum, Kadina SA 136
Fern Glade Platypus Reserve, Burnie Tas. 294
Fighter World, Williamtown NSW 13
Finch Hatton Gorge, Eungella National Park Qld 244
Fingal Vic. 87, 89
Fish Creek Vic. 96
Fish Tales, Fish Creek Vic. 96
Fishermans Point, Lincoln National Park SA 143
fishing
　1770 Qld 238
　Anderson Inlet Vic. 92
　Batemans Bay NSW 47
　Bermagui NSW 52
　Binydjarrnga (Daliwuy Bay) NT 212
　Bournda National Park NSW 52
　Brogo Dam 54
　Brunswick Heads NSW 36
　Burrum Coast National Park Qld 234
　Cleaverville WA 174
　Coffin Bay National Park SA 148
　Cooyong National Park SA 128
　Curtis Island Qld 239
　Derby WA 183
　Dongara WA 160
　Dunbogan NSW 18
　Eagle Point Vic. 102
　Edithburgh SA 134
　Emu Bay SA 121
　Eyre Peninsula SA 140, 141
　Fitzgerald River National Park WA 202
　Fowlers Bay SA 150
　Gnoorea Point WA 173
　Inskip Peninsula Recreation Area Qld 231
　Jervis Bay JBT 46
　King Reef Qld 252
　Lady Barron, Flinders Island Tas. 301
　Lake Reeve Vic. 102
　Lakes Entrance Vic. 103
　Lighthouse Beach NSW 12
　Lucinda Qld 250
　Mallacoota Vic. 104
　Merimbula NSW 54
　Metung Vic. 103
　Mornington Peninsula Vic. 85
　Nambucca Heads NSW 26
　Naracoopa, King Island Tas. 308
　North Stradbroke/Minjerribah Qld 220
　Parsons Beach SA 113

　Pebbly Beach NSW 29
　Point Sampson WA 174
　Point Sir Isaac SA 148
　Port Fairy Vic. 72
　Port Huon Tas. 277
　Port Macquarie NSW 19
　Port Vincent SA 132
　Rockhampton Qld 239
　St Helens Tas. 290
　Sandon River NSW 28
　Seal Rocks NSW 6
　Sydenham Inlet Vic. 104
　Tathra NSW 52
　Tea Gardens NSW 4
　Townsville Qld 246
　Venus Bay SA 148
　Waitpinga Beach SA 113
　Western River Cove SA 121
　Windy Harbour WA 199
Fishing Boat Harbour, Fremantle WA 188
Fishing Heritage Museum, San Remo Vic. 78
Fitzgerald River National Park WA 201–2, 203
Five Acres, Phillip Island Vic. 80
Flagstaff Hill, Bowen Qld 246
Flagstaff Hill Maritime Village, Warrnambool Vic. 67, 70
Flaherty Beach SA 135
Fletcher's Mutiny Cyclorama, Kingston, Norfolk Island 266
Fleurieu Peninsula SA 109–15, 117
Fleurieu Way SA 110
Flinders Vic. 87
Flinders Beach, North Stradbroke/Minjerriba Qld 223
Flinders Chase National Park SA 120–1
Flinders Island Tas. 299–303
Flinders Island Golf Club, Whitemark Tas. 301
Fluted Cape Walk, Bruny Island Tas. 275
folk museum, Bowraville NSW 26
Foodworks, Currie, King Island Tas. 306
Foreshore Promenade Walk, Warrnambool Vic. 70
Forrest Vic. 65, 67
Forrest Brewing Company Vic. 65
Forrest General Store Vic. 65
Forrest MTB Hire Vic. 65
Forresters NSW 12
Forster NSW 3, 6, 7
Fort Nepean Walk, Portsea Vic. 85
Fort Queenscliff Vic. 86
Fortescue Bay Tas. 281, 283
Fortescue Falls, Dales Gorge, Karijini National Park WA 177
Forts Walk, Yunbenun/Magnetic Island Qld 247
Fossil Bluff Tas. 294

fossils
    Gantheaume Point WA 184
    Naracoorte SA 125
Fotheringate Beach, Flinders Island Tas. 301
Foul Bay SA 134
Fowlers Bay SA 150
Foxglove Gardens, Tilba Tilba NSW 48
Francois Peron National Park WA 166
Frank Partridge VC Military Museum, Bowraville NSW 26
Franklin Tas. 276
Frankston Vic. 84
Fraser Island Great Walk, K'gari Qld 230
Fremantle WA 188, 189, 190
Fremantle cemetery WA 188
Fremantle Prison WA 189
French Island Vic. 89
Fresh Fish Place, Port Lincoln SA 139
Freshwater Lake, Great Sandy National Park Qld 231
Freycinet Lodge, Freycinet National Park Tas. 291
Freycinet Marine Farm, Coles Bay Tas. 288
Freycinet National Park Tas. 285, 288, 290, 291, 293
Friendly Beaches Tas. 288, 291
Furneaux Group Tas. 299
Furneaux Lookout, Flinders Island Tas. 301
Furneaux Museum, Emita Tas. 303
Furneaux Tavern, Lady Barron Tas. 301, 303

G
Gabo Island Vic. 55
Gadalathami (Town Beach), Nhulunbuy NT 210
Gadubanud People 61
Gäluru (East Woody) NT 210
Ganami (Wonga Creek) NT 213
Gantheaume Point WA 184
Gap, The, Balgowan SA 137
Gapuru (Memorial Park) NT 213
Garanham (Macassan Beach) NT 212
Gardens, The, Bay of Fires Conservation Park Tas. 290
Garma Festival, Nhulunbuy NT 208
Gaynaru Wetlands (Town Lagoon), Nhulunbuy NT 210
Geelong Vic. 293
Geeveston Tas. 273, 276-7
George Point, Hinchinbrook Island/Munamudanamy Qld 251
Geraldton WA 155, 160-1, 163, 164
Gerringong NSW 43
Ghostly Tour Dinners, Kingston, Norfolk Island 266
Giants Cave, Margaret River region WA 192
Gibson Steps, Great Ocean Road Vic. 66

Gillards Beach, Mimosa Rocks National Park NSW 57
Gimuy-walubarra yidi People 249, 255
Gippsland Lakes Vic. 102, 103
Gippsland Lakes Coastal Park Vic. 102, 103, 105
Gippsland Lakes Discovery Trail Vic. 103
Girramay People 249, 251
Girringun National Park Qld 251
Giya People 241
Glade Picnic Area, Dorrigo National Park NSW 27
Gladstone NSW 20
Gladstone Qld 239
Glass House Mountains Qld 217, 220
Gloucester National Park WA 196
Gloucester Tree, Gloucester National Park WA 196
Gnoorea Point WA 173
Godfreys Beach, Stanley Tas. 295
Gold and Sunshine coasts Qld 217-23
Gold Coast Qld 217, 218-19
golf
    Cape Wickham Golf Links, King Island Tas. 310
    Fingal Vic. 89
    Flinders Island Tas. 301
    Kingston, Norfolk Island 268
    Narooma NSW 45
    Ocean Dunes, King Island Tas. 310
Goolarabooloo People 183
Goolwa SA 109, 114, 115, 123, 128-9
Gooreng Gooreng People 233
Goreng People 195, 201
Gosford NSW 9, 10
Gove Boat Club, Nhulunbuy NT 210, 213
Gove Peninsula NT 207-13
Gracetown WA 192
Grafton NSW 32
Grand Mecure Basildene Manor, Margaret River WA 193
Grand Pacific Drive NSW 39-43
'Grandis' (gum tree), Bulahdelah NSW 5
Grandvewe Cheeses, Birchs Bay Tas. 276
Grandview Hotel, Bowen Qld 246
Granite Skywalk, Porongurup National Park WA 200
Granites, The SA 129
Grass Tree Hollow, Hawke National Park WA 203
Grassy, King Island Tas. 305, 308, 311
Grassy Head NSW 24
Great Australian Bight SA/WA 145-51, 195
Great Barrier Reef Qld 233, 235, 236, 239, 241-61
Great Barrier Reef Drive Qld 255-61
Great Beach Drive Qld 225-31
Great Green Way Qld 249-53

Great Lakes NSW 3-7
Great Ocean Drive, Esperance WA 202
Great Ocean Road Vic. 61-7
Great Ocean Road Heritage Centre, Lorne Vic. 64
Great Ocean Road Memorial Arch, Eastern View Vic. 64
Great Otway National Park Vic. 66
Great Oyster Bay Tas. 286
Great Sandy National Park Qld 226, 231
Great Southern WA 195
Green Cape NSW 51, 57
Green Cape Lightstation NSW 55-7
Green Cathedral, Booti Booti National Park NSW 6
Green Mountains, Lamington National Park Qld 219
Green Patch, Booderee National Park JBT 47, 49
Greenough WA 160, 161
Greens Pool, William Bay National Park WA 199
Griffiths Island Vic. 72
Griffiths Island Lighthouse Vic. 72
Griffiths Sea Shell Museum and Marine Display, Lakes Entrance Vic. 103
Gubbi Gubbi People 217, 225
Gugu-Badhun People 241, 249
Gumbaynggirr People 23, 27
Gumuniya (Buffalo Creek) NT 210
Gunaikurnai People 99, 102
Gunditjmara People 61, 69, 73
Gunnamatta Beach Vic. 87
Gurang People 233
Guugu Yimithiirr People 255, 261
Guwatjurumurru (Giddy River) NT 213

H
Half Moon Bay Vic. 86
Hamelin Bay WA 192
Hamelin Pool Marine Nature Reserve WA 166
Hamersley Drive, Fitzgerald River National Park WA 202
Hamersley Inlet, Fitzgerald River National Park WA 203
Hammerstone Sandblow, K'gari Qld 229
Hanson Bay SA 121
Hanson Bay Wildlife Sanctuary, Karatta SA 120
Harveys Return Campground, Flinders Chase National Park SA 121
Hastings Vic. 83, 88
Hastings Caves State Reserve Tas. 277
Hat Head NSW 21
Hat Head Caravan Park NSW 21
Hawke National Park WA 203
Hawks Nest NSW 4, 5

Index   317

Hazards, The, Freycinet National Park Tas. 288, 299
Head of Bight SA 151
Hearson's Cove, Murujuga National Park WA 174
Hedland Hotel, Port Hedland WA 177
Helensburgh NSW 40
Hellyers Road Distillery, Havenview Tas. 294
Heritage Aviation Museum, Evans Head NSW 33
Heritage Guest House, South West Rocks NSW 21
Hervey Bay Qld 225, 230, 233, 234–5
Hexham NSW 3
Heysen Trail SA 114
Heywood Vic. 74
Highfield Historic Site, Stanley Tas. 296
Hillarys Boat Harbour WA 156, 157
Hilli Goat, The, Norfolk Island 267
Hinchinbrook Island/Munamudanamy Qld 250, 251, 253
Hindmarsh Island SA 129
Hinkler Hall of Aviation, Bundaberg Qld 236
Hinkler House, Bundaberg Qld 236
Historic Terrace Houses, Kiama NSW 43
Historic Whaling Station, Albany WA 200
HMAS Adelaide (wreck dive site), Avoca Beach NSW 10–12
HMAS Sydney Memorial, Geraldton WA 160
Hobart Beach campground, Bournda National Park NSW 57
Hobart Tas. 273, 274, 279, 280, 285, 286, 293
Home Hill, Ranelagh Tas. 276
Hook Point Qld 225
Hopetoun WA 202
Hopetoun Falls, Beech Forest Vic. 65
Horizontal Waterfalls, Talbot Bay WA 179, 183
Horse Head Rock, Wallaga Lake NSW 52
horse-drawn tram, Victor Harbor SA 114
Horseshoe Bay, Bermagui NSW 52
Horseshoe Bay Holiday Park, South West Rocks NSW 21
Hotel Brunswick, Brunswick Heads NSW 31
Hou Wang Temple, Atherton Qld 258
Huon Valley Tas. 273, 274
Huon Valley Caravan Park, Huonville Tas. 277
Huonville Tas. 273, 274, 276, 277
Huskisson NSW 45
Hutt Lagoon WA 164
Hyams Beach NSW 46

I

Illawarra Escarpment NSW 40
Illawarra Fly, Knights Hill NSW 42
Iluka NSW 29
Iluka Nature Reserve NSW 29, 32
Imagine Cruises, Nelson Bay 13

Indented Heads Vic. 86
Indian Ocean Drive WA 155–61
Ingham Qld 250, 251
Injidup Beach WA 190
Innawonga People 177
Inneston SA 135, 137
Innisfail Qld 250, 252
Inskip Point Qld 225, 229
Inskip Point Recreation Area Qld 231
Interpretation Centre, Port Arthur Historic Site Tas. 282
Inverloch Vic. 91, 92, 96, 97
Inverloch Foreshore Camping Reserve Vic. 97
Island Fish Fry, Kingston, Norfolk Island 267
Island Quarters, Whitemark, Flinders Island Tas. 303
Isle of the Dead cemetery, Port Arthur Tas. 282
Israelite Bay WA 203

J

Jabirr Jabirr/Ngumbarl People 179, 183
Jade Motel, Cowell SA 140
Jamberoo NSW 42
Jamberoo Action Park NSW 42
James Price Point WA 179, 183, 185
Japanese cemetery, Broome WA 180
Jean Shaw Koala Reserve, Hawks Nest NSW 4
Jerusalem Creek, Bundjalung National Park NSW 32
Jervis Bay JBT 45, 46, 49
Jervis Bay and the Eurobodalla JBT and NSW 45–9
Jetty Beach, South Bruny National Park Tas. 277
Jetty Resort, The, Esperance WA 203
Jewel Cave, Margaret River region WA 192
Jiniguedera People 163
Johanna Beach Vic. 66, 67
Johnstone Shire Hall, Innisfail Qld 252
Joseph Banks Conservation Park Qld 238
Josephine Falls, Wooroonooran National Park Qld 252
Jourama Falls, Paluma Range National Park Qld 250, 253
Juat People 155
Jukun People 179
Jundaru community 173
Junior Eco Rangers, Kingfisher Bay Resort Qld 230
Jurien Bay WA 160
Jurien Bay Adventure Tours WA 160
Jurien Bay Marine Park WA 160
Juru People 241
JW Marriott Gold Coast Resort & Spa, Gold Coast Qld 223

K

Kadina SA 136
Kalamina Gorge, Karijini National Park WA 177
Kalbarri WA 163, 164, 166, 169
Kalbarri National Park WA 164, 169
Kalbarri Palm Resort WA 169
Kalbarri Skywalk WA 164
Kangaroo Island SA 112, 117–21
Kangarutha Track, Bournda National Park NSW 54
Kannaook/Cape Grim Tas. 293
Karajarri People 171
Karbeetong Lodge, Mallacoota Vic. 105
Karijini Eco Retreat WA 177
Karijini National Park WA 177
Kariyarra People 171
Karratha WA 171, 173, 174
Karri Forest Explorer Drive WA 196
Kate's Berry Farm, Swansea Tas. 288
Katherine NT 207, 208
Kaurna People 109, 117
kayaking/canoeing
    Antechamber Bay SA 118
    Batemans Bay NSW 47
    Bournda National Park NSW 52
    Brogo Dam NSW 52
    Brunswick Heads NSW 36
    Coffs Harbour NSW 27
    Coorong National Park SA 128
    Dunbogan NSW 18
    Geeveston Tas. 277
    Great Sandy Strait Qld 230
    Jerusalem Creek NSW 32
    Lake Reeve Vic. 102
    Mallacoota Vic. 104
    Nambucca Heads NSW 26
    Rockingham WA 190
    Sandon River NSW 28
    Sleepy Bay Tas. 288
    Tuross Head NSW 48
Kelp Industries, Currie, King Island Tas. 307
Kembla Grange NSW 42
Kennaook/Cape Grim Tas. 293, 297
Kennedy Bay Qld 251
Kennett River Family Caravan Park Vic. 67
Kennett River Vic. 65, 67
Keppel Kracken, Yeppoon Qld 239
Kernewek Lowender festival, Moonta SA 136
Kettering Tas. 274, 276
K'gari Qld 224, 229–30, 231, 235
KI Outdoor Action, Vivonne Bay SA 121
Kiama NSW 39, 43
Kiama Blowhole NSW 43
Kiama Coast Walk NSW 43
Kilcunda Beach Vic. 92
Kilcunda trestle railway bridge Vic. 92
Killalea Regional Park NSW 43

Killarney Beach Caravan Park Vic. 75
Killecrankie, Flinders Island Tas. 303
Killekrankie 'diamonds', Flinders Island Tas. 303
Killick Beach NSW 20
Kimberley Coast WA 179–85
King George Sound WA 199
King Island Arts & Cultural Centre, Currie Tas. 307
King Island Dairy, Currie Tas. 306, 311
King Island Distillery, Currie Tas. 306
King Island Kelp Craft, Reekara, King Island Tas. 310
King Island Museum, Currie Tas. 306
King Island Tas. 305–11
King Reef Qld 252
Kingfisher Bay Resort Qld 225, 230, 231, 235
Kingscliff NSW 36, 37
Kingscote SA 117, 118, 120, 121
Kingston, Norfolk Island 263, 264–7
Kingston, Tas. 274
Kingston SE SA 123, 128, 129
Knights Hill NSW 42
Knob, The SA 141
Knoll, The, Tamborine National Park Qld 219
Koala Conservation Centre, Phillip Island Vic. 77, 79
Koala Hospital, Port Macquarie NSW 19
Koombana Bay WA 190
Koorana Crocodile Farm, Coowonga Qld 239
Koppio SA 141
Korogora track, Hat Head NSW 21
Koroit Vic. 69, 73
Koroit Irish Festival Vic. 69
Kotgee, Canunda National Park SA 129
Krowathunkoolong Keeping Place, Bairnsdale Vic. 102
Kuku Yalanji People 255, 260
Kuranda Qld 258
Kuringgai People 9
Kurrama People 177
Kurrimine Beach Qld 252, 253
Kyogle NSW 36
Kywong Caravan Park, Nelson Vic. 75

L
Lacepede Seafood, Kingston SE SA 123
Lady Barron, Flinders Island Tas. 299, 301, 303
Lady Elliot Island Qld 236
Lady Musgrave Island Qld 236, 239
Lake Albert SA 128
Lake Alexandrina SA 128
Lake Arragan NSW 29
Lake Cathie NSW 19
Lake Cave, Margaret River region WA 192
Lake Elizabeth Vic. 65, 67
Lake Fowler SA 135
Lake McKenzie Qld 228, 230
Lake Mombeong Vic. 75
Lake Reeve Vic. 102
Lake Thetis WA 158
Lake Wabby Qld 229, 230
Lakeland Qld 258
Lakes Entrance Vic. 99, 102, 103, 104, 105
Lakes National Park Vic. 103
Lakes Way, The NSW 3–7
Lakesea Holiday Park, Durras NSW 49
Lamington National Park Qld 219
Lancelin WA 158
Lancemore Lindenderry, Red Hill Vic. 89
Lashmar Conservation Park SA 118
Launceston Tas. 293
Laura Qld 255, 261
Laura Quinkan Indigenous Dance Festival Qld 261
Laurieton 18
Laurieton to South West Rocks NSW 17–21
Lavers Hill Vic. 65
Lawrence Hargrave Drive NSW 40
Le Grand Beach, Cape Le Grand National Park WA 203
Leeuwin Estate Winery, Margaret River WA 193
Leeuwin–Naturaliste National Park WA 190, 192
Lennox Head NSW 31, 35
Lesueur National Park WA 161
Light to Light Walk NSW 57
Lighthouse Beach NSW 12
Lighthouse keepers' cottages, Cape Willoughby SA 121
Lime Bay Tas. 279, 283
Lime Bay State Reserve Tas. 283
Limeburner's Creek National Park NSW 17, 21
Limeburners Nature Reserve NSW 20
Limestone Coast SA 123–9
Lincoln National Park SA 139, 142, 143, 151
Lions Den Hotel, Rossville Qld 260
Lismore NSW 31
Little Penguin Observation Centre, Burnie Tas. 294
Little Sahara, Seal Bay Conservation Park SA 121
Live Wire Park, Lorne Vic. 65
Lobster Shack, Cervantes WA 158
Loch Ard Gorge, Port Campbell Vic. 66
Logans Beach Vic. 66, 69, 70
Lombadina WA 185
Lombuy (Crocodile Creek) NT 210
London Bridge, Port Campbell Vic. 66
Lone Pine Koala Sanctuary Qld 220
Long Point, Coorong National Park SA 129
Lorne Vic. 64–5, 67
Lorne Bush House Vic. 67
Lower Glenelg National Park Vic. 75
Lucinda Qld 250, 251
Lucky Bay, Cape Le Grand National Park WA 203
Lucy's noodle house, Mallacoota Vic. 99
Lune River Tas. 277
Lurrpukurra NT 213
Lyluequonny People 273

M
M Arts Precinct, Murwillumbah NSW 37
Macgillivray SA 119
Mackay Qld 241, 242, 244, 247
Macksville NSW 23, 24
Macksville Star NSW 24
MacLaren Point, Lincoln National Park SA 143
McLaren Vale SA 109, 110
Maclean NSW 28, 31, 32
Macleay Valley Coast NSW 17
Magic Mountain, Merimbula NSW 54
Mahogany Ship Walking Trail Vic. 70
Main Beach, North Stradbroke/Minjerribah Qld 220, 223
Mainoru Outstation Store NT 208, 213
Maitland Bay NSW 10
Maitland Bay Track, Bouddi National Park 10
Maits Rest Rainforest Trail, Otway Ranges Vic. 66
Maleny Qld 222
Maleny–Kenilworth Rd, Canondale Qld 222
Malgana People 163, 166
Mallacoota Vic. 99, 104, 105
Mallacoota Foreshore Holiday Park 105
Mammoth Cave, Margaret River region WA 192
Mamu Tropical Skywalk, Innisfail 252
Mananaymi (Scout Camp) NT 213
Mandu Mandu Gorge walk, Cape Range National Park WA 163
Mangrove Creek NSW 12
Mantarays Ningaloo Beach Resort, Exmouth WA 169
Mantra Ettalong Beach Resort, Ettalong Beach NSW 15
Mantra Mackay Qld 247
Manuka campground, Arthur Pieman Conservation Area Tas. 297
Manyimi Campground, Gove Boat Club, Nhulunbuy NT 213
Mapleton Qld 222
Mapleton Falls Qld 222
Marapikurrinya Park, Port Hedland WA 176
Marble Bar WA 171
Marcus Beach Qld 220
Mardudhunera People 174
Mareeba Qld 255, 258
Margaret River WA 187, 190, 193

Index 319

Margaret River Farmers Market WA 187
Margaret River region WA 187, 190, 192
Margarets Beach Resort, Margaret River WA 193
Margate Tas. 274
Maria Island Tas. 289, 291
Marion Bay SA 135, 137
Maritime Discovery Centre, Portland Vic. 74
Maritime Museum, Whyalla SA 140
Maritime Museum of Townsville Qld 247
Mark Point, Coorong National Park SA 129
Marlo Vic. 104, 105
Marlo Hotel Vic. 104
Maroochydore Qld 220
Martha Lavinia Beach, King Island Tas. 310
Martuthunira People 171
marvellous murals, Tumby Bay SA 141
Mary Boulton Pioneer Cottage and Museum, Macksville NSW 24
Mary Cairncross Park, Maleny Qld 222
Mary MacKillop Penola Centre, Penola SA 125
Mary Poppins Festival, Maryborough Qld 231
Maryborough Qld 231
Maslin Beach SA 110
Mason Bay, Fitzgerald River National Park WA 203
Massey Green Caravan Park, Brunswick Heads NSW 37
Matso's Brewery, Broome 194
Maya People 163
Meeniyan Vic. 94, 97
Melbourne Vic. 61, 77, 83, 84, 91, 102
Melukerdee People 273
Memory Cove, Lincoln National Park SA 142, 143
Menang People 195, 196, 197, 199, 200, 201
Meningie SA 128
Mercure Kangaroo Island Lodge, American River SA 121
Merewether NSW 12
Merimbula NSW 51, 54, 55
Merimbula Air Service NSW 55
Mernana, Flinders Island Tas. 301
Merricks General Wine Store Vic. 83
Merrijig Inn, Port Fairy Vic. 75
Mettams Pool WA 156
Metung Vic. 103
Metung Hot Springs Vic. 103
Metung Hotel Vic. 103
Miaree Pool, Karratha WA 174
Michael Lerner Lookout, Bermagui NSW 52
Mickey Bourke's Koroit Pub Vic. 73
Middle Beach NT 210
Middle Island Vic. 70
Middle Lagoon WA 185
Middle Rock, Deepwater National Park Qld 239

Middleton SA 115
Millaa Millaa Falls Qld 252
Millicent SA 124
Millstream-Chichester National Park WA 174, 177
Millstream Homestead, Millstream-Chichester National Park WA 174
Millstresm Falls, Ravenshoe Qld 252
Millyana, Millstream-Chichester National Park WA 177
Mimosa Rocks National Park NSW 52, 57
Minjerribah/North Stradbroke Qld 217, 220, 223
Minjungbal People 31
Minlaton SA 131, 135
Minlaton Bakery 131
Minnamurra Falls, Jamberoo NSW 42
Minnie Water NSW 28
Mirning People 145
Mission Beach Qld 249, 250-1, 252
Mitchell River silt jetties, Eagle Point Vic. 102
Mobys Beachside Resort, Pacific Palms NSW 7
Moggs Creek Vic. 61
Mogo NSW 47
Mon Repos Conservation Park Qld 235
Monkey Mia WA 163, 166, 168, 169
Montagu Campground, Smithton Tas. 297
Montalto Vineyard and Olive Grove, Red Hill South Vic. 88
Montville Qld 222
Mooloolaba Qld 220, 222, 223
Moonta SA 136
Moonta Mines Museum SA 136
Moonta Mines Railway SA 136
Moonta Mines State Heritage Area SA 136
Morgans Landing, Coffin Bay National Park SA 143
Mornington Vic. 85
Mornington Peninsula Vic. 83-9
Mornington Peninsula Chocolaterie and Ice Creamery, Flinders Vic. 87
Mornington Peninsula National Park Vic. 87, 89
Mornington Peninsula Regional Gallery, Mornington Vic. 85
Moruya NSW 48
Mosaic Trail, Edithburgh SA 134
Mossman Qld 256
Mossman Gorge Qld 256, 261
Mossman Gorge Cultural Centre Qld 256
Mossy Point NSW 48
Mount Bates, Norfolk Island 268
Mount Dutton Bay Woolshed SA 149
Mount Gambier SA 123, 124, 125, 129
Mount Gambier Gaol SA 129
Mount Martha Vic. 85
Mount Molloy Qld 258

Mount Oberon Vic. 96
Mount Pitt, Norfolk Island 268
Mount Tanner, Flinders Island Tas. 302
Mount William National Park Tas. 291
mountain biking
   Forrest Vic. 65
   Tathra NSW 52
Mourilyan Qld 252
Movie World, Gold Coast Qld 219
Mowanjum Aboriginal Art & Culture Centre, Derby WA 183
Mozzie Flat SA 134, 137
Mudlo Rocks, Rainbow Beach Qld 225
Mueller Inlet campground, Tamboon Vic. 105
Mulberry Lodge, Willunga SA 115
Mulgumpin/Moreton Island Qld 223
Mullumbimby NSW 36
Mungalli Falls Qld 252
Mungo Brush NSW 3, 5, 6, 7
Mungo Brush Rainforest Walk NSW 5
Murchison River Caravan Park, Kalbarri WA 169
Murphy's Haystacks, Mortana SA 148-9
Murramarang National Park NSW 47, 49
Murray River SA 129
Murrays Lagoon, Cape Gantheaume Wilderness Area SA 121
Murujuga Aboriginal Corporation WA 174
Murujuga National Park WA 174
Murwillumbah NSW 37
Museum of Geraldton WA 160, 164
Museum of the Great Southern, Albany WA 200
Museum of Tropical Queensland, Townsville Qld 247
Museum of Underwater Art (MOUA), John Brewer Reef Qld 247
Museum Village, Esperance WA 202
Mushroom Reef Marine Sanctuary, Flinders Beach Vic. 87
Mushroom Rock Nature Trail, Kalbarri WA 164
Musselroe Bay Tas. 291
Mutiny on the Bounty Show, Kingston, Norfolk Island 267
Myall Beach Qld 256, 261
Myall Lake NSW 3, 6
Myall Lakes National Park NSW 5, 6, 7
Myponga Beach SA 110
Mystics Beach NSW 43

N
Nablac NSW 7
Nal-a-wort, Canunda National Park SA 129
Nambour Qld 222
Nambucca Heads NSW 23, 24, 26, 29

Nambung National Park WA 158, 161
Nan Tien Buddhist Temple, Wollongong NSW 42, 43
Naracoopa, King Island Tas. 308
Naracoorte Caves SA 125
Naracoorte Caves Campground SA 129
Narooma NSW 45, 47, 48, 49
Narrung SA 128
Narungga People 131, 134
National ANZAC Centre, Albany WA 200
National Cartoon Gallery, Coffs Harbour NSW 27
National Motorcycle Museum of Australia, Nablac NSW 7
National Trust Museum, Victor Harbor SA 114
Naturaliste Charters, Bremer Bay WA 200
Nature's Hideaway at Middle Lagoon WA 185
Nature's Window, Kalbarri National Park WA 164
Nawu People 139, 145
Neck, The, Bruny Island Tas. 275
Nelson Vic. 69, 75
Nelson Bay NSW 13
Nelson River Cruises, Nelson Vic. 75
Nepean Bay SA 121
Nerang Qld 219
New Norcia WA 157
Newcastle NSW 3, 9, 12, 13
Newcastle Museum NSW 13
Newcastle Ocean Baths NSW 12
Newdegate Cave, Hastings Caves State Reserve Tas. 277
Newhaven Vic. 77, 78
Newland Head Conservation Park SA 113, 114
Ngajarli Deep Gorge, Murujuga National Park WA 174
Ngaku People 17
Ngarda-Ngarli land 174
Ngarla People 171
Ngarluma People 171, 174
Ngarrindjeri People 109, 114, 117, 123, 128
Ngatjumay People 195, 203
Ngilgi Cave, Margaret River region WA 192
Ngurrangga Tours WA 174
Nhanda People 163
Nhulun Lookout NT 210
Nhulunbuy NT 207, 208, 210-11, 213
Nhuwala People 171
night-time ghost tour, Port Arthur Historic Site Tas. 282
Nightcap National Park NSW 35, 37
Nimanburr People 179
Nimbin NSW 35
Ninety Mile Beach Vic. 102, 103
Ningaloo Reef WA 163, 169
Noah Beach Qld 261

Nobbies Centre, Phillip Island Vic. 77, 79, 80
Nobbys Head 12
Noongar People 189
Noosa Qld 220, 222, 224, 225, 226
Noosa Heads Qld 217, 223, 226
Noosa Heads Surf Club Qld 217
Noosa Hill Resort, Noosa Heads Qld 223
Noosa National Park Qld 220
Noosaville Qld 220
Norah Head Lighthouse NSW 12
Norfolk Bay Tas. 281, 283
Norfolk Island, South Pacific 263-9
Norfolk Island National Park, Norfolk Island 268
Normanville SA 110
Norseman WA 151, 203
North Beach, Wallaroo SA 136, 137
North Brother Mountain in Dooragan National Park NSW 18
North East River, Flinders Island Tas. 299, 302, 303
North Haven NSW 18
North Pier Hotel, Cowes Vic. 80
North Stradbroke/Minjerribah Qld 217, 220, 223
north-west, The Tas. 293-9
North West Cape Peninsula WA 163
Northern Rivers region NSW 31, 33, 35
Novotel Cairns Oasis Resort Qld 253
Novotel Newcastle Beach, Newcastle NSW 15
Novotel Sunshine Coast Resort, Twin Waters Qld 223
Novotel Wollongong Northbeach, North Wollongong NSW 43
Nowra NSW 45, 46
NRMA Murramarang Beachfront Holiday Resort, South Durras NSW 49
NRMA Myall Shores Holiday Park, Bombah Point NSW 7
NRMA Port Arthur Holiday Park Tas. 283
NRMA Port Macquarie Breakwall Holiday Park, Port Macquarie NSW 21
NRMA Stockton Beach Holiday Park, Stockton NSW 15
Nubeena Tas. 279
Nuenonne People 273, 275
Nullarbor Hotel Motel (Nullarbor Roadhouse) SA 151
Nullarbor National Park SA 151
Nullarbor Plain SA/WA 145, 150-1
Nullarbor roadhouses SA 151
Nut, The, Stanley Tas. 293, 294, 295
Nyamal People 171
Nyangumarda People 171
Nyul-Nyul Country 184
Nyunyul People 179
Nywaigi People 241, 249, 250

O
Oaks Hervey Bay Resort and Spa, Urangan Beach Qld 239
Ocean Beach, K'gari Qld 230
Ocean Beach, Wilson Inlet WA 199
Ocean Dunes, King Island Tas. 310
Ocean Park Aquarium, Shark Bay WA 167
Oceans Mooloolaba Qld 223
OceanViews, Grassy, King Island Tas. 311
Off the Wharf, Lakes Entrance Vic. 103
Old Bank B&B, The, Cygnet Tas. 277
One Mile Jetty Centre, Carnarvon WA 168
Onslow WA 171, 172
Onslow Beach Resort, Beadon Bay WA 177
Orange Roughy Cafe, Fish Creek Vic. 96
O'Reilly's Rainforest Retreat, Green Mountain section, Lamington National Park Qld 219
Orford Tas. 286
OTC Satellite Earth Station, Carnarvon WA 168
Otway Fly, Beech Forest Vic. 65
Otway Harvest Trail Vic. 66
Oxenford Qld 218
Oyster Bay Nation Tas. 285
Oyster Cove Tas. 274
Oyster Walk, Coffin Bay SA 148

P
Pacific Bay Resort, Coffs Harbour NSW 29
Pacific Palms Recreation Club, Elizabeth Beach NSW 3
Painted Cliffs, Maria Island Tas. 289
Palana, Flinders Island Tas. 302, 303
Palana Beach House, Flinders Island Tas. 303
palawa People Tas. 296, 299, 302, 305
Palm Beach NSW 9
Palm Grove, Tamborine National Park Qld 219
Palmetum, Townsville Qld 247
Paluma Range Qld 250
Paluma Range National Park Qld 250, 253
Paperbark Camp, Jervis Bay JBT 49
Parachilna Gorge, Flinders Ranges SA 114
Paradise Beach Vic. 102
Paradise Country, Gold Coast Qld 219
Pardoo Station, Pardoo WA 177
Paredarerme People 285
Paredarerme Pungenna People 279, 280
Parndana SA 121
Parnka Point, Coorong National Park SA 129
Paronella Park Qld 252, 253
Parsons Beach SA 113, 114, 135
Patonga NSW 9
Patriarch Wildlife Sanctuary, Lackrana, Flinders Island Tas. 301
Pavillions on 1770 Qld 239
Paynesville Vic. 103, 105

Index 321

Payungu People 163
Peaceful Bay WA 203
Peachtree Creek campground, Tamboon Vic. 105
Pearl Luggers, Broome WA 180
Pearshape, King Island Tas. 308
Pebbly Beach, Murramarang National Park NSW 29, 47, 49
Peedamulla WA 173
Peerapper People 293
Peggs Beach Conservation Area Tas. 297
Pemberton WA 196
Penguin Tas. 294, 297
Penguin Parade, Phillip Island Vic. 77, 78, 79–80
Peninsula Hot Springs, Fingal Vic. 87, 89
Penneshaw SA 117, 118, 121
Pennicott Wilderness Journeys, Port Arthur Tas. 279
Pennicott's Wilsons Promontory Cruise, Wilsons Promontory Vic. 97
Pennington Beach SA 118
Penny's Lagoon, King Island Tas. 310
Penola SA 123, 125
Penong SA 150
Penong Windmill Museum SA 150
Peppermint Bay, Woodbridge Tas. 276
Peppermint campground, Arthur Pieman Conservation Area Tas. 297
Peppers Moonah Link Resort, Fingal Vic. 89
Peppers Salt Resort & Spa, Kingscliff NSW 37
Peramangk People 109
Peregian Beach Qld 220
Perth/Boorloo WA 155, 156, 187, 188, 195, 203
Peterborough Vic. 66
Petrified Forest, Cape Bridgewater Vic. 75
Petticoat Lane, Penola SA 125
Phillip Island, Norfolk Island 269
Phillip Island, Vic. 77–81, 92
Phillip Island Beachfront Holiday Park, Cowes Vic. 80
Phillip Island Chocolate Factory, Newhaven Vic. 78
Phillip Island Circuit (racetrack) 80
Phoenix Art Gallery and Café, Bowraville NSW 26
Pibelmen Boodja People 187
Picnic Point campground, Mimosa Rocks National Park NSW 57
Pier Store Museum, The, Kingston, Norfolk Island 265
Pilbara Coast 171–7
Pile Valley, K'gari Qld 229
Pilgrim Lodge, Berkeley NSW 43
Pilot Beach NSW 18
Pine Islet Lighthouse, Mackay Qld 244
Pines picnic area, The, Yarriabini National Park NSW 24

Pines Surfing Academy, Mystics Beach NSW 43
Pinjarup People 187
Pink Lake SA 135
Pinnacles Desert, Nambung National Park WA 158
Pinnacles Edge Resort, Cervantes WA 161
Pinnacles Loop Drive, Nambung National Park WA 158
Platypus Walk, Geeveston Tas. 277
Plaza Theatre, Laurieton NSW 18
Point Ann, Fitzgerald River National Park WA 201
Point Hicks Lightstation Vic. 105
Point Labatt SA 149
Point Leo Vic. 88, 89
Point Lonsdale Vic. 86, 89
Point Moore Lighthouse, Geraldton WA 161
Point Plomer NSW 17, 21
Point Puer Tas. 282
Point Road campground, Boranup WA 193
Point Sampson WA 174
Point Sir Isaac SA 143, 148
Point Smythe Vic. 96
Point Turton SA 135
Polperro Dolphin Swims, Sorrento Vic. 85
Pondalowie Bay SA 131, 135, 137
Pool, The, Coffin Bay National Park SA 143
Porky Beach, King Island Tas. 310
Porongurup National Park WA 200
Port Albert Vic. 102
Port Arthur Tas. 279, 280, 281–2, 283, 286
Port Arthur Historic Site Tas. 281, 282
Port Arthur Motor Inn Tas. 283
Port Augusta SA 139
Port Campbell Vic. 61, 66
Port Campbell National Park Vic. 66
Port Davies, Flinders Island Tas. 302
Port Denison WA 160
Port Douglas Qld 255, 256, 261
Port Elliot SA 114, 115
Port Fairy Vic. 69, 70, 72, 73, 75
Port Fairy Folk Festival Vic. 69
Port Germein SA 140
Port Gibbon SA 141, 143
Port Hedland WA 171, 176, 177
Port Huon Tas. 277
Port Interpretive Walk, Port Hedland WA 174
Port Kembla NSW 42
Port Lincoln SA 139, 142, 145, 148
Port Lincoln Hotel SA 143
Port Macquarie 17, 19, 20, 21
Port Neill SA 141
Port Phillip Bay Vic. 84, 86
Port Stephens NSW 9, 13
Port Stephens Koala Sanctuary NSW 13, 15
Port Vincent SA 132

Port Wakefield SA 132
Port Willunga SA 110, 115
Port Willunga Beach Caves SA 109
Port Willy Kiosk, Port Willunga SA 110
Portarlington Vic. 86
Portland Vic. 69, 72–3, 74
Portsea Vic. 83, 85, 87
Post Office, Inneston SA 137
Pottsville NSW 36
Poverty Bay SA 141
Preservation Bay Tas. 297
Pretty Beach, Murramarang National Park NSW 49
Prickly Wattle campground, Arthur Pieman Conservation Area Tas. 297
Princess Margaret Rose Cave Vic. 75
Princetown Vic. 66
Pritchards campground, Lower Glenelg National Park Vic. 75
Promontory Gate Hotel, Fish Creek Vic. 96
Proserpine 241
Protestors Falls, Nightcap National Park NSW 35
Providore 24, Stanley Tas. 293
Pt Leo Estate, Merricks Vic. 88
Pub Without Beer, Taylors Arm NSW 24
Puppy's Point, Norfolk Island 267
Puthikwilayti People 285, 289
Putty Beach NSW 10, 15
Pyemmairrener People 285
Pyramid Rocks, Phillip Island Vic. 80
Python Pool, Millstream-Chichester National Park WA 174

Q
Q1, Surfers Paradise Qld 218
quad bikes, Stockton NSW 15
Quality Row, Kingston, Norfolk Island 266
Quandamooka People 217
Quarry Markets, Willunga SA 110
Queenscliff Vic. 86, 89
Queenscliff High Light Vic. 86
Queenscliff Low Light Vic. 86
Queenscliffe Maritime Museum Vic. 84
Quinkan Galleries, Laura Qld 261
Quondong Point WA 183, 185

R
RAC Holiday Park, Cervantes WA 161
RAC Monkey Mia Dolphin Resort WA 166, 169
RACV Cape Schanck Resort Vic. 89
RACV Inverloch Resort Vic. 97
Rainbow Beach Qld 224, 226, 229, 231
Rainbow Ocean Palms Resort, Rainbow Beach Qld 231

Rainforest Centre, Dorrigo National Park NSW 27
Ramindjeri People 109, 114, 117
Ramsay Bay, Hinchinbrook Island/Munamudanamy Qld 251
Rapid Bay SA 112, 115
Ravenshoe Qld 252
Ravenshoe Hotel Qld 252
Ravensthorpe WA 202
Raymond Island Vic. 103
Recherche Bay Tas. 277
Red Cliffs NSW 28, 29
Red Hill Vic. 89
Red Rock walking trail, Agnes Water Qld 238
Redbank Bridge, Port Hedland WA 174
Redbanks Beach SA 141
Redbill Beach, Bicheno Tas. 290
Redwood Forest, Beech Forest 65
Reef HQ, Townsville Qld 246
Region X, Mossy Point NSW 48
Remarkable Cave Tas. 282
Remarkable Rocks, Flinders Chase National Park SA 120
Rex Lookout Qld 256
Rhyll Vic. 78, 79
Rhyll Inlet Vic. 78
Ricardoes (farm), Port Macquarie 20
Ricketts Point Marine Sanctuary Vic. 84
River Heads Qld 225, 235
Riverside Tourist Park, Rockhampton Qld 239
Riviera Nautic, Metung Vic. 103
Roaming with Red Dog trail, Dampier WA 173
Robe SA 123, 126, 128, 129
Robe House SA 129
Robe old cemetery SA 126
Rockhampton Qld 233, 239
Rockhampton Art Gallery Qld 239
Rockhampton Botanic Gardens and Zoo Qld 239
Rockingham WA 190
Rocky Cape National Park Tas. 296
Rocky Point, Norfolk Island 267
Rocky River, Flinders Chase National Park SA 121
Roebuck Bay WA 180, 182
Rosebud Vic. 83, 85, 89
Ross Farm, Meeniyan 97
Rosslyn Bay Qld 239
Rottnest Island/Wadjemup WA 156, 189
Round House, Fremantle WA 188
Royal Botanic Gardens, Cranbourne Vic. 84
Royal National Park NSW 40
Royson Head, Dhilba Guuranda-Innes National Park SA 134
Rummery Park, Whian Whian State Conservation Area NSW 37
Rye Vic. 85, 89

S
Sacred Heart Church, Beagle Bay WA 184
Sails Motel & Pool Club, The, Brunswick Heads NSW 37
St Albans NSW 12
St Barnabas Chapel, Norfolk Island 267
St Francis Xavier Cathedral, Geraldton WA 160–1
St Helens Tas. 285, 290
St Helen's Bakery Tas. 285
St Helen's Beach Qld 247
St Kilda Vic. 84
St Leonards Vic. 86, 89
St Mary Inlet, Fitzgerald River National Park WA 203
St Marys Tas. 291
Sal Salis Ningaloo Reef, Cape Range National Park WA 169
Sale Vic. 99, 102
Salt, Yeppoon Qld 239
Saltwater Creek NSW 57
San Remo Vic. 77, 78, 80, 92
San Remo Fisherman's Co-op, San Remo Vic. 78
sand boarding, Stockton Dunes NSW 15
Sand Dune Adventures, Newcastle NSW 15
sand tobogganing
    Mulgumpin/Moreton Island 223
    Seal Bay Conservation Park SA 121
Sandon NSW 23
Sandon River NSW 28, 29
Sandpatch Wilderness Area, Croajingolong National Park Vic. 105
Sandy Bay Tas. 274
Sandy Cape Qld 225
Sandy Cape Track Tas. 297
Sapphire Coast, The NSW 51–7
Sarina Qld 242
Sarina Sugar Shed Qld 242
Sawtell NSW 26
Sawyers Beach, Flinders Island Tas. 302
Scarborough WA 156
scenic flights
    Buccaneer Archipelago WA 183
    Gabo Island Vic. 55
    Twelve Apostles Vic. 66
Scenic Rim Qld 219
Scotts Cove Lookout SA 121
Scotts Head NSW 24
Screw Creek Nature Walk, Anderson Inlet Vic. 92
Sculpture by the Sea, Cottesloe Beach WA 156
Sea Acres Rainforest Centre, Port Macquarie NSW 19
Sea Cliff Bridge, Grand Pacific Drive NSW 39, 40
SEA LIFE Sunshine Coast, Mooloolaba Qld 222

Seal Bay SA 117, 120
Seal Bay Conservation Park SA 121
Seal Rocks, King Island Tas. 307
Seal Rocks NSW 3, 6
Seal Rocks, Phillip Island Vic. 80
Sealy Lookout, Bruxner Park, Coffs Harbour NSW 27
Seaspray Vic. 102
Seaview Trail, Canunda National Park SA 125
seawater swimming pool, Edithburgh SA 134
Second Valley SA 112
Sedgers Reef Hotel, Iluka NSW 29
Sensation Beach, Coffin Bay National Park SA 143
Separation Point Lookout, Geraldton WA 161
September Beach, Lincoln National Park SA 143
Settlement Point View Platform, Port Davies, Flinders Island Tas. 302
Seven Mile Beach National Park NSW 43
Shannonvale Qld 258
Shark Bay WA 163, 166, 167
Shark Bay World Heritage Discovery Centre, Denham WA 166
shark-cage diving, Port Lincoln SA 142
Shell Beach WA 166
Shellharbour NSW 43
Shelly Beach NSW 12
Sheoak Falls, Lorne Vic. 65
Ship Inn Stanley Tas. 297
Shipstern Bluff Tas. 283
Shipwreck Creek campground, Wingan Vic. 105
Shipwrecks and Safe Havens maritime trail, King Island Tas. 310
Shipwrights Point Regatta Ground Campground, Port Huon Tas. 277
Shoreham Vic. 89
Shot Tower, Taroona Tas. 274
Shothole Canyon Road, Exmouth WA 169
Shute Harbor Qld 247
Silky Oaks Lodge, Mossman Gorge Qld 261
Silverwater Resort, San Remo Vic. 80
Singing Bridge, Tea Gardens–Hawks Nest NSW 4
Sirius Museum, Kingston, Norfolk Island 265
Sisters Beach, Rocky Cape National Park Tas. 296
Sky Window, Eungella National Park Qld 244
Skybury Coffee Plantation, Mareeba Qld 258
Skywalk, Dorrigo National Park NSW 27
Sleaford sand dunes, Lincoln National Park SA 142
Sleepy Bay Tas. 288
Slim Dusty Centre and Museum, South Kempsey NSW 20
Smalleys Beach, Cape Hillsborough National Park Qld 247

Smiths Beach WA 190
Smiths Lake NSW 3, 6
Smithton Tas. 297
Smithy Museum, Koppio SA 141
Smoky Bay SA 149
Smoky Cape Lighthouse NSW 21
Snake Lagoon Campground, Flinders Chase National Park SA 121
Snelling Beach SA 121
snorkelling
  Baranguba (Montague Island) NSW 48
  Blue Pool, Bermagui NSW 52
  Edithburgh SA 134
  Emily Bay Lagoon, Norfolk Island 268
  Lady Musgrave Island Qld 236
  Mettams Pool WA 156
  Ningaloo Reef WA 169
  Ricketts Point Marine Sanctuary Vic. 84
  Sawyers Beach, Flinders Island Tas. 302
  Second Valley SA 112
  Sleepy Bay Tas. 288
  Solitary Islands Marine Park NSW 27
  Wop-pa/Great Keppel Island Qld 239
  Yunbenun/Magnetic Island Qld 247
Snottygobble Loop, Hawke National Park WA 203
Snowy River Cycling, Orbost Vic. 103
Snowy River Estuary Walk, Marlo Vic. 104
Snug Tas. 274
Sodafish, Lakes Entrance Vic. 103
Solitary Islands Marine Park NSW 27
Somers Vic. 88
Somersby NSW 12
Sorell Tas. 280, 286
Sorrento Vic. 85, 86, 89
Sound and Light Tour, Norfolk Island 267
South Bruny National Park Tas. 277
South Cape Bay Tas. 277
South End, Curtis Island Qld 239
South Head walking trail, Venus Bay SA 148
South Kempsey NSW 17, 20
South Mission Beach Qld 251, 253
South West Edge, The WA 195–203
South West Rocks 17, 21
Southend SA 125, 129
Southern Ocean Lodge, Hanson Bay SA 121
Sovereign Resort Hotel, Cooktown Qld 261
Spalding Cove, Lincoln National Park SA 143
Spencer NSW 12
Spiky Beach Tas. 286
Spiky Bridge, Swansea Tas. 286
Spirit of the Coorong, Goolwa SA 128
Spirit of Tasmania 293
Splash Town, Moonta SA 136
Squeaky Beach Vic. 96
SS Maheno (wreck), K'gari Qld 229
SS Speke (wreck), Phillip Island Vic. 80
'Staircase to the Moon', Broome WA 182

'Staircase to the Moon', Onslow WA 172
Stanley Tas. 293, 294–6, 297
Stanwell Tops NSW 40, 43
Star of Greece, Port Willunga SA 110
Stargazers, Millstream-Chichester National Park WA 177
State Coal Mine, Wontaggi Vic. 94
SteamRanger Cockle Train SA 115, 129
Steep Point WA 166, 167
Stenhouse Bay, Dhilba Guuranda-Innes National Park SA 137
Stewarts Bay Lodge, Port Arthur Tas. 283
Stirling Range WA 200
Stirling Range Road WA 200
Stobie pole art trail, Tiddy Widdy Beach SA 132
Stockton NSW 15
Stockton cycleway nSW 15
Stockton Dunes NSW 15
Stokes Bay SA 121
Stokes Point, King Island Tas. 305, 308
Stoney Point Vic. 89
Story Bank, Maryborough Qld 231
Strand, The, Townsville Qld 246
Strathalbyn SA 114
Streaky Bay SA 149, 151
Streaky Bay Hotel SA 151
Streets Beach, Brisbane Qld 222
Stringybark camping area, Deep Creek National Park SA 115
Strzelecki National Park, Flinders Island Tas. 303
Strzelecki Peaks, Flinders Island Tas. 301
Stuarts Point NSW 24
Stumpys Bay, Mount William National Park Tas. 291
Suffolk Park NSW 35
Sugarloaf Light Station NSW 3, 6
Sumac Tas. 297
Summerland Farm, Alstonville NSW 35
Summerlands Vic. 77, 79, 80
Sun Pictures, Broome WA 180
Sunny Ridge Strawberry Farm, Main Ridge Vic. 88
Sunrise Beach, Onslow WA 172
Sunset Beach, Onslow WA 172
Sunshine Beach Qld 220
Sunshine Coast Qld 217, 220–1
Superbike World Championship, Phillip Island Vic. 77, 80
Surf Coast Walk Vic. 64
Surfers Paradise Qld 217, 218
surfing
  1770 Qld 238
  Angourie Point NSW 28
  Anson Bay, Norfolk Island 267
  Bargara Qld 235
  Bells Beach Vic. 64

Berry Bay SA 135
Brunswick Heads NSW 36
Coaramup Bay WA 190
Colliers Beach, King Island Tas. 308
Corny Point SA 135
Crescent Head NSW 20
Daly Head SA 135
Disappointment Bay, King Island Tas. 310
Dongara WA 160
East Coast Tas. 290
Forresters NSW 12
Friendly Beaches Tas. 288
Gunnamatta Beach Vic. 87
Injidup Beach WA 190
Jervis Bay JBT 46
Killick Beach NSW 20
Lancelin WA 158
Margaret River Main Break WA 190
Martha Lavinia Beach, King Island Tas. 310
Mystics Beach NSW 43
North Haven NSW 18
North Stradbroke/Minjerribah Qld 220
Parsons Beach SA 113
Point Plomer NSW 21
Porky Beach, King Island Tas. 310
Red Banks Beach SA 141
Shelly Beach NSW 12
Shipstern Bluff Tas. 283
Smiths Beach WA 190
The Farm, Killalea Regional Park NSW 43
Waitpinga Beach SA 113
Wamberal NSW 12
Werri Beach NSW 43
Yallingup WA 190
Yamba NSW 28
Surfleet Cove, Lincoln National Park SA 143
Swansea Tas. 286, 288
Swimming Lagoon and Children's Water Playpark, Mackay Qld 244
Sydenham Inlet Vic. 104, 105
Sydney NSW 3, 4, 39, 40
Symbio Wildlife Gardens, Helensburgh NSW 40

T
Table Cape Lookout, Table Cape Tas. 294
Table Cape Tulip Farm, Table Cape Tas. 293, 294
Tae Rak Aquaculture Centre, Budj Bim Cultural Landscape, Heywood Vic. 74
Tagon Coastal Trail, Cape Arid National Park WA 203
Tahune AirWalk, Geeveston Tas. 277
Tahune Forest Reserve, Geeveston Tas. 277
takayna/Tarkine wilderness area Tas. 293, 297
Talbot Bay WA 183
Talia Caves, Talia SA 148

Tallow Beach NSW 10
Tamboon Inlet Vic. 105
Tamborine Mountain Qld 219
Tamborine National Park Qld 219
Tamborine Rainforest Skywalk, Tamborine Mountain Qld 219
Tangalooma Island Resort, Mulgumpin/Moreton Island Qld 223
Tannum Sands, Boyne Island Qld 239
Tanonga Luxury Eco-Lodges, Charlton Gully SA 143
Tantanoola Tiger Hotel, Tantanoola SA 124
Tapanappa Lookout, Deep Creek National Park SA 113, 115
Taranna Tas. 281, 283
Taribelang People 233
Tarkine Drive Tas. 297
Taroona Tas. 274
Tasman Arch, Tasman National Park Tas. 281
Tasman Bay Lookout Tas. 280
Tasman Blowhole, Tasman National Park Tas. 281
Tasman Holiday Parks – South Mission Beach Qld 253
Tasman National Park Tas. 281, 283
Tasmanian Devil Unzoo, Taranna Tas. 283
Tasmanian Fruits Farm Gate Guide Tas. 273
Tathra NSW 51, 52, 57
Taylors Arm NSW 24
Taylors Landing, Lincoln National Park SA 143
Tea Gardens NSW 4, 7
Teddy's Lookout, Lorne Vic. 65
Teewah Beach Qld 226, 231
Ten Mile Beach NSW 32, 37
Teralina/Eaglehawk Neck Tas. 279, 280
Terrigal NSW 12, 15
Tessellated Pavement Tas. 280
Tewantin Qld 220, 226
Thala Beach Nature Reserve, Oak Beach Qld 261
Thalanyji People 163, 169
Thaua People 51
The Apple Shed, Grove Tas. 276
The Boathouse, Birks Harbour SA 129
The Boathouse, Currie, King Island Tas. 306
The Bounty Centre Toy Shop, Burnt Pine, Norfolk Island 268
The Channon Craft Market NSW 35
The Channon NSW 35
The deep south Tas. 273–7
The Entrance NSW 9, 12, 15
The Farm, Killalea Regional Park NSW 43
The Gap, Balgowan SA 137
The Gardens, Bay of Fires Conservation Area Tas. 290
The Granites SA 129

The Hazards, Freycinet National Park Tas. 288, 299
The Hilli Goat, Norfolk Island 267
The Jetty Resort, Esperance WA 203
The Knob SA 141
The Knoll, Tamborine National Park Qld 219
The Lakes Way NSW 3–7
The Neck, Bruny Island Tas. 275
The north-west Tas. 293–9
The Nut, Stanley Tas. 293, 294, 295
The Old Bank B&B, Cygnet Tas. 277
The Pier Store Museum, Kingston, Norfolk Island 265
The Pines picnic area, Yarriabini National Park NSW 24
The Pool, Coffin Bay National Park SA 143
The Sails Motel & Pool Club, Brunswick Heads NSW 37
The Sapphire Coast NSW 51–7
The South West Edge WA 195–203
The Strand, Townsville Qld 246
The Truganini Lookout, Bruny Island 275
The Tub, Talia Caves, Talia SA 148
The Whale Inn, Narooma NSW 49
The White Albatross, Nambucca Heads NSW 29
Thirroul NSW 42
Thomas River, Cape Arid National Park WA 203
Thorsborne Trail, Hinchinbrook Island/Munamudanamy Qld 251
Three Capes Track Tas. 281
Three Mile Pool WA 177
Thurra River campground, Croajingolong National Park Vic. 105
Tidal River Vic. 91, 96, 97
Tidal River Campground Vic. 97
Tiddy Widdy Beach SA 132
Tilba Bakery, Central Tilba NSW 49
Tilba Real Dairy, Central Tilba NSW 49
Tilba Tilba NSW 45, 48, 49, 52
Timbertown, Wauchope NSW 19
Timboon Vic. 66
Tin Can Bay Qld 226
Tin City, Stockton Bight NSW 15
Tintoela, Cascade Bay, Norfolk Island 269
Tiona NSW 6
Tiparra Rocks, Balgowan SA 137
Tomaree Headland, Port Stephens NSW 13
Tommeginne People 293
Torquay Vic. 61, 64
Tourist Drive 8, Taree via Wingham and Wauchope NSW 19
Tower Hill Wildlife Reserve Vic. 73
Town Green, Port Macquarie NSW 19
Townsville Qld 241, 246, 249, 250

Tranquility Bay of Fires, Binalong Bay Tas. 291
trawulwai Nation 299
Tree Top Walk, Walpole–Nornalup National Park WA 196
Triabunna Tas. 286, 289, 291
Trial Bay Campground, Arakoon National Park NSW 21
Trial Bay Gaol, Arakoon NSW 21
Trial Bay Kiosk, Arakoon National Park NSW 17, 21
Trial of the 15, Kingston, Norfolk Island 267
Trig camping area, Deep Creek National Park SA 115
Trigg WA 156
Troubridge Hill lighthouse SA 134
Troubridge Point SA 131
Trousers Point, Flinders Island Tas. 299, 300–1, 303
Trowutta 297
Truganini Lookout, The, Bruny Island 275
Tully Qld 251
Tully Gorge Lookout Qld 252
Tumbling Waters Retreat, Stanwell Tops NSW 43
Tumby Bay Hotel SA 143
Tumby Bay SA 139, 141, 142
Tunarama Festival, Port Lincoln SA 142
Tuncurry NSW 6
Tuross Heads NSW 48
Tuross Lake NSW 48
Turrakana/Tasman Peninsula Tas. 279–83, 286
Turtle Centre, Mon Repos Conservation Park Qld 235
Tweed Heads NSW 31, 36
Tweed Range Scenic Drive NSW 36
Tweed Regional Gallery and Margaret Olley Art Centre, Murwillumbah NSW 37
Tweed Valley NSW 36
Twelve Apostles Vic. 66, 70
Two Chimneys Reserve, Norfolk Island 263, 268
Two Chimneys Wines, Norfolk Island 268
Tyerrnotepanner People 285

U
Ulverstone Tas. 294
Umpherston Sinkhole, Mount Gambier SA 124
Unavale Vineyard, Lady Barron Tas. 301
Underwater Observatory, Busselton Jetty WA 190
Urunga NSW 26
Urunga Honey Place NSW 26
Urunga Lagoon boardwalk NSW 26

V

Valley of the Giants, K'gari Qld 229
Valley of the Giants, Walpole–Nornalup National Park WA 196, 199, 203
Venus Bay SA 148, 151
Venus Bay Beachfront Tourist Park SA 151
Vera's Water Garden, The Entrance NSW 12
Victor Harbor SA 109, 113, 114, 115
Victoria Cove, King Island Tas. 310
Victoria Park Nature Reserve, Alstonville NSW 33
Vincentia NSW 46
Vivonne Bay SA 121
Vlamingh Head Lighthouse, Exmouth WA 169
Voyager Estate, Margaret River WA 193

W

Wadandi People 190
Wadawurrung People 61, 83
Wadbilliga National Park NSW 54
Waddy Point, K'gari Qld 230
Wadjemup Museum, Rottnest Island WA 189
Waitpinga Beach SA 113, 114
Wakka Wakks People 233
Walk with the Birds boardwalk, Dorrigo National Park NSW 27
Walk the Yorke SA 134
Walkabout Lodge, Nhulunbuy NT 213
Walkers Lookout, Flinders Island Tas. 301
Walkerville Vic. 91
Wallaga Lake NSW 52
Wallagoot Lake NSW 54
Wallaman Falls, Girringun National Park Qld 251
Wallaroo SA 131, 135, 136, 139
Wallaroo Marine Apartments SA 137
Wallingat National Park NSW 7
Wallis Lake NSW 3, 6
Walpole WA 196
Walpole–Nornalup National Park WA 196
Wamberal NSW 12
Wanggoolba Creek Qld 225
Wanuway (Cape Arnhem) NT 207, 212–13
Wardandi People 187
Warren National Park WA 196
Warrgamay People 249
Warrnambool Vic. 61, 66–7, 69, 70, 73, 75
Warrnambool to Port Fairy Rail Trail Vic. 73
Waterfall Bay Tas. 281
Waterfall Circuit Qld 252
Waterfall Way NSW 27
Wathawuy (Goanna Lagoon and Latram River) NT 213
Watsacowie Brewery, Minlaton SA 135
Waubs Beach, Bicheno Tas. 290
Wauchope NSW 19
Waverley House Cottages, Lakes Entrance Vic. 105

Way Way Creek Drive, Macksville NSW 24
Weano Gorge, Karijini National Park WA 177
Wellington SA 128
Werri Beach NSW 43
West Bay SA 121
West Cape Vic. 104
West Cape Lighthouse SA 134
Western Beach, K'gari Qld 231
Western River Cove SA 121
Wet Tropics World Heritage Area Qld 250, 255, 256
Wet'n'Wild Water World, Gold Coast Qld 219
Whadjuk People 155, 156, 187, 189
Whale Inn, The, Narooma NSW 49
Whale Watch Western Australia, Bremer Bay WA 200
whale-watching
 Baranguba (Montague Island) NSW 48
 Bicheno Tas. 290
 Bremer Bay WA 200
 Cape Jervis SA 112
 Cape Leeuwin WA 192
 Cape Naturaliste WA 192
 Cape Tourville Tas. 288
 Cape Woolamai Vic. 80
 Coffs Harbour NSW 27
 Copacabana NSW 10
 Eden NSW 55
 Fitzgerald River National Park WA 202
 Great Sandy National Park Qld 226
 Head of Bight SA 151
 Hervey Bay Qld 230, 233, 234
 Iluka Bluff NSW 32
 Iluka NSW 29
 Jervis Bay JBT 45
 K'gari (Fraser Island) Qld 225, 230
 Logans Beach Vic. 66, 69, 70
 Merimbula NSW 54
 Nambucca Heads NSW 24
 Nelson Bay NSW 13
 Newland Head Conservation Park SA 113
 Pebbly Beach NSW 29
 Point Ann, Fitzgerald River National Park WA 201
 Port Stephens NSW 9
 Portland Vic. 73
 Seven Mile Beach National Park NSW 43
 South West Rocks NSW 21
 Sugarloaf Light Station NSW 3
 Tathra NSW 52
 Venus Bay SA 148
Whalers Bluff Lighthouse Vic. 72
Whalers Way, Port Lincoln SA 142
Wharf to Wharf walk (Merimbula to Tathra) NSW 52
Whian Whian State Conservation Area NSW 37

Whisky Beach Vic. 96
White Albatross, The, Nambucca Heads NSW 29
white-water rafting
 Coffs Harbour NSW 27
 Tully River Qld 251
Whitehaven Beach Qld 244, 247
Whitemark, Flinders Island Tas. 299, 300, 302
Whitsunday Coast Qld 241–7
Whitsunday Islands Qld 241, 244
Whoota Whoota Lookout, Wallingat National Park NSW 7
Whyalla SA 139, 140
Widi People 244
Widjabul People 31
Wild Harvest Restaurant, Grassy, King Island Tas. 308
Wilderness Coast Walk Vic. 105
wildflowers
 Badgingarra National Park WA 161
 Cape Le Grand National Park WA 203
 Coalseam Conservation Park WA 161
 Fitzgerald River National Park WA 201
 Lesueur National Park WA 161
 Myall Lakes National Park NSW 5
 Parndana SA 121
 Stirling Range WA 200
 Wadbilliga National Park NSW 54
Wildlife Habitat, Port Douglas Qld 256
wildlife-watching
 Adelaide Bay bird hide, Flinders Island Tas. 301
 Australian Reptile Park, Somersby NSW 12
 Baranguba (Montague Island) NSW 48
 Bicheno Tas. 290
 Billabong Koala Wildlife Park, Port Macquarie NSW 19
 Booderee National Park JBT 47
 Bournda National Park NSW 54
 Broken River, Eungella National Park Qld 244
 Bruny Island Tas. 275
 Burnie Tas. 294
 Cape Barren Island Tas. 301
 Cape Woolamai Vic. 80
 Coorong National Park SA 128
 Curtis Island Qld 239
 Dhilba Guuranda-Innes National Park SA 135
 Dolphin Marine Conservation Park, Coffs Harbour NSW 27
 Dooragan National Park NSW 18
 East Coast Natureworld, Bicheno Tas. 290
 Etty Bay Qld 252
 Flinders Chase National Park 120–1
 Francois Peron National Park WA 166
 French Island Vic. 89
 Green Cape Lightstation NSW 57

Griffiths Island Vic. 72
Hamelin Bay WA 192
Hanson Bay Wildlfe Sanctuary, Karatta SA 120
Jurian Bay Marine Park WA 160
Kangaroo Island SA 117, 120
K'gari (Fraser Island) Qld 230
Koala Conservation Reserve, Phillip Island Vic. 78
Koombana Bay WA 190
Lady Elliot Island Qld 236
Lady Musgrave Island Qld 236
Lone Pine Koala Sanctuary, Brisbane Qld 220
Mackay Qld 244
Mallacoota Vic. 104
Maria Island Tas. 289
Middle Island Vic. 70
Mission Beach Qld 250-1
Mon Repos Conservation Park Qld 235
Monkey Mia WA 166
Mornington Peninsula Vic. 85
Mornington Peninsula National Park Vic. 87
Murramarang National Park NSW 47, 49
Myall Lakes National Park NSW 5
Ningaloo Reef WA 169
Patriarchs Wildlife Sanctuary, Lackrana, Flinders Island Tas. 301
Penguin Tas. 294
Penneshaw SA 118
Phillip Island, Norfolk Island 269
Phillip Island, Vic. 77, 78, 79–80
Point Labatt SA 149
Port Davies, Flinders Island Tas. 302
Port Douglas Qld 256
Port Lincoln SA 142
Port Stephens Koala Sanctuary NSW 13
Port Stephens NSW 13
Port Vincent SA 132
Raymond Island Vic. 103
Rockingham WA 190
Rottnest Island WA 189
Seal Bay SA 120
Seal Rocks 6
Stanley Tas. 295
Symbio Wildlife Gardens, Helensburg NSW 40
Tasmanian Devil Unzoo, Taranna Tas. 273
Tower Hill Wildlife Reserve Vic. 73
Wilsons Promontory 97
Wingham Brush NSW 19
Yanchep National Park WA 156
Younghusband Peninsula SA 129
Wildsights, Monkey Mia WA 166
William Bay National Park WA 199
Williamtown NSW 12-13

Willie Creek Pearls WA 180
Willunga farmers market SA 110
Willunga SA 110, 115
Wilson Inlet WA 199
Wilsons Promontory Vic. 91, 96-7, 299
Wilsons Promontory Lightstation Vic. 96
Windy Harbour WA 199, 203
Wineglass Bay Tas. 285, 288
wineries
    Albany WA 195
    Berry NSW 43
    Coonawarra SA 125
    East Coast Tas. 288
    Flinders Island Tas. 301
    Huon Valley Tas. 276
    McLaren Vale SA 109, 110
    Margaret River region WA 187, 190, 192, 193
    Mornington Peninsula Vic. 88
    Norfolk Island 268
    Port Lincoln SA 142
    Wingan Inlet Vic. 105
    Wingham Brush NSW 19
Wirangu People 139, 145
Wirrawuy NT 210
Wiseman's Ferry NSW 12
Witches Falls, Tamborine National Park Qld 219
Wittelbee Conservation Park SA 151
Wollongong NSW 39, 42-3
Wollongong Harbour NSW 42
Wollumbin (Mount Warning) NSW 36
Wonambi Fossil Centre, Naracoorte SA 125
Wonboyn NSW 105
Wonboyn Lake NSW 51
Wong-Goo-Tt-Oo People 174
Wonthaggi Vic. 92, 94
Woodbridge Tas. 276
Woodcutters Beach SA 143
Wooden Boat Centre, Franklin Tas. 276
Woody Hill campground, Bundjalung National Park NSW 37
Woolgoolga NSW 28
Wooli NSW 23, 28
Wooroonooran National Park Qld 252
Wop-pa/Great Keppel Island Qld 239
Worimi Conservation Lands NSW 15
Worimi People 3, 5, 9, 15
Wreck Rock, Deepwater National Park Qld 239
Wudjari People 195, 201, 203
Wujal Wujal (Bloomfield Falls) Qld 260
Wula Gura Nyinda, Monkey Mia WA 166
Wulgurukaba People 241, 249
Wybalenna, Flinders Island Tas. 302
Wye River Vic. 65
Wynyard Tas. 294

Y
Yaburara People 171, 174
Yallingup WA 190, 192, 193
Yamatji People 155
Yamba NSW 23, 28-9, 32
Yambuk Vic. 74
Yanchep WA 156, 158
Yanchep National Park WA 156
Yangie Bay, Coffin Bay National Park SA 143, 148
Yarriabini Lookout, Yarriabini National Park NSW 24
Yarriabini National Park NSW 24
Yawuru Country 180
Yawuru People 171, 179
Yaygirr People 23, 31
Yellow Beach, Flinders Island Tas. 301, 303
Yellow Rock Beach, King Island Tas. 310
Yeppoon Qld 233, 239
Yeppoon Lagoon Qld 239
Yidinjdji People 249
Yindjibarndi People 174
Yinigurdira People 163, 169
Yirrganydji People 255
Yirrkala NT 211
Yirrkala Church Panels NT 211
Yolngu People 207, 208, 211, 212
Yorke Peninsula SA 131-7
Yorketown SA 135
Younghusband Peninsula SA 129
Yuat People 158
Yued People 156
Yuggera People 217
Yuibera People 244
Yuin People 42, 45, 51, 54
Yunbenun/Magnetic Island Qld 246, 247
Yungaburra Qld 258
Yunupingu clan 208
Yuraygir National Park NSW 23, 28, 29
Yuwibara People 241, 244

Z
Z-Bend, Kalbarri National Park WA 164
Zamia Grove, Tamborine National Park Qld 217
Zillie Falls Qld 252
zoos
    Australia Zoo, Beerwah Qld 222
    Mogo Wildlife Park, Mogo NSW 47
    Rockhampton Botanic Gardens and Zoo Qld 239
    Symblo Wildlife Gardens, Helensburg NSW 40

PHOTOGRAPHY CREDITS

All images © Lee Atkinson, with the exception of the following:

Front cover: Jessica Prince

Back cover: iStock Photo

Pp xiv, 4, 5, 6, 8, 12, 14 (top left, bottom left and right), 19 (top), 28, 33, 36 (top), 42, 43 (bottom), 46, 48 (left), 50, 52, 54, 55, 56 (top left, bottom left and right) Destination NSW; pp 26, 27, 40, 114, 127 (top and bottom right), 143 (top), 149 (bottom), 164 (right), 172, 175 (bottom), 292, 296, 306, Shutterstock; p 38 David Finnegan/NSW National Parks and Wildlife Service; p 56 (top right) courtesy of Sapphire Coast Destination, David Rogers Photography; pp ii, v, 60 (top left and bottom right), 64, 65, 67, 70, 73, 76, 81 (top left and bottom right), 84, 85 (top), 86, 88, 90, 95 (top right), 98 (top right), 104 Visit Victoria; p 81 (top right) courtesy Phillip Island Tourism; p 89 (left) Anson Smart; pp 95 (bottom left), 97 Pennicott Wildernesss Journeys; pp 116, 120, 137, 144, 148, 15, 152, 156, 157, 158, 164 (left), 167, 168, 175 (top), 182, 191 (top left), 192, 197, 198 (top right), 198 (bottom left), 199, 200, 264, 265 (bottom), 267 Tourism Australia; pp iii, 111 (bottom), 127 (top left), 162, Alamy; p 173 (top) Tourism Western Australia; p 176 becauz gao / Shutterstock.com; pp xi, 214, 218, 219, 222, 226, 228 (top), 229, 230, 234, 238, 245 (top left), 245 (bottom right), 246, 251, 253, 254, 270, 276, 286, 288, 289, 290 (right), 297 Tourism and Events Queensland; p 194 Sean Scott; p 228 (bottom) courtesy Fraser Coast Tourism; p 231 (right) Kingfisher Bay Resort; pp 224, 231 (right) TravMedia Australia; p 236 courtesy Bundaberg Tourism, Jeremy Somerville; p 237 (top) courtesy Capricorn Coast.

ABOUT THE AUTHOR

One of Australia's most experienced travel writers, and two-time winner of the prestigious Australian Society of Travel Writers Best Adventure Story Award, Lee Atkinson has been writing about her adventures on and off the road for Australian newspapers, magazines and travel guides since 1991. A self-confessed road trip junky who loves getting away from the crowds in wild and remote places, she believes "that any excuse to hit the road is a good one."

Lee is the author of 14 travel books and two smartphone apps about travelling in and around Australia and co-editor of two anthologies of travel writing, as well as a contributor to Explore Australia's *Camping Around Australia* guide and the road tripping bible, *Explore Australia*. Her most recent books published by Hardie Grant Travel are *Ultimate Road Trips Australia*, *The Definitive Bucket List* and *Australia's Best Nature Escapes*. See www.leeatkinson.com.au

Published in 2023 by Hardie Grant Explore, an imprint of
Hardie Grant Publishing

Hardie Grant Explore (Melbourne)
Wurundjeri Country
Building 1, 658 Church Street
Richmond, Victoria 3121

Hardie Grant Explore (Sydney)
Gadigal Country
Level 7, 45 Jones Street
Ultimo, NSW 2007

www.hardiegrant.com/au/explore

All rights reserved. No part of this publication may be reproduced, stored in a retrieval system or transmitted in any form by any means, electronic, mechanical, photocopying, recording or otherwise, without the prior written permission of the publishers and copyright holders.

The moral rights of the author have been asserted.

Copyright text © Lee Atkinson 2023
Copyright concept, maps and design © Hardie Grant Publishing 2023

The maps in this publication incorporate data from © Commonwealth of Australia (Geoscience Australia), 2006. Geoscience Australia has not evaluated the data as altered and incorporated within this publication, and therefore gives no warranty regarding accuracy, completeness, currency or suitability for any particular purpose.

Incorporates or developed using [Roads Feb 2022, Hydrology Nov 2012] © Geoscape Australia for Copyright and Disclaimer Notice see geoscape.com.au/legal/data-copyright-and-disclaimer

Maps contain parks and reserves data which is owned by and copyright of the relevant state and territory government authorities. © Australian Capital Territory. www.ACTmapi.act.gov.au Creative Commons Attribution 4.0 International (CC BY 4.0), © State of New South Wales (Department of Planning, Industry and Environment) Creative Commons Attribution 4.0 International (CC BY 4.0), © State of New South Wales (Department of Primary Industries) Creative Commons Attribution 4.0 International (CC BY 4.0), © State of Victoria (Department of Environment, Land, Water and Planning) Creative Commons Attribution 4.0 international (CC BY 4.0), © State of South Australia (Department for Environment and Water) Creative Commons Attribution 4.0 Australia (CC BY 4.0), © State of Western Australia (Department of Biodiversity, Conservation and Attractions) Creative Commons Attribution 3.0 Australia (CC BY 3.0 AU), © Northern Territory Government of Australia (Department of Environment, Parks and Water Security) Creative Commons Attribution 4.0 International (CC BY 4.0), © The State of Queensland (Department of Environment and Science) Creative Commons Attribution 4.0 International (CC BY 4.0), © Commonwealth of Australia (Great Barrier Reef Marine Park Authority) Creative Commons Attribution 4.0 International (CC BY 4.0), © State of Tasmania (Department of Primary Industries, Parks, Water and Environment) Creative Commons Attribution 3.0 Australia (CC BY 3.0 AU)

Maps contain Aboriginal Land data which is copyright of the relevant state and territory government authorities. Attribution 3.0 Australia (CC BY 3.0 AU), © Northern Territory Government (Department of Infrastructure, Planning and Logistics), © State of Western Australia (Department of Planning, Lands and Heritage), © Government of South Australia (Department for Energy and Mining) Creative Commons Attribution 3.0 Australia (CC BY 3.0 AU), © State of New South Wales (Department of Planning, Industry and Environment) Creative Commons Attribution 4.0 International (CC BY 4.0), © State of Queensland (Department of Resources) Creative Commons Attribution 4.0 International (CC BY 4.0)

A catalogue record for this book is available from the National Library of Australia

Hardie Grant acknowledges the Traditional Owners of the Country on which we work, the Wurundjeri People of the Kulin Nation and the Gadigal People of the Eora Nation, and recognises their continuing connection to the land, waters and culture. We pay our respects to their Elders past and present.

For all relevant publications, Hardie Grant Explore commissions a First Nations consultant to review relevant content and provide feedback to ensure suitable language and information is included in the final book. Hardie Grant Explore also includes traditional place names and acknowledges Traditional Owners, where possible, in both the text and mapping for their publications.

Traditional place names are included in *palawa kani*, the language of Tasmanian Aboriginal People, with thanks to the Tasmanian Aboriginal Centre.

Ultimate Coastal Road Trips: Australia
ISBN 9781741178258

10 9 8 7 6 5 4 3 2 1

Publisher
Melissa Kayser
Project editor
Megan Cuthbert
Editor
Alice Barker
Proofreader
Rosanna Dutson
First Nations consultant
Jamil Tye, Yorta Yorta
Cartographer
Emily Maffei and Claire Johnston

Design
Andy Warren
Acknowledgement of Country symbol design
Relative Creative
Typesetting
Kerry Cooke
Index
Max McMaster
Production coordinator
Simone Wall

Colour reproduction by Megan Ellis and Splitting Image Colour Studio

Printed and bound in China by LEO Paper Products LTD.

FSC MIX Paper | Supporting responsible forestry FSC® C020056

The paper this book is printed on is certified against the Forest Stewardship Council® Standards and other sources. FSC® promotes environmentally responsible, socially beneficial and economically viable management of the world's forests.

Disclaimer: While every care is taken to ensure the accuracy of the data within this product, the owners of the data (including the state, territory and Commonwealth governments of Australia) do not make any representations or warranties about its accuracy, reliability, completeness or suitability for any particular purpose and, to the extent permitted by law, the owners of the data disclaim all responsibility and all liability (including without limitation, liability in negligence) for all expenses, losses, damages (including indirect or consequential damages) and costs which might be incurred as a result of the data being inaccurate or incomplete in any way and for any reason.

Publisher's Disclaimers: The publisher cannot accept responsibility for any errors or omissions. The representation on the maps of any road or track is not necessarily evidence of public right of way. The publisher cannot be held responsible for any injury, loss or damage incurred during travel. It is vital to research any proposed trip thoroughly and seek the advice of relevant state and travel organisations before you leave.

Publisher's Note: Every effort has been made to ensure that the information in this book is accurate at the time of going to press. The publisher welcomes information and suggestions for correction or improvement.